The Family and the Sexual Revolution

THE FAMILY
AND THE
SEXUAL
REVOLUTION

SELECTED READINGS

Edited by

EDWIN M. SCHUR

20135

1964

INDIANA UNIVERSITY PRESS

BLOOMINGTON & LONDON

Preface

Since sexual and family relationships are so central to the human experience, it is understandable that they are of immediate and personal concern to most people. Recently, together with this individual interest, there has been a significant increase in open discussion and controversy about such matters. Patterns of sexual and family behavior, and the institutions and values underlying and surrounding them, increasingly are recognized as legitimate topics for public analysis and debate. Widespread concern about sexual "laxity," best-selling books on the "roles of women," and heated disputes about birth control policy, represent but a few of the many indications of heightened public attention to sex and family life.

Yet in standard works on sex and family problems written by social scientists and medical men, the reader is likely to encounter either of two less-than-helpful approaches. One is an oversimplified "guidance" orientation, in which the author implies he can specify *the* rules or techniques for achieving dating happiness, marital harmony, or sexual adjustment. The other is a scrupulously "objective" presentation of facts and research findings—highly informative, but often peculiarly unsatisfying to any but specialist readers. While each of these approaches has undoubted merits, both tend to neglect basic ethical dilemmas and issues of broad social policy.

This volume is intended to provide neither direct guidance on specific personal or interpersonal problems, nor a compendium of scientific information. Rather I have tried to bring together some provocative materials relating to three hotly disputed topics that lie at the center of key changes affecting the modern family—sex standards, women's roles, and birth control. As a sociologist I believe strongly that scientific research and analysis are important ways of increasing our knowledge. Yet, as I also point out below, no amount of sex and family research is going to eradicate the need to make important value choices and policy decisions in these areas. The emphasis throughout this book is on these elements of value and policy; indeed, many of the readings are more in the nature of considered opinions, statements of values, or even polemics than of scientific reports. Additional facts and figures can easily be obtained elsewhere. Similarly, although I have tried to include diverse viewpoints, the volume is somewhat weighted toward unconventional views—on the assumption, again, that the conventional ones already predominate in existing works as well as constituting the outlooks which most Americans have more generally been conditioned to accept. It is hoped that these materials will prove illuminating and thought-provoking—for the general reader as well as for students in courses on the family, social problems, or contemporary American society. If this collection in some small measure exposes readers to a variety of challenging outlooks (the confrontation of which is so essential to the vitality of a democratic system) it will have served a useful purpose.

For first arousing my interest in the study of the family I am grateful to Fowler V. Harper, whose socio-legal casebook, *Problems of the Family* (recently revised with Jerome H. Skolnick) remains a pioneering interdisciplinary effort to illuminate key issues in this field. I am further indebted for specific ideas and general perspectives to various of my teachers at Yale Law School, New School for Social Research, and the London School of Economics, and to both colleagues and students first at Wellesley College and now at Tufts University. I would like also to acknowledge the thoughtful and skilled assistance of Bernard B. Perry, Miriam S. Farley, and others at Indiana University Press, and the fine work of Mabel F. Adams in typing the manuscript. Some final steps in preparing this volume were undertaken as I was beginning a year's leave of absence from Tufts in residence at the Center for the Study of Law and Society, University of California, Berkeley. I am grateful to Tufts and to the Russell Sage Foundation for making that opportunity possible.

EDWIN M. SCHUR

Medford, Massachusetts

Contents

PART THREE: *Birth Control*

MARION BASSETT has for many years been a penetrating analyst of marriage and family problems.

SIMONE DE BEAUVOIR, whose book *The Second Sex* has won world-wide acclaim, is the celebrated existentialist philosopher and novelist.

BRUNO BETTELHEIM, director of the Sonia Shankman Orthogenic School at the University of Chicago, is the author of many works dealing with child-rearing and related topics.

ALBERT ELLIS, a practicing psychotherapist, is the author of numerous books dealing with sexual problems.

FREDERICK ENGELS, the Communist theoretician, was co-author with Marx of *The Communist Manifesto*.

MARYNIA FARNHAM is a practicing psychiatrist and teaches psychiatry at Columbia University. Her other works include *The Adolescent*.

PAUL GOODMAN is a well-known writer of social commentary—as well as being a novelist, a poet, and the co-author of a volume on gestalt therapy.

ALAN F. GUTTMACHER, until recently director of obstetrics and gynecology at Mt. Sinai Hospital, New York, is currently director of the Planned Parenthood Federation of America. He has taught at Columbia University, and has written widely on birth control and other socio-medical topics.

SEWARD HILTNER is professor of theology and personality at Princeton Theological Seminary. He is the author of *Sex Ethics and the Kinsey Report* and other works.

ALFRED C. KINSEY founded the Institute for Sex Research, Inc. located at Indiana University, a nonprofit scientific research organization devoted to the study of human sexual behavior.

LESTER A. KIRKENDALL is professor of family life at Oregon State University, and the author of *Premarital Intercourse and Interpersonal Relationships*.

RICHARD H. KLEMER, a marriage counselor and researcher in the field of marital problems, is also on the faculty of the University of Washington.

MIRRA KOMAROVSKY is chairman of the sociology department at Barnard College of Columbia University, and is well known for her research in the family field.

FERDINAND LUNDBERG is the author of *America's 60 Families and The Coming World Transformation*.

DAVID MACE, a leader in the marriage counseling movement, is co-author (with Vera Mace) of *Marriage East and West* and *The Soviet Family*. He has written widely on sex and family topics.

BRONISLAW MALINOWSKI was a key figure in the development of scientific anthropology. Major works by him include *The Sexual Life of Savages* and *Sex and Repression in Savage Society*.

MARYA MANNES is the author of *More in Anger,* as well as of numerous articles on current affairs.

MARGARET MEAD is a well-known anthropologist. Her many books include (besides *Sex and Temperament*), *Male and Female* and *Coming of Age in Samoa*.

ALVA MYRDAL is a leading Swedish social scientist. She is co-author (with Viola Klein) of *Women's Two Roles: Home and Work*.

A. S. NEILL, founder and director of The Summerhill School in England, is an active proponent of radically progressive educational methods.

MORRIS PLOSCOWE was formerly a judge of the Magistrate's Court of the City of New York, and is at present practicing law and teaching at New York University's law school. His various publications include *The Truth about Divorce* and *Crime and Criminal Law*.

THOMAS POFFENBERGER is a professor of child development at Iowa State University, currently on leave directing research in that field at the University of Baroda, India.

BLAINE R. PORTER is chairman of the department of family life education at Brigham Young University.

IRA L. REISS is a professor in the department of sociology and anthropology at the State University of Iowa. He is the author of *Premarital Sexual Standards in America*.

BERTRAND RUSSELL is the renowned British philosopher, writer, and social reformer.

NORMAN ST. JOHN-STEVAS has written widely on legal and political topics, and has lectured at Kings College, London, and tutored in jurisprudence at Christ Church and Merton College, Oxford. His other books include *Obscenity and the Law* and *Women in Public Law*.

PATRICIA CAYO SEXTON is a professor of educational sociology at New York University and has written widely on the problems of working women.

PITIRIM A. SOROKIN, the renowned author of *Social and Cultural Dynamics*, is a professor emeritus at Harvard University, and currently president of the American Sociological Association.

WALTER R. STOKES is a prominent marriage counselor, and the author of many works on sex, marriage, and family problems.

The Family and the Sexual Revolution

Social Science and the Sexual Revolution

Is Western industrial society today experiencing a "sexual revolution," and if so what is its nature? The term has been used by some writers to suggest a startling and cataclysmic disruption, a sharp decline in morals and in family stability that is symptomatic of broader social disintegration. Thus Pitirim Sorokin (in one of the readings presented below) deplores recent trends in family and sexual behavior; a similar aversion to our supposedly "atomistic" family system has been expressed by Carle Zimmerman.[1] The revelations of the Kinsey reports have lent added fuel to this alarmist theme—and in fact represent one of the indicators of "disaster" to which Sorokin points.

Critics of these analyses have objected first that (inferences from Kinsey to the contrary nothwithstanding) there really may not have been any startling change in sexual behavior in the very recent years; and more generally that the vision of a society disintegrating with the decline of old-style family life is quite inaccurate. Does this mean, then, that it is incorrect to speak of a family or sexual revolution? I think not. Students of the family are almost all agreed that the major fact about this social institution, for the United States today and perhaps for the entire world, is that it is undergoing profound change. Textbooks on the family are replete with discussion of the impact of industrialism, urbanism, and secularism on family functions. The economic interdependence and self-sufficiency the family once had have all but disappeared; traditional husband-wife roles are in a state of flux; the reproductive function has declined (in the sense of family size decreasing); care of children and the transmission to them of basic societal values are increasingly delegated by the immediate family to outside agencies; the family no longer is the center of recreation, education, and moral guidance and support. These trends often are summed up by saying that there has been a decline in "familism" (or family-centeredness) with a corresponding increase of individualism in family behavior. While these changes have been gradual rather than sudden, their occurrence cannot be questioned; likewise the more explicitly sexual aspects of change are also beyond dispute.

In this volume attention is focused on three particular issues relating to social changes affecting the family: sex standards (with special reference to the question of premarital intercourse); the social roles of women; and the control of fertility. Many other areas of sexual and family behavior are also of great social significance and deserve the attention of students of society. For example, the matter of the public's attitude toward (and the legal measures taken against) various forms of sexual deviation has recently been subjected to some careful scrutiny from legal and ethical standpoints. The assertion by the Wolfenden Committee in Great Britain[2] that in the realm of sexual behavior the function of the criminal law is only "to preserve public order and decency, to protect the citizen from what is offensive or injurious, and to provide sufficient safeguards against exploitation and corruption of others, particularly those who are specially vulnerable. . . ." is a notable indication of new thinking in this area. (This was the rationale for their proposal that homosexual behavior between consenting adults in private should no longer be a criminal offense; a similar proposal has been included in the American Law Institute's Model Penal Code.)

Another important aspect of the changes that are taking place involves the reform of marriage laws, particularly those relating to divorce (and alimony), but this can barely be touched on in the present volume. Trends in child-rearing, psycho-sexual aspects of husband-wife relations, problems of sexual censorship, the question of illegitimacy, the social problem of prostitution—one could go on at great length to list the numerous important dimensions of sexual and family change. As already noted, this collection of readings does not attempt any such comprehensive coverage. The three topics chosen deserve special emphasis for several reasons: they lie at the heart of the changes that are occurring; they have frequently received either insufficient or unreflective treatment in conventional discussions; they all raise major issues of public controversy. Let us consider briefly the general significance of these topics and what social investigations have contributed to our understanding of them.

A recent family textbook succinctly refers to "the radical re-definition of sex that has been under way for at least 40 years."[3] While there may be some dispute about the exact nature and extent of this redefinition, there is little doubt that important changes in outlook and behavior have occurred. These changes involve a fairly apparent interrelationship between sex standards, women's roles, and birth control—many aspects of which are touched on in readings presented below. As Walter Lippmann noted, in his classic analysis *A Preface to Morals* (1929), when chaperonage became impossible and the fear of pregnancy was all but elimi-nated, the entire conventional sex ethic was shattered. "The whole revolution in the field of sexual morals turns upon the fact that external control of the chastity of women is becoming impossible."[4] The possibility of women supporting themselves economically completed the circle. Sexual and financial dependence were no longer woman's only paths—even if the pressures leading her in those directions continued to be strong. To the impact of feminism and the revolutionary implications of widespread contraceptive knowledge were added the pervasive influence of Freudian psychology and the moral relativism implicit in an age of seculari-zation. The consequences were hardly surprising: a reaction against the double standard; a demand among women that they too experience satisfying sexual relationships; a refusal to accept unsatisfactory marriages; an increased recognition of the possibilities of "sex as play."[5] Above all, individuals (both men and women) increasingly came to make their own decisions regarding sex and marriage. Lippmann noted that, at the time he was writing, it was impossible to know whether increased openness about sex reflected more promiscuity or less hypocrisy. But he went on to write, "what everybody must know is that sexual conduct, whatever it may be, is regulated personally and not publicly in modern society. If there is restraint it is, in the last analysis, voluntary; if there is promiscuity, it can be quite secret."[6]

While there may always be some limits on the completeness of research in the sexual realm, scientific investigators have done much to broaden our perspective on sexual behavior. To the work of the early pioneers in the study of sex and family life (Freud, Havelock Ellis, and others) we are beginning to add the somewhat more rigorously conducted studies of modern researchers—which have already produced much data regarding sexual behavior in our culture and elsewhere. Particularly useful in pointing up the great diversity of sexual standards and practices have been some of the anthropological and historical surveys.[7] These studies bring out the important point that in no society does sex go entirely unregulated; at the same time they make clear that our particular system of sex standards and ways is not necessarily essential for the maintenance of a stable family system. The Kinsey reports undoubtedly constitute the major effort to accumulate data on sexual behavior in the United States. These studies have been subjected to considerable methodological and substantive criticism from social scientists; yet as reasonably systematic and careful attempts to increase our knowledge in this area they remain unparalleled. A subsidiary gain from this research has been in the efforts by social scientists to interpret the findings, and the stimulus the reports have provided generally to further analysis of American sex standards and behavior.[8] Other significant research efforts in this field—focusing on responses of high school and college students—have provided much information about and considerable insight into the nature of premarital sex practices, the patterned sequence of increasing physical involvement, and the meaning of the practices for the individuals involved and in terms of the system of dating prevalent in America.[9]

This kind of research may well lead to a questioning of conventional thinking about premarital relationships. Reiss has concluded, for example, that not all premarital sex is "body-centered," that the developing standard in America seems to be "permissiveness with affection." Development of such descriptive categories based on research findings seems more valuable than the traditional and uncritical categorization of all sexual relations into marital (all good) and other (all bad). Similarly, conventional assumptions about a "lack of morals" among the lower classes have been contradicted by research such as that of Whyte—demonstrating that in a slum neighborhood, just as in the middle-class, sexual behavior is governed by a distinct and organized set of norms.[10] Numerous other studies, which cannot be mentioned specifically in this brief discussion, have thrown light directly or indirectly on the patterns and meaning of sexual behavior.

In comparison with changes in sex standards, problems relating to the roles of women have received even more attention from social researchers. As the selections presented in Part II indicate, there is a good deal of dispute, even among scientific observers, as to just what is "natural" behavior for women. Cross-cultural research demonstrates that in every society there is a division of labor by sex; on the other hand, there appears to be little uniformity as to which specific tasks are handled by which sex. Similarly, while sociological analysis of small groups suggests a basic division between the performance of "integrative-expressive" and "adaptive-instrumental" functions,[11] evidence regarding the inevitability or necessity of particular details of such differentiation is limited.

Understandably the sociologist has focused especially on the social role aspects of male and female behavior; social conditioning of sex-roles has been amply demonstrated. Several analysts have discussed the conflicting expectations facing the young woman in modern American society, and have pointed to the multiplicity of roles the married woman must fulfill.[12] Social scientists also have traced out the specific changes in woman's participation in the labor market, and the numerous adjustments (legislative, attitudinal, interpersonal) these changes imply.[13] Such studies recognize that extensive social services (particularly in the realm of child-care facilites) will be necessary if women are to undertake more full-time employment outside the home. In this connection American observers have been particularly interested in the experience of certain other societies—most notably the Scandinavian countries, Russia, and Israel (each of which receives some attention in the present collection of essays). The Israel kibbutz, as a radical experimental effort to free all adult women for productive labor in the community, has received special attention.[14]

As noted above, social scientists have been aware too of the significant attitudinal and interpersonal implications of women's changing roles in society. It is emphasized by family experts that changes in women's statuses and roles produce or are related to changes affecting the male's position in the family and in society. Just as male attitudes are seen to be crucial to the successful implementation of woman's widening opportunities, so too there is an awareness of the likely effects of these changes on the power structure or patterning of authority relations within the family. The ramifications of these changes on husband-wife relations—even to the extent of threatening the male's sense of sexual adequacy—may be very far-reaching indeed.[15] Numerous other aspects of woman's situation—including the vocational aims of female students, the effects on children of mothers' employment, and the influence of such employment on marital adjustment—are topics for continuing research. The recent publication of a book, *The Employed Mother in America*,[16] bringing together various research reports on such matters, indicates the strong interest social scientists are displaying in this area.

The matter of family planning has also received considerable attention from social scientists, because of the long-standing tradition of demographic studies (that is, scientific research on population). Work in this field has included broadly based analyses of world population trends, detailed analyses of the population composition and trends in specific countries (including underdeveloped societies), and within this country several large-scale surveys of family planning practices and attitudes.[17] Social scientists have worked closely with government agencies in this area, and have often spoken out forcefully in public policy debates on birth control. Their studies have been responsible for the now widespread awareness of "differential fertility" (that is, the inverse relationship between socio-economic position and fertility), and also for the growing public realization of the urgency of curbing the world population explosion. Although the amount of social research and analysis on such topics as abortion has been limited, there has been some. And a national conference on abortion in 1955 (conclusions of which are presented in Part Three) demonstrated that social scientists do share with other specialists an interest in coming to grips with pressing social problems of this sort. Social analysts have been in the forefront of the call for development of coherent national population policies (see the Myrdal excerpt below), and also have worked for statutory and other governmental action where they have felt that to be desirable. Above all, however, in the area of population, social research has produced a vast quantity of factual data regarding the composition of populations, past and present trends in population, and relationships between population and other social conditions.

As can be seen from the above (highly selective) discussion, one major contribution of social research is to increase our reservoir of information about sexual and family behavior. Perhaps an even more significant contribution lies in the development (among as wide an audience as possible) of a sociological orientation to these matters. Many people believe not only that sex and family are sacred and inviolable, but also that behavior in these realms is purely individual and unpredictable, and hence defies scientific analysis. Sociological studies clearly demonstrate that there are patterns, that such behavior can be understood to an appreciable degree (even if a complete feeling for any one particular relationship can be captured only by the individuals involved).

But beyond this, a sociological approach shows that the various practices and values in a society are not haphazard and unconnected. Any specific aspect of family and sexual behavior must be seen in its total social context, and changes in such behavior can be analyzed only in terms of their interplay within a broad constellation of social forces.[18] Furthermore, just as nonproblematic family behavior is structured socially, so the family and sexual "problems" of a society are closely related to the society's approved social arrangements and values. As Kingsley Davis noted, in a perceptive analysis of illegitimacy. "the contramoral is always functionally related to the moral. . . ."[19] It is because of these structural interrelationships that the sociologist tends to be wary of those "solutions" to social problems that stress reforming of supposedly wayward individuals, or which attribute the difficulties entirely to individual psychological disturbance.

An added potential contribution of social analysis is to provide a basis for informed private judgments and public policy decisions. Individuals in our society are continually making important decisions about their own sexual and family lives and at the same time they are judging (in varying degrees of informal and formal censure or approbation) the sexual and family behavior of others. Public policy in this area also is continuous, as witness the multitude of legal regulations governing sex and marriage behavior in the United States. The major topics covered in this book are all to some extent public issues. Reports of "immorality" have ignited concern about the sex behavior of American college students; last year a federal law was put into force extending the right to equal pay for women workers; and fierce disputes have arisen in a number of localities (including Cook County, Illinois, and Alameda County, California) regarding public provision of birth control information.

Sociologists often like to think that their task is merely to uncover the facts; as disinterested, objective, scientific observers it would be improper to allow their own values to color their work. While the desire to maintain "ethical neutrality" and to prevent personal bias from distorting scientific analysis is largely commendable, methodical fact-finding can never completely preempt the domain of value choices. The sociologist cannot use the rationalization of "value-free science" as a means of evading responsibility for his choice of research topics, for his selection of substantive criteria of evaluation, and for the uses to which his studies may be put (and the resulting social effects they may have).[20] In the area of sex and family studies, value judgments are particularly likely to insinuate themselves into ostensibly nonevaluative analysis. This point was admirably suggested by William Kolb some years ago in a pungent critique of marital success prediction studies.[21] As Kolb pointed out, often the sociologist has measured marital "happiness," "stability," "integration," or "adjustment," with little regard for the actual content or nature of the marriages in question. He rightly complained that evaluation of marital success using such criteria would also have to specify just what successful families are happy *about*, what they are adjusted *to*, and so on. One can be adjusted to socially undesirable conditions as well as to desirable ones, and it is therefore erroneous to automatically confer upon a "vacuum-value" like "adjustment" a positive meaning. In not questioning the content of adjustment the sociologist, as Kolb indicated, really is "supporting some system of family norms upon which he has not reflected"—in this case those of the conventional middle-class family.

The preoccupation with adjustment and stability displayed in some of these family studies very likely reflects what at least until recently was a dominant mode of thinking in sociology generally— an overemphasis on supposed integration and equilibrium in the social system, a tendency to see conflict and disruption as alien to the system rather than as an inevitable aspect of social life.[22] As noted above, there is very little doubt that major social changes have been taking place in sexual and family life; it is merely the evaluation of these changes that is in dispute. On this point the relation between disruption and conflict on the one hand and social change on the other is a vital consideration. For example, with the advent of new opportunities for women have come new confusions, conflicts, contradictions, and tensions—partly owing to the unevenness of change in various institutions and social values. To recognize the existence of such conditions, however, does not require that they be given a negative evaluation. Such difficulties may well be the price that has to be paid in the process of achieving what many would consider a desirable type of social change. In other words, how one feels about equal rights for women must enter into one's determination of the relative merits of stability and instability in this area. Similar kinds of considerations apply to our conclusions about other changes in sexual and family life.

A good deal of the material typically presented to students of the family embodies conventional assumptions, and some of these (as the Kolb anaylsis reveals) creep in surreptitiously. Another good example of this conventional bias, and one particularly relevant for purposes of this book, is the textbook treatment of pre-marital sex. In an interesting content analysis,[23] Ira Reiss noted certain "structural assumptions" shared by many of the marriage-and-family text writers: "they seem strongly to believe that pre-marital intercourse is almost always a lustful, selfish, and promiscuous relation, barren of affection and tenderness. They treat pre-marital intercourse as if all of it were this 'physical' type and as if no 'psychical' type existed." As he points out, this is inconsistent with the "ample evidence that many young people engage in intercourse with people whom they deeply love." Similarly, the text writers made statements concerning the psychological effects of premarital coitus and the relation of such behavior to engagement and marital failure which were "far too extreme to be justified by the available research evidence. . . ." Reiss concluded that the authors "were so occupied by their distaste for this type of activity and their attempt to 'prove' their values that they often neglected the objective approach to this area of behavior." Although I have not made a detailed study of family texts appearing since the Reiss article, it is safe to say that such card-stacking in the direction of conventionality is still prevalent. Even textbooks designed for "social problems" courses—which might be especially expected to subject conventional assumptions to critical scrutiny—tend to be either silent or conventional on the question of sexual standards.[24]

In a recent study, Erich Fromm suggests that the work of Marx and Freud (and it might well be said of other modern thinkers and schools of thought too) grew out of a certain common ground. He mentions as representing fundamental and common premises three short statements: "1) *De omnibus es dubitandum* (Of all one must doubt). 2) *Nihil humanum a mihi alienum* (I believe nothing human to be alien to me.). 3) *The truth shall make you free.*"[25] It seems to me that these premises (of skepticism, humanism, and the value of stripping away illusions) are particularly relevant to sex and family matters—and that this is the credo we are following in attempting scientific study and critical analysis in this area. One of the problems, however, is that the scientific approach sometimes seems to be telling us that there is no scientifically provable "truth," that everything is relative. The social scientist would like to be able to provide all the "right" answers, and undoubtedly both the student and the general public would be pleased to "learn" them—this would be much pleasanter than the confrontation of diverse and conflicting "views." But no matter how much social research we do, major value choices relating to sex and family life are going to persist. The social scientist cannot "prove" values—he simply cannot demonstrate scientifically what is right and what is wrong. He can hopefully (and nonscientific analysts can help here too) provide us with as broad an understanding as possible from which to make whatever determinations face us. While we often tend to resist the effort to think things through for ourselves, sex and family are topics of such importance to us all that in these matters at least making the effort becomes imperative.

NOTES

1. Carle C. Zimmerman, *Family and Civilization* (New York: Harper, 1947).

2. See *The Wolfenden Report*. Report of the Committee on Homosexual Offenses and Prostitution, Introduction by Karl Menninger (New York: Stein and Day, 1963); also this writer's review in *American Sociological Review* 28 (December 1963): 1055.

3. Ruth Shonle Cavan, *The American Family* (New York: Thomas Y. Crowell, 3rd ed., 1963), p.346.

4. Walter Lippmann, *A Preface to Morals* (New York: Macmillan, 1939; Beacon Press ed. 1960), p.228.

5. Nelson Foote, "Sex as Play," in Jerome Himelhoch and Sylvia Fleis Fava, eds., *Sexual Behavior in American Society* (New York: Norton, 1955), pp.237-243.

6. Lippmann, p.286.

7. Clellan S. Ford and Frank A. Beach, *Patterns of Sexual Behavior* (New York: Harper, 1951); George P. Murdock, *Social Structure* (New York: Macmillan, 1949); see also Richard Lewisohn, *A History of Sexual Customs* (New York: Longmans, Green and Harper, 1958).

8. See Jerome Himelhoch and Sylvia Fleis Fava, eds., *Sexual Behavior in American Society* (New York: Norton, 1955); Donald P. Geddes, ed., *An Analysis of the Kinsey Reports* (New York: E. P. Dutton, 1954).

9. Winston Ehrmann, *Premarital Dating Behavior* (New York: Henry Holt, 1959); Ira L. Reiss, *Premarital Sexual Standards in America* (Glencoe: Free Press, 1960); Lester A. Kirkendall, *Premarital Intercourse and Interpersonal Relations* (New York: Julian Press, 1961).

10. William Foote Whyte, "A Slum Sex Code," *American Journal of Sociology*, XLIX (July 1943): 24-31.

11. See Talcott Parsons and Robert F. Bales, *Family, Socialization and Interaction Process* (Glencoe: Free Press, 1955).

12. Mirra Komarovsky, "Cultural Contradictions and Sex Roles," *American Journal of Sociology*, 52 (1946): 184-189; and "Functional Analysis of Sex Roles," *American Sociological Review*, 15 (1950): 508-516; also Talcott Parsons, "Age and Sex in the Social Structure of the United States," *American Sociological Review*, 7 (1942): 604-616.

13. For a good general discussion see Alva Myrdal and Viola Klein, *Women's Two Roles: Home and Work* (London: Routledge and Kegan Paul, 1956).

14. Melford E. Spiro, *Kibbutz: Venture in Utopia* (Cambridge: Harvard University Press, 1956); and "Is the Family Universal?" *American Anthropologist*, LVI (1954): 839-846.

15. Helen Hacker, "The New Burdens of Masculinity," *Marriage and Family Living*, 19 (1957): 227-233.

16. F. Ivan Nye and Lois W. Hoffman, eds., *The Employed Mother in America* (Chicago: Rand McNally, 1963).

17. For an indication of the scope of this work consult Kingsley Davis, "The World's Population Crisis," in Robert Merton and Robert Nisbet, eds., *Contemporary Social Problems* (New York: Harcourt, Brace and World, 1961), pp. 291-323; Conrad and Irene Taeuber, *The Changing Population of the United States* (New York: Wiley, 1958); Ronald Freeman, P. K. Whelpton, and A. A. Campbell, *Family Planning, Sterility, and Population Growth* (New York: McGraw-Hill, 1959); P. K. Whelpton and C. V. Kiser, eds., *Social and Psychological Factors Affecting Fertility* (New York: Milbank Memorial Fund, 1950); and Lee Rainwater with Karol K. Weinstein, *And the Poor Get Children* (Chicago: Quadrangle Books, 1960).

18. For studies representing the structural-functional approach to the family see Norman W. Bell and Ezra Vogel, eds., *A Modern Introduction to the Family* (Glencoe: Free Press, 1960); Rose Laub Coser, ed., *The Family: Its Structure and Function* (New York: St. Martin's Press, 1963); also Parsons and Bales, cited.

19. Kingsley Davis, "Illegitimacy and the Social Structure," *American Journal of Sociology*, 45 (1939): 215-233.

20. For differing views on this matter see Robert Lynd, *Knowledge for What?* (Princeton: Princeton University Press, 1939): George Lundberg, *Can Science Save Us?* (New York: Longmans, Green, 1947, 1961); Alvin Gouldner, "Anti-Minotaur: The Myth of Value-Free Sociology," *Social Problems*, 9 (1962): 199-213.

21. William Kolb, "Sociologically Established Family Norms and Democratic Values," *Social Forces*, 26 (1948): 451-456.

22. For a critique of this tendency see Lewis A. Coser, *The Functions of Social Conflict* (Glencoe: Free Press, 1956); Ralf Dahrendorf, "Out of Utopia: Towards a Reorientation of Sociological Analysis," *American Journal of Sociology*, 64 (1958): 115-127.

23. Ira L. Reiss, "The Treatment of Pre-Marital Coitus in 'Marriage and the Family' Texts," *Social Problems*, 4 (1957): 334-338.

24. See Edwin M. Schur, "Recent Social Problems Texts: An Essay-Review," *Social Problems*, 10 (1963): 287-292.

25. Erich Fromm, *Beyond the Chains of Illusion* (New York: Simon and Schuster, 1962), p. 13.

PART ONE

Changing Sex Standards

PREMARITAL COITUS: SOME ARGUMENTS AND ATTITUDES

Sexual Behavior in the Human Male *(1948) and* Sexual Behavior in the Human Female *(1953) were the first two major publications arising out of the work of the Institute for Sex Research at Indiana University. Without doubt these volumes (together with the further work of the Institute) constitute a landmark in the growth of a systematic body of scientific knowledge regarding sexual behavior in modern Western society. Reactions to this work have been extremely mixed. Some popular commentators have compared Kinsey's work to that of Freud and Darwin, others have viewed the Reports as a frontal assault on moral values and indeed on the family as a basic social institution. Professional observers have questioned sampling and other procedures employed in the studies, and have criticized the Reports on the ground of biological reductionism. Yet almost all scientific workers have welcomed the studies as an impressive effort to increase our knowledge of a vital area of human life.*

One of the most controversial findings of the studies was the disclosure that about half of the females questioned had engaged in premarital intercourse. Critics inferred from the publication of such findings that the authors approved of what they found, or else that whatever the authors' intentions, the revelations would have a snowball effect, leading to a further "decline in morals." Most scientific students of sex believe, however, that the advantages of fact-finding and fact-facing by far outweigh any dangers that might result from such research.

Premarital Coitus:
Some Arguments and Attitudes

ALFRED C. KINSEY, W. POMEROY,
C. MARTIN, AND P. GEBHARD

Arguments for or against the acceptance of coitus before marriage have been based, for the most part, on emotional reactions which reflect the cultural tradition. However, these reactions are ordinarily supported or rationalized by arguments which may be summarized as follows:

AGAINST PRE-MARITAL COITUS. Most marriage manuals, treatises on sex education, moral philosophies, and much of the technical literature agree in emphasizing the disadvantages and general undesirability of pre-marital coitus. They point out the damage it may do to the individual, to the sexual partner, and to the social organization. Specifically, they emphasize:

1. The danger of pregnancy
2. The danger if abortion is used to terminate a pregnancy
3. The possibility of contracting a venereal disease
4. The undesirability of a marriage which is forced by a pre-marital pregnancy
5. The traumatic effects of coitus which is had under the inadequate circumstances which are supposed to attend most pre-marital relations
6. The damage done by the participant's guilt over the infringement of the moral law
7. The guilt at the loss of virginity, and its subsequent effect on marriage

Reprinted from Alfred C. Kinsey, W. Pomeroy, C. Martin, and P. Gebhard, *Sexual Behavior in the Human Female* (Philadelphia: W. B. Saunders Co., 1953), pp. 307-310 and 314-321; footnotes and figures omitted.

8. The fear that males lose respect for and will not marry a female with whom they have had coitus

9. The damage done when guilt feelings are reawakened after marriage

10. The guilt resulting from fear of public disapproval

11. The risk and fear of social difficulties that may follow discovery of the relationship

12. The risk and fear of legal difficulties that may follow any discovery of the relationship

13. The possibility that pre-marital coitus which is satisfactory may delay or altogether prevent the individual from marrying

14. The possibility that the coitus may make one feel obligated to marry the sexual partner

13. The possibility that guilt over the coitus may break up an otherwise desirable friendship with the sexual partner

16. The overemphasis which pre-marital experience may place on the physical aspects of friendship and marriage

17. The likelihood that pre-marital irregularities will lead to later extra-marital infidelities, with consequent damage to the marriage

18. The possibility that the female will be less capable of responding satisfactorily in her marital coitus because of the traumatic effects of pre-marital experience

19. The fact that pre-marital coitus is morally wrong

20. The principle that abstinence from such activities may develop one's will power

FOR PRE-MARITAL COITUS. The reasons for having pre-marital coitus have rarely been marshaled in any comparable order, perhaps because of the general disapproval in our culture of any extenuation of such behavior, or perhaps because those who do not disapprove consider that the reasons for having any coitus are self-evident. Nevertheless, the following advantages have been claimed for such experience:

1. It may satisfy a physiologic need for a sexual outlet

2. It may become a source of immediate physical and psychologic satisfaction

3. If there is no guilt, it may increase one's ability to function more effectively in other, non-sexual fields

4. It is more valuable than solitary sexual activity for developing one's capacity to make emotional adjustments with other persons

5. It may develop one's capacity to make the particular sorts of emotional adjustments which are needed in marital relationships

6. It may provide training in the sorts of physical techniques that may be involved in marital coitus

7. It may test the capacities of two persons to make satisfactory sexual adjustments after marriage

8. It is easier to learn to make emotional and physical adjustments at an earlier age; they are learned with greater difficulty after marriage

9. Failure in a pre-marital relationship is socially less disastrous than failure after marriage

10. Heterosexual experience may prevent the development of a homosexual pattern of behavior

11. Pre-marital coitus may lead to marriage

12. In at least some social groups, an individual may acquire status by fitting into the group pattern of behavior

All of these arguments, pro and con, are met by denials from those who believe to the contrary. There are obvious biases on both sides of the fence. On the one hand, it is claimed that the objections to pre-marital coitus are primarily moral, even when they are presented in ostensibly technical manuals emanating from professionally trained persons. On the other hand, it is claimed that arguments for pre-marital coitus are based on hedonistic desires rather than upon any consideration for the ultimate good of the participating partners or of the social organization. On the one hand, there is an insistence that the mores were born out of ancient experience which remains valid for the present day. On the other hand, it is claimed that conditions have changed, and that many of the older objections to pre-marital coitus are no longer valid in a world which has acquired the means of controlling conception and venereal disease, and some scientific understanding of the nature of emotions and of the problems that underlie human relationships. There have been few attempts to accumulate anything like scientific data.

The resolution of these conflicting claims can come only through some recognition that certain of these problems lie in areas which belong to the biologic, psychologic, and social sciences, while others are moral problems which the student of moral philosophies must solve.

Even the scientific aspects are too many for any immediate solution; but the data brought together in the present chapter may contribute to a more objective understanding of certain aspects of the problem.

[In a subsequent section the Report discusses respondents' attitudes concerning permarital relations and some other psychological aspects of the question. Part of this discussion is reproduced below.]

ATTITUDES. Whether a female decides to begin pre-marital coitus, or to continue it after she has once had it, must depend on a multiplicity of physical, situational, social and other factors, on some of which we have specific information and on others of which we do not yet have sufficient data for analyses. Interestingly enough, the most significant correlation seems to have been with the presence or absence of experience. Among the unmarried females who had never had coital experience, 80 per cent insisted that they did not intend to have it before marriage; but among those who had already had such experience, only 30 per cent said that they did not intend to have more. . . . A selective factor must have been involved; but it may be noted again that experience dispels many of the fears that gather about the unknown, especially when it is an unknown type of sexual activity.

In their own analyses of the factors which had restricted their pre-marital coitus, 89 per cent of the females in the sample said that moral considerations had been of primary importance. . . . Some of these individuals had identified these factors as moral. However, some of them insisted that they were not accepting the traditional codes just because they were the codes, and believed that they had developed their attitudes as a result of their own rational analyses of what they considered to be expedient, decent, respectable, fine, sensible, right or wrong, better or best. This represented an interesting attempt on the part of the younger generation to proclaim its emancipation from the religious tradition, but most of them were still following the traditions without having found new bases for defending them. It is to be noted that the females of the younger generations had recognized moral restraints on their pre-marital activities about as often as the females born some thirty or forty years before. But the increased incidences of coital activity, more than the expressed opinions, indicated that the moral codes had been less effective among the younger generations.

Some 45 per cent of the females in the sample recognized that their lack of sexual responsiveness had been a factor in limiting their pre-marital activity. . . ; but it seems clear that a lack of responsiveness or an inability to respond was even more important than the females themselves understood. As someone long ago recognized, it is easier to abstain from sin when one is not physically or physiologically endowed with the capacity—or with much capacity—to sin.

Fear of pregnancy ranked next, with 44 per cent of the females considering that this had been one of the factors which had limited their pre-marital coitus. . . .

As many females (44 per cent) said that fear of public opinion had been an important factor in limiting their behavior. . . . On the other hand, most of them were confident that no one except their sexual partners would know of any coitus which they might have.

Some 22 per cent frankly recognized that they had abstained from coitus, at least in part, because they had not encountered the opportunity to have it. . . .

Fear of venereal disease had been only a minor factor in limiting the pre-marital coitus of the females in the sample. It was reported as a factor in only 14 per cent of the sample. . . .

These were the expressed reasons which the females gave for their lack of coitus, or for their decisions to limit their further coitus. In many cases, these probably were the factors which had been involved; but in some cases these appeared to be nothing more than rationalizations of the real reasons. Taking all of our experience into account, we are inclined to list, in order of importance, the following as the primary factors which had limited the pre-marital activity of the females in the sample:

1. The sexual unresponsiveness of many younger females
2. The moral tradition of our American culture
3. Lack of experience, and the individual's fear of engaging in an unfamiliar activity.

REGRET AFTER EXPERIENCE. That pre-marital coitus is often unsatisfactory is commonly believed by most persons and asserted with considerable positiveness by many who consider such activity morally wrong. Many of those who have written on the subject (*e.g.,* Margaret Culkin Banning, Robert Foster, Evelyn Duvall, and others noted elsewhere) assert that pre-marital activity always brings psychologic disturbance and lasting regrets. The positiveness of these assertions might lead one to believe that they were based on sufficient investigations of the fact, but data which might sufficiently support such statements have never been accumulated by these writers or by other students in this field.

As a matter of fact, some 69 per cent of the still unmarried females in the sample who had had coitus insisted that they did not regret their experience. . . . Another 13 per cent recorded some minor regret. An even larger proportion, some 77 per cent of the married females, looking back from the vantage point of their more mature experience, saw no reason to regret their premarital coitus. Another 12 per cent of the married females had some minor regret. These figures differ considerably from those usually presented in public discussions of such pre-marital activity. They illustrate the difference between wishful thinking and scientifically accumulated data. There are, of course, more cases of regret among the disturbed persons who go to clinicians for help.

The regret registered by a portion of the sample appeared to depend on the nature of the pre-marital experience. . . . For the most part, those who regretted it most were the females who had had the least experience. Our data, for instance, show that 25 per cent of those who had had the smallest amount of pre-marital coitus seriously regretted their experience, while only 14 per cent of those who had had such experience for two or three years, and only 10 per cent of those who had it for something between four and ten years registered such regret. . . . This is borne out by the fact that the married females, with their more extended coital experience, regretted their pre-marital coitus in only 11 per cent of the cases. This is especially interesting because the statement is often made that the quality of a marital relationship is so far superior to a pre-marital relationship that married women usually regret such experience. That statement is not confirmed by our data.

Similarly, regrets were inversely correlated with the extent of the promiscuity in the pre-marital activity. . . . Among the females in the sample who had confined their coital contacts to a single male, 15 per cent seriously regretted their experience. On the other hand, of those who had extended their coitus to something between eleven and twenty males, only 6 per cent regretted their experience. It may be that experience reduces the psychologic disturbance, or it may be that those females who are least inclined to worry are the ones who become most promiscuous. It is probable that both factors contribute to these correlations.

Whether pre-marital experience was regretted or not did not, interestingly enough, seem to depend upon the generation to which the individual belonged. . . . Actually, the data show a large number of the youngest generation regretting their pre-marital coitus, but this probably depends on the fact that they had had more limited experience at the time they contributed their histories. Initial regrets are often resolved as an individual matures and acquires more experience.

Whether one regrets her pre-marital experience seems to depend to only a small degree upon the complications which a pregnancy may produce. In the sample, some 17 per cent of those who had become pregnant . . . as a result of their pre-marital experience seriously regretted that they had had coitus, while 13 per cent of those who had not become pregnant registered such regret. . . . It is more surprising to find that 83 per cent of those who had become pregnant registered little or no regret.

Regrets were correlated to only a small extent with the complications which venereal infections had introduced. Although 16 per cent of the females who had had infections seriously regretted their pre-marital coitus, some 13 per cent of those who had not been infected registered similar levels of regret. . . .

Pre-marital coitus which was had with the future spouse was least often regretted. Serious regret had occurred in only 9 per cent of the histories of the females who had had at least some of their pre-marital coitus with the males whom they subsequently married. . . . But if the pre-marital coitus had not included the fiance, there had been serious regret in 28 per cent of the cases.

There were no factors which were more closely correlated with guilt, among the females in the sample who had had pre-marital coitus, than their religious backgrounds, and the extent to which they felt that such experience was morally wrong. The data show, for instance, that 23 per cent of the devout Protestants but only 10 per cent of the inactive Protestants seriously regretted their pre-marital experience. . . . Some 35 per cent of the devout Catholics but only 9 per cent of the inactive Catholics in the sample recorded such regrets. The more limited sample of Jewish females showed the same trends. The clinician might very well advise the individual who is strongly convinced that coitus before marriage is morally wrong to hesitate about having such experience, for she is more likely to be emotionally disturbed by it. We have also shown . . . that the possibility of the pre-marital coitus reaching a satisfactory conclusion in orgasm is definitely lower for females who are religiously devout. It might be argued, however, that the religious attitudes were as responsible as the coitus for these psychologic disturbances.

ACCEPTANCE. That a considerable portion of the pre-marital coitus is psychologically satisfactory is, of course, evidenced by its continuation and considerable prolongation in the histories of many of the females who begin such activities. We have already noted that 69 per cent of the single females in the sample had accepted their coital experience, and 77 per cent of the married females had recalled their pre-marital experience without evident psychologic disturbance. . . .

The psychologic significance of any type of sexual activity very largely depends upon what the individual and his social group choose to make of it. The disturbances which may sometimes follow coitus rarely depend on the nature of the activity itself, or upon its physical outcome. An occasional unwanted pregnancy, a rare instance of venereal disease, or a very rare instance of physical damage are about the only undesirable physical after-effects. But if the behavior leads to some open conflict with the social organization of which the individual is a part, then the consequences may be serious and sometimes disastrous. The so-called traumatic effects of sexual experience often depend on the individual's inability or refusal to recognize the satisfaction that he or she actually found in the experience, or on his or her persistence in believing that the experience should not have been satisfactory, or that it must, in some way, have undesirable consequences; but these, again, reflect the attitudes of the community in which the individual was raised.

The truth of this thesis is abundantly evidenced by our thousands of histories which among them, include every conceivable type of sexual behavior without subsequent psychologic disturbance, while the same sort of behavior in other histories may bring shame, remorse, despair, desperation, and attempted suicide. The simplest matter can be built into an affair of gigantic proportions. Failing to comprehend that their own attitudes and the social codes generated these disturbances, most persons identify them as direct evidence of the intrinsic wrongness or abnormality of the sexual act itself.

In one or another of the cultures of the world, nearly every type of sexual behavior has been condemned, while in other cultures the same activities have been considered desirable sources of pleasure and socially valuable. Heterosexual coitus is extolled in most cultures, but forbidden to Buddhist and Catholic priests. Homosexual activity is condemned in some cultures, tacitly accepted in others, honored as a religious rite in others, and allowed to Buddhist priests. Behavior which is accepted by the culture does not generate psychologic conflicts in the individual or unmanageable social problems. The same behavior, censored, condemned, tabooed, or criminally punished in the next culture, may generate guilt and neurotic disturbances in the non-conforming individual and serious conflict with the social organism. This seems to be the source of most of the disturbances which we have found in the histories of American females and males who masturbate, who engage in heterosexual petting, or in homosexual relations or animal contacts, or utilize sexual techniques, which, biologically normal enough in themselves, are taboo in our particular culture. This is the explanation of most of the psychologic disturbances that come out of pre-marital coitus.

THE FOLKLORE OF SEX

If one were to attempt to summarize in one word the nature of American attitudes on sex, perhaps "ambivalence" would be the most appropriate choice. Americans seem persistently plagued by contradictory notions regarding anything sexual. Sex is at the same time viewed as marvelous (the epitome of happiness, the source of ultimate ecstacy) and as dirty (something to be hidden, unmentionable, enjoyed by "bad" persons, etc.) We subject our children to such conflicting interpretations at an early age (see the selection from A. S. Neill below) and the contradictions follow us throughout our lifetimes— reflected in our general values, our interpersonal relations, and the mass media to which we are continually exposed.

The following reading summarizes findings in a study (undertaken by a well-known psychotherapist) of the treatment of sexual topics in a sample of mass periodicals. There is considerable debate among social scientists regarding the extent to which the mass media influence attitudes and behavior. Some analysts find that media effects are only slight and secondary; others see the media as exerting a significant if subtle long-term influence. But whatever conclusions one draws about media impact, there is little doubt that systematic analysis of media content does tell us something important about the values of the culture from which the media derive.

The Folklore of Sex

ALBERT ELLIS

Some of the facts brought forth in the course of the present study were to be expected and their explanations obvious. Some are surprising and their explanations subtle or unknown. We shall now try to answer the main questions raised by these facts.

1. *Why are so many references, both liberal and conservative, to extramarital relations and to sex organs, desires, and expressions found?*

Probably because millions of Americans, in fact the great majority of them, actually do engage in fornication or adultery sometime during their lives; and because, when they do not do so, they still have distinct desires thus to engage and are concerned with the propriety of their desires. Also, American attitudes toward extra-marital as well as marital relations seem to be changing in a more liberal direction; but because the older and more conservative attitudes are by no means yet eradicated, considerable controversy still exists and tends to make the issue a lively one.

There is a tendency for mass media to portray the masculine viewpoint as a liberal one and the feminine view as conservative. Thus, male characters in both men's and women's magazine stories, novels, and motion pictures more often express favorable attitudes toward adultery and fornication than female characters. These mass media presently reflect a dichotomously trended male-female viewpoint in regard to extramarital affairs and, to a lesser degree, sex enjoyment in marriage.

2. *Why are most attitudes regarding kissing and petting liberal rather than conservative?*

Reprinted from Albert Ellis, *The Folklore of Sex* (New York: Grove Press, 1961; Black Cat edition, published in the U.S.A. and Canada by Grove Press, and in England by Evergreen Books, Ltd.), pp. 240-255.

Probably because kissing and petting are relatively mild forms of sex behavior and are virtually ubiquitous in our society. On the other hand, while kissing and petting are frequently mentioned in mass media, masturbation is one of the least mentioned sex acts. This tends to indicate that modern Americans are far more ashamed of masturbating than they are of engaging in kissing and petting and that, in spite of our sex books condoning masturbation (while still often emphasizing the dangers of petting, fornication, and adultery), the nineteenth-century attitude toward autoerotism lingers on in our mores.

3. *Why are attitudes toward abortion, birth control, illegitimacy, and pregnancy relatively few?*

Probably because these are not "romantic" sex topics and therefore not as likely to be included in fictional presentations as are more "respectable" subjects. While attitudes toward pregnancy and abortion seem to be loosening up recently in our society, they have not yet sufficiently done so for fiction writers to accept them too enthusiastically and use them for romantic effects.

4. *Why are so many attitudes toward nudity and sex organs extant and why are they so preponderantly liberal?*

Because nudity and references to sex organs apparently represent, in our communities, toned-down modes of sex activity which may be favorably espoused, while more direct modes of sex behavior are often greeted with more mixed or unfavorable reactions. Thus, viewing a nude woman or thinking about her hips and breasts is a step removed from *having* sex relations with her and is apt to arouse less guilt in a prim person.

5. *Why are relatively few attitudes toward incest, sex crimes, and sex "perversions" found, and why do they tend to be relatively conservative?*

Probably because these acts are still considered so heinous that they can directly be mentioned with only relative infrequency—especially in "respectable" outlets such as the women's magazines and general magazines. In this respect, our mass media doubtless mirror the contemporary attitudes of the majority of Americans who violently oppose most manifestations of sex crimes or "perversions."

6. *Why are so many attitudes, and especially liberal attitudes, found in relation to women's sexuality?*

Probably because, owing to the large amount of sexuality appearing in contemporary literature, readers have become somewhat jaded and can more easily be titillated by, say, a heroine's lustiness and unconventionality than by similar behavior on the part of a hero. Just as sadistic and other extreme types of sex activity are now being used to arouse sex-glutted novel and story readers, so, for purposes of sensationalism, promiscuous women are to some extent replacing promiscuous men as the protagonists of popular fiction.

7. *Why are sex attitudes in the 1960's so much more predominantly liberal than those in the 1950's?*

Largely because of the much greater freedom now apparent in fictional best-sellers and in the men's magazines. Particularly in relation to attitudes toward sex organs, desires, and expressions these two outlets have become amazingly more permissive in the last decade; though in regard to almost all other forms of sex behavior they have also become more prosexual. Whereas the women's magazines have remained similar in sexual tone to those of the 1950's, and other kinds of media have changed only moderately, the men's magazines and the best-selling novels are now radically different from their forebears and seem to be becoming still more openly sexual every year.

8. *Why are some kinds of mass media, such as best-selling novels and men's magazines, considerably more liberal than other kinds of media?*

Probably for several reasons. First of all, some outlets, such as the men's magazines, are patently read by male rather than female readers; and there is no question that a double standard of sexual morality still exists in the United States, with males generally more prosexually oriented than females.

Secondly, there would seem to be a considerable educational

and intellectual difference in the readers of various types of publications. The best men's magazines, such as *Esquire* and *Playboy*, and the most literate novels, such as those of William Faulkner, Robert Penn Warren, D. H. Lawrence, and Vladimir Nabokov, are almost certainly perused by a reading public that is distinctly more educated and intelligent than readers who generally dip into the motion picture and TV magazines and the true-confession type of periodicals. In consequence, publications which cater to the more educated and more intelligent reader seem to be, on the whole, vastly more liberal and prosexual than those which cater to duller teen-age readers.

Thirdly, several types of mass media, such as motion pictures and general magazines, are more widely read or witnessed than other types of media such as humor or men's magazines. Various groups of readers of these most popular media—for example, Catholics and hard-shelled Baptists—tend to complain to editors and producers when sexually permissive ideas are presented; and, being economically dependent on their vast audiences, these media feel (rightly or wrongly) that they cannot afford to antagonize even minority groups. Consequently, they tend to stay much more sexually "pure" than do publications or productions with a more select type of audience.

Fourthly, some modern publications, such as the men's magazines, seem to be particularly designed to provide sexual release for the members of the public who are strongly denied titillation and education in the more "respectable" type of outlets. Just as various types of prostitutes will tend to flourish when "good" women are strict about denying their sexual favors to males, so will various highly sexualized publications develop when publications such as the *Saturday Evening Post,* the *Ladies' Home Journal,* and the *Reader's Digest* remain rather prim about their sex attitudes.

Fifth, as Ivor Williams has recently shown in a perceptive article in *Playboy* ("The Pious Pornographers," reprinted in Ray Russell's

The Permanent Playboy), although today's women's magazines are still conservative about their formal presentations, they actually contain considerable lascivious portrayals and allusions in their stories, articles, and advertisements, which make some of the more honest (and hence less salacious) material in the men's magazines seem a little cloistered by comparison.

9. *Why is there still relatively less acceptance of extramarital relations and sex deviations and crimes than there is of other forms of sex behavior?*

As far as extramarital relations are concerned, the antisexualists are still fighting a strong, if losing, battle. The very heart of the Judeo-Christian sex ethic is that men and women shall remain virginal until marriage and that they shall be completely faithful after marriage. In regard to premarital chastity, this ethic seems clearly on the way out, and in many segments of the populace is more and more becoming a dead letter. Premarital coitus or petting to orgasm are now being experienced by the great majority of American males and females. The churches and other social institutions, however, are still battling this tendency and their influence is strong in popular literature, especially in general and women's magazines.

Adultery is less practiced and condoned today than are premarital sex relations—partly because it is more likely to be disruptive of marriage and family ties. Although there is probably a trend toward increasing adultery (including adulterous petting) on the part of many men and, especially, women today, this trend is not half so pronounced as the trend toward increasing premarital affairs. Again, the churches and other social institutions are waging a heavy war against adulterous relations and still wield a considerable amount of influence in this connection.

Sex deviations (when properly defined) and crimes are certainly not healthy or happy in their own right; and even though negative attitudes toward deviants and sex offenders have ameliorated in recent years, it is not to be expected that they will ever become enthusiastically approving. Moreover, many puritans who today cannot effectively rant against premarital intercourse, petting, kissing, nudity, and other forms of sex behavior seem to be making the most of the fields where their efforts are still effective—namely, in the fields of deviation and sex crime.

10. *What are some of the main factors that influence contemporary sexpressions as they appear in our mass media?*

1. The factor of human psychobiological *needs* and *desires:* which, sexually speaking, cannot easily be downed and which, when sexually unsatisfied, encourage the presentation of considerable liberal sex attitudes and salacious sex materials that, officially and traditionally, are supposed to be taboo in our society.

2. The factors of social change in general, and change in sex codes and ideas in particular, which encourage confusion, doubt, and ambivalence concerning a good many of our current sex views.

3. The factors of sexual discomfort and inconvenience, even when basic sex needs are partly satisfied, which motivate millions of Americans to act differently than they think and unconsciously to think differently than they consciously permit themselves to think they think.

4. The factors of individualism, democracy, and secularism, which discourage men and women from uniformly following traditional, authoritarian, religiously based sex tenets.

5. The factors of fear, guilt, and inhibition, which influence readers and auditors to resist and discourage the publication of many direct sexual representations and which encourage, instead, their indirect (and often salacious) presentation.

6. The factor of modern romanticism, which bolsters traditional sex mores on the one hand, but leaves loopholes, under certain circumstances, for more liberal codes and modes on the other hand.

7. The factor of differing masculine-feminine standards in our society, which encourage one kind of sex attitudes and usages for males and quite a different, often conflicting, kind for female readers and auditors.

8. The factor of unconscious feelings, urges, desires, and beliefs, which encourage men and women, sexually and generally, to think one way and to act another and even think they think one way, while actually thinking another.

9. The factor of exceptionally strict, puritanical, and traditional sex views which linger on in such a straitlaced fashion as to necessitate some semi-automatic counterbalancing tendencies on the part of many people who try most rigorously to hold to the letter of these traditional views.

10. The factor of certain strong pressure groups, particularly church groups, which stoutly defend conservative sex mores and attempt to bar and censor liberal or salacious sex references in public media.

11. The factor of capitalist enterprise, which views sex as another commodity which may be profitably sold for public consumption and which therefore encourages highly salacious presentations in those media which are hospitable to them.

12. The factors of sexual displacement and erogeneity, which make it possible for highly genitalized sex acts (like intercourse and incest) to be symbolized by quasi- or non-genital modes of sex behavior (like kissing or gazing at nudity) and which thereby allow for a good deal of public presentation of toned-down sexuality that, in more direct modes of presentation, would otherwise be banned.

13. The factor of the prevalence of modern humor, which also enables much sex material of a liberal or salacious nature to be publicly displayed that, if presented in more serious guise, would not be allowed.

14. The factors of modern technology, scientific discovery, literacy, and universal education, which are making it increasingly difficult for traditional-conservative views of any type, including sexual views, to flourish unchallenged, unopposed, and unalloyed.

15. The factor of cultural lag, which permits many highly illogical, inconsistent, and immature sex views to linger on decades and

centuries beyond their original usefulness and logical applicability to human affairs.

Now that we have seen what the facts of sexpression in America are, and why they are, the question arises: What are the behavioral implications of these facts? Or, in other words, what do these facts mean in terms of the thoughts, feelings, and actions of the average American man and woman?

The most important implications would seem to be the following:

1. *The average American—in fact, virtually every living American—is completely muddled-, mixed-, and messed-up in his sex views, feelings, and acts. Much of the time he is quite consciously confused and knows that he does not know sex "right" from "wrong." Or else he keeps changing his mind about what is sexually proper and improper. Or he engages in sex acts which he feels he should not perform but which he would feel even more uncomfortable about not performing. When—occasionally—this average American does manage to get consciously straight in his sex views, he still remains unconsciously caught and tangled in beliefs that are frequently as consistent with his conscious thoughts as Isadora Duncan was with Anthony Comstock. The result, in terms of the modern American's external and internal sex harmony, is a degree of peacefulness remarkably like that now existing between the United States and the Soviet Union. (This goes, incidentally, for the consciously libertarian sexualist, who normally—in our culture—has underlying puritanical attitudes and feelings, as well as for the consciously straitlaced antisexualist, who underlyingly has distinctly libertine impulses.)*

(a) In consequence, the typical American male or female has no monolithic sex attitude, but only very pluralistic attitudes. And, while his or her attitudes on politics, religion, economics, or what you will may tend to be fairly consistent and self-harmonious, his or her sex beliefs normally tend to be self-contradictory and, in many ways, self-defeating.

(b) Officially, legally, and traditionally most of the sex views of our society are negativistic and disapproving, and (consciously) the majority of Americans appear to adhere to these traditional antisexual viewpoints. Unofficially, extralegally, and actually, however, the sex attitudes of millions of Americans (and particularly of male Americans) are at least partially positive, approving, and prosexual.

2. *Whenever official and legal American sex views tend to become too rigid, negative, and puritanical, an unofficial and extralegal reaction against these views appears to arise and to take one or more of the following forms:*

(a) The views on the banned mode of sex behavior itself may become (unofficially or semi-officially) more liberalized. For example, ultra-strict views on fornication may give way to more liberal views.

(b) The views on the banned form of sex behavior may remain fairly constant, but views on related, substitutive, or sexually toned-down forms of behavior may become more liberalized. Thus attitudes toward fornication may remain conservative, but attitudes toward kissing and petting may become more liberal.

(c) The views on the banned sex act may remain consciously constant, but unconsciously they may become more liberalized. Thus people may continue to *say* that adultery is wrong but may remain relatively guiltless when they actually commit adultery.

(d) The views on the interdicted mode of sex behavior may remain the same as far as one's personal behavior is concerned but may become more liberalized when the behavior of others is at issue. Thus a girl may think it wrong for her to lose her own virginity but may think it perfectly all right for her girl friends to lose theirs.

(e) The views on the "bad" sex activity may remain steadfast, but the actions concerning it may be decidedly more liberal. Thus people may think it quite wrong to be "obscene" in public—and may then continually recount the most "obscene" kinds of jokes.

(f) The official interdictions against certain types of sex activity may be unofficially channelized into certain restricted areas and may be liberalized or ignored in other areas. Thus bans against telling "dirty" stories or jokes may be upheld when one is in mixed company, but relaxed in men's smokers or women's dressing rooms.

(g) Specific outlets may arise where more liberalized sex attitudes and acts are unofficially tolerated, even though they are officially taboo. Thus burlesque and night-club shows may be permitted to display nudity openly, and "lovers' lanes" may spring up where heavy petting is unofficially tolerated.

(h) Where liberal expressions of sex viewpoints are not permitted, substitutional salacious uses of sex material may arise instead. Thus those who dare not *say* that masturbation or adultery is a good mode of sex behavior may continually write about them in a lascivious way or greatly enjoy reading or hearing salacious reference to them.

(i) Sex activity that is banned and condemned may easily become "naughty" as well as "wicked"—and its naughtiness may give it a spice that makes both its discussion and its participation more enjoyable, and perhaps more frequent, than would otherwise be true.

(j) When specific sex acts (like masturbation or fornication) are banned, non-sexual or semi-sexual acts (like defecation or urination) may take on a super-sexualized meaning and may serve as sexual outlets.

(k) When direct, normal sex acts—e.g., masturbation or heterosexual intercourse—are banned or discouraged, indirect, abnormal acts—e.g., exhibitionism or sexually assaulting young children—may tend to rise in their stead.

(l) Violent, anti-sexual protests on the part of some individuals may provoke and serve as a mask for bizarre, prosexual acts by them. Thus people who are most vituperative and crusading against sexual "vice" may pruriently be indulging their sexual sadism.

(m) When extreme forms of anti-sexuality become rampant—such as asceticism or inquisitional persecution of sexual nonconformists—the energy and drives behind the anti-sexual crusading tend to take on a highly sexualized character and to serve as an (unconscious) sexual outlet. Thus the anti-sexual fervor of certain religious sectarians seems to result in orgasm-like releases.

3. *When specific modes of sex behavior are officially banned, they often tend, by the very virtue of their banning, to become particularly pleasurable and inviting to many of our citizens.*

(a) Prohibited sex acts may become unusually exciting in themselves. Thus kissing seems to be a fairly mild form of sexual entertainment where it is freely permitted—so mild, in fact, that many peoples of the world do not engage in it at all—but to become unduly sexually arousing and enjoyable when it is discouraged.

(b) Proscribed kinds of sex behavior may take on aspects of novelty and adventure which otherwise they would scarcely hold. Thus American men and women frequently seem to desire adulterous relations not because their mates are no longer sexually satisfying to them, but because there is an element of danger, thrill, and novelty in illicit adultery which adds to its pleasures.

(c) Tabooed sex behavior frequently enhances the pleasure of substitutive modes of sex activity which ordinarily would not be too exciting for their own sake. Thus enjoining fornication often puts a premium on kissing and petting, which are normally found to be far less satisfying when fornication is freely permitted.

4. *When certain modes of sex behavior are interdicted, people often resort, instead, to various types of neurotic symptomatic behavior.*

(a) Prohibitions of sex acts may lead to repression of sex desires —with consequent frigidity, impotence, fear of marriage, unconscious hatred of one's spouse, et cetera.

(b) Prohibiting certain modes of sex conduct may lead to guilt about very normal sex desires, to an intensification of normal desires. The result may be neurotic symptomatology of many different kinds.

(c) The bottling up of certain modes of sexual expression may force normal persons to turn to compulsive modes of behavior and to do precisely those sex acts which they are most (consciously) ashamed of doing. They may compulsively, and joylessly, perform normal illicit sex acts (e.g., fornication or masturbation), deviational sex acts (e.g., homosexuality or intercourse with animals), or offensive or criminal sex acts (e.g., exhibitionism or forcible rape).

(d) Discouragement of sex pleasures, and designation of them as "disgusting" and "revolting," may lead to neurotic loss of feeling and enjoyment in normal sex acts—including loss of pleasure in marital intercourse.

(e) Discouraging or toning down sex education may lead many men and women to become irrationally and neurotically fearful of normal sex acts like masturbation, nocturnal emissions, menstruation, et cetera.

(f) Interdicting various sex acts may lead to neurotic overemphasis on and preoccupation with these acts and may result in compulsive promiscuity, prurient obsessions on "obscenity," backhanded preoccupations with scatology, continual lascivious thoughts, et cetera.

(g) Damming up sex urges may lead to all kinds of unconscious personality distortions and impulsions. Thus preventing a man from having adulterous relations may cause him to hate a wife whom he otherwise loves, and may even eventually induce him to harm or kill her. Forcing women to live in accordance with a double standard of sex morality may cause them to become obsessively jealous, or to become compulsively enamored of aggressive, masculine life goals.

(h) The essence of good mental hygiene is to enable people to face squarely their desires and behavior and to understand their conscious and unconscious impulses. But banning sex acts normally involves concomitantly banning the discussion of many of these acts, and thus banning the individual's facing his underlying sex feelings and urges. Hence, good mental hygiene procedure and even effective psychotherapy are not given a chance, and sexually impelled or aggravated neurosis tends to run rampant in our society.

(i) Banning a sex act frequently makes it, at the same time, more desirable (because of the scarcity, novelty, and danger thereby attached to it) and less desirable (because of the guilt, anxiety, and fear thereby attached to it). This concomitant heightening and lessening of its desirability inevitably leads to serious conflict on the part of many individuals who have psychobiological impulses to perform a banned sex act. And since conflict is one of the main sources of neurosis, an unhealthy mental situation thus arises for many of our countrymen and countrywomen.

(j) Once a sex act that is still phychobiologically urgent is banned, it is bound to cause mental anguish and conflict: for if we frankly enjoy the act, on the one hand, we will still feel guilty about it underneath; and if we strictly abjure the act, on the other hand, we will feel distinctly deprived and will have (conscious or unconscious) cravings for it. In either eventuality, we will tend to build up (largely unconscious) feelings of doubt, anxiety, and depression—which may easily encourage neurotic outbursts and symptomatology.

(k) The banning of certain sex outlets—e.g., homosexuality—which would be, under normal circumstances, merely peculiar and idiosyncratic modes of behavior, serves to make the users of these outlets neurotic—and to make neurotics use these outlets. In this sense, sex "perversion" does not render society sick, but society makes sick people out of "perverts"—and induces disturbed individuals to use "perversions" as neurotic symptoms.

5. *Debarring certain modes of sex behavior often results in individual and social hypocrisy, evasion, and downright lying.*

(a) Sex behavior may be wholly excoriated when it is frankly enjoyed, and hypocritically accepted when it is mildly disguised. Thus prostitution is roundly condemned when it directly involves a man paying a woman for sexual favors, but is quite acceptable when the same man indirectly spends money on the same woman or supports her in legal marriage only to gain sex favors from her.

(b) Sex behavior may be tolerated when its genital aspects are disguised, but condemned when they are obvious. Thus a woman may publicly display most of her breasts, but she dare not show the tiniest bit of her labia. And, among certain elements of the American populace, heavy petting up to and including mutual orgasm is not considered to be engaging in sex relations, while the slightest interpenetration of the male and female genitalia, even without orgasm, is definitely so considered.

(c) Those who are no longer capable of various types of sex behavior may tend hypocritically to assume smug, holier-than-thou attitudes and to look down upon those who are still desirous of engaging in banned sex acts—and do. Thus judges who might have been sex hellions in their youth may hand out stiff sentences for minor sex infractions by the current younger generation.

(d) A double standard of sex behavior tends to grow up, under which certain acts are tolerated for one group but not for another. Thus a man who openly has a mistress roundly condemns his wife for taking a lover. Or a wealthy girl is envied her sexcapades, while a salesgirl is excoriated for hers.

(e) In actual practice, banning sex acts in our country has often resulted in (i) an increased desire for them and (ii) little lessening of participation in them. This means that millions of Americans consciously *think* one way (e.g., that adultery is "bad") and then *desire* and/or *act* quite another way (e.g., actively commit or desire to commit adultery). Such Americans frequently (consciously or unconsciously) look upon themselves as arrant hypocrites.

(f) Since direct approval of many banned sex acts is impossible in our society, and since the desire for these acts remains high (and often is, ironically, aggravated by the ban), many quasi-serious or humorous allusions to these acts are publicly presented —and this indirect form of presentation constitutes another mode of social hypocrisy. Thus bald-faced "obscenity" is rarely employed in America—but humorous stories, the very essence of whose wit lies in their "obscene" core, are ubiquitous.

(g) Rigorous puritanical sex codes, as we have seen, frequently encourage prurience and lead to the most hypocritical forms of sex behavior. Thus, in order to collect "obscene" material legitimately, men and women may become "vice" crusaders.

6. *Interdicting various types of sex conduct normally leads to considerable individual and group antagonism between those who conform to the interdictions and those who do not.*

(a) In contemporary American society there seems to be a good deal of antagonism between the sexes, part of which stems from the fact that our double standard of morality allows much greater sex freedom to males than to females. Thus girls resent boys' trying to seduce them—and then insisting on marrying virgins.

(b) Within individual couples there presently appears to exist much antagonism and much inhibition of potential love as a result of differing sex goals. Thus girls try to get boys to marry them before having intercourse, and boys try to get girls to have intercourse with them before marriage. Frequently masculine and feminine sex goals are so diverse that, primarily on that count, boy-girl romances never get started or break up quickly after they do start.

(c) Individuals and groups who are forced to conform to prohibitory sex codes frequently become antagonistic to other individuals and groups who manage to evade these codes to some extent. Thus married individuals may tend to resent the comparative sexual freedom of single individuals and violently to condemn the latter.

7. *The contrabanding of various sex acts often leads to illogical and self-contradictory individual and social sex philosophies.*

(a) Some aspects of sex behavior may be discouraged which, were they not banned, would help uphold the bans on other aspects of sex behavior. Thus masturbation, which normally acts as something of a substitute for and inhibitor of fornication, is illogically interdicted along with fornication itself. And birth control, which would prevent abortions and illegitimate pregnancies, is excoriated along with the latter aspects of sex behavior.

(b) Some sex acts (e.g., illegitimate pregnancy) are unofficially prosecuted although not legally banned, while other sex acts (e.g., fornication) are legally banned (in some states of our union) but unofficially highly tolerated.

(c) Some intrinsically harmless sex acts (e.g., masturbation and homosexual relations between adults) are placed in the same condemned category as other intrinsically harmful acts (e.g., assaultive rape).

(d) Publicly anathematizing a given mode of sex conduct may, ironically, give additional status and esteem to some of those who frankly partake of this mode of conduct. Thus men become envious of other men who are notorious fornicators or whoremongers; and even women may prefer promiscuous men for their bedmates. Again, being able to employ "obscenity" or scatological language in a frank and open manner may become a mark of sophistication or hardboiledness and be thereby duly (and even unduly) esteemed.

(e) Emotionalized, illogical sex attitudes grow up because of banning certain activities; and these emotionalized attitudes often lead to inadequate, emotionalized types of sex education, which, in turn, maintain the original emotionalized, illogical sex attitudes, thus effectuating a continuing vicious circle.

(f) Men and women, because of sex bans, often crave the sexually impossible. Thus current sex contradictions cause men to want wives who are "pure"—and wanton; and cause women to want husbands who are good economic supporters—and unpredictable, exciting lovers.

(g) Sex prohibitions encourage obscurantism and sex superstitions, which are most idiotic and illogical. Thus lack of adequate sex education encourages people to believe in astrological influences on their love lives, or to hold to sex rites—e.g., taboos on intercourse during menstruation—which have long been scientifically invalidated.

8. *Forbidding various modes of sex conduct frequently results not in the disappearance or even lessening of that conduct, but in its continued performance—with concomitant self-punishment, guilt, anxiety, pain, and anguish on the part of those who practice it.*

(a) Even when people "get away with" banned sex conduct and go "scot-free" for violating the bans, they are usually (consciously or unconsciously) guilty over their behavior and suffer direct pangs of conscience or indirect unpleasant psychophysical effects.

(b) Sometimes the banning of a sex act directly or indirectly *causes* dire consequences for its perpetrators. Thus banning fornication logically leads to banning birth control and venereal disease control—and these latter bans provide distinct penalties (e.g., illegitimate pregnancy, abortion, and syphilis) for many fornicators.

(c) When society bans a sex act for which many of its members still feel strong psychobiological urges, these members have the choice of (i) consciously favoring the sex act, and feeling unconsciously guilty and shameful about it, or (ii) consciously disfavoring the act, and feeling unconsciously compelled to resort to it nevertheless. In either eventuality, the banned act is usually, in one degree or another, actually *performed*—and then regretted. Thus birth control, in contemporary America, is utilized by the great majority of us; but the negative propaganda that is subtly or frankly dispersed in connection with it forces us unconsciously to feel guilty though we consciously accept it, or consciously to feel guilty when we reject it in theory but are nevertheless driven to its practice. In either event, we perform it with pain, trouble and qualms.

The foregoing behavioral sequelae of our contemporary sex prohibitions, and of the utterly conflicting and confused attitudes which we have acquired in relation to them, are, it will be noted, virtually all dismal and unfortunate. Are there, then, no advantages to prohibiting or discouraging certain modes of sex behavior?

Doubtless there are, since obviously our civilization seems to be better off for banning sex acts like assaultive rape than it would be if it encouraged this practice. It may also be argued—and, indeed, often, and at great length, has been—that societal prohibitions against sex activities like fornication, adultery, promiscuity, and prostitution have a distinctly salutary effect on civilized life.

Perhaps so. But the findings of this study offer no supportive evidence in this connection. What they do show—and that fairly conclusively—is that in contemporary America most of our official and legal sex bans are *not* very effective, *are* being continually and widely flouted in both theory and practice, and *are* accepted by our citizenry in an incredibly conflicting and confused manner. Under *these* conditions, the behavioral results, when viewed in terms of thoughts, feelings, and actions of the everyday common garden-variety American male and female, are truly dreadful and depressing. To say otherwise would be completely to contradict the main findings of this study.

WHAT MAY BE DONE ABOUT THE FACTS DISCOVERED?

The facts of this study seem clearly to point to one main moral; namely, that human sexuality cannot easily be downed and that even—perhaps especially—in a society like our own, which is officially and legally sexually repressive and inhibited, human psychobiological sex drives remain sufficiently high and undownable, causing endless individual and societal conflicts, confusions, and contradictions.

Otherwise stated: whatever the intrinsic demands of human sexuality may or may not be, it seems clear, in this day and age, that when we attempt to push sex down here it tends to rise up there, and that all our attempts to outlaw, penalize, and denigrate various modes of sex behavior have resulted mainly in liberalizing reactions against conservative proscriptions; in pluralistic instead of monolithic sex views; in sex acts which directly contradict sex theories; in unconscious sex urges which effectively sabotage conscious motivations; in people's finding heightened interest and pleasure in many banned sex acts; in the growth and abetting of multitudinous forms of sexual and general neuroses; in the prevalence of widespread sexual hypocrisy; in the promotion of formidable amounts of sex antagonism; in the formation of numerous illogical and idiotic sex philosophies and rules; and in the production of enormous degrees of sexual and general pain, dissatisfaction, anxiety, and woe for literally millions of Americans.

The question, therefore, obviously arises: What should be done to alleviate or correct our current sexual embarrassments, inconsistencies, inequities, and chaos?

Since this purports to be a scientific study, moralistic *shoulds* and *musts* are probably out of place in it. The writer, partly because of his findings in the course of this research, and partly because of his own emotional prejudices and biases, has as pronounced views on these *shoulds* and *musts* as has anyone. Scientifically, however, these views may not be entirely relevant and should perhaps appear in a different context rather than in the present volume. (Since writing the first edition of this book, many of my personal sex views have appeared in *The American Sexual Tragedy* and *Sex Without Guilt*.)

Sticking, however, to the objective findings of this study, and avoiding (for the nonce) moralistic *shoulds* and *musts*, it may still be legitimately noted what Americans *may* do to resolve, to some extent, their contemporary disordered, deranged, and disheveled attitudes and acts relating to different modes of sex behavior.

In general, it would appear that we have the choice of: (1) learning to tolerate our present contradictory, liberal-conservative sex views in a more democratically accepting manner; (2) continuing to change our sex attitudes so that they become more consistently liberal; or (3) returning to a distinctly conservative, rigorously monolithic state of sexual philosophy and activity, and ruthlessly uprooting all the sexual laxity, liberality, and lasciviousness which we have allowed to creep into our present-day mores.

The first alternative—that of our learning to tolerate both liberal and conservative sex viewpoints and allowing them to exist side by side in our society—is probably impractical for several reasons: (1) It leads, as we have been seeing throughout this book, to conscious and unconscious confusion, guilt, and grief on the part of both liberals and conservatives. (2) It cannot be tolerated by sexual arch-conservatives—such as the religious pressure groups— since it at least allows *some* individuals and groups to preach and to practice sexual liberalism. (3) Consequently, it will lead to a continual—and perhaps total—warfare, which will result, in all probability, in the victory of alternative 2 or alternative 3—consistent sexual liberalism *or* conservatism eventually becoming the order of the day.

The ultimate choice, then, seems to be between our going forward to be as consistently liberal in our sex views and acts as the limitations of human nature will allow—or in our going back to consistent, ultraconservative sex attitudes and activities. Both these alternatives comprehend human risks and dangers, and involve the development of patterns of thinking, feeling, and living which are radically different from those most of us follow today. One of them, it may fairly safely be predicted, will ultimately prevail among those elements of humanity who somehow manage to survive our present troubled times.

Which do you suppose it will be?

GROWING UP ABSURD

*As noted in the introduction, a major point stressed by
sociologists is the interrelatedness of the different values
and institutions of a given society. The reading that follows,
while not specifically sociological, illustrates this tenet of the
sociological approach. Literary and social critic Paul Goodman has been in the forefront of a recent critical appraisal of
the dominant values and patterns of life in America today. In
his analysis, any problems we have regarding sex represent
but one aspect (albeit an important one) of what is more generally wrong with our society.*

*The situation of young people is of special interest to Good-
man, who has forcefully condemned the way in which "the
organized system" stifles healthy and socially desirable inclinations. Goodman believes that modern youth understandably rebels or retreats in the face of an impersonal, market-
oriented way of life that offers no enduring values and no
meaningful ways of livelihood. In the sexual realm as in
others, he suggests, we are squelching what is good and
healthy in the individual, in the interests of what is in many
respects a sick society. One of Goodman's major concerns has
been over the loss of a sense of "community" engendered by
industrialization, urbanization, and the growth of bureau-
cracy. Although it may be somewhat utopian to hope for communal feelings within a way of life inevitably geared to the
modern industrial city, few would argue with the general
aim of reducing superficiality and meaninglessness in social
relationships (including sexual ones).*

Growing Up Absurd

PAUL GOODMAN

Let us next talk about marriage and so-called "animal" functions of the social animal.

Everyone agrees that an important condition for the troubles of growing up is the troubles between the parents at home, brutal quarrels and drunkenness, coldness, one or the other or both parents getting away as often as possible and being withdrawn while present, and marriages breaking up. The most common popular, and mayoral, prescription for delinquency is "more parental supervision." In the usual circumstances this would likely *increase* the tension and the trouble, but be that as it may: the question remains, how? how to have reasonable supervision when the marriages themselves are no good? for presumably the good marriages don't have the problem children. (The frequent recommendation to fine or jail the parents is a lulu.)

I do not think the public spokesmen are serious. For powerful and well-known modern reasons, some of them inevitable, the institution of marriage itself, as we have known it for several hundred years, cannot work simply any longer, and is very often the direct cause of intense suffering. Urbanism, the economic independence of women, contraception, relaxing the inhibitions against unmarried and extramarital sexuality, these are inevitable. A dispassionate observer of modern marriage might sensibly propose, Forget it; think up some other form of mating and child care. The pastor of a large church in an ordinary Midwestern town told me that, in his observation, not one marriage in twenty was worth while; many were positively damaging to the children. If very many marriages could simply let themselves dissolve after a few years, the partners would suddenly become brighter, rosier, and younger. But of course, in this field there are no dispassionate observers. We are all in the toils of jealousy of our own Oedipus complexes, and few of us can tolerate loneliness and the feeling of being abandoned. Nor do we *have* any other formula for secure sex, companionship, and bringing up children.

This is not a newsy story. Is it kept in mind by the Mayor of New York whose canned voice says every night on the radio that parents who are not affectionately supervising the children are failing in responsibility? Has the Mayor not seen an harassed mother hysterically and unmercifully whacking a three-year old in the sand pile?

Does he think it is some different parent he is now appealing to? (I heard one mother scream, "I ask you only one simple thing, to obey me!")

"Most of the children we see [in King's County Domestic Relations Court] have been so seriously damaged by their environment that they need 24-hour-a-day corrective treatment. I'll say unequivocally that most of the children we see should be separated from their parents for their own health and welfare." (Dr. J. M. Fries.)

Consider some incidents of sex and marriage in a more "privileged" and a more "underprivileged" situation. For the first, we can return to the remarkable boom in early marriages and child bearing that we mentioned in the last chapter, occurring especially among the economically privileged who previously would have married late. No doubt this has been partly due to the war and Cold War, clinging to life and clutching to something safe in an era of anxiety. But it seems to be also partly a strong reaction to the drift toward formlessness which these young persons could observe in their own parents.

These young-marrying, contemporaries or juniors of the Beat Generation, have often expressed themselves as follows: "My highest aim in life is to achieve a normal healthy marriage and raise healthy [non-neurotic] children." On the face of it, this remark is preposterous. What was always taken as a usual and advantageous life-condition for work in the world and the service of God, is now regarded as an heroic goal to be striven for. Yet we see that it *is* a hard goal to achieve against the modern obstacles. Also it is a *real* goal, with objective problems that man can work at personally, and take responsibility for, and make decisions about —unlike the interpersonal relations of the corporation, or the routine of the factory job for which the worker couldn't care less.

But now, suppose the young man is achieving this goal: he has the wife, the small kids, the suburban home, and the labor-saving domestic devices. How is it that it is the same man who uniformly asserts that he is in a Rat Race? Either the goal does not justify itself, or indeed he is not really achieving it. Perhaps the truth is, if marriage and children are the *goal*, a man cannot really achieve it. It is not easy to conceive of a strong husband and father who does not feel justified in his work and independent in the world. Correspondingly, his wife feels justified in the small children, but does she have a man, do the children have a father, if he is running a Rat Race? Into what world do the small children grow up in such a home?

It is advantageous to the smooth functioning of the organized system if its personnel are married and have home responsibilities. (E.g., it's much harder for them to act up and quit.) But the smooth functioning of the organized system may not be advantageous to the quality of the marriage and the fatherhood. It is a troubling picture. On the one hand, early marriage is excellent and promising, especially in the probable case that both the young people have had sexual experiences and could have others, and they have chosen the marriage as a reasonably steady and jealousy-free alternative. And having the children early is admirable, rather than delaying for the empty reasons that middle-class people used to give. On the other hand, to take on such early responsibilities indicates an early resignation: the marriage seems partly to be *instead of* looking ambitiously for a worth-while career.

If the highest aim in life is to achieve a normal marriage and raise healthy children, we can understand the preoccupation with Psychology, for the parents do not have much activity of their own to give rules to the family life. The thousand manuals of sex technique and happy marriage, then, have the touching dignity of evangelical tracts, as is indeed their tone; they teach how to be saved and there is no other way to be saved.

On the children is lavished an avalanche of attention. They cannot possibly reward so much attention, and the young father, at least, soon gets pretty bored and retires to his Do-It-Yourself. Now it used to be said that middle-class parents frustrate the children more, to meet high standards, but the frustration is acceptable because it leads to an improved status, esteemed by the children; the lower classes, on the contrary, are more permissive; nor would the discipline be accepted, because the father is disesteemed. What then is the effect, in the ranch houses, if the discipline is maintained, because the standard is high, but the status is disesteemed, first by the father himself, who talks cynically about it; then by the mother, who does not respect it; then by the growing children? *Is it possible to maintain and pass on a middle-class standard without belief in its productive and cultural mission?*

I wonder if we are not here describing the specific genesis of a Beat Generation: young men who (1) cannot break away from the father who has been good to them, but who (2) simply cannot affirm father's values; and (3) there are no other dominant social values to compensate. If this is the case, where now there are thousands of these young men, there will be hundreds of thousands. *The organized system is the breeding ground of a Beat Generation.*

Among poor young men, quitting school early and perhaps meeting discrimination in the better unions, or other obstacles to making something of themselves, the more permitted and widely stimulated sexuality can work as a deadly trap. For there is desire and sexual opportunity at the same time as the older adolescent's sense of personal worth is diminishing. He must act the man when he does not feel like a man. This may come to the impotence of the unemployed or the self-disapproving alcoholic. It is not helped, either, if the desirable women seem to choose "successful" fellows, or if a young man has the convention that dating costs money. The contrary alternative is that sex itself become a proof of manly worth, a form of conquest without lust or love, or not even conquest, but simply potency. For instance, young Navy sailors who on the ship are griping but docile children, on shore regard the women as their "pigs" and do not let themselves get "involved." Among the Spanish poor, too, the tradition of *macho*, masculinity, that they have brought with them, seems to be especially a means of proof that a young man is not a contemptible boy.

On either alternative, his sexual need can get a fellow into plenty of trouble. To get the money and be a success, he may steal. If he proves himself by sex, brutality or promiscuity will get him into sexual scrapes. If sex gets him into too much trouble or if his doubt of potency is too strong, he may withdraw altogether, into gambling or being a tough guy, or passively into narcotics.

There are class differences; but through all classes, it is hard to grow up when the general social attitude toward sexuality is inconsistent and unpredictable. (It is hard to exist as an adult too.) In this respect our society is uniquely problematical. Broadly speaking, there are three universally widespread and incompatible attitudes toward sexual behavior, and two of these are inconsistent in themselves.

In the ideal theory and practice, sexuality is one of the most important natural functions and the attitude toward it ranges from permissive to enthusiastic. This is the position of all Thinking, of public spokesmen and women's magazines, and of the Supreme Court in its decisions on classics of literature; and it is somewhat put into practice by psychological parents, mental hygienists, nursery schools, and bands of adolescents and adults. Yet there are puzzling inconsistencies. What applies to brother does not apply to sister, though every girl is somebody's sister. What is affirmed and tacitly condoned, must still not be done overtly. For instance, although all Serious Thought is agreed on the simple natural function and there are colorful little abstract treatises for children, it is inconceivable for a publisher to print a sober little juvenile story about, say, playing doctor or the surprising discovery of masturbation.A character in a juvenile (or adult) adventure story may not incidentally get an erection as he may wolf a sandwich or get sleepy. It seems obvious that, here as everywhere else, the only antidote for the sadistic-sexual comic books that are objected to, is the presentation of factual truth and a matter-of-fact tone; whereas what we have, permissiveness combined with withdrawal from real contact, precisely produces the sadistic-sexual need. This is the bread-and-butter of psychological theory; why it is not said in the annual investigations of the comic books? Again, although most public spokesmen are for a "healthy frankness," the public schools are run quite otherwise. Let me recall a typical incident recently in California (spring of '59). A high school science teacher employed the bright-idea project of tabulating the class's sexual habits as an exercise in fact finding. This got him into terrible hot water, and the School Board carefully explained, "What we teach is human reproduction, much as we discuss the functions of the human eye or ear," that is, without mentioning light or sound, color or harmony, or any other act or relation.

(I am writing this equably and satirically, but the stupidity of these people is outrageous.)

The treatment of sexuality in the popular culture and the commodities and advertising is less puzzling: it is to maximize sales. Existing lust is exploited and as far as possible there is created an artificial stimulation, with the justified confidence that the kind of partial satisfactions obtainable will involve buying something:

cosmetics, sharp clothes, art magazines, dating entertainment. And since, for very many people, lust is at present accompanied by embarrassment, shame, and punishment, these too are exploited as much as possible. I do not think there is here any inconsistency. One simply goes along with the widespread melodramatic fantasy of lust and punishment. E.g., the public sentiment for Caryl Chessman's execution, 70 per cent, expressed itself with terrifying frequency in sadistic, pornographic, and vindictive language: the plays of Tennessee Williams are the deep poetry of these people. It would be inconsistent if the popular culture tried to be factual, analytic, or compassionate. But there is an absolute incompatibility between this sexuality of popular culture and the ideal theory and practice of the "simple natural function."

If we ask, however, what is acceptable public behavior in the neighborhoods or with the neighbors, the confusion is baffling. There are islands of contradictory practice, even though these may have the identical Culture and almost the same Thought. Kids masturbating may be smiled on or ignored, or they may be barred from one's home, or they may be arrested as delinquent. Among the boys themselves, up to the age of thirteen mutual masturbation is a wicked thrill, but after thirteen it is queer and absolutely to be inhibited. Adolescent couples must pet or it is felt that something is wrong with them; but "how far?" Sometimes they may copulate, if they can get away with it; or they absolutely must not. You may admire and speak to strange girls on the street, it is flattering and shows spirit; or you may not, it is rude and threatening. But if you whistle at them while you huddle in your own group, that's bully. You may pet in public like the French; you may not pet in public, it's disgusting; you may on the beach but not on the grass. Among the boys, to boast of actual or invented prowess is acceptable, but to speak soberly of a love affair or a sexual problem in order to be understood is strictly taboo; it is more acceptable among girls. It is assumed that older teen-agers are experienced and sophisticated, but they are legal minors who must not be corrupted. More important, any relation between an older teen-aged girl and a man even in his twenties, or between an older teen-aged boy and an experienced woman, is shocking and ludicrous, though this is the staple of sexual education among the civilized.

In this tangle of incompatible and inconsistent standards, one strand is sure and predictable: that the law will judge by the most out-of-date, senseless, and unpsychological convention, even though it is against the consensus of almost every family in the neighborhood and the confessional attitude of the parish priest. They will arrest you for nude bathing a mile away on a lonely beach. (But this tendency to maintain the moral-obsolete is, of course, inevitable in our kind of democracy. A legislator may believe what he pleases, but how can he publicly propose the repeal of a statute against sin?)

I am describing again an interrupted revolution, the so-called Sexual Revolution. We see again how the organized system of production and sales manages to profit by the confusion of the interruption, whereas a finished revolution would be economically a dead loss, since good sexual satisfaction costs nothing, it needs only health and affection.

Special mention must be given to male homosexuality, which preoccupies adolescents and young men of every class from bottom to top. The preoccupation appears either as gnawing doubts that oneself might be a "latent homosexual," or as reactive contempt and ridicule, or hostility and even paranoia. Among young people every kind of nonconformism in a contemporary tends to be thought of as homosexual, whether it be a passion for music or a passion for social justice.

Inevitably in the stimulating and hectic sexual atmosphere, including overtly expressed homosexuality, repressed homosexual thoughts also begin to break through. Remnants of unfinished normal homosexual situations reappear, and one is sharply aware of new temptations in the culture. The shared narcissism of dandy hair-do's is astonishingly prevalent; the affectionate body-contact of buddies is obsessionally inhibited or immediately commented on and "interpreted"; and one sees queers everywhere.

The question must be asked why the breakthrough into awareness seems to balk and circle at just this point on just this issue? why, in the present, just the homosexual temptations and threats loom so large? One important answer, I think, is the theme I have been developing in this book. The fellows are interrupted in growing up as men; their homosexuality threatens them as immaturity. They are afraid of going backward to boyhood status, admiring the model penises and powers of their seniors and adults. Or they regress further to a safe narcissism and would want their own penises and bodies to be loved as their personal worth, but this reversion to infantilism is fiercely resisted.

In the difficulty of growing up, the young man psychologically regresses to an earlier stage because it is easier, he cannot take on the responsibiltiies of heterosexual love and masculine conflict. But then, doubting his potency and to avoid ridicule and danger, he becomes obsessionally heterosexual and competitive; or alternatively, he may become apathetic and sexually not there.

PREMARITAL SEXUAL BEHAVIOR: A SYMPOSIUM

The control of premarital sexual behavior has been a matter of great concern in our society—both anxious parents and confused young people attest to the fact that this problem generates much uncertainty and tension. However one views the apparent long-term trend toward greater premarital permissiveness, it has to be recognized that one cannot simply turn the clock back and reinstitute unquestioning adherence to earlier norms. The automobile, if nothing else, has rendered extensive chaperonage impossible; at the same time the widespread availability of contraceptives has effected an irrevocable change in the likely consequences of (and in attitudes toward) premarital relations.

Since pious platitudes will not significantly alter this situation, it may be a good deal more useful to examine carefully the various sexual standards that have existed in the past and that seem to be developing at the present time. The following symposium represents a diversity of views regarding premarital sex, held by a number of family specialists. While none of them has any monopoly on truth in these matters, all such considered statements on such a crucial issue deserve our attention.

Premarital Sexual Behavior:
A Symposium

The Control of Adolescent Premarital Coitus:
An Attempt at Clarification of the Problem

THOMAS POFFENBERGER

The November, 1960 issue of Marriage and Family Living published an article by L. A. Kirkendall which elaborated on his thesis that the decisions of a couple regarding premarital coitus should be made by them on the basis of how they believe the act will affect their interpersonal relations. In the same issue, the writer published critical papers concerning the Kirkendall concept, pointing out among other things the problem a young couple would have foretelling the effects of coitus as well as the likelihood that such a concept would be used as a rationalizing mechanism. These papers were in turn commented upon by Kirkendall and all published in the same issue. Professor Klemer subsequently conducted a study of some of his college students asking them to express their attitudes about the issues raised. The present paper is in response to a request to comment further upon the subject and to attempt a clarification of the writer's views.

The first section will include both a further critique of Kirkendall's position and responses to his comments on the writer's earlier paper. The second part will attempt to clarify the issues and offer a positive approach to the problem.

I. REPLY AND CRITIQUE

1. *Humanistic concepts are not the antithesis of mores*
Kirkendall feels that the present author's position is not clear,

Reprinted from *Marriage and Family Living*, 24 (1962), 254-278; footnotes omitted.

that first there is expressed a belief in the value of a humanistic basis for sex morality and that then a brief for the mores is indicated. The apparent cause of the confusion is because there *has* beeen expressed a belief in both. In fact, this was a major point in the original article on "morality" and "piety"—that for the survival of any society, individuals representing both positions are needed. It is true that the humanistic concepts often come into conflict with the mores of a society as we well know, but it is another thing to indicate that they cannot exist together. As much as some might desire it, few humanists would claim that man will ever be able to live in a society without political structure.

2. *"Interpersonal relationships" is not a complete concept of "moral" behavior.*

Kirkendall defines moral experiences as "those which promise to enlarge the number of persons or groups with which we are able to cooperate." He states further, "Cohesion and solidarity between persons or within small groups obtained by methods which create barriers, block communication, or, in the long-run, wall off others in their outreaching realationships reflect an immoral approach to human relationships."

Many have expressed concern about the organization man and the other directed person. Should we now label a person as immoral just because he acts in ways which do not promise to "enlarge the number of people he is able to cooperate with?" If a society is to be dynamic, do we not need some people who are *not* willing to cooperate in the conventional sense? There were many professors at the University of California who would not sign the so-called loyalty oath and thus caused numerous problems of an interpersonal nature. According to Kirkendall's definition, such persons would be regarded as immoral, but is the country not better off because a few men were strong enough in their beliefs in freedom of expression to be outspoken, in spite of the fact that they not only created dissonance in a large institution, the state, and in a sense, in the nation at large?

Certainly we all must agree that in a world of conflict, better interpersonal relationships are not only desirable; they are a necessity! However, we may question whether or not this should be the *only* criterion for determining the morality of behavior. For example, this exchange may not better interpersonal relationships, but it may produce other results which will make it worth while. Such a debate is neither moral nor immoral. Just as there are premarital sex relationships which could be regarded as amoral, there are certainly many situations in which there is no misrepresentation, no exploitation, and where both persons benefit from a sexual encounter, yet the lives of neither are significantly affected.

3. *Improved "interpersonal relationships" should not be the only criterion of satisfactory sex behavior*

Judging from this point of view, Kirkendall would ask us to evaluate every sex act in marriage as well as before marriage, in terms of his list of criteria. Aside from the complications of the pocket check list which immediately comes to mind, this approach can present other difficulties. Males in our society have already been told that it is their responsibility to produce an orgasm in their women, and that if they don't it is somehow their fault, when this actually may or may not be the case. We have husbands who seek counseling because they are disturbed about this when the cause of the difficulty can be helped only by long psychotherapy with the wife, if indeed it can be helped then. In spite of the fact that the male, at present, is still conditioned to regard sex as one thing and love as something else, he must now consider whether or not the sex act will deepen his partner's relationship with him. Is it not possible that a preoccupation with "interpersonal relations" will tend to increase male guilt and concern? In some cases a certain amount of concern on the part of the man would be helpful to the woman, but in other cases the male is so guilt-ridden that any increase in concern would only create greater conflict. It seems that if we *must* make general recommendations a more specific approach might be of more value. The present day sex manuals are often helpful and reassuring, although their approach is not new. The *Kamasutra* educated Hindus two thousand years ago about the importance of a refined mutual relationship for the sexual satisfaction of both partners and described in detail how this might be accomplished.

Other criteria come to mind other than "interpersonal relations" in judging the satisfactory nature of sex behavior. Sex as play, engaged in for fun and relaxation as well as for physical satisfaction, is an example. Foote has offered some realistic observations on this subject, including its relationship to premarital coitus.

4. *"Interpersonal relationships" is a contradictory concept*

In regard to the high school age group, Kirkendall tells the adolescent that premarital coitus is not wrong in itself; it is wrong only if it is disturbing to the couple's interpersonal relations. Yet in his "reply" he states, "In my current article and in other of my writings a clear and firm position has been taken against exploitive, advantage-taking attitudes and behavior. This position, in my judgment, eliminates, both now and probably for a long time to come, the use of premarital intercourse as a solution to the sex problems of youth." He goes on to say, "We must, nevertheless, be able to face the possibility that ways may be found to use sex in premarital relationships in a positive, meaningful way. This we will be able to do if we can focus on the really important issue—the creation of sound interpersonal relations."

Is it advisable that we recommend that parents and teachers tell young people that all the research shows premarital coitus among high school students is ill-advised, but on the other hand, that in certain instances coitus can and should deepen a couple's interpersonal relationship? We need to consider the possibility that not only may the interpersonal relations concept not be helpful, it may be actually harmful from a mental health standpoint.

Klemer has pointed to O. H. Mowrer's position that neurosis is more often produced by anxiety over what is correct behavior than by the curbing of physical desires. This, of course, does not mean that physical desire is denied nor that some release may not be found.

In his rebuttal, Kirkendall says, "Both Mowrer and Poffenberger seem to regard sexual control as a matter of continual struggle and as a sort of running battle between consuming desires and one's social self."

Limited social research indicates that the problem varies with societies and individuals, but at present the writer takes the position that sexual control *does* involve a conflict between sex drive, both biological and conditioned, and one's social self.

Abram Kardiner speaks to this point when he says, ". . . it always seems that the pursuit of individual happiness and satisfaction must yield to the welfare of society in which everyone has a stake but for which no one on his own wishes to take the responsibility. The individual cannot see that sex morality purports to protect his interests as well as that of society. It may be that the protection he gets is not appreciated because the price he pays for it is too high, and society, through obligatory custom, seems to him more like the obstructor of his freedom than the guardian of his interests. This has always been, and still is, the dilemma of sex morality."

It is true that when behavior is sanctioned there will be many who behave in ways counter to the mores. This fact alone, however, does not justify the removal of the sanctions.

Ausubel points out, "Once sex drives have been actualized from their physiological substrata they become much too urgent and insistent to be repressed in the majority of individuals." He states further, "When social sanctions or moral scruples prevent sexual gratification through premarital intercourse, some direct substitutive outlet such as masturbation or petting is the general practice." From a mental health standpoint he believes that, "As long as the adolescent does not *internalize* moral obligations to abide by these taboos, and as long as opportunities for clandestine gratification are available, no more mental conflict is generated than under conditions of unrestricted freedom as in Samoa." One cannot be sure how valid this statement is, but a case can be made for justifying such sex outlets as prostitution. It is well to bring up this point for consideration because of Kirkendall's concern over boys' visits to prostitutes. He bases this concern on the fact that 19, or half his sample of 38 boys who had visited them, said that the experience was unsatisfactory. In considering his results, an examination of the study is indicated. In the first place, there may be a selective factor in boys who are willing to tell an adult about their sex experiences. From a psychological standpoint the interviews may serve several outlets: one of them being the need to confess wrong doing. After the confessional, one is expected to expiate himself. The parent figure nature of the relationship the boys had with Kirkendall would tend to cause them to give him the answer they felt he would like, and so one might expect them to play up the negative aspects of their experiences. It is then not unexpected that these boys reported their experiences with prostitutes as having been unsatisfactory. However, having been unsatisfied with the experience does not necessarily imply that there may have been serious psychological effects as a result. The very impersonal nature of such a relationship would make it very questionable that any lasting emotional effects would ensue unless the youth were already disturbed in his psycho-sexual development.

Kirkendall further suggests the possibility of adding to the schools' sex education programs a discussion of "the significance and meaning of prostitution, and masculine participation in it." Let us proceed cautiously for two reasons. We are *now* having problems with sex education. For example, in the spring of 1961, a newspaper in a large city reported the fact that the teacher, in a mixed class of 16-year-olds had handed out a well-known sex inventory which was thereupon filled out and exchanged between boys and girls. If all the facts were presented correctly, the signed complaint of 1,000 parents was justified. The author has said before that to have co-educational sex education on the basis that sex should be treated like any other subject is questionable. The position can be taken that it is *not* like any other subject and will not be in the foreseeable future. Also, because we all have our blind spots in regard to sex, great care must be taken in examining our motives with regard to how we handle the subject. Specifically we may need to be concerned about the possible unconscious erotic stimulation that some gain from teaching sex which motivates them to behavior that is harmful to the program. Children become confused by such teachers' preoccupation with the subject. However, the main reason for questioning Kirkendall's plan to teach about prostitution is that within the framework of the school system, there is only one way in which it could be taught, and that is from the negative standpoint. The old profession would not get a "fair shake." More seriously, it would be just one more situation in which boys would be made to feel more guilty than they already do about their sex feelings.

This is not to be construed as a recommendation that teen-age boys visit prostitutes. The point is, that in the absence of conclusive research data it is unwise to make *any* recommendations.

5. *The interpersonal relationships concept may be used prematurely by parents and teachers*

Some care needs to be taken in giving advice to parents and teachers. While a non-directive approach is not the complete answer, parent education might have avoided many of its past difficulties by accepting more of the Rogerian method of counseling. Certainly we in the profession have been freer in the past with our advice to parents than subsequent research and experience have justified. Perhaps the major theme should be caution.

The writer was much concerned last year when a teacher said to him that Kirkendall's ideas had been such a help to her. She said, "Now I have an answer; I just tell the girls and boys that they have to consider both sides of the question: Will sexual intercourse strengthen or weaken their relationship?" It isn't known how she follows up this approach, but one might imagine from her comment, that since it was a difficult subject for her to deal with, she dropped it as soon as possible. Her answer, however, kept her from being regarded as an "old fuddy," which she feared she might have been considered if she had said high school students should not have coitus. The teacher felt she had *an answer,* but it is doubtful that any of the students felt they had been given one.

6. *The "interpersonal relationships" concept is not one that either can or should be used in a public high school*

As Kirkendall evaluates adolescent coitus, it is neither good nor bad in itself. This evaluation is, like it or not, counter to the present mores of the society. Secondary schools are one of the major institutions of this society, and they play a significant role in the social conditioning of our youth; as such they must uphold the mores. As long as adolescent premarital coitus is not approved of by the majority of the members of the society, the schools can take only the position that it is not approved of and not approved of under any circumstances. To the extent that high school teachers deviate from the mores in this regard, they do harm to the cause of sex education. A Swedish sex educator, Professor C. W. Herlitz, Chief Doctor to Schools in Sweden, expressed it this way, "It is true that sex education should not be unrealistic, but, on the other hand, it should not advocate principles or a manner of life which are unworthy or undesirable either to society or to the individual. Education should make it quite clear what is undesirable and what standards are not to be adopted."

II. COMMENTS ON A POSITIVE APPROACH
TO THE PROBLEM

1. *The inculcation of values regarding proper conduct can best be done by a non-authoritarian approach*

Kirkendall said in his rebuttal, "Suppose instead of sexual decisions we had been discussing irresponsible auto driving—would Drs. Mowrer and Poffenberger then advance the same points?" The answer for the latter at least is "yes!" Kirkendall says the author is concerned with "permissiveness" while he, on the other hand, has repeatedly said that youth today are full of "pious dictates" which have shown themselves not to be effective. Although we need more data on the subject, some of the studies of juvenile delinquency indicate we may need a bit more of the pious dictates which Kirkendall derides. A friend of the author was recently released from a two-weeks' recuperation in a hospital because a car driven by a teen-age boy, traveling at an excessive speed, smashed into his car from the rear. The boy was returning from picking up his 1961 Impala where it had been in a repair shop as a result of a collision he had had two weeks earlier. The boy's parents had given him a car so he could drive six blocks to high school. This boy has been given everything he ever wanted, and he has no respect for himself, his parents, or anyone else. Yet his parents would be regarded by most persons as being "fine people," and they have repeatedly talked to him about the effect of his behavior on others. They have failed, however, to make clear to him that not only is there behavior that is not acceptable, but that he must pay for transgressions that endanger the welfare of others. This is a reality of life, and it seems advisable for the welfare of the child as well as for the society that children learn it early and that they learn it from their parents.

In the aforementioned article of the exchange, Kirkendall said that the writer believes our "best control is a good resounding 'no'." He went on to say, "The writer cannot agree with Poffenberger that we must retreat to the old approach which has failed us so often and so badly in the past." A vain search was made to find where a return to the past was suggested. Also, although the writer admits to taking the position that at present it is best for professional persons in the field to continue to support society's opposition to premarital coitus among junior high and high school students, it is misleading to say that this is being authoritarian. We are considering here the inculcation of attitudes regarding proper conduct. This is an area in which there is some research, but as everywhere in the field of human relations, we are just beginning to understand the infinite complexities of the conditioning process. In the author's previously quoted article it was said that in a democratic society we are interested in developing individuals who are able to base much of their behavior on principle rather than responding to the dictates of an overly rigid superego or only upon external controls.

Hartmann has pointed out that every moral value system has its origins in the relations of the child to adults who are not only loved and hated but who are also persons in authority. The evolving value system may run the gamut from authoritarian to antiauthoritarian character but regardless, the system usually appears in the form of imperatives or commands. A parent may be quite antiauthoritarian, but because his child identifies closely with him and so wants to be like him, the values and beliefs of the parent become the values and beliefs of the child, and they tend to guide him all of his life.

2. *An understanding adult can aid the adolescent in developing firmer moral convictions by helping him develop self-insight*

We have learned better ways to handle moral training than those which were used in the past. We now know that increased self-awareness can have an effect upon one's moral code. Broadening of self-knowledge, including motivations, can lead to a broadening of the sense of responsibility and the avoidance of easy rationalizations. A clearer awareness of one's actual value structure, as well as insight into the implication of one's behavior will not make an immoral person moral but it can tend to lead to greater consistency of conduct which in itself is an essential part of morality. Parents can add to such self-understanding on the part of the child, as can other understanding adults in the child's world. However, the parent has a double function. He must play the role of friend and counselor, and at other times the role of one who controls behavior.

We recognize the problem of conflict in these roles when both are attempted by a school official such as a dean of students. The person who is responsible for control of behavior usually finds few students willing to confide at any great length. Before confiding, the student wants someone whose response will be sympathetic and understanding rather than disciplinary. In recognition of the conflict in the two roles, schools attempt to vest different individuals with them. Less attention has beeen paid to the fact that parents are expected, as a matter of course, to play both roles. This can be done, but there needs to be a clear recognition on the part of the parent that these are different roles, and it helps if the child understands this also. There are many times when a parent must take an unpopular stand on an issue, say he is sorry, but that the answer is 'no,' and that is that! He tries his best to explain his position so that the child understands his reasons, and sometimes he is rewarded by the comment a little later, "You were right, Dad." As the children grow older, there is increasing give and take, and the parent must occasionally retreat when he hears a child's logical arguments for something he wants to do. When there is disagreement, father, mother and adolescent can discuss the issue, but there should always be an attempt to discuss a problem until a definite conclusion has been reached as to the proper behavior or course of action.

At the present time it seems advisable that parents take the stand that they do not want their daughters to have coitus while they are in the school years because they feel it is their duty to protect them as best they can. Parents are aware that in our society at the present time, a teen-age girl is vulnerable in such relationships. Parents can create opportunities to discuss sex-social situations with daughters as frankly and openly as possible, making an attempt to point out conflicts in regard to sex behavior in our culture, the developing nature of the sex drive in boys and girls, and the values currently held by the society. It is doubtful that parents should advise daughters to make up their own minds about coitus on the basis of "interpersonal relationships." It seems preferable to discuss the problems created by premature but intense sex-social involvements, pointing out the fact that such situations create problems for everyone concerned. Along with this, parents should be encouraged to supervise carefully their daughters' dating relationships.

Parents should recognize that sex-social problems of sons differ from those of daughters. Assuming that boys as well as girls are raised with loving understanding, they will be concerned about the feelings and welfare of others because of such home conditioning. As a result, there will tend to be a carry-over in their relationships with the other sex. Parents should continue to help their sons view the world, the world they must live in and be a part of, as realistically as possible—feeling that the better it is understood, the more adequately they can deal with the situations which will confront them. Parents can try not to make their sons feel guilty over their developing sex drive (again both basic and conditioned), but they should expect their boys to control it to the extent that they and others will not be hurt.

3. *Cultural change in values is possible and a desirable goal*

In the article in the exchange the writer said that the present preoccupation with sex in the culture needs to be replaced with other values. We need to create motivation for educational and intellectual achievement as well as occupational and professional productivity in our adolescent young people. In an unpublished manuscript, the authors have reported a study at the University of California at Davis, which gives evidence of change in motivation of incoming freshmen between 1955 and 1960. As is well known, during that period a great effort was made on the part of our society to increase the achievement motive in high school students. The significant difference in motivation shown between the two samples indicated that such efforts were successful, which should give us all encouragement to continue our efforts. It seems quite reasonable to say to the adolescent that we expect him/her to be concerned with preparing for the work he/she is to do in the world and the contributions one is expected to make rather than to spend night after night of the high school years with a steady date. All parents may not be successful, but the above study found a significant relationship between parental expectations and high school achievement

As far as a long term solution is concerned, we might consider one proposal made by Ausubel some years ago. He wrote ". . . we have already seen that there is no single, inevitable, or universal pattern of psycho-sexual development and that the suppression of physiological sex urges is not invariably associated with the psychological conflict. In the light of this finding, it is possible to suggest a more realistic solution which is also more appropriate to the emotional and aesthetic ideals of our society. And the finding that the Arapesh are able to prevent effectively the development of physiological sex drives merely through a passive deemphasis and to channel all sex urges and consciousness along affectional lines lends credence to the belief that a psycho-affectional goal of sex behavior is neither unrealistic nor impossible (with proper sex education) in our culture". If this is what is desired we must remember that such an approach goes to the very heart of the conditioning process and involves the same type of warm affectional, non-aggressive upbringing that is characteristic of the Mountain Arapesh people of New Guinea. Children who are thus conditioned are more likely to be considerate in all their dealings with others, not only in their sex relationships. However, even in such a culture, we can expect, as indeed Mead found among Arapesh, individuals who require sanctions to keep their behavior within the expected norm of the society.

CONCLUSION

Hopefully it has been made clear that the author fully supports the morality behind Kirkendall's approach. Consideration for others as a fundamental basis of human behavior goes back at least 24 centuries, to Prince Sidhatta, Gautama the Buddha and to Confucius, and was perhaps taught by some in the Euphrates Valley, two thousand years before that. However, four thousand years of civilization indicate that it is not enough to teach a code of behavior, that it must be reinforced by sanctions.

It was interesting to see the clear recognition of this point by the students in the Klemer study. He reports: "Only one out of the entire sample of men believed that Kirkendall's methods were presently sufficient in themselves to ensure sexual morality, and only nine out of 86 women would be willing to try to control premarital sexual activity by the interpersonal relationships motivation alone."

So we come full circle, concluding again, that 1) if a society is to survive it must enforce its mores, folkways, and laws. 2) These codes are most effective when the moral logic behind them is understood and accepted by those who are expected to conform. 3) This understanding and acceptance can best be gained through identification with sympathetic and understanding adults whose own values are made clear to the child and adolescent.

Student Attitudes Toward Guidance
in Sexual Morality

RICHARD H. KLEMER

Recent reports of large simultaneous increases in the rate of illegitimate pregnancies and of venereal disease among teen-agers, combined with other persistent evidences of increased premarital sexual activity, have refocused attention on the difficult problem of moral education for young people in our complex and sophisticated space-age society. To many people—both educators and parents alike—it seems clearly apparent that if we are to revive and/or maintain sexual morality in our time, something must be done in our educative process. But what should be done? And, equally as important, how?

A significant and challenging exchange of views on how best to promote sexual morality among young people was published in the November, 1960, issue of *Marriage and Family Living*. The main protagonists were Dr. Lester Kirkendall and Dr. Thomas

Poffenberger, but an additional critique was provided by Dr. O. Hobart Mowrer.

In this exchange, Dr. Kirkendall advances his thesis that in order to achieve greater sexual morality, parents and educators should abandon their negative and authoritarian prohibitions on premarital sexual activity and instead promote a positively-oriented sexual ethic based on the importance of more satisfying interpersonal relationships.

Under the Kirkendall proposals, a young person would be conditioned to decide what he should do about premarital intercourse on the basis of what behavior would improve the relationship with the potential partner, rather than "on the goodness of specified behavior or acts in terms of mores, taboos, commands or abstract logic." Since most premarital sexual intercourse tends to be exploitative for one partner or the other and thus damaging to the interpersonal relationship, such intercourse would usually be avoided under his proposal, Kirkendall believes.

While Kirkendall feels that there are many difficulties to be faced in reorienting our young people to the good interpersonal relationships standard, he points to the failure of our present system based on rigid dictates (which because of the automobile, among other things, are now all but unenforceable) as justification for trying something different.

Poffenberger, on the other hand, holds that behavior becomes stable and predictable *only* when it is a part of the mores. He feels that strong sanctions are still necessary to control the young person's sexual behavior. He warns that if each individual were allowed to determine his behavior on the basis of its effect on interpersonal relationships, we could "predict with some degree of certainty that this might often be used to justify entering into sexual relationships rather than refraining from them. . . ." Poffenberger feels that it is necessary for society to take the authoritarian position that young people must hold chastity as a value at least until they reach a relative social and economic maturity and that it is the parents' responsibility to communicate this value to their children.

For the publication of the Kirkendall-Poffenberger Exchange, Mowrer provided a thought-provoking critique which tends toward the Poffenberger point of view. In this critique, Mowrer emphasizes a major Poffenberger implication by saying that young people today are "sick of our efforts merely to 'explain' things to them and would *welcome* more definite limits than we commonly think we have a right to impose."

Early in 1961 it occurred to the writer that the significance of the Kirkendall-Poffenberger Exchange might be increased by some further evaluation from those most concerned by it—the young people themselves. After all, the proof of the pudding is in the eating. To find out what one group of young people who had just been space-age teen-agers themselves might think of the relative merits of the Kirkendall and Poffenberger proposals, a study was undertaken at the University of Alabama by the writer. All of the young people in this study were completely unknown to either Kirkendall or Poffenberger.

One hundred and seventeen students in Marriage Family Relationship classes taught both by the writer and by his colleague, Dr. Joseph Rowland, were asked to read the Kirkendall-Poffenberger Exchange and then answer evaluating questions about it. All but a very few of these students were Protestant, from unbroken homes, from Alabama or states contiguous to Alabama, and from middle or upper-middle class homes as indicated by father's occupation.

Four of the answer sheets were eliminated because these respondents were considerably older than the other students. Of the 113 students whose replies were finally included in the survey, 86 were women and 27 were men. The age range was 20-25. These students replied to four questions which had both a dichotomous answer possibility and an invitation to open-end comment. The first question asked whether the respondent believed that Kirkendall or Poffenberger offered the more convincing methods for achieving morality in our time.

In reply, 41 per cent of all the respondents said that they thought Kirkendall's interpersonal relationships approach was the more convincing; 45 per cent felt that Poffenberger's methods were the more convincing; and 14 per cent indicated that they could not make a choice because both authors presented ideas which should be incorporated in the training of young people. Of the men, 48 per cent agreed with Kirkendall and 41 per cent with Poffenberger. Of the women, 40 per cent agreed with Kirkendall and 46 per cent with Poffenberger.

But in reply to the second question, a 90 per cent majority felt that Kirkendall's "positive goals" are not *now* sufficient by themselves to maintain sexual morality among young people and that Poffenberger's "negative restraints" are also very necessary at the present time. Only one out of the entire sample of 27 men believed that the interpersonal relationships approach could work by itself at this time, and only nine out of 86 women would be willing to try to control premarital sexual activity by Kirkendall's methods alone.

In answer to a third question, 48 per cent of the men and 54 per cent of the women felt that someday in the future it might be possible to educate young people to reject premarital sexual experience because of their desire to protect interpersonal relationships.

Asked in the fourth question for agreement or disagreement with Mowrer's statement that young people would welcome more definite limits on their sexual behavior, 67 per cent of the men and 80 per cent of the women, indicated agreement. Thus some 76 per cent of all these respondents apparently believed that young people want more conviction and more proscription on the part of parents and educators.

It appeared from the arrayed data that some of the students' answers might be associated with their sex or their affectional status—dating, engaged, or married. But when tested, while some of these associations approached significance, none actually reached the five per cent level of confidence.

The replies to the open-end questions provided even greater insight into the attitudes of the respondents. It was clear from their comments that Kirkendall and Poffenberger each had some very intense adherents among the students. Many of those who favored Kirkendall cited their belief in the self-respect and mental health superiority of Kirkendall's positive approach and the failure of the traditional negative restraints.

But there were others who said Kirkendall's methods were absolutely unworkable because they were too idealistic and/or unrealistic. It is interesting that the older male students especially seemed to hold this view and several, not knowing of the depth of Dr. Kirkendall's research with very realistic young men, implied that Kirkendall must be, like their parents, blissfully unaware of how really wicked and hedonic the world is today. Representative is the comment of a 25-year-old male student. He said:

> "Premarital sex will be rampant if we use Kirkendall's approach. He is unrealistic. . . . I believe that more permissiveness as to the moral choices of youth will lead to greatly increased rates of premarital intercourse and I am thankful that both Drs. Mowrer and Poffenberger have undertaken to show the fallacies of Dr. Kirkendall's reasoning. The interpersonal relationships of Kirkendall would be workable only for a minute percentage of the American adolescent and youthful population. My authority is my own youth and the knowledge of the lack of concern for moral issues in the majority of college students, especially males. The minority who would accept and practice the theory are those young people who already have high moral standards usually by virtue of their upbringing and parents who said 'no!' and meant it."

It is true that the students in this sample are among the more religious and more highly socialized in the U.S. and therefore probably biased toward the traditional approach to sexual morality.

However, it may also be true that this is the kind of young person who is the most susceptible to the belief in the importance of good interpersonal relationships which is necessary for Kirkendall's approach. It would be interesting to see the results of a similar survey made among the students at a Northeastern or West Coast metropolitan university where, it is rumored, the students are somewhat more sophisticated, uninhibited, and iconoclastic.

In addition to those Alabama students in this survey who rejected Kirkendall because they thought his ideas were universally impractical, there were a considerable number who backed off from the interpersonal relationships approach because they thought that while it might work for mature college students, it couldn't possibly work with young adolescents. Several pointed out that it was significant that Kirkendall and Poffenberger had based their ideas on data from two different age groups—Kirkendall worked with college students, Poffenberger with high-schoolers.

The general impression received from reading the total group of papers was that almost all of the students in this sample would certainly *like* to live in a world where better interpersonal relationships were the basis for premarital sexual decisions, if only they could believe that it could really happen. When they turned away from Kirkendall, many students did so with wistful reluctance. One 20-year-old student summed it up this way:

> "Unfortunately, I have to agree with Poffenberger," he said. "I think it would be ideal if this important decision could be made on the basis of individual reasoning and beliefs, but I don't think it can be done at present . . . young people tend to rationalize to obtain the answers that allow them to yield to temptation." Then he added, "People today are too concerned with 'what they can get out of it' and 'what the fellows will think' to be able to see the need for moral uprightness and honesty."

But while many were wary of accepting Kirkendall's proposal, a large majority of the students enthusiastically agreed to the

Mowrer statement that young people would welcome more definite limits for their moral behavior. Said one 21-year-old female student:

> "I believe that it is certainly true that young people would wel- come more definite limits on their moral behavior. Of course the teen-ager will object to these limitations because his peer group expects him 'to gripe' about his parental limitations. But actually these limitations give him a sense of security, for then the teen-ager knows what is expected of him. He can also put the blame for any moral decisions on his parents and will escape the scorn of his peers."

Many of the other respondents warned, however, that for the new limits to be really welcome, they must be "sold" to the young people on some modern and practical—yet at the same time idealistic—basis, and not be rooted in older metaphysical or theological concepts which are out of synchronization with present-day reality.

Since so many young people, all over the country as well as in Alabama, agree that some kind of more vigorous guidance is desired, why in the world isn't it provided for them? Manifestly, the answer to this question is crucial to any real evaluation of a proposal for bettering the moral understanding and behavior of young people.

It seems reasonable to speculate from even casual observation, that one major reason why many parents and educators fail to provide the guidance children desire is that they are perplexed by the apparent inapplicability of many of the older codes and conventions to the realities of space-age living. Yet they have no better guides to suggest. Recent technological and social changes ranging alphabetically from "Automobile, dating function of" to "Women, equality for", have tended to create disagreements, ambivalences, and confusions within and among parents and educators as to what kind of moral behavior will best serve and protect the child.

An integral (but sometimes overlooked) part of the problem of social change is the fact that many people, both young and old, have now arrived at a point where they have accepted change— change in any form—as a value in itself. For them, that which is traditional has become suspect. This has led to value conflict and even more difficulty for parents who would like to preserve something of our cultural heritage of sexual morality, yet at the same time don't want to appear old-fashioned or, if you will, "square" by sternly denouncing all premarital sexual activity.

Moreover, some of the same social changes which have conditioned our society continually to upgrade the value of change itself, have increasingly caused many people to downgrade the value of premarital chastity. Increased cross-class associations, theoretically better contraceptive devices, supposedly improved venereal disease control, the all-pervasive commercial glorification of sex, and the general "eat, drink, and be merry" philosophy of these times of boom and crisis, have all contributed to the demotion of premarital continence from its former status as a first-class cultural value. One need look no further than some of our marriage relations books which include sections on "positive values of premarital intercourse" to see how far the quasi-official downgrading of chastity has gone. By contrast, it is still almost unthinkable that any American book would have a section on the positive values of blasphemy, trampling the flag, or eating human flesh.

But in place of chastity, no widely acceptable "modern" standard of sexual behavior has been offered from any souraze. "Permissiveness with affection," identified by Ira Reiss as a contemporary observed "standard", actually has very little that is standard about it. There is no standard for the degree of permissiveness to be offered and no standard for the degree of affection to be required. Moreover, the distinction between permissiveness with affection and outright sexual exploitation is dependent upon a knowledge and perception of adult motivation and emotional reaction that is almost unteachable to inexperienced children. Thus many parents are left in a quandary, confused and unsure about the sexual morality they suggest hesitantly—if at all—to their even more confused offspring.

And most of the suggestions from professional counselors and educators—both moralist and anti-moralist—in recent years have done little to help parents with their practical problems in moral education, regardless of the theoretical merits of those suggestions. Robert Harper, along with Albert Ellis, has been insistent that parents, in dealing with children, should "stop teaching them that premarital sexual intercourse is bad" and instead ". . . . teach them how to exercise their own critical faculties about deciding under what sorts of circumstances and with what sorts of partners it is likely to be functionally desirable for all parties concerned." But even the parent who is emotionally able to adjust to the unconventionality of these directions and who is able to accept their implications both for child and for society, soon finds that the proponents have few practical suggestions to offer as to how such teaching may be effectively accomplished with normal, sexually-curious but emotionally immature, children. Moreover, Ellis himself concedes that parents who try to carry out such directions ". . . not only have to explain their view to their own children (which is difficult to do when the children are quite young), but they also have to explain that other people think differently, and that there might be difficulties in presenting their views to these others. Raising children in a non-conformist manner, therefore, is much harder than raising them to conform to the sexual prejudices [*sic*] of their community."

Ultimately, however, perhaps the most insidious of all the confusions impeding more effective moral guidance, is the widely believed allegation that premarital sexual intercourse has become so general that we can no longer hope for *any* real premarital sexual morality on the part of young people. The implication of this is that no fair-minded parent or educator should expect his child to buck the trend and stand up against the alleged majority in defiance of the supposedly steady march toward complete sexual freedom. No one actually knows for sure how far this trend has gone in the main stream of our society. But many people, fearing the worst, seem to feel that about all they can do now is to help children protect themselves from unwanted pregnancies by handing out contraceptive advice.

While there may be wide regional and subcultural differences, this complete defeatism concerning young peoples' current sexual morality seems unwarranted for our society as a whole. After some years of counseling and teaching and after examining the complete returns from the Alabama survey which is the main subject of this paper, it seems clear to the writer that individual young people (especially young women) can still be taught to believe in the personal importance of premarital continence to the point where these beliefs are not negative inhibitions, but positive values from which they can gain self-esteem. One 22-year-old woman student told how she thought it should be done in the survey. She said:

> "Parents must teach their children in such a way that they will not want to go counter to what they believe to be right and just and good. Done this way, taboos become willful self-restraints. They are not set out as things the child must not do or can not do but rather they are things that under the prevailing circumstances the child himself wishes not to become part of him. This has worked for me; I would not want it otherwise."

The experiments of Solomon Asch and others have shown that most of those young people who have made a judgment that short is short will change that judgment when confronted by a majority which vehemently contends that short is long. But, Asch found, there are always some who will stand up and speak the truth as they see it regardless of the unanimity of opposing judgments. Asch's conclusions indicate that this kind of resolute independence has its basis in the depth of the individual's conviction and the strength of his self concept.

This suggests that to really help young people to become self-actualizing, resolute, secure individuals, perhaps the methods of both Kirkendall and Poffenberger are needed simultaneously. The authoritative forcefulness of Poffenberger's mores give security and stability and self-respect to the young person who abides by them. At the same time, Kirkendall's idealism can give meaning to conviction and his concern for interpersonal relationships can help parents avoid over-dominating the young people while giving them authoritative guidance.

There is another reason, too, for not despairing for sexual morality in our time. There is considerable historical precedent for believing that moral trends can be modified and even reversed—especially with our present media for mass education. It seems reasonable to believe that if counselors and educators could agree among themselves, even within sub-cultural groups, on some acceptable and practical space-age standard of sexual morality—be it old or be it new, be it noble or be it normative—there might be a good chance of that standard becoming a reality.

And it appears to the writer that there are some evidences, including the discussions of the recent North American Conference on Church and Family, of a renewed interest among professional people in achieving some agreement on moral standards. This, in itself, is hopeful. For when we have ended some of our disagreement at the professional level, we may then be able to provide parents with the greater security of conviction that will enable them to begin to give their children the kind of guidance that the children apparently desire. Thus any trend toward complete nonmorality can be halted.

Consistency and Sexual Ethics

IRA L. REISS

The study of the ways in which values relate to each other and to other parts of human society is of prime importance to sociology. The purpose of this paper is to examine one area of social values in order to discern the extent to which one may find inconsistencies and the relation of these inconsistencies to the strength of the belief concerned. The area chosen for examination is that of premarital sexual standards. Four major premarital sexual standards will briefly be examined for inconsistencies among the values connected with each standard. It should be clear that it is beyond the scope of this paper to exhaustively examine our sexual standards for inconsistencies. Our effort is aimed merely at discerning some basic characteristics of these standards. In this attempt we hope we will help build a foundation for further conceptualization in this area.

THE DOUBLE STANDARD

The double standard in premarital sexual intercourse basically is composed of the belief that women should not engage in premarital coitus but such behavior for men is acceptable. This code is an informal, covert, sexual standard since it does violate our official formal standard of abstinence. The inconsistencies in this sexual code are relatively easy to locate. The basic inconsistency develops from the situation that if women fully abided by this code and abstained then men would not be able to abide by the code for there would be no female sexual partners. Historically this clash was handled by the existence of a class of prostitutes and by a dichotomous view of women which held that virgins were "good" women and non-virgins were automatically "bad" women. A man was supposed to obtain his partners for sexual intercourse from the "bad" group of women. This is still the basic mechanism in the functioning of the double standard in American culture. Nevertheless, this modification still means that no man can abide by the double standard unless a woman violates the double standard and thereby becomes a "bad" woman.

One related inconsistency in the double standard may also be mentioned. Since double standard males value virginal women they seek to find such women as mates. Despite this valuation the same males are reducing the supply of virginal women by their sexual behavior. Now one may contend that such males are reducing the number of virgins in groups other than those into which they intend to marry. However, double standard males disagree as to which group of females are "marriageable" and thus virtually all groups of females come under "attack" from some group of double standard males. Thus, by encouraging the double standard one does cut down in general the available number of virgins and thereby lessens one's chances of obtaining a virginal mate.

These examples of internal conflict in the double standard should be sufficient to show the basic clashes involved here. It should be borne in mind that the adherents of this code have various rationalizations developed to "explain" such inconsistencies or to block out such things from their awareness. As I shall attempt to show, adherence to a sexual code seems to seldom depend on how consistent the code is. The double standard is not unique in its inconsistencies as we shall soon see. Its inconsistencies may be more obvious than others' but that is likely due to the fact that the newer sexual codes have publicized these features. Also the double standard is the oldest sexual standard we have and time has a way of allowing inconsistencies to develop.

ABSTINENCE

Our formal premarital sexual standard is abstinence. This is the code one hears from the pulpits and in formal declarations of belief. As it has evolved in our present day society it too can be seen to have inconsistencies. As Margaret Mead has pointed out, there is conflict between the idea of premarital restraint and marital sexual enjoyment. To bring individuals up for the first 20 or 30 years of their life and teach them to restrain and control their sexual desires or to prevent their developing too intense sexual appetites and then to expect that they will be able to regularly achieve orgasm in marital coitus is to desire two conflicting things. Kinsey did present evidence that those females who enter marriage without any orgasmic experience from *either coitus, petting or masturbation* are much less likely to experience orgasm in marriage. Kanin and Howard cite evidence that restrictive sexual backgrounds are a hindrance to rapid sexual adjustment in marriage. The evidence is, of course, not conclusive, and in any case, it surely does not mean that every virginal female would be at such a disadvantage in achieving marital sexual satisfaction. But it does tend to support the view of the researchers cited above that some such casual connection between premarital and postmarital orgasm, although not fully established by the evidence, is likely. Thus, the abstinent female is caught between two values, her value on virginity and her value on marital sexual enjoyment. Her standard instructs her to achieve both and it is not always easily accomplished.

Now, of course, as Kinsey's data indicate, a girl who pets to orgasm but remains virginal is more likely to achieve orgasm in marriage than are her more chaste sisters. Thus, some abstinent women may try and resolve the value-clash by this means and still avoid the risk of pregnancy involved in coitus. But to the extent that this is done, the value of virginity, at least in its traditional meaning of inexperienced, untouched, and discriminate, is increasingly sacrificed. Petting of a more intimate nature than simple kissing and hugging seems increasingly very common among abstinent women. My own current research on several high schools and colleges indicates that the great majority of abstinent women accept intimate petting under conditions of a stable affectionate relation. This "solution" to the above value-conflict does modify the meaning of what is "being saved for marriage" but at the same time seems to increase the chances for marital orgasm.

THE NEWER SEXUAL CODES

The double sandard and abstinence are ancient sexual codes with histories going back thousands of years. There are two newer sexual codes which have grown considerably in the 20th century.

These newer codes do avoid some of the inconsistencies which lack of equalitarianism and emphasis on restraint has brought to the double standard and abstinence. However, they have their own brand of inconsistency. The adherents of these new sexual standards are quite vocal, and have made particular efforts to point out how these newer sexual codes are "natural" and "culture-free" and avoid the biases that go with the older traditional codes. Since this is one of the chief emphases of the adherents of these codes, let us see to what extent their codes are consistent, as their adherents claim, with the avoidance of tradition and with the emphasis on a natural approach to sex.

PERMISSIVENESS WITH AFFECTION

Of the two newer covert sexual standards this one is by far the more common. My own current research indicates the growth of this code especially on our college campuses. This standard sanctions coitus if it occurs in a stable affectionate relationship. From my own questioning of these people I would say that the majority of them believe they are emancipated from the past puritanical sexual attitudes and view their sexual standards as culture-free codes arrived at by reason. Let us now see if their sexual standard is consistent with these beliefs.

The formal puritan conception of sex said that all sex outside of marriage was bad. The believers in permissiveness with affection are not fully rejecting this puritan notion—they are modifying it to read: "Only sexual intercourse which lacks in deep affection is bad." In short, there is still the ancient stigma on sexual relations engaged in purely for pleasure. The Puritan pleasure-sin connection is not broken but it is modified.

In fact, if we look more closely at Puritan America we find that even the Puritans made some similar sort of modification of their "pleasure-sin" doctrine. Although the Puritans were formally opposed to premarital coitus it occurred rather frequently according

to their church records and was not as severely censured if it occurred between an engaged couple. The records of one Massachusetts church in the late 18th century show confessions of fornication
by 66 of 200 couples married there. We could, of course, go back
further in history and show that the Anglo-Saxons also levied lower
fines on engaged couples having coitus than on other couples.

Now, the acceptance today of premarital coitus among engaged
couples and other couples involved in stable affectionate relations
is no doubt more overt and less qualified than it was in the 18th
century. The acceptance also is possibly more generally widespread. However, the claims of the permissiveness with affection
adherents that their standard is "culture-free" and fully rejects our
puritan heritage and that it is an individual standard arrived at
via reason alone—these claims cannot be accepted for they are not
consistent with the evidence concerning this standard.

The popularity of this standard today can be explained by its
integration in our present culture as well as its links to our past.
It fits in with our more hedonistic emphasis, our greater freedom
for young people, our stress on love, etc. These strong cultural and
social pressures have no doubt encouraged the growth of this new
premarital sexual standard. It is thus in this sense too, no more lacking in socio-cultural roots and no more "individualistic" or "culture-
free" than the double standard or abstinence. It is rather best
viewed as representing a different aspect of our society and culture
than as representing something free from our socio-cultural influence. Thus, there is an inconsistency between the values of this
standard which profess the necessity of a culture-free belief and
the values which profess a relation between love and sex which
is quite well-rooted culturally.

PERMISSIVENESS WITHOUT AFFECTION

This is the last of our four major premarital sexual standards.
In terms of number of adherents in my current research study of

high school and college students, it is the smallest of all the standards. I believe one of the key reasons for its lack of support is its
violation of the very powerful norm associating affection with sexual behavior. In permissiveness without affection sexual intercourse
is allowed regardless of the amount of affection present. The major
prerequisites are free choice, physical desire and some precautions
to avoid pregnancy or disease.

One of the commonest beliefs held by the adherents of this code
is that their approach is a "natural" and "biological" approach to
sexual behavior. They believe that humans are similar to other
animals sexually and thus they should copulate whenever the
desire is mutual, providing precautions are taken against undesired
consequences such as pregnancy. Sexual relations are viewed as
similar to good wine. Both should be indulged in whenever one
desires but typically one should avoid emphasizing the importance
of the behavior. Let us now examine this belief and see how consistent it is with what this standard actually represents.

There is a wealth of evidence to support the view that human
sexual behavior is learned to a degree far exceeding that of any
other animal species. The similarity in sexual behavior found within
each animal species is lacking in man. We have evidence of cultures
existing today in which women outdo men in sexual aggressiveness
and performance; cultures in which men and women are equally
sexually motivated; and cultures, such as our own, where men outdo women in sexual motivations. Although our own kind of culture
is the most common, the existence of these other types means that
a great deal of our sexual nature is learned. The peoples in all societies are virtually the same biologically. But culturally, the peoples are quite diverse.

What this learned aspect means is that when two humans feel
sexual desires for each other they can be sure that much of the
specific nature of this desire is derivable from the culture in which
they were brought up. What physical traits are sexually appealing
varies considerably by culture. In many non-literate cultures a

woman's breasts are not at all a sexual symbol. In our own society they are one of the chief sources of erotic imagery.

In addition, there are moral ideas that each culture teaches concerning what is proper sexual behavior. No known society allows complete sex freedom. Thus when two people feel desire for each other not only has learning entered in respect to the erotic imagery but also whether they think it proper to carry out their desires will depend upon their cultural upbringing. Every society teaches that one cannot satiate his sexual desires with full freedom. Incestuous desires are not permitted to be consummated except in very rare circumstances; adulterous desires are carefully restricted in most societies; sexual relations involving people of grossly different ages are very frequently censored; sexual intercourse involving people of grossly different social classes is often proscribed or permitted only under special circumstances as in the double standard or a mistress system. Thus, even the most liberal culture we know of does not allow two people to engage in coitus merely because they happen to satisfy each other's culturally learned erotic imagery. The rules restricting sexual relations are in many cases based on the functional requirements of the social organization. Of course, this is not always the case and one many always question the necessity of any particular sexual restriction but that some restrictions are necessary in order to maintain the integrity of the family unit, the class system, the clan system, etc. goes without question.

Thus, in two ways even the adherents of permissiveness without affection are kept from responding to each other in any "natural" or "biological" sense. First, they are taught erotic imagery and this differs by culture, not by biology. And secondly, there are certain restrictions which any social organization demands in order to maintain the continuity of its structure.

It seems quite unlikely that human beings will ever live in a society where they can indulge their sexual desires at will. Neither sexual desires nor their indulgence can be freed from the social context in which they occur. In actuality the permissiveness without affection standard blocks its own value of "biological sex" for it restricts coitus in terms of incest, pregnancy, etc., and also stresses certain learned sexual behaviors. In sum, biological sex is incompatible with the cultural aspect of human behavior.

SUMMARY AND CONCLUSIONS

I have tried to point out certain inconsistencies in each of our four major sexual standards. We have seen that the double standard is involved in a clash between its goal of women remaining virginal and its desire for sexual partners. Abstinence is involved in the clash between the value placed on virginity and the value placed on marital sexual satisfaction. Permissiveness with affection is involved in a clash between its goal of a "culture-free" sexual belief and the culture-bound characteristics of its association of sexual behavior with affection. Permissiveness without affection is involved in the lack of consistency between its goal of a "natural" biological type of sex and its restriction on this by the culturally accepted erotic imagery and the culturally taught avoidance of incest, pregnancy and the like.

Certain qualifications are in order. As stated earlier, I am only dealing briefly with these four codes and the characteristics I point out by no means fully delineate the positions being discussed. Also, not all adherents of these standards will be involved in the clashes of values which were discussed. My effort is simply aimed at pointing out that *all* of our sexual standards have somewhat basic inconsistencies of one sort or another.

Now, the reasons for inconsistency are many—for one it is a result of time and the infinite attempts to adopt a belief system to many different circumstances. Again, it results from different rates of change or new additions in other parts of society which then clash with our older beliefs. Finally, it results from the fact that our knowledge is almost always at least a few steps short of being the most accurate available and we are not always aware of the full consequences of our beliefs.

My aim has been to show the defects in the rationalistic view of social behavior which suggests that individuals choose their beliefs on the basis of the consistency of the beliefs involved. At least in the area of sexual standards such choice is not possible among the four major standards for they *all* involve inconsistencies and contradictions of one sort or another. One would have to weigh the importance of the various types of inconsistency. It seems more likely that people will *think* their views are consistent rather than that they will actually *be* consistent. Whether people actually do or could accept or reject beliefs on the basis of some measure of consistency is, to my mind highly doubtful. I would hypothesize that basic value assumptions are much more crucial to choice of standards than the consistency of beliefs. For example, I would submit that the permissiveness without affection adherents have basic values of sexual freedom and lack of restraint on pleasure. This basic value set seems to do more to attract and hold adherents than the consistency of the beliefs that go with these basic values. In the case of permissiveness with affection one can denote that the value of physical pleasure is present but it is dominated by the value placed on affection as a prerequisite to such sexual pleasure. Here, too, acceptance of these basic values seems more likely to be the crucial reason for people adhering to this standard.

The two older sexual standards also have their core values which set them apart. The double standard stresses physical pleasure as much as permissiveness without affection does but it restricts the rights to such pleasure to men. Abstinence more than the other standards stresses the basic values of restraint and moderation. My own research supports the importance of these basic values in the adherence to a standard.

Ultimately when I pressed for an answer as to why a person accepted a sexual standard that had so many inconsistencies, my informants would invariably resort to the basic values named above and use them to justify their beliefs. I would contend that in any area of belief, due to lack of time, lack of ability or lack of desire, people will not usually examine the full nature and implications of their beliefs. Rather they will accept their beliefs on largely emotional grounds because of their integration with certain basic values. Inconsistencies of belief usually enter into social life as a criticism of someone else's beliefs. Individuals may take them quite seriously as criticism of other people's beliefs but not as seriously as criticisms of their beliefs.

In sum then, I would say that the review of these four standards and their beliefs has afforded us some initial evidence that consistency is commonly lacking in sexual standards, and that basic values seem more involved in one's adherence to a standard than the rational considerations of consistency. In short, I am hypothesizing that consistency within a sexual standard is not the most important variable in predicting the future strength of that sexual standard. Basic values regarding sexual behavior and the integration of these values with some of our key cultural values seem more important for indicating present and future strength than the internal consistency of a standard. It seems likely that the most self-consistent standards do not necessarily flourish best, nor the least consistent go out of existence. This entire area of the relation of reason and emotion, of consistency and values, of choice in general is at the heart of much of the field of sociology. A great deal of what I have put forth here is surely not more than suggestive. It is hoped that future research will further test and clarify the ideas presented here.

Our Changing Sex Ethics

WALTER R. STOKES

In undertaking this discussion of our changing sex ethics it is not meant to suggest that sex ethics have not always been in process of change, for they have in fact ever been subject to the altering forces of cultural evolution. What is here proposed, and documented in some detail, is that within the present century the rate of change in our sex ethics has been so accelerated as to assume the character of a revolutionary upheaval, with the next leveling off period still some generations ahead.

Instead of joining those prophets of disaster who see only trouble before us, and who demand a return to the "good old days," it is advocated that we acknowledge the changes that are upon us and accept responsibility for directing them with all the rationality, foresight and skill of which we are capable.

By the time Freudian psychology offered its challenge, our culture had amassed a truly weird array of irrational attitudes about sex. Most of them seem to have stemmed from the Judco-Christian doctrine of sex as original sin. Specific examples of the irrationalities produced by this mystical concept are: (1) a generally guilty feeling about all erotic emotion (2) a violent fear of autoerotic enjoyment, especially masturbation (3) repression or denial of childhood sexuality (4) restriction of teen-age sexuality to an unreal, romantic, de-sexualized idealism that ignores the erotic emotions and physical realities of sex (5) establishment of monogamous marriage as the sole permissible setting for the expression of sex (6) creation of a pattern of weak, stereotyped sexual behavior within the marital framework and (7) formulation of a tradition that sex is, at best, a questionable and transient activity of early and middle adult life, with little or no place in later life.

Havelock Ellis, Freud, Robert L. Dickinson, and Alfred Kinsey personify our modern critical re-evaluation of the old assumptions and ethical views concerning sex. These men questioned the earlier assumptions and began to build a scientific case against them. Freud performed a tremendous service by showing how damaging to personality development it is to drive sexual and other assertive impulses of childhood into the underground of the unconscious. He made us aware, for the first time, of the relationship of this process to neurosis, psychosis and disorders of the sexual function. However, despite Freud's remarkable analysis of the sex morbid-ities of his time, he can by no stretch of imagination be considered a distinguished prophet of man's best sex potential. His own life appears to have been a rather austere and melancholy one, and he was not optimistic about man's capacity for future happiness and security. His faith in the union of sex with tenderness and affection seems to have been limited and his view has not been brightened by the work of Kinsey, who chose to present his keen observations about sex behavior in isolation from the emotions. This is not to imply that either Freud or Kinsey had no personal concern about such a linkage. It is simply to stress that their peculiar contribution lay in their analytical and critical observations. However, they cleared the way for new and rational approaches for making the most of sex in human life. For this we have reason to be grateful.

Freud opened the way to a new philosophy of human nature that is rapidly changing man's image of himself. The new thinking derives from the Freudian concept that man's emotional nature is made up of conflicting drives which need not be looked upon as either good or bad but simply as posing problems that can be compromised or adjusted without reference to the ancient formula of good and evil. This means that man is no longer coerced by tradition to look upon himself as an innately sinful person but is free to accept himself for what he really is: a creature of many ambivalent or opposing desires and motives. This view forces man to acknowledge much confusion and insecurity about himself but at the same time sets him free, as his own master, to resolve or to compromise his conflicts with the aid of all the abundant and improving tools furnished through his scientific endeavors.

Rational man is becoming aware that he need not presuppose a hopeless war between his primitive narcissistic impulses and his social aspirations. But he is becoming equally aware that there is no way for a human being to grow and mature without acknowledging the ambivalences of life and accepting full personal responsibility for living with them and gaining skill in their management.

It has recently become apparent to many that here is our rational road to feelings of relative security and happiness.

Freud, Kinsey and others have contributed useful facts and theories concerning man's sexual nature. But they have not, as previously suggested, done a very inspiring job of expressing faith in where the road leads or what may be encountered along the way. Here it will be sought, with the aid of much personal faith and imagination, to pursue this road into the future and comment upon some of the things to which it may lead us.

First, I would affirm the belief that the human potential for happily integrating primitive biological needs with sound social aspirations is boundless and perhaps nearer to substantial achievement than most might suppose.

At the core of further progress lies "the doctrine of extending to all persons, of every race, age and sex, the dignity of being a good and lovable person, to be treated with respect and with the right to an identity of his own. Each should understand the folly of exploitation of others and abhor it." Obviously, this is a slight elaboration of the Golden Rule that has been with us since the days of Confucius. But there is now one extremely significant difference: Confucius and Christ grasped the idea but not the psychodynamics of how to make it work. Here we have recently made notable progress through the multi-disciplined efforts of social science. Surely, we can not yet claim to have all the answers, but we have a lot of them and are swiftly improving these and adding new ones.

Many of us see great promise in our growing effort to understand the emotional development of babies and children in an empathic way, instead of continuing a traditional policy of jamming into their minds a variety of grotesque assumptions about their nature. The new approach to child development may well prove the crucial element in reducing the hostility and friction which youth so often feels against the adult world. Unless we somehow greatly decrease the morbid and unnecessary hatreds generated in children by irrational elements in our culture there is simply no chance for the mass of humans to live successfully by the wise and loving words of anyone.

One of the most hopeful changes now at work is a tendency to abandon the old negative attitudes about masturbation. It seems likely that we shall soon be giving young people frank and warm endorsement of autoerotic pleasure as an end completely acceptable and desirable in itself and as the self-respecting basis upon which other sex experiences are built. The self-discovery and self-enjoyment of sex will be tainted by no depreciation, direct or indirect, for to do so is to create guilt, damage the self-image and impair the potential for affectionate heterosexual relations.

Today it is increasingly advocated that adults owe it to children, as an element in the shaping of our culture and the promotion of mental health, to give them clear information about the man-woman enjoyment of sex, thus providing material upon which they may build realistic and socially integrated masturbation fantasies. If we do not accept this responsibility children are left at the mercy of having to use in their fantasies the distorted impressions of sex that are so abundant in our culture: pornography, sado-masochistic concepts or the erotically sterile romantic sex of Hollywood. They will be influenced by these distortions to some extent, despite all that we can do in our time, but we should not default as to what we are capable of doing to give them a basis for developing ideals and fantasies in which erotic emotions and genital sexuality are frankly integrated with ideals of mutual affection and social responsibility.

If we succeed in doing this it must be acknowledged that we are preparing children for a world considerably different from the one in which they are to live. This creates some confusion for them and some problems, but I see no other sensible route toward progress.

There is much evidence that we are now in process of drastically modifying our ancient ideas about sex freedom for children and teen-agers. Clearly it will require some generations to modify our old ways and to grant young people the degree of sex freedom optimal to attainment of their full maturity. In this program we shall need contraceptive skill much beyond our present attainment, but that is on the way.

The entire problem of liberating mankind from our heritage of sex fears is profoundly dependent, at every level, upon our complete triumph over the tyranny of unwanted pregnacy. This problem we shall soon solve, if for no other reason just because of the fierce pressure of world over-population.

We are living in a time of generally unhappy marriages and things seem likely to get worse before they get better, but I have confidence that our discontents are moving us toward new standards that will bring marriages of far superior quality. I am sure that as men and women come more realistically to value their own and each other's sexuality, and learn fully to associate physical sexuality with tenderness and affection, marriage will become quite generally a relationship of rich reward and fulfilment, instead of the jailhouse of disillusionment and frustration that it now so often is.

While I can not feel certain that our present system of permanent, monogamous marriage is to survive, nevertheless I am strongly persuaded that it will, when it can be placed upon a more honest and mutually rewarding basis such as I have suggested.

Many of our current plagues of adult sexual life will rapidly be reduced as we improve our job with children and raise the quality of marital satisfaction. Such things as extramarital relations, prostitution and sex deviation will decline and when encountered will be dealt with in terms of empathy and constructive aid rather than by our present punitive means.

In the pursuit of more accurate understanding of how sexual and other emotional disturbances originate, family studies are being undertaken designed to shed light upon how certain kinds of emotional disorder arise from morbid family tradition. Current unpublished studies being conducted by the National Institute of

Mental Health (Bowen, Wynn) and by Harvard University (F. Kluckhohn, Spiegel) are pioneer efforts of this kind. It may be readily foreseen that in centuries ahead such studies will be numerous and will be followed through many successive generations in order to establish the truth about many things as to which we now merely speculate.

It seems quite reasonable to imagine that before long, as part of our cultural engineering plans, we shall be setting up experimental communities of selected volunteer families to embark upon important experiments in cultural change, involving such matters as greatly increased sex freedom for children and young people. It is not difficult to visualize that such experiments, carefully planned and participated in by our best professional talent, could provide immensely valuable clues toward eliminating morbid elements in our culture and speeding up the capability of humans to approach their full potential for happy and constructive living. Ventures of this sort are likely to appear within the next century.

To undertake projects of this kind obviously would mean a drastic abandonment of ancient tradition as the chief guide to ethical conduct and replacement of it by faith in the ingenuity and resourcefulness of man's ability to create new ethical concepts founded upon the understanding and wisdom provided by his emerging behavioral and social sciences.

Within a few generations we should have an effective science of human ecology, or the relationship of man to his external environment. Under this discipline the size of human population will be everywhere maintained within bounds most favorable to human well being.

Allied with ecology is the lately developing science of comprehending the physiology of human response to stress, both external and internal. This is a much wider subject than sex, yet sex is an important part of it. What I wish to touch upon is the remarkable scientific work that has been done toward understanding the effects of stress upon the human organism and of the disorders that result when successful response to stress can no longer be maintained. This is the research pioneered by Dr. Hans Selye. It is perhaps the most exciting contribution of our generation to the fundamental understanding of man and his needs and limitations.

It is predicted that as present research in this field reaches maturity we shall be impelled to give up most of our irrational ways of killing or crippling ourselves by unnecessary and avoidable stresses, including those imposed by sexual puritanism.

Looming upon our immediate horizon is a vast increase in leisure time. The way in which we use it will be of the greatest importance, and our new sciences of ecology and of the regulation of stress will provide guides in devising wise patterns for the use of our growing leisure. We shall come to recognize that mere freedom from illness and noxious stress is not enough, nor is freedom from labor necessarily an advantage. We shall develop a science concerned with aiding humans to live in such a way that their maximum capacity for happiness can be substantially achieved and the best genetic strengths of the species encouraged. In all of this I feel sure there will emerge a much accentuated place for sex in human life and that the new outlook upon sex will closely integrate it with the warmest enjoyment of mutual affection, altogether free from our present tendencies toward sexual antagonism and exploitation.

In the not too far distant future, within a few centuries, we should have a dependable science of human genetics and should be employing our knowledge clinically. I do not think it at all fantastic to anticipate that prospective parents may eventually choose to have the wife nurture an egg cell obtained from an ovum bank and fertilized by semen from a selected donor. Eventually much and possibly all human reproduction may be accomplished through a reproductive cell bank that will use only the ova and sperms of genetically highly selected donors. Donor artificial insemination has already come into wide use in animal industry and many thousand human pregnancies have been brought about by this means.

At present we have a somewhat paranoid tradition that makes

it difficult for many men and women to accept children who are not a direct biological extension of themselves. That we can abandon this attitude is indicated by the fairly widespread present acceptance of both adoption and artificial insemination by donor. When we are more mature we shall readily perceive the greater joy and satisfaction of sponsoring and loving genetically superior children. Meanwhile, however, because of salvage of the genetically unfit by modern medicine, we are likely to be in for a troublesome period of producing increased numbers of genetically defective children. This will prod us toward overcoming our prejudice against "test tube babies" and will lead to greatly increased use of surgical sterilization for genetic reasons.

If I have been saying things that sound like idle science fiction, I would remind that my professional background is that of a practical clinician, a physician for more than 30 years, experienced in wrestling with the problems mentioned. With understanding and technique presently at hand, and given the sort of relatively enlightened people with whom most of my work has occurred, we have even now solved or made substantial progress with solution of the human needs here reviewed. That it has been possible to do so much already argues well for the future.

It is hoped that this somewhat personal, unorthodox, imaginative presentation may provoke new thinking about matters of such prime concern to everyone who works in the field of marriage and the family.

Critique

LESTER A. KIRKENDALL

It is a privilege to have the opportunity to participate in the constructive thinking which I believe will come from the articles by Drs. Poffenberger, Reiss, and Stokes.

Dr. Poffenberger's article has been stimulated in good measure by the interchange in *Marriage and Family Living* (November, 1960), which involved the two of us and Dr. O. H. Mowrer. In this exchange I suggested that moral decisions and judgments should be based upon a concern for the quality of interpersonal relationship which might result from whatever behavior or attitudes were being considered. I quoted a statement from an article written by Curtis E. Avery and myself. The statement read:

> Whenever thought and choice regarding behavior and conduct are possible, those acts are morally good which create trust, and confidence, and a capacity among people to work together cooperatively. Such acts are morally bad which build barriers and separate people through creating suspicions, mistrust and misunderstanding. Such acts destroy integrity in relationships and decrease the individual's sense of self respect.
>
> This means that acts in themselves are neither moral nor immoral—good or bad. In thinking and choosing we focus attention on the quality of relationships between persons rather than on the goodness or badness of specified behavior or acts in terms of *mores,* taboos, commandments, or abstract logic. . . . *in general, conduct which strengthens the good relationship between the individual and society or any segment of society is good; and that conduct which strengthens relationships between two individuals is good, provided it does not weaken relationships between the individuals and society.* (The italicized portion of this paragraph was not quoted in the original interchange.)

This approach grew out of Mr. Avery's and my conviction that in a world which has grown tremendously complex, markedly cosmopolitan, and very small it had become necessary to find the very bedrock upon which moral considerations rest. We believe this bedrock to be the quality of interpersonal relationships produced by our behavior and attitudes.

This view is often interpreted as a laissez-faire, highly permissive attitude in which all concern for the control or direction of conduct is abandoned. This seemingly is Dr. Poffenberger's interpretation. But he is talking about "controls". I am attempting to answer the question, "Upon what foundation should our moral judgments rest?" Once this question has been answered, we can see more clearly the nature of the standards needed, the character of the controls necessary, and the strictness with which they should be enforced. Suppose we conclude a concern for interpersonal relationships *is* a sound basis for moral standards. Surely it is not illogical then to say, once we are clear about the probable consequences of certain acts for interpersonal relationships that our attitudes toward engaging in them may be either highly restrictive, quite approving, or neutral.

Other than that we seem to be focusing our concern at different points, I have difficulty in determining what fundamental disagreement exists between Dr. Poffenberger and myself. In Part I of his article he construes the concept I have advanced in such narrow terms that I feel my meanings are distorted. In Part II, however, he moves essentially to the same view I hold. Thus he indicates that he is "interested in developing individuals who are able to base much of their behavior on principle rather than responding to the dictates of an overly rigid superego or only upon external controls." There is no disagreement here.

He speaks of "developing firmer moral convictions" through broadening "self-knowledge, including motivations" which "can lead to a broadening of the sense of responsibility and the avoidance of easy rationalizations." This outcome is exactly what I was seeking in my book, *Premarital Intercourse and Interpersonal Relationships,* cited by Dr. Poffenberger.

He argues for a "clearer awareness of one's value structure." This is what I too hope for; this is my reason for writing these articles. He says when "boys as well as girls are raised with loving understanding they will be concerned about the feelings and welfare of others because of such home conditioning." This is another way of stating the framework I have advanced.

So far as sexual behavior is concerned Dr. Poffenberger quotes approvingly the following statement from Ausubel, "it is possible to suggest a more realistic solution [to the sex standards problem] which is also more appropriate to the emotional and aesthetic ideals of our society . . . [we may believe] that a psychoaffectional goal of sex behavior is neither unrealistic nor impossible (with proper sex education) in our culture." This is my position also.

And so I think I can welcome Dr. Poffenberger on board as navigator. We're going in the same direction and aiming for the same goal.

Drs. Stokes and Reiss help document the need for a value system which will enable us to cope with changing conditions in a meaningful and consistent way so far as sex is concerned. Dr. Reiss found in his work that when individuals had become aware of the logical inconsistencies involved in the sex standards they supported they "invariably" resorted to certain basic values which they held to justify their beliefs. In other words, their behavior was actually determined by these values rather than by logical consistency. This observation emphasizes the overriding importance of one's value system, for this is the determinant of behavior.

Dr. Reiss did not attempt to isolate the values which should underlie our sexual standards. He does note however, and I agree, that unrestricted freedom cannot and will not be tolerated. The restrictions, he suggests, will be in the interest of preserving the family or a similar social unit.

Dr. Stokes indicates how profound and how penetrating are certain changes now altering our views toward sex. He has noted several developments—a reevaluation of Freudian concepts, a mounting realization that the sexual impulse can be directed, the developing sciences of human ecology and human genetics, and an interest in eugenic reproduction. To these he could have added others such as a decline in the power of the fear-evoking deterrents which have been used to support chastity, and the declining need always to use sexual functioning in the service of reproduction. All these developments are forcing us toward a reappraisal of our attitudes toward sex.

Dr. Stokes strongly and clearly supports the interpersonal relationships criterion when he advocates "the doctrine of extending to all persons, of every race, age and sex, the dignity of being a good and lovable person, to be treated with respect and with the right to an identity of his own. Each should undertsand the folly of exploitation of others and abhor it."

The Stokes position is based on a positive concept of human nature, and a deep faith in the potentialities of people. The importance of these points cannot be overemphasized. They are cardinal points in my own thinking. The concept one holds of the nature of human nature practically determines what he believes can be attained and what he expects when working with people. From my study and observation I believe that man is by nature predominantly a social being. While progress may be slow and erratic, it is upon that aspect of his nature which we can and must rely for an ultimate solution to our problems. If I am wrong at this point my whole structure falls; if I am correct the view I suggest seems to follow inevitably.

Critique on Symposium of Reiss, Stokes and Poffenberger Papers

BLAINE R. PORTER

Few, if any, facets of human behavior deserve the serious consideration of man more than the re-evaluation of our moral codes and the development of a sound, functional, ethical orientation regarding sex. The obvious discrepancies between conduct and traditional morals, particularly in American society, give evidence that we are often confused and inconsistent.

Because human beings have sex impulses, society has found it necessary to order and regulate sex activities and relations, and therefore every cultural group has established some set of rules and patterns to which its members were expected to conform. In our culture, we have inherited moral codes and prohibitions regarding sexual activities based primarily upon the Judaic-Christian doctrine, many of which grew out of a religious reaction to the interpreted immorality of the times. From the point of view of modern behavioral science, many of the regulations and restrictions were rigid and penalties for infractions of the moral sexual code were harsh. Some of the traditional attitudes and beliefs about sex have focused upon the negative view that sex was unclean—something to be denied and rejected. The church and state took upon themselves the responsibility of establishing regulations and attempted to enforce adherence to these regulations in order to preserve the values of the society or group.

Problems develop, both in the areas of the enforcement of moral codes and the feelings of members of the group about moral codes when major inconsistencies exist betweeen professed standards and actual behavior. Reiss has focused his attention upon the extent to which one may find inconsistencies in the area of premarital sexual standards and has attempted to relate these inconsistencies to the strength of the belief or standard concerned.

The double standard in premarital sexual intercourse has been increasingly questioned and criticized in modern America. Reiss points out that "This code is an informal, covert, sexual standard since it does violate our formal standard of abstinence." There is evidence that a decreasing percentage of our population claims to endorse the double standard. There are those who believe in and observe a single standard of chastity, and an apparently increasing number who are accepting premarital coitus for both male and female. Reiss states that "since double standard males value virginal women, they seek to find such a woman as a mate." Further consideration of this statement necessitates an evaluation of the degree of value placed upon virginity. The number of nonvirgins (both male and female) at time of marriage has constantly increased over the past several decades. The practices of both men and women, plus the expressed attitudes regarding virginity and premarital coitus suggest that virginity at the time of marriage may not be valued to the extent that it has previously been valued.

In his discussion of abstinence, Reiss, while qualifying the findings of Mead, Kinsey, Kanin and Howard, leans toward accepting the point of view that premarital coitus enhances and abstinence hinders good sexual adjustment in marriage. In the opinion of the reviewer, research data supporting this position are sparse and questionable. Other data, particularly clinical studies, suggest that attitudes and feelings regarding sex are probably more significant than actual behavior (premarital) in their influence upon sexual adjustment. Even if such research data were valid, other issues should be considered in making a decision about what one's behavior should be.

The author makes an interesting point that intimate petting short of coitus has been a "solution" for a "great majority" of abstinent women. However, clinical data reveal that a great many women have problems both before and after marriage that are associated with such behavior.

Reiss clearly describes the inconsistencies in the standards of "Permissiveness With Affection," and "Permissiveness Without Affection." In his consideration of all four standards he has presented evidence that consistency is a common lack in sexual standards. I agree that people—particularly young persons facing decisions regarding sexual behavior—will not usually examine the full nature and implications of their beliefs. Many, if not most of them, lack the knowledge and maturity necessary to fully understand the long range implications. They will likely be more concerned about the immediate satisfaction of needs and desires and give insufficient thought to possible unintended consequences. Perhaps the main contribution of this paper is the hypothesis "that consistency within a sexual standard is not the most important variable in predicting the future strength of that sexual standard."

Much more attention needs to be devoted to seeking an explanation of the inconsistency between professed values and actual practice.

Stokes, in his paper, "Our Changing Sex Ethics," makes a plea that we free ourselves of the shackles of the past regarding myths and taboos about sex and accept a rational approach which will put us on the road to relative security and happiness. I object to his laying most of the blame for "a truly weird array of irrational attitudes about sex," at the doorstep of Judeo-Christian doctrine. While admitting that the interpreters of religious doctrine have sometimes applied unhealthy, distorted, weird attitudes about sex, we should acknowledge the worthy goal of religious prohibitions about sex; namely, the protection of the individual and the preservation of the family. In comparison with the practice of modern medicine, some of the ancient physicians used some crude and weird treatments and prescriptions, but that is no reason to suggest that we discard the field of medicine.

The Hebraic-Christian view has held that sex is potentially both good and evil. Religious groups are making real strides today in developing realistic and humanistic views about sex. Religion can make significant contributions in the field of sexual ethics, particularly to the people who embrace a religious philosophy. Our goal, then, is to capitalize upon the good that it has to offer. I'm sure Stokes would agree with this because he has said on other occasions, "I have no real quarrel with religious teaching that does not do violence to humanistic values."

I have had the pleasure of discussing these issues with Dr. Stokes on several occasions, and I become more convinced that we are seeking similar goals, but champion different means for attaining them. Certainly, few if any, of us would disagree with his statement, "At the core of further progress lies the doctrine of extending to all persons of every race, age, and sex the dignity of being a good and lovable person, to be treated with respect and with the right to an identity of his own. Each should understand the folly of exploitation of others and abhor it."

Along with Stokes, I too "have confidence that our discontents are moving us toward new standards that will bring marriages of far superior quality." But I do not agree with him that this goal can best be achieved by "giving young people frank and warm endorsement of autoerotic pleasure as an end completely acceptable and desirable in itself." It is the idea of "pleasure as an end completely acceptable and desirable in itself," that I object to. I hold profoundly to the conviction that sex in its rightful place should be a means to an end: A means to self-fulfillment, a way of saying to another human being, with dignity and respect, I love you. I believe that sex relations outside of marriage are almost always engaged in as ends in themselves. The endorsement of autoerotic pleasure as an end completely acceptable and desirable in itself could easily develop the attitude that other, and perhaps all, sex behavior is to be engaged in as an end in itself. Such behavior may occasionally be justified, but in my opinion, should not represent our ultimate goal.

The problems relating to sex fears are numerous and complex. I therefore cannot agree that "The entire problem of liberating mankind from our heritage of sex fears is profoundly dependent, at every level, upon our complete triumph over the tyranny of unwanted pregnancy."

Stokes states, "I am sure that as men and women come more realistically to value their own and each other's sexuality, and learn fully to associate physical sexuality with tenderness and affection, marriage will become quite generally a relationship of rich reward and fulfillment, instead of the jailhouse of disillusionment and frustration that it now so often is." Again, I agree with the goal to be achieved, but am not convinced that the means for achieving this end is via the road of encouraging autoeroticism, premarital coitus, and sanctioning extra-marital affairs.

The conduct of one's sex life should be focused on how it contributes to helping an individual become a person—a more complete person. Judgment and decision must be based on sound principles of human growth and development and not on the pleasure principle. This conduct should be such that it will contribute to growth, increased maturity, respect for self and others, and the well-being of everyone involved. An ethical orientation is a concern for what one's actions will mean or do to others; it poses the question whether what one does or expects to do will be injurious, humiliating, or otherwise damaging to the other person's integrity and dignity, and will be damaging or undesirable to one's self as a personality. An ethical action, therefore, is one that rejects the use of another person as an instrument or object to be used or coerced for any purpose, no matter how socially or personally desirable that purpose may seem.

Our goal, then, it seems to me, is to establish a sex ethic and a methodology of sex education to help young people accept their bodies, understand their feelings, and integrate the totality of their life and being into something meaningful and satisfying. I do not believe we achieve this via the path of our Victorian ancestors nor the philosophy of "have fun when and with whom you can find it" which represents the attitude of many modern American teen-agers.

The experimental projects suggested by Stokes have interesting possibilities, but several other related factors must also be considered besides the human genetic one. What would this mean to the family, to the process of self-actualization, to marriage interaction, and to parent-child relationships? Before any such projects could safely be initiated, it seems to me they must be preceded by much serious thought and a wealth of high quality research.

We need to not only raise the question of ethics regarding sexual relationships before or outside of marriage, but also within marriage itself. Many young people today are developing high aspirations and are marrying with the hope that they can improve upon the level of achievements of their parents. But again, they are inheritors of a tradition of ethical conduct. Much humiliation, degradation and unhappiness has been inflicted upon a spouse with no feelings of compunction because it could occur within the limits of the moral and legal codes. Attention must be focused on an ethical orientation that seeks to add to the dignity, integrity, well-being and happiness of the individual in any and all circumstances.

That our sex ethics are rapidly changing is frankly acknowledged, and that this issue needs the serious attention of responsible persons is wholeheartedly granted. Many of us need to be prodded out of our ruts and biases. Many professional persons may not agree with some of the recommendations of Dr. Stokes, but if they are stirred into doing some serious thinking about this problem, he will have made a significant contribution.

Poffenberger has devoted over half of his paper to directly answering questions raised by Kirkendall's rebuttal in a previous exchange. This might be classified as a rebuttal to a rebuttal.

There are two defendable points of view regarding the issues at stake. Both Kirkendall and Poffenberger have merits to their positions, but neither are right on all points or wrong on all points. There is value in such exchanges, but I feel in some instances in this paper that Poffenberger is grasping for any minute point which will defend his position and undermine his opponent, e.g. "The interpersonal relationships concept may be used prematurely by parents and teachers." This criticism could be leveled against almost any theory or concept. The fact that someone may misuse or prematurely use ideas, concepts, or truths does not challenge their validity. A teen-ager may be given the privilege of driving an automobile before he has the judgment for its proper use, but that does not mean we should condemn automobiles. Rather, it suggests the need for more responsibility on the part of the adults who are directly involved.

Poffenberger makes the statement "that in the absence of conclusive research data, it is unwise to make *any* recommendations," yet later states, "the writer admits to taking the position that at present it is best for professional persons in the field to continue to support society's opposition to premarital coitus among junior high and senior high school students." I'm not necessarily disagreeing with Poffenberger's latter position, but merely pointing out what appears to me to be an inconsistency.

The author should be complimented in attempting to state a positive approach to the problem. I agree that "an understanding adult can aid the adolescent in developing firmer moral convictions by helping him develop self-insight," but the statement, "Parents can try not to make their sons feel guilty over their developing sex drive, but they should expect their boys to control it to the extent that they and others will not be hurt," could be interpreted as condoning a double standard of morality as long as "they and others will not be hurt." I doubt, however, that this is what Poffenberger had in mind.

Our discussion of these three papers leads us to the conclusion that the main question is one of comparative values. The choices we make are affected by the values we consider worth-while and important. Anyone who does not care about the pattern of his life and conduct beyond getting what he wants when he wants it, cannot contribute much to developing a constructive sexual ethic.

The basic question is how can the individual work out the full meaning and implications of his enduring goal values, how does he discover the ways he must act in order to attain inner freedom, live according to his own inner integrity, and protect the dignity of other persons? Inconsistencies in our sexual standards have been pointed out, arguments presented regarding the why and how of achieving the control of adolescent premarital coitus, and a plea for a more rational approach to our changing sex ethics including an "unorthodox" suggestion regarding a possible future direction for the science of human genetics.

These authors have helped us take a look at our present situation and have challenged some of our present standards. However, in my opinion, the task of re-evaluating our sexual standards and establishing a code of sexual ethics which will gain more numerous and more ardent followers than our present code has enlisted, is still before us. This latter task is not primarily concerned with the

pattern of behavior which individuals are exhibiting in our own
or other cultures, but with the goals and objectives to be followed
if life is to realize the highest values in sex, love and marriage. The
practical implication is that in all our sex relations, certain considerations must be made regarding enduring values since a disregard or violation of these will be detrimental to an individual's
personal integrity and worth, to other persons involved, to the
family, to the community, and to the world. Once the values are
agreed upon, then the standards of behavior can be developed
which will most optimally contribute to achieving one's own potentialities, to experiencing fulfilling human relationships, and
to the improvement of family life.

Reply to Porter and Kirkendall

WALTER R. STOKES

It has been suggested by Blaine Porter that there is no need to
discard the field of medicine because ancient physicians used crude
and weird treatments and prescriptions. I agree. However, I would
vigorously oppose an implication that modern medicine is in any
way bound to accept the wisdom or worth of anything found in
ancient medicine. Yet when we come to religious tradition and
traditional sex ethics a great many insist that ancient wisdom is
superior to our best modern thinking. This I question and most
certainly I would not exempt religious or traditional authority
from the same kind of challenging rational criticism that has proved
so valuable in building modern medical science.

Professor Porter questions the ethical soundness of my position
in "giving young people frank and warm endorsement of autoerotic
pleasure as an end completely desirable and acceptable in itself."
Unfortunately he omitted the rest of the sentence, which provides
the following qualification: "—and as the self-respecting basis
upon which other sex experiences are built." This is of critical

importance. Up to age two or three a child can not well grasp the social implications of sex. Any effort to discourage his interest in it can only make him feel that it is "bad." If allowed to accept erotic feeling as "good" the growing child's sex awareness should become enriched by association with affectionate and responsible social aspirations. But in no event can I see anything unethical or anti-social in the simple joy of autoerotic pleasure or, for that matter, in enjoyment of sexual intercourse as an experience delighted in by two affectionate and responsible people and requiring no other justification, even though other purposes may sometimes be served.

I suggest that the most basically erroneous of all our ancient ethical concepts is the one which makes personal sensuous delight seem sinful and antisocial. I consider this to be a false, hypocritical view which is destructive alike to sound personal identity and to truly loving human relatedness. I feel very deeply that man can achieve his best social potential only when he has a guiltless ability to share his narcissistic delights with other human beings in whom he senses similar qualities. It is my observation that people who fairly well attain this have minimum difficulty accepting the really essential disciplines of social living.

Professor Porter sees me as "encouraging autoeroticism, pre-marital coitus and sanctioning extramarital affairs." I would note briefly that my position as to the first two is qualified in important ways and that never have I endorsed the wisdom of extramarital relations. In my recent book, *Married Love in Today's World,* I say of extramarital relations "—the hazards are great, no stable satisfaction is attained, and a third party may be greatly injured. —If the marriage can not be made happy, a divorce is the self-respecting and constructive step that can eventually lead to remar-riage and a stabilized emotional life."

At the end of his commentary he expresses confidence in the need for enduring, dependable ethical values (presumably along traditional religious or cultural lines.) I am wary of this, both from dislike of many traditional values and mistrust of becoming bound to dogma of any kind. I believe there is greater promise in adopting the thesis that all our values shall be regarded as working hypotheses whose worth and usefulness shall be under constant test and subject to modification according to experience. I think this view constitutes a value more important than any other.

I am pleased that Lester Kirkendall finds so much to approve in what I have said and I am altogether delighted with the central theme of his own approach to sex ethics.

To both Professors Porter and Kirkendall I offer warmest appreciation for their thoughtful comments. And as the former has observed, all of us are going in very substantially the same direction. None should lose sight of this as we honestly air our differences. I am sure I express pride for all of us that we have so well avoided the pitfalls of arrogance and kept our focus upon human need.

THE DOUBLE STANDARD

Double standards regarding sex behavior (i.e., more freedom allowed for men than for women) have been with us for a long time, and the ramifications of differentially evaluating the behavior of the two sexes are far-reaching indeed. It has been noted, for example, that actually what is involved is a "double double" standard. Since the male needs females with whom to enjoy his greater freedom, the double standard necessarily implies the further differentiation of two classes of women—"good women" and "bad women"—and this is the rationale for viewing prostitution as a complement of conventional marriage, as many writers have done.

As the author of the following selection (an experienced family expert) shows, sexual standards relate closely to the over-all social roles of men and women in a given society; indeed, this reading could have been included in Part II of this collection almost as easily as in Part I. While numerous justifications for the double standard have been presented over the years, today (as Miss Bassett makes clear) they appear less than impressive except as obvious rationalizations of the male's position of dominance. As a result the male's greater sexual "prerogatives" are no longer accepted unquestioningly, but rather this whole matter is being subjected to intensive reconsideration.

The Double Standard

MARION BASSETT

"You lead up to the great stumbling block for successful marriage, Eve. This is the double standard under which our society still largely operates. It is at the root of innumerable laws, customs and problems."

"Yes, it's a subject often avoided when discussing the family as too delicate, too complex—so let us give it first place."

ADAM APPROVES A SINGLE STANDARD
—WITH VARIATIONS

"I would say that since the man is allowed only one wife at a time and his affairs before and after marriage are kept under cover we ostensibly live under a single standard. I approve of a single standard—but of course a certain amount of leniency for man should be allowed since his nature demands some freedom and variation in mates," Adam continued. "On the surface we must maintain for our children's and wives' sakes the appearance of a strict and monogamous society. You know, Eve, since the woman carries the unborn child she is the one who may bear evidence of relations outside of marriage. That provides the basis of the double standard."

Eve did not agree but thought a while as to just how to answer. Then she began slowly "Let us consider a situation outside our country so that we may see it with perspective. There may be a society in South America where women wear tightly fitting dresses and the men loose capes or ponchos. Let us imagine a few of each

Reprinted from Marion Bassett, *A New Sex Ethics and Marriage Structure* (New York: Philosophical Library, 1961), pp. 28-46; footnotes omitted.

sex at times went shop lifting in the vegetable and poultry market of their village. The men hid their stolen goods neatly under their ponchos but the women often were 'caught with the goods.' The attitude in this society might well develop that it is nowhere nearly as serious for men to go shoplifting as for women and a double standard on shoplifting result. Even their gods were called in to sanctify the double standard and impress it upon the women. Men pretended not to shoplift but they certainly did at times and neatly got away with it.

"The logic of your reasoning to support the double standard on sexual behavior, that women may carry evidence of their actions and therefore must be more restricted, is exactly the same as that of these simple people for their double standard on shoplifting."

Adam didn't answer. He was buried in thought. Then he ventured, "There is a similarity, I admit."

Eve took his hand to show her friendship while she went further. "You say that respected women must walk a straight and narrow path, because if they don't, they may 'get caught with the goods,' to make a comparison with this South American group, while men approving the strict pattern for themselves can step aside from its restrictions and never carry any clear evidence of their action. If we are frank, isn't your theory that men like to *pretend* they obey the same pattern as their wives while they cherish the advantage of being able to break away without being discovered?"

"Well, that's part of it. I hate to admit it. But there are other factors."

"Yes, let's consider them all. It seems to me that many men don't want to face the situation. They are perplexed and run away from any analysis. Have you read that part of James Boswell's diary in *London Journey* which was recently published? Boswell in his amazing frankness tells not only of his experiences but also of his reactions." Eve passed the book to Adam with certain passages marked.

Adam ran through some of Boswell's accounts of relations with prostitutes and then read to himself a description of how on the night of the King's birthday Boswell dressed like a blackguard, carried an old oaken stick and went into the park. There he made an agreeement with a "little profligate wretch" for sixpence and tells how he "abused her in blackguard style."

Later in the diary Adam reads about the servant girl, Peggy Doig, the mother of Boswell's illegitimate son who died when fifteen months old. She is in London. "I have seen her and advised her not to fall into such a scrape again. I really don't know how to talk on such a subject, when I consider that I led her into the scrape."

Another description he scanned told of going into the park and "performing concubinage with a strong plump . . . girl." The next day he "went to Temple Church and heard a very good sermon. . . . This with music and the good building put me into a very devout frame and after service my mind was left in a pleasing, calm state."

"What a man to write all that," Adam breathed. "He sees no inconsistency between using a prostitute, then gaining 'a pleasing, calm state' from a church service. It does make one think. He admits being perplexed about his feelings toward the mother of his illegitimate child."

"If we only had similar frank diaries by most men we'd be able to know the real situation," Eve said as Adam smiled. "I don't think it's a healthy state of affairs to have one standard ostensibly held by society while a lot of deception is carried on.—The fact that men don't get caught with evidence of their sidestepping doesn't really justify a freer standard for them. That reasoning, and the other side, that since women may show the results of breaking from the supposed behavior of society they must be more careful is all based on a great hypocrisy and the matter of who can be more hypocritical. It claims the men may, and therefore we should accept different behavior from them. But it just doesn't go with a society that stands for truth, for honesty, for sincere human relations, a society which supports churches and sends its children to Sunday schools.

—One may think the effects of these two standards are minor influences in our social life. But I hold that they ramify through all areas."

"Well, I'm open minded about it, Eve. I really only expressed a common attitude. It would be good to dig into the situation."

"It is time it was frankly pulled apart and exposed under a bright light and a microscope as scientists do in laboratories. That is the way new knowledge has been gained in physics and chemistry. Scientists constantly reconsider past beliefs and old attitudes and constantly discard many of them. Some ceased to honor the old idea that an atom could not be split and that is why they stepped into a vast new world of knowledge.

"Our human relations must also be studied if we are to make progress," Eve continued. "If we close our eyes and cling to the old folklore and unsound attitudes still supporting some of our ways we are heading for more tragic times ahead. If certain ideas about social behavior work against people's well-being they should be discarded. New attitudes must take their place even though we hesitate to embrace them because they are strangers.

"People have found it difficult to build new patterns for life. The process is filled with fear. The good old ways always offer us a false sense of security. Yet as we read history we realize that those before us were forced to work out new patterns of life to go with new knowledge and new conditions. Their lives would have been in greater danger if they had clung to old customs after electricity, new continents, new medical knowledge had been discovered. The same is true today. We are safer if we study today's folklore and develop new and appropriate attitudes than if we fearfully hold to the ways of our ancestors."

A knock at the door interrupted them. Adam's cousin, John de Dios, entered. They invited him to join their discussion. After telling him their subject and their views they asked for his.

He was a confident, outspoken fellow so he declared forthrightly, "I believe in a double standard and in its entire acceptance. No pretense of a single standard, no hypocrisy about it. Children should expect their fathers to have affairs with other women and wives should adjust to them.—I therefore do not base my reasoning on the fact that men can get away with breaking a single standard because they don't become pregnant. I base my reasoning on the fact that women become attached to their babies, want to care for them and bring them into their homes—where another man than the child's father may raise them. Men don't have these mother instincts. There's no chance they will bring illegitimate children into the homes of their wives. Nature gave men this advantage which allows their sexual freedom. And men have used it through history."

Adam's Cousin Openly Supports the Double Standard

Adam could see that Eve was holding on to herself and figuring how to be tactful in her reply. She had heard such arguments before. "That's a good clear statement, John, of what many think. Let's stop to analyze it.—Every baby starts its life by the joining of a reproductive cell from a man with one from a woman. His body just as much as hers enters into the conception of new life. Likewise, his actions, just as much as hers, lead to the starting of this new child. By no twisting of logic can he claim that the new life is more the result of her actions than of his. And also by no reasoning can he hold that when the child is born it is more her responsibility to care for. The child in all truth is the product of two, is flesh of their flesh, and carries the inheritance of both into the next generation. Men know all this but don't want to apply it.

"If the man is equally mature he will want his child to have opportunities for growth, just as much as the mother does, and he'll want to assume his full half-share of providing these. Of course, however, if he does not regard himself as an equally mature and responsible person as the woman, he can put his head in the sand and ignore his illegitimate child. Remember though, he can logically uphold the double standard only if he believes the man is a less responsible person and approves of his remaining so.

"That is, a man has a choice of these two attitudes. He can consider himself a person as responsible as the woman, in which case he would acknowlege his child 'under the rose,' support it as his own, either in his own home or in another's. If he holds this to be the course for a respected and honored man—then he would be as careful as a woman not to start a child whom he didn't want to raise. The caution of both man and woman would be the same and we'd have a single standard regarding sexual relations.

"On the other hand, the man may hold himself as a less responsible person than a woman, one who doesn't recognize the value of human life as she does. Therefore, he is not so concerned about possible conception and the life of his own child. Then, and only then, can he approve man's greater sexual liberties and the two different standards."

John thought for a while, then turned to a way out and said with spirit. "Well, Eve, we are willing to be regarded as less responsible persons than women. We just are—we want to continue to be so— nature made us this way. We want the double standard, our own freedom, but not that for our wives!"

Eve calmly replied, "How about our laws and customs which assume men are wiser, more responsible than women, and therefore men become the officers of companies, heads of most churches and projects of all kinds, hold the important government positions, make the laws for all and are the legal heads of our families? Should all this be changed?"

John looked a little sheepish. He wanted men to hold all these prerogatives based on their greater virtue, and also wanted the double standard which can be based only upon their lesser virtue— their valuing human life less than the women do. He couldn't think of a good reply.

Eve broke the silence. "There is still another pattern which could be followed. A society could approve a single standard, and both men and women would be equally unconcerned about possible conception out of marriage and equally indifferent to the well-being of any illegitimate children. Such a society might well practice infanticide, killing or exposing such babies or selling them as prostitutes or slaves, as has been done."

"That would be of course a society gone to seed, degenerate, chaotic—out of the question! We rely on women not to let it go this way," John vigorously replied.

"Perhaps men give women far too heavy a job through the double standard which assumes men should not do their part in caring for all their children."

John calmed down and said quietly, "But, Eve, let's be frank, you know it is far more difficult for a man than a woman to walk the narrow path and always to be concerned with consequences."

"You think so, but, remember, you don't know how great women's urges are to step aside. You like to imagine they aren't so strong as yours. What ground have you for such a belief? True, men have held it. Adam and I the other day looked at the medical book by Acton which says women have no sexual feelings or urges. But we know better now. Most intelligent men today recognize that women are full human beings physically and psychologically with hungers as strong as men's for delicious food and delicious experiences."

"I always thought myself an intelligent man."

"Excuse me, John! I should have said a man who has kept up on recent thinking and writing in this field. Of course most don't. They often think this is a subject which should not be written about.—There is an excellent study by Ford and Beach which brings some light on the matter. It shows that among many human societies where pressure is not placed on women to suppress and conceal their interests they show as much desire for sexual satisfactions as the men, and in some societies even more. Likewise, we are coming to the realization that when women have not been trained to fear and avoid sexual experience in youth and are treated lovingly by their mates their enjoyment is likely to be fully as great as men's. Thus, approval of a double standard on the ground that the man has greater difficulty in controlling himself than the woman does not hold."

Eve saw that he was not hurt by what she was saying. Instead he was intrigued by the new ideas of women being innately more desirous of a complete, full life than society allowed them—even the old maids and the widows. He glimpsed a pattern that might be more fun for all than this double standard. He urged her to tell more of her thoughts.

"You have never guessed how far-reaching are the effects of this one-sided arrangement. Even most women have not stopped to recognize this, John. You men create two classes of women in order to meet your wishes for strictly controlled wives and also women who will be free for your affairs outside of marriage.

"We could say that woman's two dominant needs give men great power over her. One is her need for a sexual life, the other her need for assistance in raising children. Men have, in their subconscious and unplanned urge to control her, used both these needs. They have said in effect through their laws to the women, 'If you want me to be a responsible father then you must acknowledge my complete sexual ownership of you. On the other hand, if you take any freedom in sex, then you will not have a responsible father for your child.' That is, they divide women according to their sexual actions into wives and those of a lower caste, the 'sinful' and the 'fallen'. Men's feelings about this 'sinful' group are ambivalent. When they are talking in the company of wives or married couples they scorn this lower caste, but when men alone are talking they often admit how much they love their present mistresses or friends 'under the rose'. But the laws place these latter women in a precarious position. They can be arrested if prostitution is established, they are given practically no assistance through the courts in winning proper assistance from the father if one has a child. The father may help her due to a kind impulse but our laws actually seldom force him to carry his half share. Because she is considered 'sinful' she has almost no basic rights as we shall later note.—Corresponding to these two groups of women what do we find among men?"

John hesitated, then Adam said, "Just one group, yes. They are not divided according to whether they take some freedom or not. Men's varied behavior does not so much concern others. In fact, most all are expected to show their masculine nature by stepping aside sometime in their lives."

"And our laws protect them amazingly, even as the customers of prostitutes."

"Yes, when that house of prostitution was raided by the police last week all the men customers were freed and the women arrested," Adam observed.

"Actually this double standard which makes women 'sinful' for the same action which is considered natural for a man has a vicious influence. It extends its effects through all phases of all women's lives hanging the 'sword of Damocles' over their heads. It provides grounds for husbands' unreasonable criticism of wives often based on suspicion alone. It also provides a ready method for anyone who wants to hurt a woman. He or she need only to start a rumor. It places every woman who is in a relatively weak position, through her low economic position or simply her single state, where she can be badly injured. The effects, in short, force her to be cautious and fearful, which means less courage and self-confidence in many ways. Her insecurity, if she has a suspicious husband, often affects her self-confident poise necessary to wisely handle her children. I have known several cases of this. And simple suspicion by a husband can lead to her divorce, for we know divorces can be obtained without substantial grounds in various special places. The whole tone and tenor of every woman's life is shadowed by this 'sword of Damocles' causing her to walk in kind of a strait jacket. Some may not feel this since they have never imagined a different status.

"She is subject to all of this of course while she is often frustrated as a celibate single or widowed woman, or married to a husband who no longer loves her. The contrast between her position and that of a man who enjoys his wife and also without much fear tastes some adventure and novelty with other attractive women, you cannot fully realize."

Eve looked at John and found him slumped in his chair. He was a good sport to listen attentively and try to understand. After a few minutes he said, "True we think women lacking in courage to do this and that, over-cautious about appearances and the middle aged ones often with no sparkle.—You know, when we give attention to some young women and propose a little affair, we forget we're offering to place her in a tough position."

"Yes indeed! I'm glad you see that," Eve said enthusiastically. "Her risks of rumor, of detection—and of pregnancy with her whole life often influenced by such a drastic experience, sometimes, you know, even leading to suicide, place her in a totally different position from the man.—You men often complain of women being too cautious, too strait-laced, yet you have done almost everything you can to make them that way. You have put them in an agonizing position. Here is a lovely young woman who is eager to marry a congenial man, who proposes relations. What is she faced with? She may desire these as much as he, but she knows all these overhanging risks. If she refuses he may drop her for another friend, although he may be just the man for her husband. He would like to marry a virgin, yet he wants his sweetheart to join him now as his full sexual companion! He is asking contradictory things of her, as do those frequently who are in a position of advantage. Besides his contradictory wishes, she is not sure if he wants to marry her. This young woman may be your daughter. Shouldn't we face her perplexities and try to help?"

Since John had two daughters he understood and nodded, yes.

Eve was encouraged to continue, "What an uproar we would hear if someone suggested to an audience that in bridge the rules be made so that an ace would be the highest card for men and the lowest ranking card for women players. Or that in tennis a man's ball should be counted in when three feet beyond the outer lines of the court but a woman's ball must be within the boundary lines. To slightly change the picture, how about rules that the shorter men, under five feet six inches, must pay income taxes at twice the rate for men over this height? Yet all these weighted, one-sided rules would not effect the player's lives as much as do the warped rules called the double standard of morals."

John and Adam looked at each other with a feeling that there was some sense in what Eve was saying. "This is really interesting," John commented. "I don't know where we're being led, but you don't seem to think, Eve, that, if women are as interested in sexual pleasures as men, *we all* should be put under a rigid, confining single standard. I'm glad I dropped in."

"Nor do you think we all should be granted extensive freedom, for that would bring chaotic conditions," Adam said.

Eve laughed. "You are both right. It's most complex. We can't come to a conclusion yet."

WIVES, PROSTITUTES, HETAERAE

"As we have mentioned," Eve continued, "today, when one asks, 'What kind of a man is he?' one does not mean, 'What is the pattern of his sexual life?' That is considered to be of his own private concern. Yet 'What kind of a girl is she?' often means just this. Her sex life is the rightful concern of all, which is another indication that she is regarded largely as a sexual person or object. The questioner wants to know to what degree she is free or strict. In our discussion we have brought out that women are placed in two main groups according to their sexual lives: one, those who keep within the prescribed restrictions; the other, those who provide partners for men outside of marriage and who are called all sorts of names— loose woman, prostitute, harlot, whore and many others. Thus, men have their proper wives and also others, whom they must condemn at least to mixed groups, and whom the law also in effect condemns.

"Now something interesting is happening," Eve went on, "and

it is most significant. A third group is developing, which could be called the hetaerae, women who are somewhat independent of men and the sexual restrictions placed on them. During one period of the Greek Empire there were women of education and refinement who were economically independent. They did not marry but enjoyed friendships and relations with those they chose. Thornton Wilder's *Woman of Andros,* gives us a vivid picture of the beauty and character of some of the Greek hetaerae. Sappho of immortal lyrics was one among many leading hetaerae who were authors, musicians, philosophers and teachers. Some of their companions with whom they passed long years were Menander, Pericles and Alexander the Great. Their minds were developed, their imaginations stimulated and they had knowledge of their world, so they could make some of the outstanding contributions of their age. In contrast were the wives whose days were filled with household chores and heavy childbearing, whose spirits were often broken. Demosthenes cogently expressed the men's view toward women and their classification according to the sexual use made of them. 'We have courtesans (hetaerae) for pleasure, concubines (palladides) for daily use, and wives to provide us with legitimate children and to grow old faithfully in the interior of the house.'

"At present in western countries I think we now find three similar divisions of women determined by their sexual life: the married; the prostitutes earning a livelihood mainly through prostitution; and those we might call the hetaerae, who are financially independent though unmarried—and who have relations of their own choosing. They may be independent through their earnings, or property. Also among these are young unmarried college women supported by their families who have affairs with college men not for any economic purpose but for the same reason as their bachelor partners. The number of hetaerae is probably increasing.

"Their development is one step away from sexual bondage, either as the sexual possession of a husband or as a sexual servant of the man customer in prostitution. The hetaerae may consent to relations or refuse them; may approve a particular partner and later refuse him. They, in short, are in control of their own bodies."

"That's a striking statement, Eve," Adam interjected.

"Yes, I know it is. Later we should look into it further."

"I'd like to join you in some of your later talks if I may. You've got me thinking," John said as he passed around cigarettes and helped the others light them.

"We'd like to have you, John, I see you have an open and un-prejudiced mind—are willing to look under the surface."

"I'm interested in what you were saying about the problems of girls today."

"Yes—their problems are crucial. It looks as though we are in a period of change, feeling our way out of a pattern, perhaps too restrictive—and involving too much hypocrisy. To have a small number of hetaerae who own their own bodies is a significant step but this pattern doesn't include the important factor of children and child-care. That is what offers complications."

"Oh, indeed," Adam murmured.

"During these days girls and women are bearing the brunt of both the confusion of changing attitudes and the double standard. For instance, we mentioned the single girl who knows that to yield to her sweetheart's pleas for relations may cause her to be rejected as his later wife. On the other hand, if she refuses him she may be discarded as his present companion. All, while her parents unmindful of her real problem, are constantly warning, 'Oh, darling, do be careful.'—Later after marriage when her husband leaves her for a lengthy trip he may say, 'Dearest, while I'm gone be a good wife for me.' And then she may hear from a childhood beau, 'Mary, I'm sailing for the front overseas. Have a heart, dear! For old friendship's sake!' These are a few of the contradictory pressures through which women wind their way.

"If the young unmarried woman has relations with her particular friend or friends, many influences lead her into the class of he-taerae. She may become popular, confident and sparkling since her life is complete," Eve went on. "Her men friends, on the other hand, often pick some less popular virgins for their future house-keeping wives. Yet some hetaerae marry, and some properly re-strained virgin young women are never asked. Many women try both patterns at different times during their lives endeavoring to discover what men really want. Although some college men are becoming more tolerant toward the non-virgin as a bride, the young men who are casual in their relationships do not want their brides to have followed the same code. That is, the most fair-minded still hold a form of double standard.

"There are many men who have as sex partners wives, hetaerae and perhaps prostitutes within a short space of time. Man may play double or triple roles but few women can play more than one role at once, and few are not handicapped by their 'past.' I say 'handicapped' regardless of what their past is. The conservatively reared and restricted young woman may be limited and handi-capped by her experience just as truly as is she who has enjoyed some sexual freedom. A woman must usually choose a limited sex 'policy' and take the disadvantages tied to each pattern while a man can be a sexual opportunist."

"Yes, Eve, that's right. One of my daughters now in high school is a serious-minded and proper little girl. There's only one boy friend who takes her out occasionally. He is rather bashful and serious, too. My other daughter now in college, I often wonder about. She is very popular. During vacation sometimes when she comes home at night after a dance her face is radiant beyond description, her hair and dress badly ruffled. I worry about each of them, for as you say each is building a pattern and reputation which will aid or hinder a good marriage. My wife and I discuss it, but come to no conclusions as to just what's the wise course for girls today," John observed between puffs on his cigarette.

"That's it," agreed Eve, "Now let's consider the choice presented women during their years of maturity. Let's see if we can use our imaginations sufficiently to make this real. Here is a turned-about society in which men play women's present roles and women take the men's. Men would have to choose between these two courses, determined by their sex policy:

A man could take a partner in marriage which would mean:

a. A home with mate and children.

b. Fitting himself into a prescribed occupation, that of house-keeping. His housework would provide services for his family, but he and his children would be financially dependent upon his mate who earned outside.

c. Having some sexual satisfaction with his wife but with her alone. (She, however, might have affairs with a man secretary or other handsome single man, younger than her husband, not restricted to home and children.)

"Now let me think about that," Adam interposed. "The man would be the house-husband. The funds to run the family and for his own clothes he'd receive from his wife."

"Yes, and he'd give extensive time to the children," Eve continued. On the other hand, he could choose a pattern corresponding to that of the single woman, which would mean:

a. No home with a mate, no children.

b. Freedom to enter other vocations than housekeeping, but probably in a less responsible job and at a lower income than if he were a woman.

c. All sexual life forbidden by our laws and customs.

John wanted time to think about this. "If the roles were reversed you think women would marry men younger than themselves. Also, under the double standard, they might have affairs with younger men."

"I don't doubt it, John.—We'll talk about this later, too.—Which of these patterns would you choose?"

"I don't like either of them! I want a home and children but I don't want to be a house-husband. And I wouldn't comply with my wife's restrictions, never to go with another woman—especially if she were having an affair," John said pounding the arm of his chair.

"I agree with John," Adam joined in indignation. "I wouldn't submit to either choice. The second one's as bad as the first. I want both a home and an occupation outside in which I can specialize and feel I have a part in the world's progress."

"But, my dears, you are in this society and most women would say, you can't eat your cake and have it too, you *must* choose! —This is just what I wanted you to feel—and feel strongly—that neither of these choices would you accept. They are too restrictive for most full-blooded persons. They deny basic human needs for *both* family and activity in the outside world.

"If men, however, did submit so they experienced these two patterns, some choosing marriage and housekeeping, other bachelorhood and business, they would, as you claim, soon revolt. The men house-husbands would sally forth with aprons and rolling pins, while the bachelors would come from their one-room apartments with wet clothes hanging to dry, and in the flashing eyes of both groups could be read the words: 'We won't stand for this.'"

Adam and John laughed. "I'm sure you're right," Adam said.

"You wonder why women submit to living within these two choices, I suppose.—But actually a woman in our culture is hardly allowed to live at all if she doesn't largely submit to one of these patterns. That is, if she refuses marriage restrictions but earns her own living and has a child or two, just what does society do to her? Have you known a case of this kind? I have. The mother is rejected socially and her children also to a degree. Her earning opportunities are limited, at the same time she carries the double job of housekeeper and bread-winner. She's far worse off than the women who fit into one of those choices.—Of course a woman may not flaunt the marriage laws but less radically refuse the restrictions offered her. A few, usually those with plenty of funds so they may engage servants, can manage to have a husband and children along with real interesting outside responsibility." Eve paused to light a new cigarette.

"And some mothers of moderate means hold earning jobs outside when their children are in school or college, but of course they carry on their housework too," Adam observed, "and, as you say their jobs are not the most interesting ones, they usually work as secretaries or clerks in stores, or as substitute teachers. I suppose that since they drop out of any former earning occupation or special field while their children are babies this breaks a line of progress to the better jobs."

"Yes, and when they take a job after some years at home, since they are still housekeepers they must choose something that eliminates long commuting trips." Eve added. "As to why women don't revolt, the way you men think you would, I can venture this. Older women, who have known through experience the various inadequacies of these two main choices, have insufficient power to change them. Sexual customs and marriage constitute the most delicate and explosive of all areas in which women can work for reform. Most young women don't know the full effects of this forced choice and since their lives are centered on keeeping husbands happy they can't risk analyzing the marriage institution.

"And does not society use the blinding power of Cupid as it explains all these restrictions to the woman? She is largely assigned to housework, it is said, because this symbolizes her love for her husband. Likewise, her small opportunity for responsible outside positions is justified because her main job is at home to help her husband. A desire to have economic independence implies she does not properly trust him. Any freedom in her sexual life, even when her husband is away for years and has affairs of his own, is clear indication, society says, that she no longer loves him. All these limitations are explained by tying them to Cupid—if she is a proper loving woman she gladly accepts them, she is told. Few are those who will analyze or revolt at the risk of being considered

cold, uninfluenced by Cupid. And where is the mother in this institution founded absolutely on mutual love when the husband's love
flies out the window? It is humanly impossible for her then to carry
on all these duties under a genuine feeling of love for him. In such
an eventuality our society seems to assume that *she* has failed. It has
made no proper provision for her and her children's future.—
Young, single women often weigh these restrictions of marriage,
but their natural desire for a companion, children and the fullness
of life lead them to shut their eyes and move hopefully into the
world of the family.

"Let us notice what our culture requires of the young woman
as she enters marriage. She has been wooed for months or years
while she has been denied any full sexual satisfaction. Then when
she is in an ecstatic state of tension, hope and faith, having decided
that she trusts this man sufficiently to give herself to him 'until
death do us part,' the inherited law of the past descends upon her.
After the wedding march has echoed through the church and the
bride swathed in satin and old lace has whispered her vows, 'the
law steps in and holds the parties to various obligations and liabilities,'—according to the words of the Supreme Court. She is quite
unconscious under Cupid's influence of the rigidity, demands and
power of the laws which now surround her, as the two kiss each
other under the palms."

"Very interesting and significant," Adam observed.

"Oh yes, almost unconsciously, society has developed a situation where the young woman has a mass of obligations dropped
on her head—maybe that puts it too strongly. Those with funds
can of course buy themselves out of future difficulties, but others
cannot. The bride assumes the 'wifely duty' of submitting to her
husband; the task of bearing as many children as chance may start,
the job of caring for all their needs with no assurance that she will
have sufficient funds for this. Likewise she has no assurance, as
she bears babies, that her husband may not leave her with this task
to shoulder largely by herself. No government or private agency

has given her an understanding of the features of reproduction, nor helped her see into the future, for instance, that her family could be placed in a desperate position with eight or nine children. And various state governments have laws which interefere with her knowledge of effective contraception."

"But, Eve," John asked, "can any other arrangements be made? It is hard to figure them out."

"If one looks at the present family setups in other countries and also variations in the past, he recognizes that innumerable changes could be made. To most of us it seems impossible that a woman could have all these things: freedom to choose her vocation, economic independence, children and life with a mate without being his sexual possession. Yet some society may well develop such a pattern. There are no contradictions here which could not be overcome if men were willing. Might a society which allowed women these basic things enjoy a new vitality? Might these liberated women—whose influence would bear weight in high places —who have great concern for the nurture of human beings, help us reorient our lives?"

They did not now attempt to answer all this but went out to lunch together. It was decided that Eve should write the next chapter since they couldn't talk further for some time. Adam was to read it over and make suggestions before their next discussion.

TRIAL MARRIAGE

On the basis of his contacts with young people in the Juvenile Court of Denver, Judge Ben Lindsey proposed (in the 1920s) a system of "companionate marriage." The gist of the scheme was divorce by mutual consent for childless couples who were incompatible; Lindsey's proposals were an amalgam of "trial marriage" ideas, wider dissemination of birth control information, reform of divorce and alimony laws, and state-supported sex education. Despite his insistence that he was merely calling for a facing of facts—for young people, he maintained, were already in "revolt"—his plan was violently assailed as approving "free love" and "promiscuity."

In the selection printed below, the noted philosopher Bertrand Russell supports Lindsey's basic reasoning and proposes a similar plan—under which no marriage would be legally binding until the wife's first pregnancy. Russell also came under strong fire for such proclamations; in 1940 his teaching appointment at the City College of New York was canceled upon complaints that such views rendered him unfit to teach. It is interesting that while Marriage and Morals *was highly critical of conventional marriage, Russell stated that given certain conditions (equality, intimacy, similarity of standards), "I believe marriage to be the best and most important relation that can exist between two human beings." The book, originally published in 1929, still stands as a major critique of traditional sex standards, a refusal to accept hypocrisy by a scholar who has never hesitated to speak his mind.*

Trial Marriage

BERTRAND RUSSELL

In a rational ethic, marriage would not count as such in the absence of children. A sterile marriage should be easily dissoluble, for it is through children alone that sexual relations become of importance to society, and worthy to be taken cognizance of by a legal institution. This, of course, is not the view of the Church, which, under the influence of St. Paul still views marriage rather as the alternative to fornication than as the means to the procreation of children. In recent years, however, even clergymen have become aware that neither men nor women invariably wait for marriage before experiencing sexual intercourse. In the case of men, provided their lapses were with prostitutes and decently concealed, they were comparatively easy to condone, but in the case of women other than professional prostitutes, the conventional moralists find what they call immorality much harder to put up with. Nevertheless, in America, in England, in Germany, in Scandinavia, a great change has taken place since the war. Very many girls of respectable families have ceased to think it worth while to preserve their "virtue," and young men, instead of finding an outlet with prostitutes, have had affairs with girls of the kind whom, if they were richer, they would wish to marry. It seems that this process has gone further in the United States than it has in England, owing, I think, to Prohibition and automobiles. Owing to Prohibition it has become *de rigueur* at any cheerful party for everybody to get more or less tipsy. Owing to the fact that a very large percentage of girls possess cars of their own, it has become easy for them to escape

From *Marriage and Morals* by Bertrand Russell (New York: Bantam Books, 1961), pp. 106-113. By permission of Liveright, Publishers, New York, and George Allen & Unwin, London. Copyright © R, 1957, by Bertrand Russell.

with a lover from the eyes of parents and neighbors. The resulting
state of affairs is described in Judge Lindsey's books.* The old
accuse him of exaggeration, but the young do not. As far as a casual
traveller can, I took pains to test his assertions by questioning
young men. I did not find them inclined to deny anything that he
said as to the facts. It seems to be the case throughout America that
a very large percentage of girls who subsequently marry and become of the highest respectability have sex experience, often with
several lovers. And even where complete relations do not occur,
there is so much "petting" and "necking" that the absence of complete intercourse can only be viewed as a perversion.

I cannot say myself that I view the present state of affairs as satisfactory. It has certain undesirable features imposed upon it by conventional moralists, and until conventional morality is changed,
I do not see how these undesirable features are to disappear. Bootlegged sex is in fact as inferior to what it might be as bootlegged
alcohol. I do not think anybody can deny that there is enormously
more drunkenness among young men, and still more among young
women, in well-to-do America, than there was before the introduction of Prohibition. In circumventing the law there is, of course,
a certain spice and a certain pride of cleverness, and while the law
about drink is being circumvented it is natural to circumvent the
conventions about sex. Here, also, the sense of daring acts as an
aphrodisiac. The consequence is that sex relations between young
people tend to take the silliest possible form, being entered into
not from affection but from bravado, and at times of intoxication.
Sex, like liquor, usually has to be taken in forms which are concentrated and rather unpalatable, since these forms alone can
escape the vigilance of the authorities. Sex relations as a dignified,
rational, wholehearted activity in which the complete personality
cooperates, do not often, I think, occur in America outside marriage. To this extent the moralists have been successful. They have

* "The Revolt of Modern Youth," 1925. "Companionate Marriage," 1927.

not prevented fornication; on the contrary, if anything, their opposition, by making it spicy, has made it more common. But they have succeeded in making it almost as undesirable as they say it is, just as they have succeeded in making much of the alcohol consumed as poisonous as they assert all alcohol to be. They have compelled young people to take sex neat, divorced from daily companionship, from a common work, and from all psychological intimacy. The more timid of the young do not go so far as complete sexual relations, but content themselves with producing prolonged states of sexual excitement without satisfacion, which are nervously debilitating, and calculated to make the full enjoyment of sex at a later date difficult or impossible. Another drawback to the type of sexual excitement which prevails among the young in America is that it involves either failure to work or loss of sleep, since it is necessarily connected with parties which continue into the small hours.

A graver matter, while official morality remains what it is, is the risk of occasional disaster. By ill luck it may happen that some one young person's doings come to the ears of some guardian of morality, who will proceed with a good conscience to a sadistic orgy of scandal. And since it is almost impossible for young people in America to acquire a sound knowledge of birth-control methods, unintended pregnancies are not infrequent. These are generally dealt with by procuring abortion, which is dangerous, painful, illegal, and by no means easy to keep secret. The complete gulf between the morals of the young and the morals of the old, which exists very commonly in present-day America, has another unfortunate result, namely, that there can be no real intimacy or friendship between parents and children, and that the parents are incapable of helping their children with advice or sympathy. When young people get into a difficulty, they cannot speak of it to their parents without producing an explosion—possibly scandal, certainly a hysterical upheaval. The relation of parent and child has thus ceased to be one performing any useful function after the child

has reached adolescence. How much more civilized are the Tro-
briand Islands, where a father will say to his daughter's lover: "You
sleep with my child; very well, marry her."*

In spite of the drawbacks we have been considering, there are
great advantages in the emancipation, however partial, of young
people in America, as compared with their elders. They are freer
from priggery, less inhibited, less enslaved to authority devoid of
rational foundation. I think also that they are likely to prove less
cruel, less brutal, and less violent than their seniors. For it has been
characteristic of American life to take out in violence the anarchic
impulses which could not find an outlet in sex. It may also be hoped
that when the generation now young reaches middle age, it will not
wholly forget its behavior in youth, and will be tolerant of sexual
experiments which at present are scarcely possible because of the
need of secrecy.

The state of affairs in England is more or less similar to that in
America, though not so developed, owing to the absence of Prohibition and the paucity of motorcars. There is also, I think, in
England, and certainly on the Continent, very much less of the
practice of sexual excitement without ultimate satisfaction, and
respectable people in England, with some honorable exceptions,
are on the whole less filled with persecuting zeal than corresponding people in America. Nevertheless, the difference between the
two countries is only one of degree.

Judge Ben B. Lindsey, who was for many years in charge of the
juvenile court at Denver, and in that position had unrivalled opportunities for ascertaining the facts, proposed a new institution
which he calls "companionate marriage." Unfortunately he has lost
his official position, for when it became known that he used it rather
to promote the happiness of the young than to give them a consciousness of sin, the Ku Klux Klan and the Catholics combined to
oust him. Companionate marriage is the proposal of a wise con-

* "The Sexual Life of Savages," p. 73.

servative. It is an attempt to introduce some stability into the sexual relations of the young, in place of the present promiscuity. He points out the obvious fact that what prevents the young from marrying is the lack of money, and that money is requested in marriage partly on account of children, but partly also because it is not the thing for the wife to earn her own living. His view is that young people should be able to enter upon a new kind of marriage, distinguished from ordinary marriage by three characteristics. First, that there should be for the time being no intention of having children, and that accordingly the best available birth control information should be given to the young couple. Second, that so long as there are no children and the wife is not pregnant, divorce should be possible by mutual consent. And third, that in the event of divorce, the wife should not be entitled to alimony. He holds, and I think rightly, that if such an institution were established by law, a very great many young people, for example, students at universities, would enter upon comparatively permanent partnerships, involving a common life, and free from the Dionysiac characteristics of their present sex relations. He brings evidence to bear that young students who are married do better work than such as are unmarried. It is indeed obvious that work and sex are more easily combined in a quasi-permanent relation than in the scramble and exictement of parties and drunken orgies. There is no reason under the sun why it should be more expensive for two young people to live together than to live separately, and therefore the economic reasons which at present lead to postponement of marriage would no longer operate. I have not the faintest doubt that Judge Lindsey's proposal, if embodied in the law, would have a very beneficial influence, and that this influence would be such as all might agree to be a gain from a moral point of view.

Nevertheless, Judge Lindsey's proposals were received with a howl of horror by all middle-aged persons and most of the newspapers throughout the length and breadth of America. It was said that he was attacking the sanctity of the home; it was said that in tolerating marriages not intended to lead at once to children he was opening the floodgates to legalized lust; it was said that he enormously exaggerated the prevalence of extramarital sexual relations, that he was slandering pure American womanhood, and that most business men remained cheerfully continent up to the age of thirty or thirty-five. All these things were said, and I try to think that among those who said them there were some who believed them. I listened to many invectives against Judge Lindsey, but I came away with the impression that the arguments which were regarded as decisive were two. First, that Judge Lindsey's proposals would not have been approved by Christ; and, second, that they were not approved by eminent divines in the present day. The second of these arguments appeared to be considered the more weighty, and indeed rightly, since the other is purely hypothetical, and incapable of being substantiated. I never heard any person advance any argument even pretending to show that Judge Lindsey's proposals would diminish human happiness. This consideration, indeed, I was forced to conclude, is thought wholly unimportant by those who uphold traditional morality.

For my part, while I am quite convinced that companionate marriage would be a step in the right direction, and would do a great deal of good, I do not think that it goes far enough. I think that all sex relations which do not involve children should be regarded as a purely private affair, and that if a man and a woman choose to live together without having children, that should be no one's business but their own. I should not hold it desirable that either a man or a woman should enter upon the serious business of a marriage intended to lead to children without having had previous sexual experience. There is a great mass of evidence to show that the first experience of sex should be with a person who has previous knowledge. The sexual act in human beings is not instinctive, and apparently never has been since it ceased to be performed *a tergo*. And apart from this argument, it seems absurd to ask people to enter upon a relation intended to be lifelong, without any previous knowledge as to their sexual compatibility. It is just as absurd as it would be if a man intending to buy a house were not allowed to view it until he had completed the purchase. The proper course, if the biological function of marriage were adequately recognized, would be to say that no marriage should be legally binding until the wife's first pregnancy. At present a marriage is null if sexual intercourse is impossible, but children, rather than sexual intercourse, are the true purpose of marriage, which should therefore not be regarded as consummated until such time as there is a prospect of children. This view depends, at least in part, upon that separation between procreation and mere sex which has been brought about by contraceptives. Contraceptives have altered the whole aspect of sex and marriage, and have made distinctions necessary which could formerly have been ignored. People may come together for sex alone, as occurs in prostitution, or for companionship involving a sexual element, as in Judge Lindsey's companionate marriage, or finally, for the purpose of rearing a family. These are all different, and no morality can be adequate to modern circumstances which confounds them in one indiscriminate total.

THE AMERICAN SEX REVOLUTION

While many critics have been labeling conventional sex standards irrational, confused, and repressive, other analysts (including the eminent sociologist Pitirim Sorokin) have been expressing grave concern over what they view as an unfortunate decline in moral standards. These analysts stress that there is much of value in a family-centered social system, and that we are currently witnessing a breakdown of family stability that is but an indicator of wider social calamity. Many observers consider Sorokin's book The American Sex Revolution *extremely fainciful in its prognostication of the imminent collapse of American society due to its "sexualization." There is considerable evidence, though, that Americans may well be "obsessed" by sex in some of the ways Sorokin describes.*

Sorokin's critique of what he terms a "sensate" culture calls attention again to the interdependence of different aspects of a social system. Trends in the family and in sexual values and behavior are indeed closely linked to our other social values and institutions. Whether or not one agrees with the author's dire predictions, his comments are noteworthy as representing one important type of reaction to our present way of life.

The American Sex Revolution

PITIRIM A. SOROKIN

GROWING SEX ADDICTION

Increasing divorce and desertion and the growth of prenuptial and extramarital sex relations are signs of sex addiction somewhat similar to drug addiction.

Through the use of drugs an addict strives to relieve his painful tensions and to experience the intensest forms of sensual pleasure. The more one indulges in the use of drugs, the deeper he is caught by their tentacles. The more he uses them, the more substantially they change the total personality of the drug addict.

Sex addiction does not represent an exception to these rules. Dedication of an individual to the pursuit of sex pleasures means a growth of the sex drive at the expense of the power of other factors determining his total activity, and radically changes the whole system of forces governing human behavior. It is similar to a change of an engine and of the total motor mechanism of a car. Externally the car may look the same, but its inner system and driving performance become quite different from what they were before. Likewise, a tangible modification of the system of forces conditioning human behavior transforms the total personality of the individual, his body and mind, his values and actions. The deeper this change, the greater the transformation of the person involved.

This means that changes in the sex behavior of our men and women presuppose a parallel change of their biological and psychosocial properties, of their scientific, philosophical, religious, moral, aesthetic, and social values; and, also, a change of the com-

Reprinted from Pitirim A. Sorokin, *The American Sex Revolution* (Boston: Porter Sargent, 1956), pp. 14-18 and 131-134.

parative motivational effectiveness of each of these factor-values. The central biological transformation consists of a set of anatomical and physiological modifications that result in an over-excitation of sex appetite and sex activities. This over-stimulation may be due either to biological (glandular, and other) alterations in the organism, or to the changes in the psychological factors that inhibit and control sex impulses and activities. If, for instance, the motivational control and inhibition of these psychosocial factors weakens, or if instead of inhibiting, they begin to approve, glorify, and justify the greater and more promiscuous sex freedom, the biological sex drive becomes progressively disinhibited and acquires a much greater "motivational power" in propelling the individual toward less and less restrained sex relations. In almost all sex revolutions on a mass scale, the increase of motivational power of sex drive is due mainly to the weakening of the controls of the psychosocial factors or values, and the replacement of the inhibitive psychosocial factor-values by those that approve sex passion, sex prowess, and more varied sex relations.

This seems to be true also of the American sex revolution discussed. We do not have sufficient evidence of strictly anatomical and physiological changes directly and indirectly related to sex activity which would explain the increased motivating power of the sex drive. But we do have sufficient proof of a disinhibition of sex drive from the controls of the restraining psychosocial factor-values. The force of many religious, moral, aesthetic and social values that taboo all the prenuptial and extramarital sex relations has been progressively weakened during the last few centuries, and the last few decades especially. And many of these inhibitive values have been replaced by the values that commend and recommend a more free satisfaction of sex passion. In my *Social and Cultural Dynamics*, the *Crisis of Our Age*, and the *Reconstruction of Humanity*, the basic change of all the main values of the Western World in this direction is demonstrated in detail. A vast body of evidence given in these works conclusively proves the basic substitution of the dominant Medieval (Religious) values by the Sensate (Secular) values during the past five centuries. This evidence also shows that these Sensate values are disintegrating at the present time.

While the Ideational values tend to restrain unlawful sex activities, the Sensate values aim to disinhibit and approve them. At their distintegrating stage the Sensate values tend to approve potentially an unrestrained sex freedom, and recommend the fullest possible satisfaction of sex love in all its forms. This basic change in phychosocial factors has manifested itself in revaluation of the previous standards by modern American (and Western) men and women. The sex drive is now declared to be the most vital mainspring of human behavior. In the name of science, its fullest satisfaction is urged as a necessary condition of man's health and happiness. Sex inhibitions are viewed as the main source of frustrations, mental and physical illness and criminality. Sexual chastity is ridiculed as a prudish superstition. Nuptial loyalty is stigmatized as an antiquated hypocrisy. Father is painted as a jealous tyrant desirous of castrating his sons to prevent incest with their mother. Motherhood is interpreted as a "mommism," wrecking the lives of children. Sons and daughters are depicted as filled with the "complexes" of seduction of their mother and father, respectively. Sexual profligacy and prowess are proudly glamorized. *Homo sapiens* is replaced by *homo sexualis* packed with genital, anal, oral, and cutaneous libidos. The traditional "child of God" created in God's image is turned into a sexual apparatus powered by sex instinct, preoccupied with sex matters, aspiring for, and dreaming and thinking mainly of, sex relations. Sexualization of human beings has about reached its saturation point. Such in black and white has been the psychosocial change of the modern man's mentality, aspirations, emotions, and values paralleling the sexual revolution in his behavior.

If the mind, behavior, and values of contemporary men and women have been notably sexualized, similar sexualization of our entire culture and of every social institution must be expected. And if this is so, then the depth and extent of the current sex revolution must be incomparably more than a mere change in the personality and conduct of our contemporaries. . . .

In a final chapter, entitled "America at the Crossroads," Sorokin writes:

As a nation we are usually quite alert to the dangers threatening our well-being. We notice their early symptoms in time, and properly take the necessary countermeasures.

DANGEROUS LISTLESS DRIFT

Our listless drift towards sex anarchy seems to be an exception to this rule. Aside from a few old-fashioned voices crying in the wilderness, no alarms are sounded by the nation's leaders in the press or over radio or television. On our life-ways, no posters warn us with: "Danger! Slow Down! Sex Anarchy Ahead!" No nation-wide educational campaign brings home to our citizens the grim consequences of an overdeveloped sex freedom. No big drive has been launched to combat promiscuity, premarital and extramarital relations, divorce, and desertion.

Still less attention is paid to the progressive sexualization of our culture, institutions, and way of life. We often spend vast amounts of money, energy, and time, in fighting various social maladies, yet we do little to stop any further increase of sex freedom. We do not tolerate excessively dangerous political, social, or economic anarchy, yet we seem to be tolerant of sex disorders.

Does our apathy in this matter mean that we are unaware of the drift? Or does it signify our approval of the growing sex obsession, an acceptance of it as another step toward a fuller freedom and a happier life? Or, perhaps, does it represent a symptom of our incapacity to free ourselves from deep addiction to promiscuity?

If we are unaware of the real situation, it is high time we awakened from our ignorance. If we have lost the capacity to resist, it is urgent that we regain it. If we expect blessings from sex anarchy, it is vital that we cast aside this foolishness and look soberly at the sorry state of affairs. For there is a dangerous hue of serious trouble on the horizon. Our sex freedom is beginning to expand beyond the limits of safety, beginning to degenerate into anarchy.

Preceding chapters have shown a rapid increase of divorce, desertion, and separation, and of premarital, and extramarital relations, with the boundary between lawful marriage and illicit liaisons tending to become more and more tenuous. Still greater has been the deterioration of the family as a union of parents and children, with "fluid marriages" producing a super-abundance of the physically, morally, and mentally defective children, or no children at all.

As a consequence, in spite of our still developing economic prosperity, and our outstanding progress in science and technology, in education, in medical care; nothwithstanding our democratic regime and way of life, and our modern methods of social service; in brief, in spite of the innumerable and highly effective techniques and agencies for social improvement, there has been no decrease in adult criminality, juvenile delinquency, and mental disease, no lessening of the sense of insecurity and of frustration. If anything, these have been on the increase, and already have become the major problems of our nation. What this means is that the poisonous fruits of our sex-marriage-family relationships are contaminating our social life and our cultural and personal well-being. They have already passed beyond the phase of being possibly dangerous, and have become ugly and deadly realities as solid and certain as any facts can be.

Our trend toward sex anarchy has not yet produced catastrophic consequences. Nevertheless, the first syndromes of grave disease have already appeared.

The new sex freedom, of course, is only one factor, in the drift toward social revolution and political disorder, toward international conflict, toward a general decline of creativity and irremediable decay of our culture. There is a whole constellation of other factors: organization, social mobility, overdeveloped social differentiation, rapid cultural change, and especially the disintegration of the sensate system of values of Western culture. However, the sex factors and the accompanying disorganization of the family are among the most important contributions to these pathological phenomena. In the analysis which follows, the reader should bear in mind that the growth of sex freedom is a significant cause, but by no means the only one.

At the present time, the magnificent Sensate house built by Western man is crumbling, and the new Integrated system of values is not yet built. Hence the crises, tensions, and conflicts of this age (See my *Crisis of Our Age* for further details)....

A MODERN CHRISTIAN VIEW

Because of the unthinking way in which some of us use the terms "moral" and "immoral," and because of lingering beliefs that sexual behavior is somehow intrinsically "bad," the values of religion and sex have in our society frequently been considered antithetical. Today many theologians, however, resist overly dogmatic conceptions in this area and instead attempt to spell out reasonable criteria for determining moral behavior in the sexual realm. In this connection, it is increasingly accepted that sexuality (at least in marriage) must be considered a quite legitimate and even a valuable aspect of human behavior.

There are, of course, doctrinal differences in the approaches to sex taken by the various churches in America. As is well known, the teachings of the Roman Catholic church include important statements regarding sex and marriage (see, for example, the encyclical of Pius XI reprinted below in Part III). Orthodox Judaism, Mormonism, and other religious groups as well could also be pointed to as having distinctive theological tenets in this area. In the book from which the following selection is taken, Dr. Hiltner draws on his more detailed analysis of the Kinsey reports and of the problems those publications have raised. His essay constitutes a synoptic statement of what might be called a "liberal Protestant" approach to sexual behavior.

A Modern Christian View

SEWARD HILTNER

Here an attempt will be made to state a modern Christian view of the place of sex in the Christian life. This is based firmly in the biblical view, but it takes into account the modern knowledge symbolized by "developmental understanding," as well as the developments within Christian history since Bible times. As far as possible, the statements themselves are put in the language of the modern world as well as in the traditional language of Christian thought.

1. *Since man is a whole or total being, sex is good if it serves the fulfillment of man as a total being, that is, if it serves God's will for man.* As a whole or total being, a personal spirit, or a self-transcending organism, man is not essentially something ethereal with body temporarily attached. Nor is he an animal with the misfortune of a lately-developed brain that complicates an otherwise simple biological existence. Sex for him is not an unhappy reminder of the link that binds him to an animal ancestry. Nor is sex for him more real or essential in its biological than in its psychological, social, or religious aspects.

Because man is a total personal spirit (including body), his sex life can never be merely animal in nature even when he tries to make it so. On the other hand, since man's body *is* man seen from one perspective, man's sex life is not something alien linked to an otherwise free being. God seeks the fulfillment and realization

Reprinted from Seward Hiltner, *Sex and the Christian Life* (New York: Association Press; A Reflection Book, 1957), pp. 72-94; footnotes omitted.

of his creatures according to his will for them, and so he blesses sex that it may be used toward that fulfillment. Man is neither animal nor angel in his essential nature, but personal spirit and self-transcending organism.

It is of the utmost importance to recognize that sex in the service of the will of God does not refer to something alien or imposed. God's will simply provides the necessary objective reference, whose subjective counterpart is man's fulfillment as a total being. One of the reasons that the biblical and sacramental conception of sex has been so largely neglected in the modern world (that is, that something of the divine is communicated through biological experience) has been the unjustified suspicion that any reference to God means an unpleasant, external, and alien imposition. That is bad Christian theology.

Even the responsible humanistic views of sex today hold that sex is for man's fulfillment as a total being, rather than merely as a creature of biology, or a disembodied ghost, or as an unstable combination of the two. In its thrust, the Christian view does not, on the subjective side, differ in principal from the best humanistic views. It doubts, however, that the full dimensions of human fulfillment are likely to be kept in mind if the reference to God is omitted. Nevertheless, any recognition of sex as relevant to the total dimensions of man's existence, and not just to some segment of that existence, is implicitly in line with the Christian view. Conversely, any view that confines sex to one or another aspect of man's being, as if it were hermetically sealed off from other aspects and dimensions, is implicitly a contradiction or foreshortening of the Christian view.

2. *Man's total self or being (spiritual or organismic) has its very existence in the community of other selves; and it is the aim of all human interrelationships in all their aspects (including the sexual) to foster the love in which spiritual or organismic selfhood is nurtured.* It has never been an easy task for Christianity to find effective ways of stating that we are members one of another, that it is

our "membership" in one another that is the source and, in some respects, the end of our selfhood. Many kinds of metaphors and analogies have been used for this purpose. No man is an island, said John Donne. We are members of the body of Christ, said Paul. Our relationships to others are not merely external, as if we were what is inside our skin and other people were to us only as external environment.

Some modern tools, discoveries, and concepts have now come to our aid at this point. A "field theory" of personality is developing, according to which each man's individuality is real but is to be seen as the "focus" of a whole "field" or network of interrelationships. Without such a network or field, there could not be a focus. Focus and field are related internally and not merely accidentally.

Our very selfhood is made up of "reflective appraisals" of other people in the course of our development, wrote George Herbert Mead. It is equally essential to man as man that he express his "homonomous" needs (for relationship) as that he develop his "autonomous" ones (for personal expression and integrity), writes the psychiatrist, Andras Angyal. These modern tools, insights, and concepts are genuinely original, and they provide a technical knowledge of the processes of personality formation never before available. They are immensely valuable in filling in the Christian conviction that men are members of one another.

Along with all other types of relationship, contact, and human expressiveness, sex too is to promote the love which is the matrix of human personality itself. Human living is inevitably a matter of relationship. In addition to acknowledging this fact, the Christian view immediately states that what counts about the relationship is its quality. The goal of all relationship is love in the Christian sense; and sexual relationships are no exception.

This interpersonal or members-one-of-another conception of human life is not, we should note, a swallowing up of personhood or individuality in some collectivity. When the relationships operate as intended by God, they sharpen individuality. If it had no such relationships, individuality would be of poor quality, if it could exist at all. There have sometimes been sentimental interpretations of the "one-flesh union" idea found in the Bible, as if two persons becoming one cease to be individuals. This is not the Christian insight. Perhaps peculiarly with sex, one's personhood is "opened up," and individuality is accentuated. One looks at all of life with a new look.

The Christian view is not sentimental or unrealistic about the conflicts and discrepancies that are bound to arise between our individuality and the interpersonal setting in which it exists. Applied to sex, for instance, there is no guarantee, in the Christian view, that the choice of the best possible partner will solve all the needs and wants of either individual who is involved. Ultimately, Christianity traces most of these discrepancies to man's sin. But such a recognition, while liberating, does not automatically change the character of individuality nor of relationships to bring them into a magical kind of romantic harmony.

Sexual relationships, like other relationships, constantly strive toward the realization of a love quality (although the person may be unaware of this). Yet there are always severe limits to the realization of this quality (although he may be unaware of this also). Thus sex, in a particular but not isolated way, always has a paradoxical element about it. Although he may try to deny it, the person receives something more from it than he had anticipated. It proves to be a gift transcending what he had deliberately set out to achieve. At the same time, even his best efforts to make it fulfill its high potentialities reach, inevitably, some level of frustration or alienation.

No one can find perfect peace by sinking into some "great All" of sexual relationship with another. Yet he who cannot "let go" and accept the gift transcending his expectations is not moving toward love at all. From the Christian point of view, man is a sinner. Yet God forgives him, and that forgiveness may be manifested in many ways, including the gift coming to him through sex of a kind and quality he had neither planned nor anticipated. The reception of this gift does not mean that individuality disappears, nor does it give complete release from the problems and even the isolation that inhere in the fact of individuality.

If the Christian view rests on our being members one of another, seeking that quality of relationship that is Christian love, but sharpening rather than qualifying our individuality, then it must be stated and interpreted developmentally if it is not to be just an "end-point morality" heedless of the stages by which human growth takes place. The little child does not learn the love quality of relationship at once but through very complicated stages of actual relationship. Many of these stages bear little resemblance, on the surface, to adult love. In addition, people may become "fixated," as Freud said, at various stages of such development. They may thus move into chronological adulthood with the base capacity for love greatly impaired.

Unless we understand something of what is going on within the person and his relationships (including the sexual), we are not in a position to know to what extent he is or is not moving in the direction of a love quality of relationships. With this insight, the Christian view thus entertains a kind of clinical caution without impairing its vision of the basic principle. If we ask when this or that person is so moving, the answer is difficult. In answering it, casual observations and snap judgments have no place.

3. *The developmental aim of sex in human life is toward a progressive integration of the several necessary levels of sexual purpose or function.* Biologically speaking, sex reduces tension. Psychologically, through sex we find unsuspected aspects of our selfhood. Socially, we discover depth in another and, by implication, the potential depth of all other persons. Ethically, we find the relationship between fulfillment and responsibility. Theologically, we see sex ultimately as a mystery, but a mystery whose meaning is revealed to us in part.

Perhaps we can assume that to God, all these aspects or purposes of sex are one; for, from the Christian view, they are all necessary as aspects of the will of God for man in relation to sex. But since we are human, we come to comprehend them as if they were separate "things." Their meaning comes into our experience at different times and seasons. We are forever tempted to isolate one or more of them from the others, or to fail to accept the insight of a new level of apprehension lest it disturb the satisfactions of the old. But the *development* of human sex life, normatively speaking, is toward an increasing integration of these purposes and perspectives.

The end-point of this integration of sexual purposes may be relatively clear—a mature adult whose sexual life releases biological tensions, moves him toward depths of self-discovery, leads him toward ever-deeper love for his partner and beyond to the depth in every person, convinces him increasingly that personal fulfillment and social responsibility go hand in hand, and reveals to him the mystery of sex so that it is at the same time serious, radical, and joyful.

But who, a sinner, has ever wholly arrived there? And who is not, in fact, wrestling at any stage of his life with one or another aspect that is stoutly resisting appropriate integration? Who has not, at one time or another, confronted such severe obstacles, from within or without, that he has, at least temporarily, given up the battle? And who has not, on some occasion, tried so hard that his very effort made the goal elude him? Who has not felt at times that he had arrived—only to realize that he has been equating dependency with mutuality, or possession with fulfillment?

This is the sexual corollary of the fact that all men sin and fall short, but it is also more than that. It is a recognition that the Christian life, while lived with the end-point in view, is always an imperfect life in process of development. Though development cannot occur without some vision of its goal, a preoccupation with the goal at the expense of the next step in the process defeats the very chance of approaching the goal.

A previous chapter emphasized how deeply the biblical view regards sex as, ultimately, a mystery, that through biology there could emerge new dimensions and realizations of man as total spirit. This is profoundly true. However, if a Christain concentrated exclusively on sex as mystery, at the expense of its other legitimate dimensions and perspectives, he might well become so inhibited or so withdrawn as to be incapable of any sex life at all. An adolescent boy who thought only of the mystery of sex would have a difficult time on his date. He and his girl may engage in much casual banter; but this does not negate the fact of sex as serious business or as mystery. What actually takes place may lead developmentally toward the ultimate integration of the several purposes of sex in their lives.

In the metaphor used through the Christian ages, the Christian life is a "school" for everyone. Even if one is in the faith and has been "saved," he is still, in the language of the Reformers, a candidate for "sanctification." No man wholly arrives, becomes a "saint." The whole of the Christian life is to be a pupil, or a "pilgrim," moving toward a goal but aware that it has not been achieved and that one cannot, therefore, look down arrogantly on other men. The vision of the goal is of great importance, but it is not a substitute for the actual process of development.

4. *In its human dimensions, sex requires both intensity and steadfastness, and a proper relationship between them.* We may consider first intensity and then steadfastness, and finally the relationship between them. That sex is presumed to have intensity implies first that the attempt to make it merely casual or flat would distort its inherent meaning. This means more than being against the view of sex that sees it as a "drink of water." It means also that sex "with reservations" is equally a distortion. In its inherent nature sex is radical and serious. If one acts sexually, but withholds in one way or another, he is in effect denying the radical and serious nature of sex. Flatness, as well as casualness, works against the intensity inherent in sex.

Intensity is desirable from each of the relevant perspectives: biologically, in the intense pleasure of the encounter and the orgasm; psychologically, in the discovery of unsuspected depths in the self; socially, in the depth of discovery of another; ethically, in the integration of fulfillment and responsibility; and theologically, in the deepening sense of the mystery. The arbitrary or permanent exclusion of any aspect of intensity foreshortens the meaning of sex.

Steadfastness is also desirable from each of these perspectives: biologically, in the form of physical fidelity to another; psychologically, in the sense of movement toward depth and not merely toward breadth or thrill; socially, in the constant recognition of new depth in the other and, by implication, in all other persons potentially; ethically, in the responsibility that, far from destroying fulfillment, goes along with it; and theologically, in the growing conviction that true faithfulness is its own reward.

But a merely flat, routine, and well-ordered but pleasureless sex life would be no more steadfast than it would be intense. If steadfastness meant only refraining from sex activity with persons other than a spouse, it might have some minimal value from the point of view of social order. That would be very far, however, from the Christian understanding of steadfastness in a full and positive sense. Steadfastness is not a negative but a very affirmative quality. It is distinguished by what it seeks, much more than by what it refrains from.

Implicit in the Christian view is the conviction that in their full human dimensions, intensity and steadfastness are likely to support and enhance each other. A movement toward full human intensity in sex will increase steadfastness; and a movement toward full human steadfastness will increase intensity. Therefore, these should be concomitant characteristics of the sex life. If there is one without the other, something is wrong. If one is so held as to exclude the other, something is still more wrong.

Developmentally speaking, the discovery of intensity and steadfastness in their full dimensions, and relating them appropriately, do not occur automatically. Very strong forces, both cultural and biological, attempt to prevent a union. A roustabout, orgasm-chasing, nothing-but-fun sex life may be wrongly represented to us as the most "intense." An anemic, unimaginative, full-of-restraint sex life may be wrongly held before us as the proper image of "fidelity." From the Christian view, both of these are carica-tures. At the same time, it goes without saying that something other than condemnation is needed in relation to actual people who are not intense or steadfast or both.

5. *The meaning and the good of any sex act or relationship are always dependent, in some measure, upon the inner meaning to the persons involved; but the sole ultimate standard for meaning or good is the judgment and love of God, of which the Christian community may at times be representative.* This means, first, that no sex act can be judged entirely in and of itself, without some reference back to the character of the one who acts. A good tree bringeth forth good fruit, and a poor tree bringeth forth poor fruit. What the act means to the person is the index of his character. What appears, on superficial examination, to be the same act in one situation as in another, may not in fact be so if the character reference is made.

This statement means, second, that the ultimate good or ill of either an act or a character is impossible to know without refer-ence to God, to that basic creating and supporting structure and power that indicates what it is in a man's character to become.

The third meaning is that the Christian community in its visible form is likely to have better ideas than most single individuals about what God's judgment and his love imply, but that there is no guarantee that this is so. According to Protestants, no visible manifestation of the church is itself without sin. The Protestant can never rest convinced that he is right merely because he does, or does not do, what his visible church tells him is right or wrong. Indeed, it is the readiness to bring everything, even the church, under the criticism of God's will that is the distinctive "Protestant principle," says Paul Tillich.

This last point is of great significance for the Christian view of sex. Again and again legalisms arise in which black-and-white definiteness is sought. Then all acts of Type A (regardless of their meaning to the person, the community, or God) are called wrong, and all acts of Type B (regardless of the same references) are called right. This situation invariably leads to more emphasis on calling wrong than on pronouncing right until, sometime, the pendulum swings, and libertinism in some form takes over.

The fact is that, however convenient it might be to pigeonhole sex acts, with no ambiguities or unclarities, this is very likely to do violence to the meanings and to the good that are involved. To be sure, some generalizations can be made, and are likely to be relevant to most situations of a similar type. But one cannot assume in advance that the mere external facts give him the necessary information about what is in the "heart."

This point implies further that if the good of any sex act rests in part upon its meaning to the person, there is a peculiarly human obligation for that person to consider the meaning of his act—to him as he is, to him as he wishes to become, and to God as he would find fulfillment through following God's will. From the Christian point of view, there can be no Christian morality that lacks reflectiveness about meaning. Man's mind and intelligence are true parts or aspects of him. To fail to use them is to foreshorten his self-discovery as a total human being. The Protestant view of sex demands, then, that the person's attitude be an "inner attitude," involving actual reflection on experience and decision about experience. There is no escape from a personal or "existential" decision to be—under God, but without an infallible guarantee of the extent to which one is acting according to God's will—a creator and molder of one's own character and selfhood.

Any community, church or otherwise, is likely to regard its own views on sex matters as being more right, or closer to the will of God, than those of any individual member. Against this tendency, which may indeed be oppressive and false, the Christian point may be interpreted as if the community had no stake in the matter.

Actually, the Christian view cannot deny the community's stake. But what it must do is to tell the community again and again that its attitude is as much under the judgment of God as is that of any individual. The mere fact of being a community does not make its judgment equal with the judgment of God.

We have attempted to set forth a Christian and Protestant view of sex in terms of general and inclusive principles, using modern language and concepts but referring back to the bases of the principles in the biblical view of sex. It may be that some unbiblical moderns will marvel at the modernity of the Bible. Biblically-minded readers may be surprised at how biblical some of the modern findings sound. In any event, it must be up to the reader to decide to what extent this modern synthesis does justice both to the biblical view and to modern knowledge.

SEX ATTITUDES

There is good reason to believe that our views on sex begin to be formed very early in childhood. Although the book from which the following selection is taken deals largely with child-rearing practices (a topic somewhat beyond the scope of this reader), this chapter on sex attitudes has more general significance and relates importantly to other topics considered in this volume. Furthermore, no student of the sexual revolution should remain unacquainted with the work of A. S. Neill. For almost forty years Neill has been director of Summerhill, an ultraprogressive school in England. The extremely nonauthoritarian and unorthodox program of the school has been a matter of considerable public and professional controversy. Even government educational inspectors in England have conceded, however, that Neill's approach to child-rearing seems to work remarkably well and at the very least constitutes a notable experiment in progressive education.

Neill's approach to sex is part of his more general orientation to children—one which stresses approval of the child, avoidance of unnecessary regimentation, recognition of basic human drives and needs, and the elimination of cant and hypocrisy wherever possible. Although Neill claims that the "free" child develops in a healthier way than under our typically "unfree" conditions, social scientists will view with caution conclusions based on his somewhat impressionistic observations. Yet even if his comments do not represent the findings of scientific research, they constitute a moving statement of beliefs by one who has long experience in working with (and an obvious affection for) children. Whatever the validity of Neill's ideas about childhood sexuality, we do know that the results of conventional caution, prudery, and downright antisexualism have been at best a mixed lot.

Sex Attitudes

A. S. NEILL

I have never had a pupil who did not bring to Summerhill a diseased attitude toward sexuality and bodily functions. The children
of modern parents who were told the truth about where babies
come from have much the same hidden attitude toward sex that
the children of religious fanatics have. To find a new orientation
to sex is the most difficult task of the parent and teacher.

We know so little of the causes of the sex taboo that we can only
hazard guesses as to its origin. Why there is a sex taboo is of no
immediate concern to me. That there *is* a sex taboo is of great concern to a man entrusted to cure repressed children.

We adults were corrupted in infancy; we can never be free
about sex matters. *Consciously,* we may be free; we may even be
members of a society for the sex education of children. But I fear
that *unconsciously* we remain to a large extent what conditioning
in infancy made of us: haters of sex and fearers of sex.

I am quite willing to believe that my unconscious attitude toward sex is the Calvinistic attitude a Scottish village imposed on
me in my first years of life. Possibly there is no salvation for adults;
but there is every chance of salvation for children, if we do not
force on them the awful ideas of sex that were forced on us.

Early in life, the child learns that the sexual sin is the great sin.
Parents invariably punish most severely for an offense against sex
morality. The very people who rail against Freud because he "sees
sex in everything" are the ones who have told sex stories, have
listened to sex stories, have laughed at sex stories. Every man who
has been in the army knows that the language of the army is a sex
language. Nearly everyone likes to read the spicy accounts of

Reprinted from A. S. Neill, *Summerhill: A Radical Approach to Child Rearing* (New York: Hart Publishing Co., 1960), pp. 205-217.

divorce cases and of sex crimes in the Sunday papers, and most men tell their wives the stories they bring home from their clubs and bars.

Now our delight in a sex story is due entirely to our own unhealthy education in sex matters. The unsavory sex interest is due to repressions. The story, as Freud says, lets the cat out of the bag. The adult condemnation of sex interest in the child is hypocritical and is humbug; the condemnation is a projection, a throwing of the guilt onto others. Parents punish severely for sex offenses because they are vitally, if unhealthily, interested in sex offenses.

Why is the crucifixion of the flesh so popular? Religious people believe that the flesh drags one downward. The body is called vile: it tempts one to evil. It is this hatred of the body that makes talk of childbirth a subject for dark corners of the schoolroom, and that makes polite conversation a cover up for everyday plain facts of life.

Freud saw sex as the greatest force in human behavior. Every honest observer must agree. But moral instruction has over-emphasized sex. The first correction that a mother makes, when the child touches his sexual organ, makes sex the most fascinating and mysterious thing in the world. To make fruit forbidden is to make it delectable and enticing.

The sex taboo is the root evil in the suppression of children. I do not narrow the word *sex* down to genital sex. It is likely that the child at the breast feels unhappy if his mother disapproves of any part of her own body, or impedes his pleasure in his own body.

Sex is the basis of all negative attitudes toward life. Children who have no sex guilt never ask for religion or mysticism of any kind. Since sex is considered the great sin, children who are fairly free from sex fear and sex shame do not seek any God from whom they can ask pardon or mercy, because they do not feel guilty.

When I was six my sister and I discovered each other's genitals, and naturally played with each other. Discovered by our mother, we were severely thrashed; and I was locked in a dark room for hours, and then made to kneel down and ask forgiveness from God.

It took me decades to get over that early shock; and, indeed, I sometimes wonder if I ever fully got over it.

How many of today's adults have had a similar experience? How many of today's children are having their whole natural love of life changed into hate and aggression because of such treatment? They are being told that touching the genitals is bad or sinful and that natural bowel movements are disgusting.

Every child who is suffering from sex suppression has a stomach like a board. Watch a repressed child breathe and then look at the beautiful grace with which a kitten breathes. No animal has a stiff stomach, nor is self-conscious about sex or defecation.

In his well-known work, *Character Analysis,* Wilhelm Reich pointed out that a moralistic training not only warps the thinking process, but enters structually into the body itself, armoring it literally with stiffness in posture and contraction of pelvis. I agree with Reich. I have observed, during many years of dealing with a variety of children at Summerhill, that when fear has not stiffened the musculature, the young walk, run, jump and play with a wonderful grace.

What then can we do to prevent sex repression in children? Well, for one thing, from the earliest moment the child must be completely free to touch any and every part of his body.

A psychologist friend of mine had to say to his son of four, "Bob, you must not play with your wee-wee when you are out among strange people for they think it bad. You must do it only at home and in the garden."

My friend and I talked about it and agreed that it is impossible to guard the child against the anti-life haters of sex. The only comfort is that when the parents are sincere believers in life, the child will generally accept the parental standards and is likely to reject the outside prudery. But all the same, the mere fact that a child of five learns that he cannot bathe in the sea without pants is enough to form some kind—if only a minor kind—of sex distrust.

Today many parents put no ban on masturbation. They feel that it is natural, and they know the dangers of suppressing it. Excellent. Fine.

But some of these enlightened parents balk at the next step. Some do not mind if their little boys have sex play with other little boys, but they stiffen with alarm if a small boy and a small girl have sex play.

If my good, well-meaning mother had ignored the sex play of my year younger sister and me, our chances of growing up with some sanity toward sex would have been good.

I wonder how much impotence and frigidity in adults date from the first interference in a heterosexual relationship of early childhood. I wonder how much homosexuality dates from the tolerance of homosexual play and the forbidding of heterosexual play.

Heterosexual play in childhood is the royal road, I believe, to a healthy, balanced adult sex life. When children have no moralistic training in sex, they reach a healthy adolescence—not an adolescence of promiscuity.

I know of no argument against youth's love life that holds water. Nearly every argument is based on repressed emotion or hate of life—the religious, the moral, the expedient, the arbitrary, the pornographic. None answer the question why nature gave man a strong sex instinct, if youth is to be forbidden to use it unless sanctioned by the elders of society. Those elders, some of them, have shares in companies that run films full of sex appeal, or in companies that sell all sorts of cosmetics to make girls more delectable to boys, or companies that publish magazines which make sadistic pictures and stories a magnet to their readers.

I know that adolescent sex life is not practical today. But my opinion is that it is the right way to tomorrow's health. I can *write* this, but if in Summerhill I approved of my adolescent pupils sleeping together, my school would be suppressed by the authorities. I am thinking of the long tomorrow when society will have realized how dangerous sex repression is.

I do not expect every Summerhill pupil to be unneurotic, for who can be complex-free in society today? What I hope for is that in generations to come this beginning of freedom from artificial sex taboos will ultimately fashion a life-loving world.

The invention of contraceptives must in the long run lead to a new sex morality, seeing that fear of consequences is perhaps the strongest factor in sex morality. To be free, love must feel itself safe.

Youth today has little opportunity for loving in the true sense. Parents will not allow sons or daughters to live in sin, as they call it, so that young lovers have to seek damp woods or parks or automobiles. Thus everything is loaded heavily against our young people. Circumstances compel them to convert what should be lovely and joyful into something sinister and sinful, into smut and leers, and shameful laughter.

The taboos and fears that fashioned sex behavior are those same taboos and fears that produce the perverts who rape and strangle small girls in parks, the perverts who torture Jews and Negroes.

Sex prohibition anchors sex to the family. The masturbation prohibition forces a child to interest himself in the parents. Every time a mother smacks a child's hands for touching his genitals, the sex drive of the child gets constellated with his mother, and the hidden attitude toward the mother becomes one of desire and repulsion, love and hate. Repression flourishes in an unfree home. Repression helps to retain adult authority, but at the price of a plethora of neurosis.

If sex were allowed to go over the garden wall to the boy or girl next door, the authority of the home would be in danger; the tie to father and mother would loosen and the child would automatically leave the family emotionally. It sounds absurd but those ties are a very necessary pillar of support to the authoritative state

—just as prostitution was a necessary safeguard for the morality of nice girls from nice homes. Abolish sex repression and youth will be lost to authority.

Fathers and mothers are doing what their parents did to them: bringing up respectable, chaste children, conveniently forgetting all the hidden sex play and pornographic stories of their own childhood, forgetting the bitter rebellion against their parents that they had to repress with infinite guilt. They do not realize that they are giving their own children the same guilt feelings that gave them miserable nights many long years ago.

Man's serious neurosis starts with the earliest genital prohibitions: Touch not. The impotence, frigidity, and anxiety of later life date from the tying up of the hands or the snatching away of the hands, usually with a spank. A child left to touch its genitals has every chance of growing up with a sincere, happy attitude toward sex. Sex play among small children is a natural, healthy act that ought not to be frowned on. On the contrary, it should be encouraged as a prelude to a healthy adolescence and adulthood. Parents are ostriches hiding their heads in the sand if they are ignorant that their children have sex play in dark corners. This kind of clandestine and furtive play breeds a guilt that lives on in later life, a guilt that usually betrays itself in disapproval of sex play when these same children become parents. Bringing sex play out into the light is the only sane thing to do. There would be infinitely less sex crime in the world if sex play were accepted as normal. That is what moral parents cannot see or dare not see, that sex crime and sex abnormality of any kind are a direct result of disapproval of sex in early childhood.

The famous anthropologist, Malinowski, tells us that there was no homosexuality among the Trobrianders until the shocked missionaries segregated boys and girls in separate hostels. There was no rape among the Trobrianders, no sex crimes. Why? Because small children were given no repressions about sex.

The question for parents today is this: Do we want our children to be like us? If so, will society continue as it is, with rape and sex murder and unhappy marriages and neurotic children? If the answer to the first question is yes, then the same answer must be given to the second question. And both answers are the prelude to atomic destruction, because they postulate the continuance of hate and the expression of this hate in wars.

I ask moralist parents: Will you worry much about your children's sex play when the atomic bombs begin to drop? Will the virginity of your daughters assume great importance when clouds of atomic energy make life impossible? When your sons are conscripted for the Great Death, will you still hold on to your little chapel faith in the suppression of all that is good in childhood? Will the God you blasphemously pray to then save your life and those of your children?

Some of you may answer that this life is only the beginning, that in the next world there will be no hate, no war, no sex. In that case, shut this book—for we have no contact.

To me, eternal life is a dream—an understandable dream indeed—for man has failed in practically everything except mechanistic invention. But the dream is not good enough. I want to see heaven on earth, not in the clouds. And the pathetic thing is that most people want the same thing. They *want,* but haven't the will to reach it, the will that was perverted by the first slap, the first sex taboo.

For a parent there is no sitting on the fence, no neutrality. The choice is between guilty-secret sex or open-healthy-happy sex. If parents choose the common standard of morality, they must not complain of the misery of sex-perverted society, for it is the result of this moral code. Parents then must not hate war, for the hate of self that they give their children will express itself in war. Humanity is sick, emotionally sick, and it is sick because of this guilt and anxiety acquired in childhood. The emotional past is everywhere in our society.

When Zoe was six she came to me and said, "Willie has the biggest cock among the small kids, but Mrs. X (a visitor) says it is rude to say *cock.*" I at once told her that it was not rude. Inwardly, I cursed that woman for her ignorant and narrow understanding of children. I might tolerate propaganda about politics or manners, but when anyone attacks a child by making that child guilty about sex, I fight back vigorously.

All our leering attitude toward sex, our guffaws in music halls, our scribbling of obscenities on urinal walls spring from the guilty feeling arising from suppression of masturbation in infancy and from driving mutual sex play into holes and corners. There is secret sex play in every family; and because of the secrecy and guilt, there are many fixations on brothers and sisters that last throughout life and make happy marriages impossible. If sex play between brother and sister at the age of five were accepted as natural, each of them would advance freely to a sex object outside the family.

The extreme forms of sex hate are seen in sadism. No man with a good sex life could possibly torture an animal, or torture a human, or support prisons. No sex-satisfied woman would condemn the mother of a bastard.

Of course, I lay myself open to the accusation: "This man has sex on the brain. Sex isn't everything in life. There is friendship, work, joy, and sorrow. Why sex?"

I answer: Sex affords the highest pleasure in life. Sex with love is the supreme form of ecstasy because it is the supreme form of both giving and receiving. Yet sex is obviously hated; otherwise no mother would forbid masturbation—no father forbid a sex life outside conventional marriage. Otherwise, there would be no obscene jokes in vaudeville halls, nor would the public waste its time seeing love films and reading love stories; it would be practicing love.

The fact that nearly every motion picture deals with love proves that sex is the most important factor in life. The interest in these films is, in the main, neurotic. It is the interest of sex-guilty, sex-frustrated people. Unable to love naturally because of sex guilt, they flock to film stories that make love romantic, even beautiful. The sex-repressed live out their interest in sex by proxy. No man, no woman with a full love life could be bothered sitting twice a week in a movie house seeing trashy pictures which are only imitations of real life.

So it is also with popular novels. They either deal with sex or with crime, usually a combination of the two. A very popular novel, *Gone with the Wind,* was a favorite, not because of the background of the tragedy of the Civil War and the slaves, but because it centered around a tiresome, egocentric girl and her love affairs.

Fashion journals, cosmetics, leg shows, highbrow sophisticated reviews, sex stories—all show clearly that sex is the most important thing in life. At the same time, they prove that only the trappings of sex are approved of—in other words, fiction, films, leg shows.

It was D. H. Lawrence who pointed out the iniquity of sex films, where the sex-repressed youth, fearful of actual girls in his own circle, showers all his sex emotion on a Hollywood star—and then goes home to masturbate. Lawrence, of course, did not mean that masturbation is wrong; he meant that it is unhealthy sex that seeks masturbation with the fantasy of a film star. Healthy sex would most surely seek a partner in the neighborhood.

Think of the enormous vested interests that thrive on repressed sex: the fashion people, the lipstick merchants, the church, the theaters and movies, the best-seller novelists, and the stocking manufacturers.

It would be foolish to say that a society sexually free would abolish beautiful clothes. Of course not. Every woman would want to look her best before the man she loved. Every man would like to appear elegant when he dated his girl. What would disappear would be fetishism—the valuing of the shadow because the reality is forbidden. Sex-repressed men would no longer stare at women's lingerie in shop windows. What a horrible pity that sex interest is so repressed. The highest pleasure in the world is enjoyed with guilt. This repression enters into every aspect of human life, making life narrow, unhappy, hateful.

Hate sex and you hate life. Hate sex and you cannot love your neighbor. If you hate sex, your sexual life will be, at the worst, impotent or frigid; at best, incomplete. Hence the common remark by women who have had children, "Sex is an overrated pastime." If sex is unsatisfactory, it must go somewhere, for it is too strong an urge to be annihilated. It goes into anxiety and hate.

Not many adults look upon the sex act as a giving; otherwise the percentage of people afflicted with impotency and frigidity would not be about seventy per cent, as quite a few experts have claimed it is. To many men, intercourse is polite rape; to many women, a tiresome rite that has to be endured. Thousands of married women have never experienced an orgasm in their lives; and even some educated men do not know that a woman is capable of an orgasm. In such a system, giving must be minimal; and sex relations are bound to be more or less brutalized and obscene. The perverts who require to be scourged with whips or to beat women with rods are merely extreme cases of people who, owing to sex miseducation, are unable to give love except in the disguised form of hate.

Every older pupil at Summerhill knows from my conversation and my books that I approve of a full sex life for all who wish one, whatever their age. I have often been asked in my lectures if I provide contraceptives at Summerhill, and if not, why not? This is an old and vexed question that touches deep emotions in all of us. That I do not provide contraceptives is a matter of bad conscience with me, for to compromise in any way is to me difficult and alarming. On the other hand, to provide contraceptives to children either over or under the age of consent would be a sure way of closing down my school. One cannot advance in practice too much ahead of the law.

A familiar question asked by critics of child freedom is, "Why don't you let a small child see sexual intercourse?" The answer that it would give him a trauma, a severe nervous shock, is false. Among the Trobrianders, according to Malinowski, children see not only parental sexual intercourse but birth and death as matters of course, and are not affected adversely. I do not think that seeing sexual intercourse would have any bad emotional effect on a self-regulated child. The only honest answer to the question is to say that love in our culture is not a public matter.

I do not forget that many parents have religious or other negative views on the sinfulness of sex. Nothing can be done about them. They cannot be converted to our views. On the other hand, we must fight them when they infringe on our own children's right to freedom, genital or otherwise.

To other parents, I say: Your big headache will come when your daughter of sixteen wants to live her own life. She will come in at midnight. On no account ask her where she has been. If she has not been self-regulated, she will lie to you just as you lied, and I lied, to our parents.

When my daughter is sixteen, should I find her in love with some insensitive man, I shall have more than one worry. I know that I shall be powerless to do anything. I hope I will have sense not to try. Since she has been self-regulated, I do not anticipate that she will fall for an undesirable type of young man; but one can never tell.

I am sure that many a bad companionship is fundamentally a protest against parental authority. *My parents don't trust me, and I don't care. I'll do what I like, and if they don't like it, they can lump it.*

Your fear will be that your daughter will be seduced. But girls are not as a rule seduced; they are partners in a seduction. This sixteen stage should not be difficult if your daughter has been your friend and not your subordinate. You will have to face the truth that no one can live another's life, that one cannot hand on experience in such essential things as emotional matters.

The basic question, after all, is the home attitude toward sex.

If it has been healthy, you can safely give your daughter her own private room and a key to it. If it has been unhealthy, she will seek sex in the wrong way—possibly with the wrong men—and you are powerless.

So with your son. You will not be so worried about him—because he cannot become pregnant. Yet with the wrong sex attitudes, he can easily mess up his life.

Few marriages are happy. Considering the infant training that the majority of people have had, it is a matter of astonishment that there should be any happy marriages at all. If sex is dirty in the nursery, it cannot be very clean in the wedding bed.

Where the sex relationship is a failure, everything else in the marriage is a failure. The unhappy couple, reared to hate sex, hate each other. The children are a failure, for they miss the warmth of the home that is necessary to their own warm life. The sex repressions of their parents unconsciously give them the same repressions. The worst problem children come from such parents.

SEX AND THE LAW

The legal aspect of sex and family problems is often over-looked in sociological analyses. This is unfortunate because sexual and marital behavior is at least partly controlled and shaped by the many varied legal provisions in this area, and provisions which do not exert direct influence on behavior may still have subtle indirect influences on attitudes. Statutes and legal holdings, moreover, provide revealing indications of the values of a society.

Although law is often said to follow public opinion, and it is argued that you cannot legislate morals (i.e., that the en-acted law must have support in the mores to be effective), one must recognize that in modern society the law has itself fre-quently been a vital instrument for promoting or reinforcing social change (minimum wage and compulsory vaccination statutes and racial desegration rulings are but a few exam-ples of this). Analysis and reform of laws relating to sex and marriage may be viewed, therefore, both as a means of keep-ing the statute books up to date and as a way of promoting attitudes and patterns of behavior believed to be rational and socially desirable. A long-time student of sex and family law with much first-hand experience of the legal problems in these fields, Judge Ploscowe is highly qualified to write on these matters. The essay which follows is a summary state-ment of conclusions based on a comprehensive and authori-tative survey of the various sex laws now prevailing in the United States.

Sex and the Law

MORRIS PLOSCOWE

Our examination of the laws relating to marriage, annulment, divorce, illegitimacy, and sex crime leaves us with a feeling that St. Paul's advice is as sound today as it was two thousand years ago. It would be a great deal better if men and women remained continent sexually or got married and then adhered strictly to their marriage vows. Much emotional disturbance, human misery, crime, disorder, and illegitimacy would be averted if humanity could abide by St. Paul's teachings. It never has. The flesh has always been weak. Organized society has always had to decide the question of the extent to which sexual activity should be regulated by propaganda, education, religion, and public disapprobation, and the extent to which it should be regulated by law. The respective areas of legal and non-legal control of sexual behavior have varied over the centuries.

Central in the law's regulation of sexual behavior are the rules regarding marriage. If marriage is made easy, then presumably the cloak of legitimacy will be thrown over much of the sexual activity of the human species. Here is the basic thought underlying common-law marriage. If a man and women are living together and having sexual intercourse, presumably they are holding themselves out to the world as husband and wife. The law, therefore, treats them as having entered into a common-law marriage relationship. The sexual intercourse becomes legitimatized by the fact of marriage. Similarly, when marriage-licensing statutes and administrative procedures throw few safeguards around entrance into marriage, they undoubtedly endow with respectability much

Reprinted from Morris Ploscowe, *Sex and the Law* (Englewood, N.J.: Prentice Hall, 1951; Ace Books edition 1962), pp. 251-264; footnotes omitted.

sexual activity which would otherwise be illicit. Youngsters can pursue the mysteries of sex in a marital rather than in a non-marital relationship. Men can enjoy their women legally, so long as there is a convenient justice of the peace around and sufficient money to pay for the marriage-license fee.

The rules with respect to the annulment of marriages also throw the cloak of legitimacy over much sexual behavior which would otherwise be illicit. The refusal of an annulment where the man and the woman engaged in sexual intercourse with knowledge of a legal impediment to the marriage is based on the notion that men and women should not be permitted to enjoy the fruits of sex except in marriage. An annulment destroys a marriage from its inception. If the annulment were granted, the sexual intercourse occurring after the marriage ceremony would be illicit. The annulment is therefore denied, and the parties are deemed to have tasted legitimate rather than illegitimate fruit.

It is questionable, however, whether the legal rules concerning marriage and the annulment of marriage do not encourage as much illicit sexual activity as they cloak with legality. This is apparent from the way the concept of common-law marriage operates in the day-to-day relationships of men and women. Because of the uncertainties involved in the creation of the marital status, common-law marriage has never had the same binding force upon the parties to the relationship as ceremonial marriage. A man and woman who obtain a marriage license and go before a priest, rabbi, minister, or justice of the peace to have a ceremony performed know that they are married. They have publicly and openly assumed the relationship of husband and wife. They know that they cannot dissolve that relationship merely by walking out on each other. But when a man and woman live together without benefit of a marriage ceremony, they may or may not be deemed to have entered into a common-law union. The law will decide the question of whether they were actually married if a contest were to arise between them or between one of the parties to the relationship and a third person. But such contests are few and far between. If the parties do not come into the courts, they may treat their relationship as a marriage, or as a temporary illicit connection as it suits their convenience. When they grow tired of each other, they may form new sexual alliances without benefit of divorce or annulment. Long before Ben Lindsey thought of the concept of companionate marriage, men and women were practicing it under the guise of common-law marriage. For a large part of our population, common-law marriage gives the pretense of legality to sexual activity, not the actuality.

Similarly, where our marriage laws encourage hasty, clandestine and immature marriages and where our annulment statutes forbid the granting of annulments, if the parties have sexual intercourse with knowledge of legal impediments the immediate sexual relationships between the parties may be cloaked with legality by legal provisions. However, in framing such legal provisions, legislators have left out of account the fact that mismated and incompatible individuals, or men and women who want their marital freedom, turn to other sexual partners for relief from domestic woes.

The fundamental difficulty with the law in the field of marriage is that it has lost sight of the fact that marriage has two primary objectives: (1) to provide a legitimate, decent, and respectable outlet for the sexual passions of men and women; (2) to provide a means whereby stable family units can be created, so that children can be brought into the world and furnished with the care, attention, education, and nurture which is their due. The law has been greatly concerned with the first objective, the provision of legitimate outlets for sexual relationships. It has tended to lose sight of its more fundamental role in furthering the establishment of stable family units.

It is true that one can find numerous expressions of judges concerning the interest of the law and of the state in the creation of stable family units. The state is said to be an interested party in every marriage contract. The welfare of the state is said to be bound up with a healthy family life. Judges point out the decisive influence on children of sound relationships between husbands and wives. Judges recognize that marriage and the monogamous family are two pillars of our civilization, and they are therefore opposed to anything that tends to undermine these institutions and express themselves as being in favor of everything that tends to conserve them.

But judicial premises and legal rhetoric, no matter how scintillating, are no substitute for detailed legal provisions and administrative procedures. In far too many instances, the latter belie the conception that the law and the state have a basic interest in the stability of marriage and the creation of a sound family life. There is a glaring disparity between the facts of our family law and judicial premises and rhetoric. It is a little difficult to see how the law favors the creation of sound and stable family units when it permits mentally diseased and mentally deficient persons to marry; when it permits mere children to undertake the burdens of matrimony without even the formality of parental consent or other adult scrutiny of their capacity to undertake the responsibilities of marriage; when it treats the entrance into marriage with about the same amount of dignity and formality as the acquisition of a dog license. Nor can one see how the law serves the interest of the state in the conservation of marriage and the stability of family life when the facts in relation to the operation of our divorce and annulment laws are examined. When every possible type of friction between husband or wife and every trivial unpleasantness can serve as the basis for a divorce on the ground of legal cruelty; when courts conveniently shut their eyes to the patent falsehoods and perjury involved in the establishment of jurisdiction and grounds for divorce; when husbands and wives can obtain binding decrees of divorce from foreign jurisdictions upon the flimsiest of grounds, merely because they go through a sham controversy; when the law of annulment is used, as it is in New York, as a convenient means of dissolving marriages on the basis of trivial or manufactured impediments, then it becomes hypocritical to spout about the law's interest in the conservation of marriage and the stability of family life.

There must be a drastic re-examination and revision of the law relating to marriage, divorce, and annulment before it can really serve the state's interest in the conservation of marriage and the stability of family life. We have indicated the lines along which the revision of our family law must proceed. The elimination of child marriages, the insistence upon parental consent in the case of the marriage of minors, the prevention of the marriage of the mentally deficient, the physically diseased, and the impotent, the elimination of hasty and clandestine marriages through the provision of adequate waiting periods between marriage-license application and marriage ceremony, the elimination of common-law marriage —these are some of the changes which the law must make if the interest of the state in the creation of sound and stable family units is to be served.

These changes in our marriage laws will tend to cut down the extent to which men and women resort to the divorce courts and annulment procedures for a solution of their domestic difficulties. Legislators have overlooked the elementary fact that lax marriage laws and procedures are one of the principal contributing factors in the demand for the dissolution of marriage through divorce and annulment. If husbands and wives were required to choose their mates more carefully, if the law made certain that the choice of a husband or wife was a free one, made after mature reflection, there would be less likelihood of incompatible matrimonial alliances and less need for the dissolution of marriages through annulment and divorce.

However, no system of marital laws or their administration can guaranteee marriages which will be free from discord and conflict. The close contact of married life brings out the best and the worst in husbands and wives. It takes strong constitutions, both mental and physical, to withstand the stresses and strains of modern life and the irritations of daily living. Individuals who appear to have been well-mated and compatible when they were married may develop disastrous differences.

Marriage under the best of circumstances is something of a gamble. One gambles upon the hope that the factors which attracted the man and the woman to each other will continue to exert their influence despite the petty frictions of domestic life. The wife may gamble upon her husband continuing to hold a good job and providing her with a modicum of economic security. The husband may gamble upon the expectation that his wife will retain her sexual attraction for him after sex has become a matter of daily routine. Both the husband and wife gamble upon the hope that there will be no obstacles in the way of procreating children and that each will make a good parent. When hopes and expectations are defeated; when alcohol, the other woman, financial inadequacy, sexual frigidity, impotency, or brutishness begins to mar the day-to-day contacts of husband and wives; when personal frustrations and inadequacies are expressed by physical brutality, bad temper, nagging, and shrewishness, then either the husband or the wife or both may seek an escape from domestic purgatory.

No system of law takes the position that no matter what the defects, disharmonies, deficiencies, and discord existing between a husband and a wife, the marriage is absolutely indissoluble and that once the choice of a husband or wife has been made, that choice is irrevocable. Even the canon law recognizes the possibility of annulling marriages where they are *not* validly entered into, or where the parties do not qualify for marriage under canon law. It is true that canon law does not recognize divorce, which would dissolve marriages for causes occurring *after* the marriage ceremony. It takes the position that once a marriage has been validly entered into, it is indissouble during the lifetime of the parties thereto. But in New York we have discovered that so-called legal impediments to a marriage ceremony, which would justify the annulment of marriages, begin to assume importance to the parties when they find that they cannot get along together. In point of fact, many requests for annulments, which are technically based on legal impediments existing at the time of the marriage ceremony, are in reality caused by the incompatibilities of husbands and wives which develop *after* the marriage ceremony. There is reason to believe that the same phenomenon occurs under the canon law, and that there, too, annulment is used as an escape from an unfortunate matrimonial situation which develops after the marriage ceremony, although the request for the dissolution of the marriage may technically rest upon a pre-existing defect.

Every system of law must provide remedies for the facts and incidents of matrimonial discord. Judicial separations, limited divorces, orders for separate maintenance and alimony, and support orders are all means for dealing with problems of family strife. Annulment and divorce are the most drastic weapons in the legal armory for a solution of matrimonial ills. It has been charged that the existence of such remedies to matrimonial difficulties contributes to the breakup of marriages. This puts the cart before the horse. Marriages are broken by all the factors which enter into matrimonial dissension and discord. When parties have reached the stage where they take their domestic troubles to a court and request a divorce or annulment, the marriage has already been badly broken by the parties themselves.

Most marriages in this country are dissolved by divorce rather than by annulment. The great problem in the field of divorce reform is how our divorce law and our divorce procedures can be organized so that the interest of the state in the conservation of marriage and the stability of family life may be adequately recognized. At first glance, divorce reform and the conservation of marriage may seem incongruous goals. As divorce laws and divorce courts are presently administered, there is little doubt of such incongruity, and it has been present for a long time. Over a century ago, the Supreme Court of Ohio was complaining of the abuses of divorce and alimony and of the injustices done to individuals by such laws:

"It seems to be considered by a great proportion of our community" states the Court, "that the marriage contract is the least obligatory of all others and that nothing more is necessary to dissolve it than that application should be made to this court to register a decree to this effect. . . . The hearings are generally ex parte. Witnesses are examined, friendly to the applicant, and it is almost, if not utterly, impossible, for the court to arrive at the real truths of the case. . . . But of the great multitude of cases which are before this court, I am confident that the greater number are—not (meritorious)."

It is doubtful whether any modification of the traditional approach to divorce can eliminate the disservice which divorce laws and divorce procedures render to the state's interest in the conservation of family life. The traditional approach to divorce fails to come to grips with the real issues involved in the breakup of marriages. Legal fault which justifies a divorce, no matter how that fault is phrased, becomes merely a convention, a legal formula which must be fulfilled before marital freedom can be obtained. The means whereby the evidence for this legal formula is supplied depends upon the squeamishness of the parties and their attorneys. It may have very little relevance to the respective faults of the husband and the wife or to their basic reasons for wanting a divorce. Nowhere in the traditional approach is there room for the question: What actually has brought the husband and wife to their present sad position? How did it happen that a marriage begun with plenty of high hopes and expectations, with good will and a spirit of sacrifice, has ended in disillusionment and failure? What qualities of personality, what social and economic factors were responsible for the breakdown of the family unit? Nor has the traditional approach to divorce worked out any serious means for attempting to solve the differences between husbands and wives by measures short of divorce.

The approach to divorce that we have suggested in Chapter IV envisions the use by courts of all the expert techniques that have been developed during the twentieth century in dealing with the troubles of individuals and problems of human behavior. Social case work, probation, psychiatry, and marriage counseling may be able to provide husbands and wives with answers to their problems which they themselves have not been able to find. These expert services may be able to rehabilitate marriages which appear to have broken down completely. By careful and thorough analysis of the difficulties and differences existing between husbands and wives, they may be able to save marriages which appear to be hopelessly destroyed. In our opinion, divorces should only be granted to husbands and wives after a thoroughgoing attempt has been made by a panel of experts to adjust the differences between them. Only when the differences are irreconcilable, only when they are so wide and deep that a viable marriage relationship is no longer possible should divorce be considered.

In recent years the ineptitude of the traditional approach to divorce has come to be clearly recognized. Even so conservative an organization as the American Bar Association has called for a complete break with the past in this field. Its Committee on Divorce and Marriage Laws has called for the adoption of the diagnostic and therapeutic approach to divorce outlined above. The Chairman of the Committee, Judge Paul Alexander has taken the lead in developing and urging this new approach to divorce. He states in one of his reports:

"What all of us want is not to open the floodgates for more divorces. . . . What every right-thinking person wants is to see our philosophy so shaped, our laws . . . so designed that it will tend to conserve, not to disserve family life; that it will be constructive, not destructive of marriage. . . ."

"Keeping ever in mind the postulates that divorce is effect not cause, the Committee proposes that we eliminate those concepts, doctrines, and procedures with which the law has shackled itself and so ineptly deflated its own ends.

"The American Bar Association Committee proposes to transform the divorce court from a morgue into a hospital, to handle our ailing marriages and delinquent spouses much as we handle delinquent children. . . . Instead of looking only at the guilt of the defendant, it proposes to examine the whole marriage, endeavor to discover the basic causative factors, seek to rectify them, enlisting the aid of other sciences and disciplines and of all available community resources."

The great merit of this new approach is that it will enable courts to come to grips with the actual facts which lead to marital discord and not the sham issues which are framed by the parties. The facts may still require the divorce to be granted. But over and over again, judges will be able, on the basis of the facts, to work out some solution to the marital problems short of divorce. In so doing, they will lend meaning to the basic legal premise that the law looks with favor upon marriage. Courts with this new approach can truly become conservators of marriage and of the home.

Where the qualifications of marriage are raised and it becomes more difficult for a man and woman or a boy and girl to become married, there is bound to be an increase in illicit sexual activity. Many who would otherwise rush into marriage to attain their sexual objectives will now try to obtain them without marriage. This sexual behavior may be a lesser evil than the necessity of dissolving rash, unwise, hasty, and immature marriages through divorce or annulment. Despite the wide-spread diffusion of knowledge of birth control one of the inevitable concomitants of illicit sexual activity will be illegitimate children. Our law should be better prepared to deal with them. We inherited the brutal and indifferent traditions of the common law toward such children. The common law paid no attention either to the fornication between unmarried men and women or to the biologic fruits of such activity. The bastard was a legal drifter; he was no one's concern and no one's responsibility.

But our law cannot be indifferent to the fate of any group of children, no matter what their origin. It must recognize what is amply demonstrated by modern psychology, that rejection is one of the surest ways of twisting personality and creating disturbed individuals. If individuals are to develop into healthy, normal human beings, they require a modicum of love, warmth, acceptance, and affection from their parents and from those around them. The illegitimate or bastard is born rejected by one parent. His mother may likewise reject him because he is the visible source of her dishonor. For the law to add its rejections to those which an illegitimate or bastard must already face is to put a premium on the growth of distorted and twisted human beings.

The law cannot undo the facts surrounding the conception and birth of the illegitimate child. But it can do more than extend him a frigid welcome after he has arrived. The law can facilitate inquiry into his paternity, so that the illegitimate child can at least know who his two parents are. It should not shackle such inquiry by technicalities and legal prudery. Such distortions as the Lord Mansfield rule, which refuses to permit husbands and wives to testify to sexual access to each other in paternity disputes, and the failure to take full advantage of the scientific values inherent in blood tests have no place in any modern system of family law.

But the law must go further, in our opinion. It must make adequate provision for the legal relationship between an illegitimate child and his parents. We have felt that the law should not create two classes of children: (1) legitimate children who have complete rights of education, support, nurture, and inheritance; and (2) bastards, who have only very restricted claims upon their fathers and mothers. In our opinion, a decent respect for the rights of human personality and the democratic conception of the equality of all persons before the law requires the elimination of the legal disabilities which are placed upon bastards and illegitimates. All children should be deemed legitimate. All children should have an equal claim upon their parents. It may be difficult to establish the paternity of a child born out of wedlock; but once it has been established by the techniques and procedures required by law and the parents of the child become known to the law, then the illegitimate child should be treated like any other child of his mother and father.

The criminal law needs a complete reorientation in the field of sex crime. The mere prohibition of an offensive act will not discourage it, particularly when it is in response to so basic a drive as sex. Moreover, a prohibited sexual act performed in private by two people who derive satisfaction from it and who will not complain is not likely to come to the attention of law-enforcement authorities. Police officers or district attorneys are not clairvoyants. They must receive notice of some kind before they can prosecute or make an arrest. As a result of ignoring these elementary principles, our statute books are cluttered with prohibitions against specific kinds of sexual behavior that are honored more in the breach than in the observance, as Professor Kinsey's statistics have amply demonstrated. Men and women copulate in sovereign disregard of penal statutes. There is little that police, prosecutors, and courts can do about it. The prohibitions are only invoked sporadically against individuals who may be a little less discreet or less fortunate than their fellows, but whose behavior is not much different. For the most part, the fornication and adultery statutes and the statutes that prohibit homosexual behavior and crimes against nature (where both parties are adults) are dead letters.

The extraordinary thing about the adultery statutes is that they are dead letters, even though the criminal behavior involved is constantly coming to the attention of law-enforcement agencies when divorce actions based on adultery are filed. It is true that the standard of proof is higher in criminal cases than in divorce cases. Divorce courts can be satisfied with a lot less evidence of adultery than criminal courts and juries. But far more fundamental in the non-prosecution of adultery cases is the feeling that the criminal law is entirely too heavy-handed a way of dealing with adultery. This may be why prosecutors do nothing throughout the country while courts grind out divorces on the basis of adultery, which is a violation of penal statutes.

It is obvious that legislators have not understood the limits of effective legal action in the field of sex crime. One cannot by means of the criminal law discourage all forms of sexual activity outside of marriage. Legislators have adopted the formula that what is objectionable must be prohibited by law, without regard to whether it is possible to enforce the prohibitions. They have failed to understand that two things are necessary for the effectiveness of legal sanctions: (1) the support of public opinion; (2) the ability of law-enforcement agencies to get at the behavior involved. Neither element is present for much of the sex behavior prohibited by the criminal law. Legislators have completely overlooked the fact that there are other agencies for the control of sexual activity which may be far more effective than the theoretical threat of a jail sentence. Among such agencies are the schools, the churches, the family, the non-commercial recreational agencies, etc. Sex behavior is a peculiarly personal and private activity. It can be influenced better by agencies which are intimately in contact with the individual than by the blunderbuss weapons of the law. Propaganda, public education, and religious teaching may be far more effective in discouraging illicit sexual activity than legal sanctions. In our opinion, many of the legal prohibitions concerning sexual activity can be dropped from the law without adversely affecting sexual morality.

The criminal law, however, has a large and important function in the field of the regulation of sexual behavior. There is certain sexual activity that a civilized community simply cannot tolerate. The threat to the individual and the community, the public outrage, the disease and the disorder involved are too great for the law to stand idly by and do nothing.

In our opinion, four different aspects of sexual activity must be prohibited by law under the threat of severe penalties, for whatever deterrent effect they have, and for whatever possibility they create for confinement of offenders for rehabilitation or social protection.

1. Heterosexual and homosexual acts in which force and violence or threats of force and violence are used to achieve sexual objectives.

2. Heterosexual and homosexual acts involving children and adolescents.

3. Heterosexual and homosexual acts which outrage public decency and give rise to public scandal.

4. Heterosexual and homosexual prostitution.

In the first two categories will be found most of the dangerous sex offenders who may be potential killers. A revision of sex-crime legislation should differentiate these offenders from others whose behavior is far less dangerous and is far less serious in character. This will require, as we have seen, a revision in the concept of rape, so that it more nearly corresponds to traditional ideas of a forcible and violent outrage on the woman's person. It will also require a lowering of the age limits in statutory rape, for it is ridiculous to speak of a man as a dangerous rapist whose only offense is a consensual act of sexual intercourse with a girl just under eighteen years in New York, or under twenty-one in Tennessee. In addition, a new concept of rape will make a clear differentiation between acts of sexual intercourse with under-age girls who are chaste and virtuous and acts of sexual intercourse with young prostitutes.

The concept of the forcible violation of an individual inherent in rape must also be extended to cover homosexual acts and crimes against nature. A man is as dangerous where he compels a woman at the point of a gun or a knife to commit fellatio or sodomy with him as when he compels her to have sexual intercourse.

It is against the relatively small number of dangerous offenders that sex-psychopath laws must be directed. Here is the group that must be submitted to intensive treatment at specialized institutions. If treatment fails of its purpose, then these offenders must be kept incarcerated for life, if necessary. But we must not make the mistake of confusing this group with the large number of minor sex offenders for whom incarceration up to life is not warranted. It is true that no community needs to put up with the vagaries of exhibitionists who exhibit their genitals in public places; frotteurs who rub their genitals against females in crowds; voyeurs who spy on women; overt homosexuals who participate in homosexual activity in public places; or fetichists who commit criminal acts in pursuit of their sexual fetich. But one need not become hysterical over these types of offenders. They do not warrant custodial incarceration for life, since most of them are not dangerous. These offenders should be submitted to psychiatric examination at clinics especially organized for the purpose. Treatment on an outpatient basis and a period of supervised liberty under probation officers might be used in the case of first offenders. Where the overt behavior continues, they must be incarcerated. If specialized institutions are established for sex offenders, they should be kept in confinement there, to serve the sentences imposed on them by the courts. If such institutions are not available, they must be sent to prison. It is to be hoped that the attempt will be made in the penal institution to change the behavior patterns of these offenders through social case work and psychiatry. But even if patterns of behavior cannot be changed, the prison may still have some restraining effect upon them. While much of the sexual behavior of these types of individuals is compulsive in character, the compulsion is not irresistible. Most of these offenders have some degree of control over their peculiar types of sexual activity. The fear of further incarceration and punishment will undoubtedly strengthen the inhibitions of many individuals whose sexual activity takes on a form which outrages public decency.

A modification of adultery and fornication statutes might also take into account the public interest in the preservation of the outward decencies. Where an adulterous affair or a sexual liaison is carried on with little regard for public sensibilities, where the parties openly flaunt their relationship and their activities to their neighbors, the criminal law may well intervene. Such open defiance of the sexual conventions is on a par with the activities of the overt homosexual who is active in public comfort stations, or the exhibitionist who shows his genitals to women and children. Thus, if the prohibitions against adultery and fornication are to be retained by the law, we would like to see them limited, as they are presently in some states, to situations which are open and notorious. The criminal law can deal with public injury to standards of decency; it is largely helpless when it is called upon to act in situations which involve a private disregard of the code of morality.

The outrage of standards of decency and the danger to health are also basic reasons for the repression of male and female prostitution. But as we have seen, the attempt to eliminate commercialized prostitution raises grave questions of law enforcement. These must be met by every community, for the cost of permitting open female prostitution or open solicitation by male homosexual prostitutes is much too great. Prostitution is the source of too much disease, crime, disorder, and wasted lives for the law to tolerate it. Honest and effective law enforcement can keep male and female prostitution under control in any community, although these activities cannot be completely eliminated. Whether a community will get such law enforcement depends upon the climate of public opinion. It is up to the citizens of every community to see that the corrupt bargains which the exploiters of commercialized vice are ever willing to enter into with public officials do not paralyze law-enforcement activity. Perhaps the better elements in any community will bestir themselves to insist upon decent law enforcement if they realize that the cynical policy of keeping the town "wide open," in defiance of state statutes, may permit men and women to indulge their sexual passions through prostitution; but it is also an open invitation for the hoodlums and mobsters who fatten upon organized criminal activity to take over the town. Not only will prostitution spread, but other types of dangerous criminal activity will proliferate throughout the city and town. A rational sexual policy for the criminal law must therefore take it as a basic premise that there can be no compromise with commercialized sexual activity—with prostitution—either male or female.

PART TWO

"The Woman Problem"

SEX AND TEMPERAMENT

Part of the "conventional wisdom" regarding sex differences has been the belief that men and women are quite different temperamentally as well as physically. Cross-cultural evidence, however, throws into question this idea that each sex has its distinctive (and universal) qualities of temperament. In the following selection, a noted American anthropologist summarizes findings regarding sex temperament in three preliterate societies of New Guinea. Her finding that the three cultures vary greatly as to the kinds of temperament approved for each sex underlines the significance of social conditioning in this area of behavior.

Although male and female are, of course, biological entities they appear to be social roles as well. Societal expectations, as reflected in social organization and child training, determine in large measure the ways in which men and women in a given society think, feel, and behave.

Sex and Temperament

MARGARET MEAD

We have now considered in detail the approved personalities of each sex among three primitive peoples. We found the Arapesh—both men and women—displaying a personality that, out of our historically limited preoccupations, we would call maternal in its parental aspects, and feminine in its sexual aspects. We found men, as well as women, trained to be cooperative, unaggressive, responsive to the needs and demands of others. We found no idea that sex was a powerful driving force for men or for women. In marked contrast to these attitudes, we found among the Mundugumor that both men and women developed as ruthless, aggressive, positively sexed individuals, with the maternal cherishing aspects of personality at a minimum. Both men and women approximated to a personality type that we in our culture would find only in an undisciplined and very violent male. Neither the Arapesh nor the Mundugumor profit by a contrast between the sexes; the Arapesh ideal is the mild, responsive man married to the mild, responsive woman; the Mundugumor ideal is the violent, aggressive man married to the violent, aggressive woman. In the third tribe, the Tchambuli, we found a genuine reversal of the sex-attitudes of our own culture, with the woman the dominant, impersonal, managing partner, the man the less responsible and the emotionally dependent person. These three situations suggest, then, a very definite conclusion. If those temperamental attitudes which we have traditionally regarded as feminine—such as passivity, respon-

From *Sex and Temperament in Three Primitive Societies* by Margaret Mead, (New York: Morrow, 1935) Mentor paperback edition, pp. 190-196. Copyright 1950 by Margaret Mead. Also available in the Apollo paperback edition. Reprinted by permission of William Morrow and Company, Inc., New York, and of Routledge & Kegan Paul, Ltd., London.

siveness, and a willingness to cherish children—can so easily be set up as the masculine pattern in one tribe, and in another be outlawed for the majority of women as well as for the majority of men, we no longer have any basis for regarding such aspects of behaviour as sex-linked. And this conclusion becomes even stronger when we consider the actual reversal in Tchambuli of the position of dominance of the two sexes, in spite of the existence of formal patrilineal institutions.

The material suggests that we may say that many, if not all, of the personality traits which we have called masculine or feminine are as lightly linked to sex as are the clothing, the manners, and the form of head-dress that a society at a given period assigns to either sex. When we consider the behaviour of the typical Arapesh man or woman as contrasted with the behaviour of the typical Mundugumor man or woman, the evidence is overwhelmingly in favour of the strength of social conditioning. In no other way can we account for the almost complete uniformity with which Arapesh children develop into contented, passive, secure persons, while Mundugumor children develop as characteristically into violent, aggressive, insecure persons. Only to the impact of the whole of the integrated culture upon the growing child can we lay the formation of the contrasting types. There is no other explanation of race, or diet, or selection that can be adduced to explain them. We are forced to conclude that human nature is almost unbelievably malleable, responding accurately and contrastingly to contrasting cultural conditions. The differences between individuals who are members of different cultures, like the differences between indivduals within a culture, are almost entirely to be laid to differences in conditioning, especially during early childhood, and the form of this conditioning is culturally determined. Standardized personality differences between the sexes are of this order, cultural creations to which each generation, male and female, is trained to conform. There remains, however, the problem of the origin of these socially standardized differences.

While the basic importance of social conditioning is still imperfectly recognized—not only in lay thought, but even by the scientist specifically concerned with such matters—to go beyond it and consider the possible influence of variations in hereditary equipment is a hazardous matter. The following pages will read very differently to one who has made a part of his thinking a recognition of the whole amazing mechanism of cultural conditioning—who has really accepted the fact that the same infant could be developed into a full participant in any one of these three cultures —than they will read to one who still believes that the minutiae of cultural behaviour are carried in the individual germ-plasm. If it is said, therefore, that when we have grasped the full significance of the malleability of the human organism and the preponderant importance of cultural conditioning, there are still further problems to solve, it must be remembered that these problems come *after* such a comprehension of the force of conditioning; they cannot precede it. The forces that make children born among the Arapesh grow up into typical Arapesh personalities are entirely social, and any discussion of the variations which do occur must be looked at against this social background.

With this warning firmly in mind, we can ask a further question. Granting the malleability of human nature, whence arise the differences between the standardized personalities that different cultures decree for all of their members, or which one culture decrees for the members of one sex as contrasted with the members of the opposite sex? If such differences are culturally created, as this material would most strongly suggest that they are, if the newborn child can be shaped with equal ease into an unaggressive Arapesh or an aggressive Mundugumor, why do these striking contrasts occur at all? If the clues to the different personalities decreed for men and women in Tchambuli do not lie in the physical constitution of the two sexes—an assumption that we must reject both for the Tchambuli and for our own society—where can we find the clues upon which the Tchambuli, the Arapesh, the

Mundugumor, have built? Cultures are man-made, they are built of human materials; they are diverse but comparable structures within which human beings can attain full human stature. Upon what have they built their diversities?

We recognize that a homogeneous culture committed in all of its gravest institutions and slight usages to a co-operative unaggressive course can bend every child to that emphasis, some to a perfect accord with it, the majority to an easy acceptance, while only a few deviants fail to receive the cultural imprint. To consider such traits as aggressiveness or passivity to be sex-linked is not possible in the light of the facts. Have such traits, then, as aggressiveness or passivity, pride or humility, objectivity or a preoccupation with personal relationships, an easy response to the needs of the young and the weak or a hostility to the young and the weak, a tendency to initiate sex-relationships or merely to respond to the dictates of a situation or another person's advances —have these traits any basis in temperament at all? Are they potentialities of all human temperaments that can be developed by different kinds of social conditioning and which will not appear if the necessary conditioning is absent?

When we ask this question we shift our emphasis. If we ask why an Arapesh man or an Arapesh woman shows the kind of personality that we have considered in the first section of this book, the answer is: Because of the Arapesh culture, because of the intricate, elaborate, and unfailing fashion in which a culture is able to shape each new-born child to the cultural image. And if we ask the same question about a Mundugumor man or woman, or about a Tchambuli man as compared with a Tchambuli woman, the answer is of the same kind. They display the personalities that are peculiar to the cultures in which they were born and educated. Our attention has been on the differences between Arapesh men and women as a group and Mundugumor men and women as a group. It is as if we had represented the Arapesh personality by a soft yellow, the Mundugumor by a deep red, while the Tchambuli female personality was deep orange, and that of the Tchambuli male, pale green. But if we now ask whence came the original direction in each culture, so that one now shows yellow, another red, the third orange and green by sex, then we must peer more closely. And leaning closer to the picture, it is as if behind the bright consistent yellow of the Arapesh, and the deep equally consistent red of the Mundugumor, behind the orange and green that are Tchambuli, we found in each case the delicate, just discernible outlines of the whole spectrum, differently overlaid in each case by the monotone which covers it. This spectrum is the range of individual differences which lie back of the so much more conspicuous cultural emphasis, and it is to this that we must turn to find the explanation of cultural inspiration, of the source from which each culture has drawn.

There appears to be about the same range of basic temperamental variation among the Arapesh and among the Mundugumor, although the violent man is a misfit in the first society and a leader in the second. If human nature were completely homogeneous raw material, lacking specific drives and characterized by no important constitutional differences between individuals, then individuals who display personality traits so antithetical to the social pressure should not reappear in societies of such differing emphasis. If the variations between individuals were to be set down to accidents in the genetic process, the same accidents should not be repeated with similar frequency in strikingly different cultures, with strongly contrasting methods of education.

But because this same relative distribution of individual differences does appear in culture after culture, in spite of the divergence between the cultures, it seems pertinent to offer a hypothesis to explain upon what basis the personalities of men and women have been differently standardized so often in the history of the human race. This hypothesis is an extension of that advanced by Ruth Benedict in her *Patterns of Culture*. Let us assume that there are definite temperamental differences between human beings which if not entirely hereditary at least are established on a hereditary base very soon after birth. (Further than this we cannot at present narrow the matter.) These differences finally embodied in the character structure of adults, then, are the clues from which culture works, selecting one temperament, or a combination of related and congruent types, as desirable, and embodying this choice in every thread of the social fabric—in the care of the young child, the games the children play, the songs the people sing, the structure of political organization, the religious observance, the art and the philosophy.

Some primitive societies have had the time and the robustness to revamp all of their institutions to fit one extreme type, and to develop educational techniques which will ensure that the majority of each generation will show a personality congruent with this extreme emphasis. Other societies have pursued a less definitive course, selecting their models not from the most extreme, most highly differentiated individuals, but from the less marked types. In such societies the approved personality is less pronounced, and the culture often contains the types of inconsistencies that many human beings display also; one institution may be adjusted to the uses of pride, another to a casual humility that is congruent neither with pride nor with inverted pride. Such societies, which have taken the more usual and less sharply defined types as models, often show also a less definitely patterned social structure. The culture of such societies may be likened to a house the decoration of which has been formed by no definite and precise taste, no exclusive emphasis upon dignity or comfort or pretentiousness or beauty, but in which a little of each effect has been included.

Alternatively, a culture may take its clues not from one temperament, but from several temperaments. But instead of mixing together into an inconsistent hotchpotch the choices and emphases of different temperaments, or blending them together into a smooth but not particularly distinguished whole, it may isolate each type by making it the basis for the approved social personality for an age-group, a sex-group, a caste-group, or an occupational group. In this way society becomes not a monotone with a few discrepant patches of an intrusive colour, but a mosaic, with different groups displaying different personality traits. Such specializations as these may be based upon any facet of human endowment—different intellectual abilities, different artistic abilities, different emotional traits. So the Samoans decree that all young people must show the personality trait of unaggressiveness and punish with opprobrium the aggressive child who displays traits regarded as appropriate only in titled middle-aged men. In societies based upon elaborate ideas of rank, members of the aristocracy will be permitted, even compelled, to display a pride, a sensitivity to insult, that would be deprecated as inappropriate in members of the plebeian class. So also in professional groups or in religious sects some temperamental traits are selected and institutionalized, and taught to each new member who enters the profession or sect. Thus the physician learns the bed-side manner, which is the natural behaviour of some temperaments and the standard behaviour of the general practitioner in the medical profession; the Quaker learns at least the outward behaviour and the rudiments of meditation, the capacity for which is not necessarily an innate characteristic of many of the members of the Society of Friends.

So it is with the social personalities of the two sexes. The traits that occur in some members of each sex are specially assigned to one sex, and disallowed in the other. The history of the social definition of sex-differences is filled with such arbitrary arrangements in the intellectual and artistic field, but because of the assumed congruence between physiological sex and emotional endowment we have been less able to recognize that a similar arbitrary selection is being made among emotional traits also. We have assumed that because it is convenient for a mother to wish to care for her child, this is a trait with which women have been more generously endowed by a carefully teleological process of evolution. We have assumed that because men have hunted, an activity requiring enterprise, bravery, and initiative, they have been endowed with these useful attitudes as part of their sex-temperament.

Societies have made these assumptions both overtly and implicitly. If a society insists that warfare is the major occupation for the male sex, it is therefore insisting that all male children display bravery and pugnacity. Even if the insistence upon the differential bravery of men and women is not made articulate, the difference in occupation makes this point implicitly. When, however, a society goes further and defines men as brave and women timorous, when men are forbidden to show fear and women are indulged in the most flagrant display of fear, a more explicit element enters in. Bravery, hatred of any weakness, of flinching before pain or danger—this attitude which is so strong a component of *some human* temperaments has been selected as the key to masculine behaviour. The easy unashamed display of fear or suffering that is congenial to a different temperament has been made the key to feminine behaviour.

Originally two variations of human temperament, a hatred of fear or willingness to display fear, they have been socially translated into inalienable aspects of the personalities of the two sexes. And to that defined sex-personality every child will be educated, if a boy, to suppress fear, if a girl, to show it. If there has been no social selection in regard to this trait, the proud temperament that is repelled by any betrayal of feeling will display itself, regardless of sex, by keeping a stiff upper lip. Without an express prohibition of such behaviour the expressive unashamed man or woman will weep, or comment upon fear or suffering. Such attitudes, strongly marked in certain temperaments, may by social selection be standardized for everyone, or outlawed for everyone, or ignored by society, or made the exclusive and approved behaviour of one sex only.

Neither the Arapesh nor the Mundugumor have made any attitude specific for one sex. All of the energies of the culture have gone towards the creation of a single human type, regardless of class, age, or sex. There is no division into age-classes for which different motives or different moral attitudes are regarded as suitable. There is no class of seers or mediums who stand apart drawing inspiration from psychological sources not available to the majority of the people. The Mundugumor have, it is true, made one arbitrary selection, in that they recognize artistic ability only among individuals born with the cord about their necks, and firmly deny the happy exercise of artistic ability to those less unusually born. The Arapesh boy with a tinea infection has been socially selected to be a disgruntled, antisocial individual, and the society forces upon sunny co-operative children cursed with this affliction a final approximation to the behaviour appropriate to a pariah. With these two exceptions no emotional role is forced upon an individual because of birth or accident. As there is no idea of rank which declares that some are of high estate and some of low, so there is no idea of sex-difference which declares that one sex must feel differently from the other. One possible imaginative social construct, the attribution of different personalities to different members of the community classified into sex-, age-, or caste-groups, is lacking.

When we turn however to the Tchambuli, we find a situation that while bizarre in one respect, seems nevertheless more intelligible in another. The Tchambuli have at least made the point of sex-differences; they have used the obvious fact of sex as an organizing point for the formation of social personality, even though they seem to us to have reversed the normal picture. While there is reason to believe that not every Tchambuli woman is born with a dominating, organizing, administrative temperament, actively sexed and willing to initiate sex-relations, possessive, definite, robust, practical and impersonal in outlook, still most Tchambuli girls grow up to display these traits. And while there is definite evidence to show that all Tchambuli men are not, by native endowment, the delicate responsive actors of a play staged for the women's benefit, still most Tchambuli boys manifest this coquettish play-acting personality most of the time. Because the Tchambuli formulation of sex-attitudes contradicts our usual premises, we can see clearly that Tchambuli culture has arbitrarily permitted certain human traits to women, and allotted others, equally arbitrarily, to men.

LEARNING THE FEMININE ROLE

Social conditioning in the area of sex roles begins very early in childhood. Numerous researchers have observed that male and female children do, at very early ages, display differences in inclinations and in behavior. Yet it is virtually impossible (even among preschool children) to abstract from the totality of the child's behavior those aspects that represent "innate" qualities, that have (supposedly) been untouched by social influence. As much research has also shown, parents have definite expectations as to how children of each sex should act—and these expectations color their reactions to, and behavior with, their own children.

In the following reading, sociologist Mirra Komarovsky uses personal history reports of college students to illustrate some of the ways in which differential expectations and treatment of male and female children pervade childhood. The author has, in her broader studies of the roles of women, been much concerned with the relation between the training girls receive in childhood and their performance of appropriate sex roles as adults. The material presented below strongly suggests that attitudes and behavioral patterns developed in the formative years (and reactions of others noted during that period) can indeed have a lasting impact.

Learning the Feminine Role

MIRRA KOMAROVSKY

The infant girl will normally grow up to behave, feel, and think in ways appropriate to her sex. The fact that she is born a female only in part accounts for the result. Heredity, of course, will determine her physical and, in as yet not too well understood ways, her psychological make-up. But she must, also, *learn* to play the role assigned to women in her society.

As the child becomes aware of the world around her, she senses that men and women behave differently. Daddy goes out to work and Mommy remains to take care of the home. Visitors seldom talk about Daddy's clothes but they often say to Mommy, "What a becoming dress!" At gatherings, men and women frequently form separate circles. The women talk about children, maids, shopping, and other homey topics, but the men use many strange words and their conversation is harder to understand.

Normally the little girl identifies herself with women and imitates them. Society (and that means Father, Mother, Aunt Jane, the nurse, the minister, the nursery rhymes, the funnies, and so on) helps her along. "Can you beat it! Sissie's hair is straight as a string and look at Buddy's curls." "What are you going to *be*," little boy? And what a pretty, sweet little sister you have." "I am going to make the grownups smile," plots the little girl, piling ribbons on her head. "Look at the little coquette!" they chuckle. But little Jimmy would be wrong to assume that his sister's trick will work for him too. "No Jimmy, don't you act silly." "Jimmy, don't wheedle; if you want something ask for it like a man." "Watch out for the little charmer," warn the proud parents. "She can coax anything out of you." But parents do not need words to carry the lesson. It is conveyed even in infancy in the very tone of the voice cooing over the cradle, in father's mock wrestling with his baby boy, and his gentler play with his daughter.

Just how the family endows girls with the feminine psyche is revealed in a study of seventy-three undergraduates in a course on the family who were asked to reminisce about their childhoods. For the most part the acquisition of the feminine personality is not conscious, and it is only when conflicts arise that the nature of the influences becomes apparent. Despite the fact that the course probably selected the most "feminine" girls, thirty out of seventy-three students recollected experiences in which their dispositions ran counter to the stereotype of femininity.

One of the earliest influences recollected by the girls related to the choice of toys and play activities. *Pressures were exerted upon the girls to select girls' toys and to be more restrained, sedentary, quiet, and neat in their play than their brothers or boys in the neighborhood.*

One such conflict may come as a surprise. Everybody knows that girls naturally prefer dolls. And yet, one quarter of the group disliked dolls sufficiently to have had and to have remembered conflicts such as the following:

> I was a member of a brownie troop when I was seven and we were to have a party one day to which each child was to bring her favorite toy. My favorite toy at the time was a set of tin soldiers. Grandmother was shocked and insisted that I would disgrace her by bringing such an unladylike toy. But I refused to take a doll, with the result that I was forced to miss the party. But Grandmother succeeded in making me feel quite "queer" because I didn't like dolls.

> I started life as a little tomboy but as I grew older Mother got worried about my unladylike ways. She removed my tops, marbles, football, and skates and tried to replace these with dolls, tea sets,

and sewing games. To interest me in dolls she collected dolls of different nations, dressed exquisitely in their native costumes. She bought me small pocketbooks, and lovely little dresses. When despite her efforts she caught me one day trying to climb a tree in the park she became thoroughly exasperated and called me a little "freak."

Once when an aunt came to visit us I took great pleasure in showing off my toys. There were no dolls among them. My aunt commented upon this fact and said that I was a strange little girl to prefer marbles to dolls. The incident must have made a deep impression upon me to be remembered for thirteen years! I can remember her saying, "I suppose you just weren't cut out to be a mother."

Adults and playmates mince no words in making these girls feel "queer." But woe to the boy who likes dolls!

My brother was caught taking a doll to bed with him. He must have seen me and my sister do it. We made fun of him and the nurse told him that if he doesn't want to be taken for a little girl he better take the teddy bear instead.

I was six when I had a playfellow with whom I often played house. One day his mother walked in and saw the boy cradling a doll. She laughed and called him a "sissy." His father, when he heard of it, was quite annoyed. This put a stop to our little game.

Interest in "boy's" toys—chemistry sets, baseball gloves, electric trains—was expressed frequently. "One of my biggest disappointments as a child," writes a girl, "happened one Christmas. I asked for a set of tools and could hardly wait for Christmas morning. I eagerly opened a package only to find a sewing set."
Others recorded similar experiences:

I have always been a model of neatness and received much praise from family and relatives. But when my adolescent brother, following in my footsteps perhaps, was observed to be very careful about his appearance he was "ribbed" no end about it.

Once I got very dirty playing and mother told me that if I didn't learn to play quietly and keep myself neat no man would ever want to marry me.

An experimental study in which young children were asked to pick toys and respond to other tests revealed that the three-year-old boys and girls were not aware of "appropriate" toys and showed incomplete recognition of sex differences. The working-class children, incidentally, manifested the awareness of sex differences earlier than the middle-class boys and, especially, middle-class girls. It is possible that working-class parents put a greater stress on differences in sex roles or that working-class children come earlier under the influences of playmates and gangs which enforce these differences.

Social pressure exerted upon the *girls to be gentler and more emotionally demonstrative than boys is illustrated by the following quotations:*

I loved to catch butterflies and mount them. One day I overheard a neighbor say that mounting butterflies was such an odd activity for a girl—girls should be gentle. I gave up my hobby because I feared people would think me queer.

I was ten years old when I attended the funeral of some relative. I was awed but I didn't cry. I remember thinking that I must *try* to cry or else people would think me very unfeeling. The irony of it was that my brother was biting his lips to keep from crying. He, too, remembered the occasion and confessed years later that he tried not to appear a "softy" by bursting into tears.

When I was ten I once wanted to take out a simple outline of the history of the world. The librarian said, "This history book is more suitable for a boy. Don't you think you'd like a book written for girls?" In our class library we had books set aside for girls and boys. By the time we graduated from elementary school most of the girls were thoroughly bored with the literature assigned to us.

I thoroughly enjoyed my high school years but I remember the real disappointment at not being allowed to take "shop," which was given only for boys, and of spending many dreary hours over a piece of cloth that somehow never quite became a skirt. [Preference for "shop" over cooking and sewing was mentioned by several students.]

When I was twelve, my mother was boasting one day to some friends about my swimming. I took lessons in preparation for a national championship meet. This friend remarked, "Don't let the child swim so much. Large muscles are very unattractive in a girl!" From then on the fear of becoming unfeminine cooled my interest in swimming.

Another difference in the upbringing of the sexes was registered by girls who had brothers. They noted that they *were given fewer opportunities for independent action and those came later than was the case with their brothers.* The boys were freer to play away from home grounds, to return later, and to pick their own activities, movies, and books. They were ordinarily allowed the first independent steps earlier than their sisters, such as the first walk to school without an adult, the first unaccompanied movie or baseball game, and later in life, the train trip or the job away from home.

The greater sheltering of the daughters was also shown in the lesser privacy allowed them in personal affairs.

One girls writes:

My mother is very hurt if I don't let her read the letters I receive. After a telephone call she expects me to tell her who called and what was said. My brother could say "a friend" and she would not feel insulted.

And again:

> My brother is 15, three years younger than I am. When he goes
> out after supper mother calls out, "Where are you going, Jimmy?"
> "Oh, out." Could I get away with this? Not on your life. I would
> have to tell in detail where to, with whom, and if I am half an hour
> late mother sits on the edge of the living-room sofa watching the
> door.

States another student:

> I have a brother of 23, and a sister of 22, and a younger brother
> who is 16. My sister and I had a much more sheltered life than my
> brothers. My brothers come and go as they please. Even my
> younger brother feels that his current girl friend is his personal
> affair. No one knows who she is but the family wants voluminous
> files on every boy my sister and I want to date. It is not easy for us
> to get the complete genealogy of a boy we want to go out with.

In a study of upper-middle-class parents of nursery-school children, it was found that 24 per cent of the parents preferred submissive to aggressive girls but only 9 per cent of them preferred
submissive to aggressive boys. There was some evidence that
fathers preferred traditional feminine behavior in girls more frequently than did their mothers.

Finally, the *daughters* of the family *are held to a more exacting
code of filial and kinship obligations.* When the grandmother needs
somebody to do an errand for her, or Aunt Jane who doesn't hear
well needs help, the girl is more likely to be called upon. The
pressure to attend and observe birthdays, anniversaries, and other
family festivals is apparently greater upon her than upon the boy.

Similarly, care of younger children is the girl's responsibility.
One student still resents the fact that while she had to mind her
five-year-old sister, her brother was free to roam all over the
neighborhood with his gang.

While many boys were expected to help with household chores, the girls had greater responsibilities in this respect. Shoveling snow, mowing the lawn, well, that was fun in comparison with daily dish wiping or cleaning up. To add insult to injury, in some cases the sisters were expected to clean their brothers' room and pick up after them. One student tells a story which perhaps is exceptional. Her brother was a gentle, considerate boy, interested in books and in art. Once her mother upon returning home found that he had straightened up the kitchen which she had left in haste. She told him that he need not have done it because men shouldn't "putter" around the kitchen. That impressed the student because she could never do enough in this respect to suit her mother.

Were we to trace the development of the feminine personality we would undoubtedly find many cumulative effects of those early influences. For example, little girls understand that they are to be sweeter, milder, gentler than the boys. But this indoctrination cannot exorcise the hostility that may exist in their hearts. Is it so far-fetched to suppose, as one writer did, that the alleged indirectness of the feminine criticism, the "I can't understand why Jane doesn't receive any phone calls," is a compromise between the imperative to be sweet and their aggression?

The differences in the upbringing of the sexes just described are obviously related to their respective roles in adult life. The future homemaker trains for her role *within* the home, but the boy prepares for his by being given more independence outside the home, by his taking a "paper route" or a summer job. A provider will profit by independence, dominance, aggressiveness, competitiveness. The greater sheltering of the girl is related to the greater biological and social risks incurred by her in sexual relations outside of marriage. Marriage for a woman is a choice not only of a mate but also of a station in life; hence the greater family control over her dating.

The parents at times explicitly recognize this functional character of their training. One girl, for example, reports that both her parents were more indulgent to her. With a little pleading she could usually get what she wanted. Her brother, on the other hand, was expected to earn money for his little luxuries because "boys need that kind of training." In a couple of cases the girls testified that their brothers were expected to work their way through college, while the girls were supported. A student writes:

> My brother is two years younger than I am. When we started going to school my father would always say as he saw us off in the morning, "Now, Buddy, you are the man and you must take care of your sister." It amused me because it was I who always had to take care of him.

Another student recollects that when her brother refused to help her with her "math" on the ground that no one was allowed to help *him,* her mother replied, "Well, she is a girl, and it isn't as important for her to know 'math' and to learn how to get along without help."

More often, however, if you asked parents to explain the different demands put upon their daughters and sons they would simply exclaim, "Why, it isn't right for a girl to do this," or, "It isn't manly." What may have been originally derived from social utility now presents itself to us as "natural" and "proper" in its own right without requiring further explanation.

We have described some differences in the upbringing of the sexes, but there is little doubt that these differences are not as great as they once were. The economic and social changes in the status of women have had repercussions upon their upbringing. As a symbol of the change witness the shorts, overalls, slacks worn by girls. Girls are encouraged to excel in athletics. Both sexes start school at the same time and attend coeducational schools. They are sent to summer camps and to out-of-town colleges. Their report cards are scanned as critically as those of their brothers; failure to be promoted is as great a blow; and an A as great a triumph. Little girls are increasingly asked, "And what are you going to be when you grow up?" "Don't be a sissy" may be addressed to Sis no less than to Buddy.

With the traditional and the modern patterns of rearing girls both present in our day, it is not surprising that confusion is rife.

The risks of the traditional upbringing reside in *the failure to develop in the girl independence, inner resources, and that degree of self-assertion which life will demand of her.*

Whatever differences in the upbringing of the sexes must remain, they need not be of the kind reported by the following young women:

> It was thought to be a part of my brother's education to be sent away to school. I was expected to go to a local college so that I could live at home. When my brother got his first job he got a room so that he would not have to commute too far. My sister at 22, turned down several offers of jobs at a high salary and took a much less desirable one only because she could live at home. She continues to be as much under parental control as she was when in college. Frankly, if anything should happen to my parents, I would be at a complete loss while I know that my brothers could carry on alone very well.

> My younger brother was not a good student and did not really want to go to college. But the family sent him, anyway, while I, who wanted passionately to continue my education, had to mark time until my grandmother finally consented to help me through college. I bitterly resented what I felt to be a great injustice.

The results of excessive sheltering of some middle-class girls may be even more serious. It produces in girls a greater dependence upon and attachment to parental families than is the case with sons. Now, our society demands that, upon marriage, adults transfer their primary emotional loyalties from parents to their own families. Many books on the family abound in such counsel as the following: "If there is a bona fide in-law problem the young couple need first of all to be certain of their perspective. The success of their marriage should be put above everything else, even above attachment to parents. Husband and wife must come first. Otherwise the individual exhibits immaturity." Another textbook affirms: "Close attachments to members of the family, whether parents or siblings, accentuate the normal difficulties involved in achieving the response role expected in marriage." Again, ". . . there is a call for a new attitude, a subordinating of and to some extent an aloofness from the home of one's childhood."

The upbringing of women does not always make it possible for them to heed such advice. To the extent that the woman remains infantile, dependent upon her parents, so closely attached to them as to find it difficult to part from them or to face their disapproval in case of a conflict between her family and her spouse—to that extent she is handicapped in making the transfer of loyalties which our culture demands. We have long recognized that the silver cord is a threat to the man's marriage. But there are reasons to suspect that failure to sever parental ties may hold (if not as acute and conspicuous) a considerable threat to the woman's marriage.

The passive, dependent woman may pass from the tutelage of the parental home to the protection of a husband without being exposed to the cold winds of the world, but the chances are increasingly against this happy outcome. It is this type of woman who, after college, moves from one blind-alley job to another and who, in case of divorce, widowhood, marital separation due to war, or another crisis, finds herself helpless and resourceless.

At the other extreme, some parents *stress achievement goals at the expense of the strictly feminine roles of girls.* The families must facilitate the acceptance on the part of the girl of her sexuality; that is, the capacity for heterosexual love and for tender motherhood. This capacity is the product of the whole complex of family relations and this is not the place to discuss it in detail. But in at least two cases among the undergraduates studied, the acceptance of femininity was hindered by parental attitudes.

One girl reported that intellectual attainments were stressed in her upbringing from childhood on, to the exclusion of everything else. She could hardly remember either parent ever mentioning that one day she would be married and would bear and rear children. If the very core of the feminine role is thus dismissed or belittled in the upbringing of the girl, and if favorable parent-child relations make for identification with such values, her acceptance of the feminine role may be impaired. In another case the adored father encouraged "boyish" behavior in his little girl to the extent that she felt "ungainly and graceless, and different from other girls." Occasionally she would slip off and play with a doll but she felt that her father would be disappointed in her if he discovered it. Even if a parent correctly considers certain conventional attributes of the "feminine" role to be worthless, he creates risks for the girl in forcing her to stray too far from the accepted mores of her time.

But in trying to mediate between the extremes of the traditional and the "modern" upbringing of the girl, parents run into other difficulties. *The steps which parents must take to prepare their daughters to meet economic exigencies and familial responsibilities of modern life—these very steps may awaken aspirations and develop habits which conflict with certain features of their feminine roles, as these are defined today.* The very education which is to make the college housewife a cultural leaven of her family and her community may develop in her interests which are frustrated by other phases of housewifery. We are urged to train women for positions of leadership in civic affairs when, at the same time, we define capacity for decisive action, executive ability, hardihood in the face of opposition as "unfeminine" traits. We want our daughters to be able, if the need arises, to earn a living at some worthwhile occupation. In doing so, we run the risk of awakening interests and abilities which, again, run counter to the present definition of femininity.

WOMAN: THE LOST SEX

The title of the book from which this selection is drawn
(Modern Woman: The Lost Sex) *suggests the considerable
discontent and uncertainty women experience today regarding their social roles and interpersonal relations. That such
malaise exists in our society nobody can doubt. The reasons
for it, however, are less certain. Lundberg and Farnham base
their reasoning on orthodox psychoanalytic theory, and take
as a point of departure the rubric "anatomy is destiny." They
argue that the basic cause of modern woman's misery has
been feminism, and state further that this social movement
was (despite some laudable surface aims) at its base as much
a sickness as a rational form of protest.*

*By seeking equality with men, the authors assert, women
have lost sight of their basic functions (which in their view
appear to be sexual and maternal). They are unhappy mainly
because they are doing tasks for which they are, as women,
ill-fitted. By doing everything she can to avoid passivity and
dependence (the true feminine qualities, according to this
treatment), woman fails to achieve sexual or other fulfillment.
This may in turn give rise to other social problems—as rearer
of children, woman is in a particularly crucial position to
affect the attitudes and behavior which dominate the society.
The reading that follows will serve to represent a school of
thought which some observers have termed "neo-anti-femi-
nism."*

Woman: The Lost Sex

FERDINAND LUNDBERG AND
MARYNIA FARNHAM

We may dispose of the legal and political aspects of woman's new position as being not significantly important in and of themselves. In these areas women gained a rightful privilege and ego-support, not dangerous to her fundamental peace of mind. It is rather in the aggressive and misdirected use to which these privileges are put that we see arising the difficulties into which many women have plunged themselves. The economic, educational, social and sexual facts of the woman's life, intertwined and interdependent as they are, are those which implement all others.

The woman arriving at maturity today does so with certain fixed attitudes derived from her background and training. Her home life, very often, has been distorted. She has enjoyed an education identical with that of her brother. She expects to be allowed to select any kind of work for which she has inclination and training. She also, generally, expects to marry. At any rate, she usually in-intends to have "a go" at it. Some women expect to stop working when they marry; many others do not. She expects to find sexual gratification and believes in her inalienable right so to do. She is legally free to live and move as she chooses. She may seek divorce if her marriage fails to gratify her. She has access to contraceptive information so that, theoretically, she may control the size and spacing of her family. In very many instances, she owns and disposes of her own property. She has, it appears, her destiny entirely in her own hands.

From *Modern Woman, The Lost Sex,* Universal Library edition, by Ferdinand Lundberg and Marynia F. Farnham, M.D., pp. 232-241. Copyright 1947 by Ferdinand Lundberg and Marynia F. Farnham. Reprinted by permission of Harper and Row, Publishers, Inc., New York; footnotes omitted.

All of this serves less to clarify and simplify her life than to complicate it with conflict piled on conflict. These conflicts are between her basic needs as a woman and the destiny she has carved out for herself—conflicts between the head and the heart, if you will.

Her necessity is to find some kind of consummation for her specific femininity and for herself as a human being. The circumstances with which she is now surrounded, as well as those of her upbringing, tend to prevent these two consummations—instinct and ego—from being fused together. Conflict and compromise are almost inevitable. Her basic needs for satisfaction as a woman would inevitably lead her in the direction of marriage and children inside the home. However, the woman who chooses this course runs into two serious obstacles: she does not obtain under present conditions satisfaction of her need for self-esteem nor does she obtain a sense of social importance. In attempting to gain these, she is led in the direction of economic independence, which carries her outside her home, away from children and childbearing. It was, of course, the failure of society after the Industrial Revolution to provide her with needed sources of self-esteem that forced her into the battle for her economic "rights" which, as we have shown, she has at least formally won. In winning them she was forced, too, into dubious battle for all the other rights auxiliary to them.

Thus she finds herself squarely in the middle of the most serious kind of divided purpose. If she is to undertake occupation outside her home with any kind of success, it is almost certain in the present day to be time-consuming and energy-demanding. So it is also with the problems she faces in her home. Certainly the tasks of a woman in bearing and educating children as well as maintaining, as best she may, the inner integrity of her home are capable of demanding all her time and best attention. However, she cannot obtain from them, so attenuated are these tasks now, the same sort of community approval and ego-satisfaction that she can from seemingly more challenging occupations which take her outside the home. Inevitably the dilemma has led to one compromise after another which we see exemplified on every hand in the modern woman's adaptation—an uneasy patchwork.

Unable to relinquish either satisfaction, she necessarily attempts to obtain both. In making the attempt, she must divide her attention and one of her occupations must be sacrificed in some measure to the other. Many women at first adopt the attitude that work will be undertaken only as a preliminary to marriage, then only as long as necessary for the economic support of the home. Later it will be abandoned when there are children and the home needs are more demanding. These women often also emphasize that they wish to have some occupation on which they can reasonably rely in case of an emergency. They are altogether too well aware of the insecurities and uncertainties of modern economic life to fail to take into account that at any time they may have to work, quite apart from inclination.

The present-day feeling regarding the impoverishment of the home is shown too in the frequent statement that women must fortify themselves with interests and occupations to which they can turn when their children no longer require their attention. Many no doubt carry out their aim and manage to obtain satisfactions inside their homes during the period of their children's dependency or even longer. For others, however, the work experience provides such satisfaction that they almost inevitably find it impossible to relinquish it. This is probably traceable to the fact that the underlying drives of these women, instilled in their childhood homes, are in the direction of such satisfactions. In present-day society, these basically masculine drives find an atmosphere which encourages rather than disapproves and deprecates their development.

It is becoming unquestionably more and more common for the woman to attempt to combine home and child care and an outside activity, which is either work or career. Increasing numbers train for professional careers. When these two spheres are com-

bined it is inevitable that one or the other will become of secondary concern and, this being the case, it is certain that the home will
take that position. This is true, if only for the practical reason that
no one can find and hold remunerative employment where the job
itself doesn't take precedence over all other concerns. All sorts of
agencies and instrumentalities have therefore been established to
make possible the playing of this dual role. These are all in the
direction of substitutes for the attention of the mother in the home
and they vary from ordinary, untrained domestic service through
the more highly trained grades of such service, to the public and
private agencies now designed for the care, supervision and emotional untanglement of the children. The day nursery and its more
elegant counterpart, the nursery school, are outstanding as the
major agencies which make it possible for women to relinquish the
care of children still in their infancy.

All these services and facilities produce what appears on the
surface to be a smoothly functioning arrangement and one that
provides children with obviously highly trained expert and efficient care as well as with superior training in early skills and
techniques and in adaptation to social relations. This surface, however, covers a situation that is by no means so smoothly functioning nor so satisfying either to the child or the woman. She must of
necessity be deeply in conflict and only partially satisfied in either
direction. Her work develops aggressiveness, which is essentially a
denial of her femininity, an enhancement of her childhood-induced
masculine tendencies. It is not that work is essentially masculine
or feminine, but that the pursuit of a career (which is work plus
prestige goal) is essentially masculine because exploitative. The
statement may cause enormous protest but it remains a fact.

Work that entices women out of their homes and provides them
with prestige only at the price of feminine relinquishment, involves
a response to masculine strivings. The more importance outside
work assumes, the more are the masculine components of the
woman's nature enhanced and encouraged. In her home and in

her relationship to her children, it is imperative that these strivings be at a minimum and that her femininity be available both for
her own satisfaction and for the satisfaction of her children and
husband. She is, therefore, in the dangerous position of having to
live one part of her life on the masculine level, another on the
feminine. It is hardly astonishing that few can do so with success.
One of these tendencies must of necessity achieve dominance over
the other. The plain fact is that increasingly we are observing the
masculinization of women and with it enormously dangerous consequences to the home, the children (if any) dependent on it, and
to the ability of the woman, as well as her husband, to obtain
sexual gratification.

The effect of this "masculinization" on women is becoming more
apparent daily. Their new exertions are making demands on them
for qualities wholly opposed to the experience of feminine satisfaction. As the rivals of men, women must, and insensibly do,
develop the characteristics of aggression, dominance, independence and power. These are qualities which insure success as co-
equals in the world of business, industry and the professions. The
distortion of character under pressure of modern attitudes and
upbringing is driving women steadily deeper into personal conflict
soluble only by psychotherapy. For their need to achieve and
accomplish doesn't lessen, in any way, their deeper need to find
satisfactions profoundly feminine. Much as they consciously seek
those gratifications of love, sensual release and even motherhood,
they are becoming progressively less able unconsciously to accept
or achieve them.

First of their demands is for sexual gratification, a problem we
discuss at some length in Chapter XI. This is the core of the goal—
sexual, orgastic equality with men. These women have intellectualized and rationalized their sexual lives, determining that they
will have for themselves the experiences and, therefore, the satisfactions that men have. So far as the experiences are concerned,
they can carry out their intentions, but where the gratifications

are concerned they meet with abysmal, tragic failure. Sexual gratification is not an experience to be obtained through the simple performance of the sexual act. To a very great extent the unconscious exertions of these women to obtain absolute parity with men have resulted in crippling them precisely for this much desired objective. Dr. Helene Deutsch, among many other psychiatrists, affirms this when she states, "In the light of psychoanalysis, the sexual act assumes an immense, dramatic, and profoundly cathartic significance for the woman—but this only under the condition that it is experienced in a feminine, dynamic way and is not transformed into an act of erotic play or sexual 'equality.'" It is precisely in development of femininity that capacity for female sexual gratification lies. The greater the denial of the feminine, in childhood and later, the surer and more extensive is the loss of capacity for satisfaction in both tenderness and sensuality: love.

The dominant direction of feminine training and development today is directly opposed to the truth of such a dictum as Dr. Deutsch's. It discourages just those traits necessary to the attainment of sexual pleasure: receptivity and passiveness, a willingness to accept dependence without fear or resentment, with a deep inwardness and readiness for the final goal of sexual life—impregnation. It doesn't admit of wishes to control or master, to rival or dominate. The woman who is to find true gratification must love and accept her own womanhood as she loves and accepts her husband's manhood. Women's rivalry with men today, and the need to "equal" their accomplishments, engenders all too often anger and resentfulness toward men. Men, challenged, frequently respond in kind. So it is that women envy and feel hostile to men for just the attributes which women themselves require for "success" in the world. The woman's unconscious wish to possess the organ upon which she must thus depend militates greatly against her ability to accept its vast power to satisfy her when proffered to her in love.

Many women can find no solution to their dilemma and are defeated in attempts at adaptation. These constitute the array of the sick, unhappy, neurotic, wholly or partly incapable of dealing with life. In a veritable army of women, the tensions and anxieties make their way to the surface in physical guise. They have always been known and dimly recognized for what they are—the miserable, the half-satisfied, the frustrated, the angered. Unable to cope with the disappointments that they have met in their emotional lives, they become ill. Their illnesses take varied forms, attack any part of the body and are often disabling. Where formerly the connection was only suspected and assumed between these multifarious physical disorders and disturbing feeling states, we are now coming to the point of really understanding their sources in the child-based emotional disorders that give rise to them. Whether it be "sick headaches," pains of indeterminable nature in the back and limbs, gastric disorders, constipation, hypertension, or the enormous collection of disorders of the reproductive system, it is all one and all arises from an inability to master unconscious feelings constantly aroused by disappointment and frustration.

Such women are constant visitors to doctors or patrons of patent medicines. They are never cured and never comfortable. They suffer as authentically as those whose complaints rest upon physically determined pathology. They are just as sick and most emphatically their illnesses are not "imaginary." They can be helped permanently only by understanding obtained through psychological insight, therefore, through psychiatry. Many of them today are beginning to find their way to such help but many, many more are not. These remain the complaining army who keep their families, friends and physicians constantly at their beck and call by their suffering.

Other women, more obviously in need of psychiatry for a solution of their troubles, do not show their difficulties in physical symptoms but present them more directly in the form of disturbances recognizably emotional. These are the "nervous," the sleepless, the depressed, the anxious, the driven, the sexually maladjusted, those who complain directly of misery and discontent.

These women are the overtly neurotic. They may have recurrent depressions which are either mild enough to be of only limited and passing concern or so severe as to require hospitalization. Whichever form they take, they are disabling for their duration and a constant threat when not actually present. A very large group of these women describe themselves as "nervous." They are often sleepless, hyper-irritable and extremely demanding of husbands and children, whom they unconsciously seek to punish for their own disabilities. There are many others with more obvious and easily categorized neurotic disorders some of whom complain of intense anxiety which renders them more or less helpless. The anxiety is often related to fear of some impending catastrophe for which they have no immediate evidence. Nevertheless, they constantly feel that they are about to suffer from some physical disorder such as cancer or heart disease for which no relief will be found.

The relatively large number of women who complain of immediate sexual and marital difficulties stands out among the neurotic. Their complaints usually revolve about the sexual act and its insufficiency or unsatisfactory nature. Often, however, the general marital relationship is under attack, the woman not being able directly to place her problem as sexual. The husband is criticized for a thousand reasons as inconsiderate, selfish, harsh or thoughtless, which he may not in fact be. These women range all the way from the frankly and completely frigid to those who complain of neglect and indifference on the part of their husbands and the feelings of loneliness and uselessness that arise from it. Many of them have the prospect of divorce prominently in mind, in hope either of finding satisfaction through removal of the irritating circumstance or, more remotely, of discovering gratification through another marriage.

A certain number of these women of inner masculine tendency are making a reasonable and satisfying adjustment. They have found, through an uneasy balance between work and home, a way of compromise that offers sufficient satisfaction in both spheres to provide happiness and completion. No doubt careful examination might discover defects in this adaptation, but it must be remembered that all adaptations are products of compromise and that where there is real satisfaction there is little reason to be captious. The difficulty lies not in the small group of women who have managed the difficult compromise, but in the much larger group who have not and who suffer from resulting frustrations.

It is not only the masculine woman who has met with an unhappy fate in the present situation. There are still many women who succeed in achieving adult life with largely unimpaired feminine strivings, for which home, a husband's love and children are to them the entirely adequate answers. It is their misfortune that they must enter a society in which such attitudes are little appreciated and are attended by many concrete, external penalties. Such women cannot fail to be affected by finding that their traditional activities are held in low esteem and that the woman who voluntarily undertakes them is often deprecated by her more aggressive contemporaries. She may come to believe that her situation is difficult, entailing serious deprivations, as against the more glamorous and exciting life other women seemingly enjoy. She may be set away from the main stream of life, very much in a backwater and fearful lest she lose her ability and talents through disuse and lack of stimulation. She may become sorry for herself and somewhat angered by her situation, gradually developing feelings of discontent and pressure. As her children grow older and require less of her immediate attention, the feelings of loss increase.

Unless she busies herself extensively with the poorly organized and generally unrewarding voluntary civic or cultural activities, she may find herself with much idle time and much frustration on her hands. Her home alone, unless it is a rural one, cannot occupy her whole time and attention because so much in it is now completely prefabricated and automatic. For amusement she is forced to resort either to the radio "soap opera," or to some other equally unrewarding use of leisure such as game playing, movie-going or aimless shopping. She is deprived of her husband's companionship during the long hours of the day when he is away from home and often the evening finds him preoccupied and disinterested in the affairs that concern her. Consequently she must construct her life out of artificial undertakings with no organic functional connection with the realities of her relationships or her interests. In this way she may easily and quickly develop attitudes of discontent and anger injurious to her life adjustment. She may begin to malfunction sexually, her libidinal depths shaken by ego frustrations.

So it is that society today makes it difficult for a woman to avoid the path leading to discontent and frustration and resultant hostility and destructiveness. Such destructiveness is, unfortunately, not confined in its effects to the woman alone. It reaches into all her relationships and all her functions. As a wife she is not only often ungratified but ungratifying and has, as we have noted, a profoundly disturbing effect upon her husband. Not only does he find himself without the satisfactions of a home directed and cared for by a woman happy in providing affection and devotion, but he is often confronted by circumstances of even more serious import for his own emotional integrity. His wife may be his covert rival, striving to match him in every aspect of their joint undertaking. Instead of supporting and encouraging his manliness and wishes for domination and power, she may thus impose upon him feelings of insufficiency and weakness. Still worse is the effect upon his sexual satisfactions. Where the woman is unable to admit and accept dependence upon her husband as the source of gratification and must carry her rivalry even into the act of love, she will seriously damage his sexual capacity. To be unable to gratify in the sexual act is for a man an intensely humiliating experience; here it is that mastery and domination, the central capacity of the man's sexual nature, must meet acceptance or fail. So it is that by their own character disturbances these women succeed ultimately in depriving themselves of the devotion and power of their husbands and become the instruments of bringing about their own psychic catastrophe.

But no matter how great a woman's masculine strivings, her basic needs make themselves felt and she finds herself facing her fundamental role as wife and mother with a divided mind. Deprived of a rich and creative home in which to find self-expression, she tries desperately to find a compromise. On the one hand she must retain her sources of real instinctual gratification and on the other, find ways of satisfying her need for prestige and esteem. Thus she stands, Janus-faced, drawn in two directions at once, often incapable of ultimate choice and inevitably penalized whatever direction she chooses.

THE SECOND SEX

Madame de Beauvoir, the well-known French philosopher and novelist, has written—in The Second Sex—*what has already become a classic study of woman's situation. This analysis is particularly notable for its attempt to draw on a wide variety of source materials—some historical, some literary, some scientific. Approaching her subject from a background influenced by Marxism, feminism, and existentialism, the author reaches conclusions almost diametrically opposed to those of Lundberg and Farnham. Far from feminism causing all the trouble, feminism (Beauvoir argues) has not really gone far enough. Only when woman is truly able to engage in freely chosen projects (and to Beauvoir, mere wifedom or motherhood will not suffice for this purpose) will she have full equality. Until then, she remains the inessential "other," ruled in almost all respects by the decisions of men.*

While some of the author's arguments may hold more meaning against the background of a conventional French middle-class upbringing than they would for typical American situations, many other points she brings out in her study have wide applicability. Beauvoir's work (to which this is the introduction) may irritate some readers, yet few will fail to be impressed by it as a highly literate and strongly felt condemnation of the subjugation of women.

The Second Sex

SIMONE DE BEAUVOIR

For a long time I have hesitated to write a book on woman. The subject is irritating, especially to women; and it is not new. Enough ink has been spilled in the quarreling over feminism, now practically over, and perhaps we should say no more about it. It is still talked about, however, for the voluminous nonsense uttered during the last century seems to have done little to illuminate the problem. After all, is there a problem? And if so, what is it? Are there women, really? Most assuredly the theory of the eternal feminine still has its adherents who will whisper in your ear: "Even in Russia women still are *women*"; and other erudite persons—sometimes the very same—say with a sigh: "Woman is losing her way, woman is lost." One wonders if women still exist, if they will always exist, whether or not it is desirable that they should, what place they occupy in this world, what their place should be. "What has become of women?" was asked recently in an ephemeral magazine.

But first we must ask: what is a woman? *"Tota mulier in utero,"* says one, "woman is a womb." But in speaking of certain women, connoisseurs declare that they are not women, although they are equipped with a uterus like the rest. All agree in recognizing the fact that females exist in the human species; today as always they make up about one half of humanity. And yet we are told that femininity is in danger; we are exhorted to be women, remain women, become women. It would appear, then, that every female human being is not necessarily a woman; to be so considered she must

Reprinted from Simone de Beauvoir, *The Second Sex*, trans. by H. M. Parshley (New York: Knopf, 1952; Bantam edition, 1961), pp. xiii-xxix; footnotes omitted. Reprinted by permission of Alfred A. Knopf, Inc. and Jonathan Cape, Ltd., London.

share in that mysterious and threatened reality known as femininity. Is this attitude something secreted by the ovaries? Or is it a Platonic essence, a product of the philosophic imagination? Is a rustling petticoat enough to bring it down to earth? Although some women try zealously to incarnate this essence, it is hardly patentable. It is frequently described in vague and dazzling terms that seem to have been borrowed from the vocabulary of the seers, and indeed in the times of St. Thomas it was considered an essence as certainly defined as the somniferous virtue of the poppy.

But conceptualism has lost ground. The biological and social sciences no longer admit the existence of unchangeably fixed entities that determine given characteristics, such as those ascribed to woman, the Jew, or the Negro. Science regards any characteristic as a reaction dependent in part upon a *situation*. If today femininity no longer exists, then it never existed. But does the word *woman*, then, have no specific content? This is stoutly affirmed by those who hold to the philosophy of the enlightenment, or rationalism, or nominalism; women, to them, are merely the human beings arbitrarily designated by the word *woman*. Many American women particularly are prepared to think that there is no longer any place for woman as such; if a backward individual still takes herself for a woman, her friends advise her to be psychoanalyzed and thus get rid of this obsession. In regard to a work, *Modern Woman: The Lost Sex*, which in other respects has its irritating features, Dorothy Parker has written: "I cannot be just to books which treat of woman as woman. . . . My idea is that all of us, men as well as women, should be regarded as human beings." But nominalism is a rather inadequate doctrine, and the antifemininists have had no trouble in showing that women simply *are not* men. Surely woman is, like man, a human being; but such a declaration is abstract. The fact is that every concrete human being is always a singular, separate individual. To decline to accept such notions as the eternal feminine, the black soul, the Jewish character, is not to deny that Jews, Negroes, women exist today—this denial does not represent a liberation for those concerned, but rather a flight from reality. Some years ago a well-known woman writer refused to permit her portrait to appear in a series of photographs especially devoted to women writers; she wished to be counted among the men. But in order to gain this privilege she made use of her husband's influence! Women who assert that they are men lay claim none the less to masculine consideration and respect. I recall also a young Trotskyite standing on a platform at a boisterous meeting and getting ready to use her fists, in spite of her evident fragility. She was denying her feminine weakness; but it was for love of a militant male whose equal she wished to be. The attitude of defiance of many American women proves that they are haunted by a sense of their femininity. In truth, to go for a walk with one's eyes open is enough to demonstrate that humanity is divided into two classes of individuals whose clothes, faces, bodies, smiles, gaits, interests, and occupations are manifestly different. Perhaps these differences are superficial, perhaps they are destined to disappear. What is certain is that right now they do most obviously exist.

If her functioning as a female is not enough to define woman, if we decline also to explain her through "the eternal feminine," and if nevertheless we admit, provisionally, that women do exist, then we must face the question: what is a woman?

To state the question is, to me, to suggest, at once, a preliminary answer. The fact that I ask it is in itself significant. A man would never get the notion of writing a book on the peculiar situation of the human male. But if I wish to define myself, I must first of all say: "I am a woman"; on this truth must be based all further discussion. A man never begins by presenting himself as an individual of a certain sex; it goes without saying that he is a man. The terms *masculine* and *feminine* are used symmetrically only as a matter of form, as on legal papers. In actuality the relation of the two sexes is not quite like that of two electrical poles, for man represents both the positive and the neutral, as is indicated by the common use of *man* to designate human beings in general; whereas woman represents only the negative, defined by limiting criteria, without reciprocity. In the midst of an abstract discussion it is vexing to hear a man say: "You think thus and so because you are a woman"; but I know that my only defense is to reply: "I think thus and so because it is true," thereby removing my subjective self from the argument. It would be out of the question to reply: "And you think the contrary because you are a man," for it is understood that the fact of being a man is no peculiarity. A man is in the right in being a man; it is the woman who is in the wrong. It amounts to this: just as for the ancients there was an absolute vertical with reference to which the oblique was defined, so there is an absolute human type, the masculine. Woman has ovaries, a uterus; these peculiarities imprison her in her subjectivity, circumscribe her within the limits of her own nature. It is often said that she thinks with her glands. Man superbly ignores the fact that his anatomy also includes glands, such as testicles, and that they secrete hormones. He thinks of his body as a direct and normal connection with the world, which he believes he apprehends objectively, whereas he regards the body of woman as a hindrance, a prison, weighed down by everything peculiar to it. "The female is a female by virtue of a certain *lack* of qualities," said Aristotle; "we should regard the female nature as afflicted with a natural defectiveness." And St. Thomas for his part pronounced woman to be an "imperfect man," an "incidental" being. This is symbolized in Genesis where Eve is depicted as made from what Bossuet called "a supernumerary bone" of Adam.

Thus humanity is male and man defines woman not in herself but as relative to him; she is not regarded as an autonomous being. Michelet writes: "Woman, the relative being. . . ." And Benda is most positive in his *Rapport d'Uriel*: "The body of man makes sense in itself quite apart from that of woman, whereas the latter seems wanting in significance by itself. . . . Man can think of himself without woman. She cannot think of herself without man." And she is simply what man decrees; thus she is called "the sex," by which is meant that she appears essentially to the male as a sexual being. For him she is sex—absolute sex, no less. She is defined and differentiated with reference to man and not he with reference to her; she is the incidental, the inessential as opposed to the essential. He is the Subject, he is the Absolute—she is the Other.

The category of the *Other* is as primordial as consciousness itself. In the most primitive societies, in the most ancient mythologies, one finds the expression of a duality—that of the Self and the Other. This duality was not originally attached to the division of the sexes; it was not dependent upon any empirical facts. It is revealed in such works as that of Granet on Chinese thought and those of Dumézil on the East Indies and Rome. The feminine element was at first no more involved in such pairs as Varuna-Mitra, Uranus-Zeus, Sun-Moon, and Day-Night than it was in the contrasts between Good and Evil, lucky and unlucky auspices, right and left, God and Lucifer. Otherness is a fundamental category of human thought.

Thus it is that no group ever sets itself up as the One without at once setting up the Other over against itself. If three travelers chance to occupy the same compartment, that is enough to make vaguely hostile "others" out of all the rest of the passengers on the train. In small-town eyes all persons not belonging to the village are "strangers" and suspect; to the native of a country all who inhabit other countries are "foreigners"; Jews are "different" for the anti-Semite, Negroes are "inferior" for American racists, aborigines are "natives" for colonists, proletarians are the "lower class" for the privileged.

Lévi-Strauss, at the end of a profound work on the various forms of primitive societies, reaches the following conclusion: "Passage from the state of Nature to the state of Culture is marked by man's ability to view biological relations as a series of contrasts; duality, alternation, opposition, and symmetry, whether under definite or vague forms, constitute not so much phenomena to be explained as fundamental and immediately given data of social reality."

These phenomena would be incomprehensible if in fact human society were simply a *Mitsein* or fellowship based on solidarity and friendliness. Things become clear, on the contrary, if, following Hegel, we find in consciousness itself a fundamental hostility toward every other consciousness; the subject can be posed only in being opposed—he sets himself up as the essential, as opposed to the other, the inessential, the object.

But the other consciousness, the other ego, sets up a reciprocal claim. The native traveling abroad is shocked to find himself in turn regarded as a "stranger" by the natives of neighboring countries. As a matter of fact, wars, festivals, trading, treaties, and contests among tribes, nations, and classes tend to deprive the concept *Other* of its absolute sense and to make manifest its relativity; willy-nilly, individuals and groups are forced to realize the reciprocity of their relations. How is it, then, that this reciprocity has not been recognized between the sexes, that one of the contrasting terms is set up as the sole essential, denying any relativity in regard to its correlative and defining the latter as pure otherness? Why is it that women do not dispute male sovereignty? No subject will readily volunteer to become the object, the inessential; it is not the Other who, in defining himself as the Other, establishes the One. The Other is posed as such by the One in defining himself as the One. But if the Other is not to regain the status of being the One, he must be submissive enough to accept this alien point of view. Whence comes this submission in the case of woman?

There are, to be sure, other cases in which a certain category has been able to dominate another completely for a time. Very often this privilege depends upon inequality of numbers—the majority imposes its rule upon the minority or persecutes it. But women are not a minority, like the American Negroes or the Jews; there are as many women as men on earth. Again, the two groups concerned have often been originally independent; they may have been formerly unaware of each other's existence, or perhaps they recognized each other's autonomy. But a historical event has resulted in the subjugation of the weaker by the stronger. The scattering of the

Jews, the introduction of slavery into America, the conquests of imperialism are examples in point. In these cases the oppressed retained at least the memory of former days; they possessed in common a past, a tradition, sometimes a religion or a culture.

The parallel drawn by Bebel between women and the proletariat is valid in that neither ever formed a minority or a separate collective unit of mankind. And instead of a single historical event it is in both cases a historical development that explains their status as a class and accounts for the membership of *particular individuals* in that class. But proletarians have not always existed, whereas there have always been women. They are women in virtue of their anatomy and physiology. Throughout history they have always been subordinated to men, and hence their dependency is not the result of a historical event or a social change—it was not something that *occurred*. The reason why otherness in this case seems to be an absolute is in part that it lacks the contingent or incidental nature of historical facts. A condition brought about at a certain time can be abolished at some other time, as the Negroes of Haiti and others have proved; but it might seem that a natural condition is beyond the possibility of change. In truth, however, the nature of things is no more immutably given, once for all, than is historical reality. If woman seems to be the inessential which never becomes the essential, it is because she herself fails to bring about this change. Proletarians say "We"; Negroes also. Regarding themselves as subjects, they transform the bourgeois, the whites, into "others." But women do not say "We," except at some congress of feminists or similar formal demonstration; men say "women," and women use the same word in referring to themselves. They do not authentically assume a subjective attitude. The proletarians have accomplished the revolution in Russia, the Negroes in Haiti, the Indo-Chinese are battling for it in Indo-China; but the women's effort has never been anything more than a symbolic agitation. They have gained only what men have been willing to grant; they have taken nothing, they have only received.

The reason for this is that women lack concrete means for organizing themselves into a unit which can stand face to face with the correlative unit. They have no past, no history, no religion of their own; and they have no such solidarity of work and interest as that of the proletariat. They are not even promiscuously herded together in the way that creates community feeling among the American Negroes, the ghetto Jews, the workers of Saint-Denis, or the factory hands of Renault. They live dispersed among the males, attached through residence, housework, economic condition, and social standing to certain men—fathers or husbands—more firmly than they are to other women. If they belong to the bourgeoisie, they feel solidarity with men of that class, not with proletarian women; if they are white, their allegiance is to white men, not to Negro women. The proletariat can propose to massacre the ruling class, and a sufficiently fanatical Jew or Negro might dream of getting sole possession of the atomic bomb and making humanity wholly Jewish or black; but women cannot even dream of exterminating the males. The bond that unites her to her oppressors is not comparable to any other. The division of the sexes is a biological fact, not an event in human history. Male and female stand opposed within a primordial *Mitsein,* and woman has not broken it. The couple is a fundamental unity with its two halves riveted together, and the cleavage of society along the line of sex is impossible. Here is to be found the basic trait of woman: she is the Other in a totality of which the two components are necessary to one another.

One could suppose that this reciprocity might have facilitated the liberation of woman. When Hercules sat at the feet of Omphale and helped with her spinning, his desire for her held him captive; but why did she fail to gain a lasting power? To revenge herself on Jason, Medea killed their children; and this grim legend would seem to suggest that she might have obtained a formidable influence over him through his love for his offspring. In *Lysistrata* Aristophanes gaily depicts a band of women who joined forces to gain social ends through the sexual needs of their men; but this is only a play. In the legend of the Sabine women, the latter soon abandoned their plan of remaining sterile to punish their ravishers. In truth woman has not been socially emancipated through man's need— sexual desire and the desire for offspring—which makes the male dependent for satisfaction upon the female.

Master and slave, also, are united by a reciprocal need, in this case economic, which does not liberate the slave. In the relation of master to slave the master does not make a point of the need that he has for the other; he has in his grasp the power of satisfying this need through his own action; whereas the slave, in his dependent condition, his hope and fear, is quite conscious of the need he has for his master. Even if the need is at bottom equally urgent for both, it always works in favor of the oppressor and against the oppressed. That is why the liberation of the working class, for example, has been slow.

Now, woman has always been man's dependent, if not his slave; the two sexes have never shared the world in equality. And even today woman is heavily handicapped, though her situation is beginning to change. Almost nowhere is her legal status the same as man's, and frequently it is much to her disadvantage. Even when her rights are legally recognized in the abstract, long-standing custom prevents their full expression in the mores. In the economic sphere men and women can almost be said to make up two castes; other things being equal, the former hold the better jobs, get higher wages, and have more opportunity for success than their new competitors. In industry and politics men have a great many more positions and they monopolize the most important posts. In addition to all this, they enjoy a traditional prestige that the education of children tends in every way to support, for the present enshrines the past—and in the past all history has been made by men. At the present time, when women are beginning to take part in the affairs of the world, it is still a world that belongs to men— they have no doubt of it at all and women have scarcely any. To decline to be the Other, to refuse to be a party to the deal—this would be for women to renounce all the advantages conferred upon them by their alliance with the superior caste. Man-the-sovereign will provide woman-the-liege with material protection and will undertake the moral justification of her existence; thus she can evade at once both economic risk and the metaphysical risk of a liberty in which ends and aims must be contrived without assistance. Indeed, along with the ethical urge of each individual to affirm his subjective existence, there is also the temptation to forgo liberty and become a thing. This is an inauspicious road, for he who takes it—passive, lost, ruined—becomes henceforth the creature of another's will, frustrated in his transcendence and deprived of every value. But it is an easy road; on it one avoids the strain involved in undertaking an authentic existence. When man makes of woman the *Other*, he may, then, expect her to manifest deep-seated tendencies toward complicity. Thus, woman may fail to lay claim to the status of subject because she lacks definite resources, because she feels the necessary bond that ties her to man regardless of reciprocity, and because she is often very well pleased with her role as the *Other*.

But it will be asked at once: how did all this begin? It is easy to see that the duality of the sexes, like any duality, gives rise to conflict. And doubtless the winner will assume the status of absolute. But why should man have won from the start? It seems possible that women could have won the victory; or that the outcome of the conflict might never have been decided. How is it that this world has always belonged to the men and that things have begun to change only recently? Is this change a good thing? Will it bring about an equal sharing of the world between men and women?

These questions are not new, and they have often been answered. But the very fact that woman *is the Other* tends to cast suspicion upon all the justifications that men have ever been able to provide for it. These have all too evidently been dictated by men's interest. A little-known feminist of the seventeenth century, Poulain de la Barre, put it this way: "All that has been written about women by men should be suspect, for the men are at once judge and party to the lawsuit." Everywhere, at all times, the males have displayed their satisfaction in feeling that they are the lords of creation. "Blessed be God . . . that He did not make me a woman," say the Jews in their morning prayers, while their wives pray on a note of resignation: "Blessed be the Lord, who created me according to His will." The first among the blessings for which Plato thanked the gods was that he had been created free, not enslaved; the second, a man, not a woman. But the males could not enjoy this privilege fully unless they believed it to be founded on the absolute and the eternal; they sought to make the fact of their supremacy into a right. "Being men, those who have made and compiled the laws have favored their own sex, and jurists have elevated these laws into principles," to quote Poulain de la Barre once more.

Legislators, priests, philosophers, writers, and scientists have striven to show that the subordinate position of woman is willed in heaven and advantageous on earth. The religions invented by men reflect this wish for domination. In the legends of Eve and Pandora men have taken up arms against women. They have made use of philosophy and theology, as the quotations from Aristotle and St. Thomas have shown. Since ancient times satirists and moralists have delighted in showing up the weaknesses of women. We are familiar with the savage indictments hurled against women throughout French literature. Montherlant, for example, follows the tradition of Jean de Meung, though with less gusto. This hostility may at times be well founded, often it is gratuitous; but in truth it more or less successfully conceals a desire for self-justification. As Montaigne says, "It is easier to accuse one sex than to excuse the other." Sometimes what is going on is clear enough. For instance, the Roman law limiting the rights of woman cited "the imbecility, the instability of the sex" just when the weakening of family ties seemed to threaten the interests of male heirs. And in the effort to keep the married woman under guardianship, appeal was made in the sixteenth century to the authority of St. Augustine, who declared that "woman is a creature neither decisive nor constant," at a time when the single woman was thought capable of managing her property. Montaigne understood clearly how arbitrary and unjust was woman's appointed lot: "Women are not in the wrong when they decline to accept the rules laid down for them, since the men make these rules without consulting them. No wonder intrigue and strife abound." But he did not go so far as to champion their cause.

It was only later, in the eighteenth century, that genuinely democratic men began to view the matter objectively. Diderot, among others, strove to show that woman is, like man, a human being. Later John Stuart Mill came fervently to her defense. But these philosophers displayed unusual impartiality. In the nineteenth century the feminist quarrel became again a quarrel of partisans. One of the consequences of the industrial revolution was the entrance of women into productive labor, and it was just here that the claims of the feminists emerged from the realm of theory and acquired an economic basis, while their opponents became the more aggressive. Although landed property lost power to some extent, the bourgeoisie clung to the old morality that found the guarantee of private property in the solidity of the family. Woman was ordered back into the home the more harshly as her emancipation became a real menace. Even within the working class the men endeavored to restrain woman's liberation, because they began to see the women as dangerous competitors—the more so because they were accustomed to work for lower wages.

In proving woman's inferiority, the antifeminists then began to draw not only upon religion, philosophy, and theology, as before, but also science—biology, experimental psychology, etc. At most they were willing to grant "equality in difference" to the *other* sex. That profitable formula is most significant; it is precisely like the "equal but separate" formula of the Jim Crow laws aimed at the North American Negroes. As is well known, this so-called equalitarian segregation has resulted only in the most extreme discrimination. The similarity just noted is in no way due to chance, for whether it is a race, a caste, a class, or a sex that is reduced to a position of inferiority, the methods of justification are the same. "The eternal feminine" corresponds to "the black soul" and to "the Jewish character." True, the Jewish problem is on the whole very different from the other two—to the anti-Semite the Jew is not so much an inferior as he is an enemy for whom there is to be granted no place on earth, for whom annihilation is the fate desired. But there are deep similarities between the situation of woman and that of the Negro. Both are being emancipated today from a like paternalism, and the former master class wishes to "keep them in their place"—that is, the place chosen for them. In both cases the former masters lavish more or less sincere eulogies, either on the virtues of "the good Negro" with his dormant, childish, merry soul —the submissive Negro—or on the merits of the woman who is "truly feminine"—that is, frivolous, infantile, irresponsible—the submissive woman. In both cases the dominant class bases its argument on a state of affairs that it has itself created. As George Bernard Shaw puts it, in substance, "The American white relegates the black to the rank of shoeshine boy; and he concludes from this that the black is good for nothing but shining shoes." This vicious circle is met with in all analogous circumstances; when an individual (or a group of individuals) is kept in a situation of inferiority, the fact is that he *is* inferior. But the significance of the verb *to be* must be rightly understood here; it is in bad faith to give it a static value when it really has the dynamic Hegelian sense of "to have become." Yes, women on the whole *are* today inferior to men; that is, their situation affords them fewer possibilities. The question is: should that state of affairs continue?

Many men hope that it will continue; not all have given up the battle. The conservative bourgeoisie still see in the emancipation of women a menace to their morality and their interests. Some men dread feminine competition. Recently a male student wrote in the *Hebdo-Latin*: "Every woman student who goes into medicine or law robs us of a job." He never questioned his rights in this world. And economic interests are not the only ones concerned. One of the benefits that oppression confers upon the oppressors is that the most humble among them is made to *feel* superior; thus, a "poor white" in the South can console himself with the thought that he is not a "dirty nigger"—and the more prosperous whites cleverly exploit this pride.

Similarly, the most mediocre of males feels himself a demigod as compared with women. It was much easier for M. de Montherlant to think himself a hero when he faced women (and women chosen for his purpose) than when he was obliged to act the man among men—something many women have done better than he, for that matter. And in September 1948, in one of his articles in the *Figaro littéraire,* Claude Mauriac—whose great originality is admired by all—could write regarding woman: "We listen on a tone [*sic!*] of polite indifference. . . . to the most brilliant among them, well knowing that her wit reflects more or less luminously ideas that come from *us*." Evidently the speaker referred to is not reflecting the ideas of Mauriac himself, for no one knows of his having any. It may be that she reflects ideas originating with men, but then, even among men there are those who have been known to appropriate ideas not their own; and one can well ask whether Claude Mauriac might not find more interesting a conversation reflecting Descartes, Marx, or Gide rather than himself. What is really remarkable is that by using the questionable *we* he identifies himself with St. Paul, Hegel, Lenin, and Nietzsche, and from the lofty eminence of their grandeur looks down disdainfully upon the bevy of women who make bold to converse with him on a footing of equality. In truth, I know of more than one woman who would refuse to suffer with patience Mauriac's "tone of polite indifference."

I have lingered on this example because the masculine attitude is here displayed with disarming ingenuousness. But men profit in many more subtle ways from the otherness, the alterity of woman. Here is miraculous balm for those afflicted with an inferiority complex, and indeed no one is more arrogant toward women, more aggressive or scornful, than the man who is anxious about his virility. Those who are not fear-ridden in the presence of their fellow men are much more disposed to recognize a fellow creature in woman; but even to these the myth of Woman, the Other, is precious for many reasons. They cannot be blamed for not cheerfully relinquishing all the benefits they derive from the myth, for they realize what they would lose in relinquishing woman as they fancy her to be, while they fail to realize what they have to gain from the woman of tomorrow. Refusal to pose oneself as the Subject, unique and absolute, requires great self-denial. Furthermore, the vast majority of men make no such claim explicitly. They do not *postulate* woman as inferior, for today they are too thoroughly imbued with the ideal of democracy not to recognize all human beings as equals.

In the bosom of the family, woman seems in the eyes of childhood and youth to be clothed in the same social dignity as the adult males. Later on, the young man, desiring and loving, experiences the resistance, the independence of the woman desired and loved; in marriage, he respects woman as wife and mother, and in the concrete events of conjugal life she stands there before him as a free being. He can therefore feel that social subordination as between the sexes no longer exists and that on the whole, in spite of differences, woman is an equal. As, however, he observes some points of inferiority—the most important being unfitness for the professions—he attributes these to natural causes. When he is in a co-operative and benevolent relation with woman, his theme is the principle of abstract equality, and he does not base his attitude upon such inequality as may exist. But when he is in conflict with her, the situation is reversed: his theme will be the existing inequality, and he will even take it as justification for denying abstract equality.

So it is that many men will affirm as if in good faith that women *are* the equals of man and that they have nothing to clamor for, while *at the same time* they will say that women can never be the equals of man and that their demands are in vain. It is, in point of fact, a difficult matter for man to realize the extreme importance of social discriminations which seem outwardly insignificant but which produce in woman moral and intellectual effects so profound that they appear to spring from her original nature. The most sympathetic of men never fully comprehend woman's concrete situation. And there is no reason to put much trust in the men when they rush to the defense of privileges whose full extent they can hardly measure. We shall not, then, permit ourselves to be intimidated by the number and violence of the attacks launched against women, nor to be entrapped by the self-seeking eulogies bestowed on the "true woman," nor to profit by the enthusiasm for woman's destiny manifested by men who would not for the world have any part of it.

We should consider the arguments of the feminists with no less suspicion, however, for very often their controversial aim deprives them of all real value. If the "woman question" seems trival, it is because masculine arrogance has made of it a "quarrel"; and when quarreling one no longer reasons well. People have tirelessly sought to prove that woman is superior, inferior, or equal to man. Some say that, having been created after Adam, she is evidently a secondary being; others say on the contrary that Adam was only a rough draft and that God succeeded in producing the human being in perfection when He created Eve. Woman's brain is smaller; yes, but it is relatively larger. Christ was made a man; yes, but perhaps for his greater humility. Each argument at once suggests its opposite, and both are often fallacious. If we are to gain understanding, we must get out of these ruts; we must discard the vague notions of superiority, inferiority, equality which have hitherto corrupted every discussion of the subject and start afresh.

Very well, but just how shall we pose the question? And, to begin with, who are we to propound it at all? Man is at once judge and party to the case; but so is woman. What we need is an angel— neither man nor woman—but where shall we find one? Still, the angel would be poorly qualified to speak, for an angel is ignorant of all the basic facts involved in the problem. With a hermaphrodite we should be no better off, for here the situation is most peculiar; the hermaphrodite is not really the combination of a whole man and a whole woman, but consists of parts of each and thus is neither. It looks to me as if there are, after all, certain women who are best qualified to elucidate the situation of woman. Let us not be misled by the sophism that because Epimenides was a Cretan he was necessarily a liar; it is not a mysterious essence that compels men and women to act in good or in bad faith, it is their situation that inclines them more or less toward the search for truth. Many of today's women, fortunate in the restoration of all the privileges pertaining to the estate of the human being, can afford the luxury of impartiality—we even recognize its necessity. We are no longer like our partisan elders; by and large we have won the game. In recent debates on the status of women the United Nations has persistently maintained that the equality of the sexes is now becoming a reality, and already some of us have never had to sense in our femininity an inconvenience or an obstacle. Many problems appear to us to be more pressing than those which concern us in particular, and this detachment even allows us to hope that our attitude will be objective. Still, we know the feminine world more intimately than do the men because we have our roots in it, we grasp more immediately than do men what it means to a human being to be feminine; and we are more concerned with such knowledge. I have said that there are more pressing problems, but this does not prevent us from seeing some importance in asking how the fact of being women will affect our lives. What opportunities precisely have been given us and what withheld? What fate awaits our younger sisters, and what directions should they take? It is significant that books by women on women are in general animated in our day less by a wish to demand our rights than by an effort toward clarity and understanding. As we emerge from an era of excessive controversy, this book is offered as one attempt among others to confirm that statement.

But it is doubtless impossible to approach any human problem with a mind free from bias. The way in which questions are put, the points of view assumed, presuppose a relativity of interest; all characteristics imply values, and every objective description, so called, implies an ethical background. Rather than attempt to conceal principles more or less definitely implied, it is better to state them openly at the beginning. This will make it unnecessary to specify on every page in just what sense one uses such words as *superior, inferior, better, worse, progress, reaction,* and the like. If we survey some of the works on woman, we note that one of the points of view most frequently adopted is that of the public good, the general interest; and one always means by this the benefit of society as one wishes it to be maintained or established. For our part, we hold that the only public good is that which assures the private good of the citizens; we shall pass judgment on institutions according to their effectiveness in giving concrete opportunities to indivduals. But we do not confuse the idea of private interest with that of happiness, although that is another common point of view. Are not women of the harem more happy than women voters? Is not the housekeeper happier than the working-woman? It is not too clear just what the word *happy* really means and still less what true values it may mask. There is no possibility of measuring the happiness of others, and it is always easy to describe as happy the situation in which one wishes to place them.

In particular those who are condemned to stagnation are often pronounced happy on the pretext that happiness consists in being at rest. This notion we reject, for our perspective is that of existentialist ethics. Every subject plays his part as such specifically through exploits or projects that serve as a mode of transcendence; he achieves liberty only through a continual reaching out toward other liberties. There is no justification for present existence other than expansion into an indefinitely open future. Every time transcendence falls back into immanence, stagnation, there is a degradation of existence into the *"en-soi"*—the brutish life of subjection to given conditions—and of liberty into constraint and contingence.

This downfall represents a moral fault if the subject consents to it; if it is inflicted upon him, it spells frustration and oppression. In both cases it is an absolute evil. Every individual concerned to justify his existence feels that his existence involves an undefined need to transcend himself, to engage in freely chosen projects.

Now, what peculiarly signalizes the situation of woman is that she—a free and autonomous being like all human creatures—nevertheless finds herself living in a world where men compel her to assume the status of the Other. They propose to stabilize her as object and to doom her to immanence since her transcendence is to be overshadowed and forever transcended by another ego (*conscience*) which is essential and sovereign. The drama of woman lies in this conflict between the fundamental aspirations of every subject (ego)—who always regards the self as the essential—and the compulsions of a situation in which she is the inessential. How can a human being in woman's situation attain fulfillment? What roads are open to her? Which are blocked? How can independence be recovered in a state of dependency? What circumstances limit woman's liberty and how can they be overcome? These are the fundamental questions on which I would fain throw some light. This means that I am interested in the fortunes of the individual as defined not in terms of happiness but in terms of liberty.

Quite evidently this problem would be without significance if we were to believe that woman's destiny is inevitably determined by physiological, psychological, or economic forces. Hence I shall discuss first of all the light in which woman is viewed by biology, psychoanalysis, and historical materialism. Next I shall try to show exactly how the concept of the "truly feminine" has been fashioned —why woman has been defined as the Other—and what have been the consequences from man's point of view. Then from woman's point of view I shall describe the world in which women must live; and thus we shall be able to envisage the difficulties in their way as, endeavoring to make their escape from the sphere hitherto assigned them, they aspire to full membership in the human race.

BOURGEOIS MARRIAGE

Although it incorporated faulty anthropological assertions (i.e., that there was a stage of "original promiscuity" which historically preceded the development of the monogamous form of family life), the Marxist approach to the family has exerted some considerable influence in the worldwide trend toward improving the material and social position of the married woman.

Since Marxian theorists have usually attributed all family problems (as indeed all social problems) to capitalism, it proved most convenient to view the bourgeois family as unnatural and artificial. Once further anthropological research had demonstrated the untenability of the promiscuity theory, the Marxist could no longer claim any special historical support for his assertions that the monogamous union was unnatural. Nonetheless, Marxian objections to woman's situation in the conventional family persisted, and these objections have strongly influenced public policy measures in Communist societies. Although modern Communist family policies (in Russia, for example) have vacillated between condemnation and encouragement of family life, the insistence on equality of the sexes has remained a constant element over the years.

Bourgeois Marriage

FRIEDRICH ENGELS

Nowadays there are two ways of concluding a bourgeois marriage. In Catholic countries the parents, as before, procure a suitable wife for their young bourgeois son, and the consequence is, of course, the fullest development of the contradiction inherent in monogamy: the husband abandons himself to hetaerism and the wife to adultery. Probably the only reason why the Catholic Church abolished divorce was because it had convinced itself that there is no more a cure for adultery than there is for death. In Protestant countries, on the other hand, the rule is that the son of a bourgeois family is allowed to choose a wife from his own class with more or less freedom; hence there may be a certain element of love in the marriage, as, indeed, in accordance with Protestant hypocrisy, is always assumed, for decency's sake. Here the husband's hetaerism is a more sleepy kind of business, and adultery by the wife is less the rule. But since, in every kind of marriage, people remain what they were before, and since the bourgeois of Protestant countries are mostly philistines, all that this Protestant monogamy achieves, taking the average of the best cases, is a conjugal partnership of leaden boredom, known as "domestic bliss." The best mirror of these two methods of marrying is the novel—the French novel for the Catholic manner, the German for the Protestant. In both, the hero "gets" them: in the German, the young man gets the girl; in the French, the husband gets the horns. Which of them is worse off is sometimes questionable. This is why the French bourgeois is as much horrified by the dullness of the German novel as the

Reprinted from Friedrich Engels, *The Origin of the Family, Private Property, and the State* (New York: International Publishers, 1942), pp. 62-66. (First published in 1884; first English translation in 1920).

German philistine is by the "immorality" of the French. However, now that "Berlin is a world capital," the German novel is beginning with a little less timidity to use as part of its regular stock-in-trade the hetaerism and adultery long familiar to that town.

In both cases, however, the marriage is conditioned by the class position of the parties and is to that extent always a marriage of convenience. In both cases this marriage of convenience turns often enough into crassest prostitution—sometimes of both partners, but far more commonly of the woman, who only differs from the ordinary courtesan in that she does not let out her body on piece-work as a wage-worker, but sells it once and for all into slavery. And of all marriages of convenience Fourier's words hold true: "As in grammar two negatives make an affirmative, so in matrimonial morality two prostitutes pass for a virtue." Sex-love in the relationship with a woman becomes, and can only become, the real rule among the oppressed classes, which means today among the proletariat—whether this relation is officially sanctioned or not. But here all the foundations of typical monogamy are cleared away. Here there is no property, for the preservation and inheritance of which monogamy and male supremacy were established; hence there is no incentive to make this male supremacy effective. What is more, there are no means of making it so. Bourgeois law, which protects this supremacy, exists only for the possessing class and their dealings with the proletarians. The law costs money and, on account of the worker's poverty, it has no validity for his relation to his wife. Here quite other personal and social conditions decide. And now that large-scale industry has taken the wife out of the home onto the labor market and into the factory, and made her often the bread-winner of the family, no basis for any kind of male supremacy is left in the proletarian household—except, perhaps, for something of the brutality towards women that has spread since the introduction of monogamy. The proletarian family is therefore no longer monogamous in the strict sense, even where there is passionate love and firmest loyalty on both sides, and maybe all the blessings of religious and civil authority. Here, therefore, the eternal attendants of monogamy, hetaerism and adultery, play only an almost vanishing part. The wife has in fact regained the right to dissolve the marriage, and if two people cannot get on with one another, they prefer to separate. In short, proletarian marriage is monogamous in the etymological sense of the word, but not at all in its historical sense.

Our jurists, of course, find that progress in legislation is leaving women with no further ground of complaint. Modern civilized systems of law increasingly acknowledge, first, that for a marriage to be legal, it must be a contract freely entered into by both partners, and, secondly, that also in the married state both partners must stand on a common footing of equal rights and duties. If both these demands are consistently carried out, say the jurists, women have all they can ask.

This typically legalistic method of argument is exactly the same as that which the radical republican bourgeois uses to put the proletarian in his place. The labor contract is to be freely entered into by both partners. But it is considered to have been freely entered into as soon as the law makes both parties equal on *paper*. The power conferred on the one party by the difference of class position, the pressure thereby brought to bear on the other party—the real economic position of both—that is not the law's business. Again, for the duration of the labor contract both parties are to have equal rights, in so far as one or the other does not expressly surrender them. That economic relations compel the worker to surrender even the last semblance of equal rights—here again, that is no concern of the law.

In regard to marriage, the law, even the most advanced, is fully satisfied as soon as the partners have formally recorded that they are entering into the marriage of their own free consent. What goes on in real life behind the juridical scenes, how this free consent comes about—that is not the business of the law and the jurist. And yet the most elementary comparative jurisprudence should show the jurist what this free consent really amounts to. In the countries where an obligatory share of the paternal inheritance is secured to the children by law and they cannot therefore be disinherited—in Germany, in the countries with French law and elsewhere—the children are obliged to obtain their parents' consent to their marriage. In the countries with English law, where parental consent to a marriage is not legally required, the parents on their side have full freedom in the testamentary disposal of their property and can disinherit their children at their pleasure. It is obvious that, in spite and precisely because of this fact, freedom of marriage among the classes with something to inherit is in reality not a whit greater in England and America than it is in France and Germany.

As regards the legal equality of husband and wife in marriage, the position is no better. The legal inequality of the two partners, bequeathed to us from earlier social conditions, is not the cause but the effect of the economic oppression of the woman. In the old communistic household, which comprised many couples and their children, the task entrusted to the women of managing the household was as much a public and socially necessary industry as the procuring of food by the men. With the patriarchal family, and still more with the single monogamous family, a change came. Household management lost its public character. It no longer concerned society. It became a *private service*; the wife became the head servant, excluded from all participation in social production. Not until the coming of modern large-scale industry was the road to social production opened to her again—and then only to the proletarian wife. But it was opened in such a manner that, if she carries out her duties in the private service of her family, she remains excluded from public production and unable to earn; and if she wants to take part in public production and earn independently, she cannot carry out family duties. And the wife's position in the factory is the position of women in all branches of business, right up to medicine and the law. The modern individual family is founded on the open or concealed domestic slavery of the wife, and modern society is a mass composed of these individual families as its molecules.

In the great majority of cases today, at least in the possessing classes, the husband is obliged to earn a living and support his family, and that in itself gives him a position of supremacy, without any need for special legal titles and privileges. Within the family he is the bourgeois and the wife represents the proletariat. In the industrial world, the specific character of the economic oppression burdening the proletariat is visible in all its sharpness only when all special legal privileges of the capitalist class have been abolished and complete legal equality of both classes established. The democratic republic does not do away with the opposition of the two classes; on the contrary, it provides the clear field on which the fight can be fought out. And in the same way, the peculiar character of the supremacy of the husband over the wife in the modern family, the necessity of creating real social equality between them, and the way to do it, will only be seen in the clear light of day when both possess legally complete equality of rights. Then it will be plain that the first condition for the liberation of the wife is to bring the whole female sex back into public industry, and that this in turn demands the abolition of the monogamous family as the economic unit of society.

FEMALE INTELLIGENCE: WHO WANTS IT?

We are today, in the United States, just beginning to realize that failure to take advantage of the working power of our female population constitutes significant neglect of a major national resource. Actually more American women are in the labor force now than ever before. By comparison with certain other countries, however, females here are heavily concentrated within a rather narrow range of job categories (e.g., secretarial and clerical work, school teaching, nursing, etc). And, by and large, women are not in this country encouraged to aim at executive and managerial careers or to enter the traditional professions—such as law and medicine. The activity of women in government also is relatively slight.

Even where women do engage in full-time productive employment outside the home, men and women rarely work in a real spirit of equality. As Miss Mannes points out in this article, American men give every indication of not wanting their women to be occupational and intellectual equals. Whether men actually are afraid of the competition such equality would entail is uncertain. In any case, however, there is little doubt that the days in which the college-educated woman was willing to play down her intellectual interests or qualities are rapidly drawing to a close.

Female Intelligence: Who Wants It?

MARYA MANNES

Every now and then there is a resounding call for a national re-source—largely untapped and unmustered—referred to as the intelligence of women, or the female brain. Editorial writers, tired of outer space, say that if we are to win the race of survival and keep up with the Russians we must not squander this precious resource but rather press it into service.

Commenting on the number of women doctors, engineers, phys-icists and laboratory technicians in the Soviet Union compared to our paltry own, citing the desperate shortages in fields where productive intellect is essential, they cry: "To the drawing-board, to the laboratories, to the computers!" And presidents of women's colleges beseech their students: "Use this brain you've got and we're training: society needs it!"

Gratifying though it may be to have the female intelligence not only publicly acknowledged but officially sought, these calls are met by a massive wave of indifference emanating from women even more than from men. We do not really believe either the acknowl-edgment or the demand for the kind of intelligence they speak of and claim they want, nor do we see any signs of a public attitude which would make its application either welcome or practical on a national scale.

The college presidents, the editorialists, the recruiters of re-sources are talking not of the intelligence which every woman needs to be a successful wife and mother or even a competent worker in office or factory or civic affairs. They are talking of the kind of free and independent intelligence which can analyze,

Reprinted by permission from *The New York Times Magazine*, January 3, 1960. Copyright by *The New York Times*.

innovate and create: the mind of the scientist and the artist, at liberty to roam in the world of abstractions and intangibles until, by will and effort, a concrete and tangible pattern is made clear.

Are women capable of this kind of intelligence? If they are not to the degree of genius—and the long history of man has produced no female Bachs or Shakespeares or Leonardos or Galileos—and although Madame Curie is in lonely company, women have in every time given to the mainstream of the arts, letters and sciences. And when even a Jesuit priest-sociologist, Father Lucius F. Cervantes—whose recent book "And God Made Man and Woman" is a long and satisfied reiteration of the sacred differences between the two sexes—writes, "As far as has been ascertained there is no inherent intellectual capacity differential between men and women," then surely women are not by nature denied the ability to think creatively and abstractly.

It is rather that this ability is unpopular with women because it is unpopular with men. Our prior need, in short, is to be loved. And if the possession of this kind of intelligence is a deterrent to love, then it is voluntarily restricted or denied by women themselves.

I have seen enough of this deterrence and this denial, since my youth, to believe it the common experience. And although it has not always been mine (I am fortunate in a happy marriage), I recognize only too well the signal of alarm in the eyes of men when a woman of intellect challenges their own.

It flashed even before I recognized it: boys at dances would forsake me soon for others, not—in Marty's language—because I was a "dog," but because I talked to them of sonnets or senses instead of about themselves. Used to a family where ideas were as much a part of the dinner table as food, I knew of no special kind of talk geared to men rather than to women. Worse, I thought that to be interesting one had to say interesting things. This was possibly the greatest miscalculation since the Charge of the Light Brigade.

For most men, I duly discovered, prefer the woman whose interest lies not in her thoughts nor her speech nor her talents, but in her interest in them. Mind, they believe, interferes with this attention, and to some extent they are right. Right or wrong, the average American male is uneasy in the presence of markedly intelligent women; and the woman who wishes to change this unease into love must spend a good part of her life reining in her wits in the reluctant admission that they do her more harm than good.

Now there is a great paradox in all this. On the one hand, more girls go to college than ever before, and more colleges are equipped to develop their minds toward whatever intellectual goals they might aspire to. On the other hand, as President Thomas C. Mendenhall of Smith College recently—and sharply—deplored, there is a 60 per cent dropout of women students before graduation and most of this is due to their early marriage and almost immediate proliferation of the species.

In an open forum recently, I asked Millicent C. McIntosh, president of Barnard, and Dr. George N. Shuster of Hunter what they considered the purpose of higher education for women if they left the campus in droves for a career of total domesticity. Their answer, roughly, was this: "Our main aim is to turn out women who can apply a trained intelligence to the problems of daily living, and whose intellectual resources can enrich their lives and those of their children."

They agreed that only a small proportion of girls manifested a genuine drive toward intellectual excellence, or a sustained dedication necessary to the mastery of any art or science, and they deplored this. But the shared opinion seemed to be that a girl who went to college would not only be a more intelligent wife and mother than the girl who did not, but that in later life and increased freedom she could draw on greater reserves of mind and spirit.

And yet an English teacher at one of the Eastern universities said: "There is a terrible waste here. I've taught girls with as much, if not more, talent than many of the boys I've had in my classes: first-class writers and thinkers. And what do they do when they leave here? Work? Not on your life. They marry and have four children, and that's that."

The argument, widely used, that a woman so trained can always return to her field when her children are grown and her time is her own, is specious, to say the least. In the sciences, if not in the arts, advances in theory and techniques are so rapid that a fifteen-year gap becomes unbreachable. Quite apart from that, the muscle of intellect degenerates with lack of use. The servantless young mother with small children has not the time, the place or the isolation necessary for any orderly process of thought or any sustained practice of the imagination.

Yet society—including most of the young women involved in this early and long domesticity—does not consider this condition even remotely tragic. On the contrary, there appears to be widespread approval of the return of women from the spurious and aggressive "independence" of their mothers to their prime function as the creators and guardians of the family.

Young girls themselves in countless numbers have chosen the security and closeness of a full household rather than the lonely road of individual fulfillment as creative identities. And although many young women work out of the home before and even after marriage, it is less for love of work than for love of a home in which a standard of living is more important than a standard of thinking.

Only a few seem to work because of an urgent need to be for once—if only part of every day—out of context and into their own skin, applying their intelligence singly toward matters not concerned with their personal lives.

Even this need, usually condoned for economic reasons ("She has to work to make ends meet") is criticized by those professionally concerned with allocating roles to the sexes, as an evasion of woman's prime responsibility and an indication either of maladjustment or of a false sense of values. And, although the country is full of educators charged with the development of the female intelligence, every social pressure is exerted on women from their childhood on toward one goal: marriage—the earlier the better— and babies, the more the better. And the girl who feels that she has something to give beyond her natural functions as a wife and mother is lonely, indeed—pitied even when she succeeds.

If television drama serials and mass magazine fiction are any indication of the national temper, there is only one "right" fulfill- ment for all women. The "career woman" may be admired for her success, but her absorption in her work—whether it be medicine, law, letters or art—is a tacit admission of her lack of fulfillment as a woman. And even if she marries and bears children, the as- sumption prevails that both her husband and her offspring will suffer from her preoccupation with the world outside.

Many housewives may secretly long for their independence, but they are secure in the knowledge that their own absorption in the home and the community is a guarantee against a continual conflict of loyalties and, indeed, against the natural hostility of men; a resentment, however covert, against the competition of the kind of female intelligence which, precisely because of its independence, is still called "masculine."

If it is true that this kind of intelligence is undesirable to the majority of men, accustomed as they are to the "liberated" woman of today, what are the reasons?

I suspect that in the stormy sea of "equality," men are uncertain of the extent and nature of their dominance—if, indeed, they be- lieve in it—and that they need a constant reassurance of their superiority in one field at least, that of the creative intellect.

They need not look far to see that it is they who formulate na- tional policies, send rockets into space and govern the world of business, art and science. The challenge from women in these fields is still negligible, but it exists; a source of discomfort rather than satisfaction. And although many men are generous in their admiration of the few women who have achieved distinction in the laboratory or in letters or in scholarship, most men have no desire to be married to them. They take too much trouble.

And here we come, I think, to the root of the matter: a masculine laziness in the ways of love which inclines them to avoid rather than surmount this particular kind of challenge. It is far easier to choose the relaxed and compliant woman than one who makes demands on the intelligence. They may be intrigued by the brilliant woman, but they rarely want her for themselves.

For the qualities that form a creative intellect are hard to live with. The woman cursed with them can retain the love of men and the approval of society only if she is willing to modify and mute them as much as she can without reducing them to impotence. As one so cursed, however modestly, I herewith submit some hard-won suggestions:

I would counsel the woman of intellect to watch her wit. Though it need not be tinged with malice, it has of necessity an astringency which many people find disconcerting. In a bland society, the unsheathed dart can draw blood, if only from vanity. And after the tide of laughter at a woman's wit has ebbed, the wrack left in the public mind is a sort of malaise: "She has a sharp tongue" or "I wouldn't want to tangle with her."

Candor is a second danger. The woman who is honest with men is so at her own risk if this honesty requires either criticism or skepticism of their position. And if she has convictions opposed to those of the man she speaks with she will be wise to withhold them or speak them so softly that they sound like concurrence.

She must, above all, have no conviction that what she has to say is of importance, but train herself instead to listen quietly to men no more knowledgeable in a given subject than herself and, what is more, to defer to their judgment. This is not always easy, but a woman cannot afford the luxury of declarations, however pertinent, if she seeks—and what woman does not?—to attract.

A man who is intense or excited about his work can be highly attractive, but woe to the woman who is either. Most people cannot distinguish between the tiresome garrulity of a woman preoccupied with her affairs and the purely abstract passion of a woman concerned with the process of thought. A state of tension is inseparable from active intelligence, but it is socially unpermissible in women.

If such women are artists—and I use this to cover all forms of creative expression—and particularly if they have achieved any stature as such, they may have the attraction of rarity. There are even men who are mature enough and secure enough to cherish in them the capacity to create abstractly as well as biologically.

But they are rarer still, for the care and cultivation of an artist is a job that wives are trained for and few husbands want. The woman artist who has a husband and children must then, to quote Phyllis McGinley, have "three hands"—a mutation still infrequent but which the irradiation of women's minds may yet produce.

Is this irradiation really desirable? Are the full resources of the feminine intelligence really needed? And if they are to be mobilized for the national good, what is to be done about a climate of opinion satisfied with the overwhelming emphasis, on the part of the younger generation, on domesticity and large families? Do we need more babies or do we need more doctors and scientists and thinkers and innovators? Is it enough that we have a great pool of college graduates applying their intelligence to the problems of their homes and towns, or do we really need more women able to come to grips with the major issues of our time?

If we do, changes will have to be made, many of which may well be unattainable at this time. But if the nation's leaders really want and need this kind of woman, the opinion molders of the mass media will have to start right now giving her an honorable place in society, and men will have to start giving her an honorable place in their hearts as well as in their professions.

For one thing, parents with daughters who show a genuine intellectual talent and aspiration in any field should not feel compelled to enter her in the infantile mating-marathon that pushes a girl toward marriage from the age of 12 on. It should be possible for such a girl to prefer an exciting book to a dull date without the censure of her family or her peers, and to continue her training through her twenties without courting celibacy.

Much has been said about the new sense of responsibility shown by the young in their early acceptance of marriage and parenthood. But time may show that the cocoon of a large-familied home is—like that of a large corporation—the best protection from the loneliness of thought and a voluntary abdication of the burdens of personal freedom.

If a woman wishes to resume her chosen work after marriage and the bearing of children, there should be no stigma attached if she can afford to hire outside help for either home tasks or the care of the young. And we might begin to consider a pattern of community-supported nurseries which would permit the woman who cannot afford help to pursue her profession at least partially free from the continuous demands of child care.

A few months ago a delegation of Russian professional women visited this country, and one of them remarked in amazement at the lack of any such service. Our profusion of labor-saving gadgets did not, it seems, blind her eyes to the domestic entrapment of the young American woman.

As for college education, there should, I believe, be a division made between students merely marking time before marriage and girls seriously bent on a career or profession, confining the domestic-minded to a two-year course of liberal arts and reserving the four-year, degree-granting course for the latter. After these have graduated, their entrance into the laboratories and offices of the country should be made on the same basis as that for equally qualified men—not, that is, as an interim occupation but as a chosen, sustained career.

And here, of course, is where the woman herself must be prepared to pay a fairly high price. If work is important to her she cannot allow herself the luxury of a large family or the kind of man who insists on one. Nor can she afford the close, and often cozy, community huddle in which women share their domestic preoccupations daily with one another. She must be prepared to fight for the freedom she wants at the risk of loneliness and the denial of a number of things dear to any woman.

As for men, they will have to stop thinking in terms of competition and think in terms of alliance instead: the alliance of companion intellects toward similar goals. If they can bring themselves to consider women primarily as human beings, they will be able to treat them intellectually as men and emotionally as women. If they do that, they will find the brilliant woman surprisingly docile and far from unfeminine.

If, however, men continue to subscribe to the prevailing belief that the American heroine must never be too intelligent for her own good and their own comfort, the cry for female brains will go largely unheeded—unless a national emergency makes it clear that we have for years been wasting one of the resources on which our strength depends and which other civilizations are using to their advantage.

WIFE OF THE "HAPPY WORKER"

Studies of the American family have been rightly criticized for concentrating almost solely on the middle class. Likewise, the public debate about women having careers has rarely concerned itself with the situation of the working-class woman—whose activities tend to be determined largely by considerations of economic necessity. Her already considerable problems are often exacerbated by continual (sometimes unwanted) pregnancies; here we can see clearly the relation between family planning and general social roles. And when she does take a job, usually it is in order to supplement the meager family income. Her "role problems," then, are quite different from those of her middle-class counterpart; yet they are certainly no less compelling for her, nor are they any less significant from the standpoint of society at large.

There has been much celebration, both among the public at large and by certain economists and other social observers, of the high standard of living we have reached in this so-called "affluent society." It is quite likely that these economic advances have relatively little meaning for the overworked and underrewarded woman of the working class. The author of this article, a college professor who has also had direct personal experience in factory work and union activities, is an acute observer of working-class culture. Her essay may serve as an antidote against too exclusive a concern with the "strains" and "maladjustments" of those not subjected to the more pressing economic crises.

Wife of the "Happy Worker"

PATRICIA CAYO SEXTON

The myth of the American woman casts her in a cheery *Saturday Evening Post* portrait, presiding over the succulent roast, with smiling offspring reaching for their portions while the husband watches benevolently from the head of the table. The myth is pleasant but totally false when applied to the wife of the average worker.

No more accurate is the European male-inspired myth of the American woman as super-privileged, pampered by luxury and attention, dominating her husband and family, and spending most of her day flitting through the cocktail-club circuit. This may be a faithful portrait of some strata of American womanhood, but not of the worker's wife.

Her day's circuit is rarely concentric with the club and social rounds traveled by her middle-class counterpart. Instead of the Junior League, her concern is mainly with Junior and his unceasing demands on her energies. Instead of presiding over a PTA meeting, arranging a charity ball at the local yacht club, entertaining week-end guests, or even collecting signatures for Adlai Stevenson, she is busy with Junior's whooping cough, the week's ironing, the plugged sink, the wet pants, the runny nose, the pay check that can't cover expenses, the kids who won't stop yelling and fighting—and the husband who offers little affection or attention in payment for her drudgery.

In observing that "the mass of men lead lives of quiet desperation," Thoreau used the traditional masculine gender to submerge the feminine. Today even those intellectuals who believe in the

Reprinted from *The Nation,* August 6, 1960.

myth of the Happy Worker will have to admit that "quiet desperation" aptly describes the life of his wife.

The worker's wife belongs to one of the largest and (paradoxically, in view of its size) most neglected groups in our population. It is even larger than our Negro minority—about 18,300,000, compared with about 17,500,000 Negroes (many of whom can't even vote). But while the Negro's collective voice is coming through loud and clear these days, shaking up our whole pattern of society, the workingman's wife has no collective voice. Indeed, there is nothing "collective" about her; she is basically unorganized, a central quality of her life. She is neither a joiner—nor a participant. Though deeply religious, she is much less likely to attend church regularly than her middle-class counterpart, and still less likely to take a more than menial role in church affairs. Similarly, her PTA activity is relatively limited, and—most tragically—she is usually a stranger, sometimes suspicious and hostile, to her husband's union, the one organization that ought to have a natural interest in her potentialities.

She is typically, a harried housewife, lonely, worried about everything from the diaper wash to world cataclysm; and—above all—she is virtually isolated from life outside the confines of her family and neighborhood. In the sociologist's language, she is a "primary" group person living in a "secondary" group society.

She does not have time or money for club life and "entertaining"; worse, she seems to lack the inner resources—the self-direction, the confidence, the assertiveness, the will—to move about freely in the larger world. Though deeply resourceful in organizing her own household with limited means, she usually doesn't have the impulse, much less the know-how, to go outside her home for help—to set up neighborhood nursery groups, for example, in order to reduce her work load. She is almost helplessly dependent on the neighborhood folkways and mores—what "other people would think" and, especially, her husband.

The middle- to upper-class American wife is perhaps the best organized, the club-joiningest person around. Of the 11 million members of 15,000 women's clubs in this country, only a light sprinkling are the wives of workingmen. And, while the club woman may be vaguely dissatisfied with her life and may turn to the psychoanalyst's couch (or someone else's) for sufficient male attention, she at least has the resources to find occasional release from the confining grip of home and husband.

The lack of resources—financial, psychic and social—of the workingman's wife may account for the discovery recently made by a mental-hygiene survey (*Americans View Their Mental Health*) that she belongs to one of the two most discounted groups in our society—the other group being male clerks.

That the worker's wife is less than dutifully contented must be surprising information to many. Writers and scholars have done little to tip us off; while plotting almost every gesture of the club woman and the working woman, they have offered barely a foot-note to the inconspicuous and undemanding workingman's wife. Like other observers, they seem to look right through and past her to those women who can be seen and heard, whose influence on the national scene is unmistakable.

A new study, *Workingman's Wife* (Rainwater, Coleman and Handel), is one of the few exceptions to the rule. Regrettably, the study is a product of market-research sociology and, as such, its central purpose is commercial rather than scholarly; adding to this deficiency is a total absence of statistics against which the reader may check conclusions. Still, the study offers some unique and illuminating insights into this unknown woman:

Vitally dependent on her husband, emotionally and financially, the workingman's wife is inclined to see him as "insensitive and inconsiderate, sometimes teasing, sometimes accusing, sometimes vulgar, always potentially withholding affection." In their sexual relations, she often feels he treats her as an "object for his own personal gratification without the kind of tenderness she so much wants."

Typically, the only recreation she enjoys are TV and visits with neighbors and relatives.

She is largely alien to her husband's life and interests. Often, when he goes off hunting and fishing with the boys, she will not even share his vacation. Unlike the middle-class woman, she tends to place "low priority on recreation and vacations as things on which to spend money." Restricted to the house, more than one out of three have "never learned to drive a car" and would be hard pressed to find recreational outlets away from home.

While the middle-class wife generally has intimate knowledge of her husband's job and working life, conceiving her main job to be that of hostess to his friends and business associates, the workingman's wife sometimes knows nothing about her husband's work —what he does or even where his job is located—and rarely thinks of herself as a means of advancing her husband's career through excellence as a hostess and "contact-maker."

The worker's wife is likely to view the world as chaotic and to feel she has no power to shape her own life or the course of civic or world events.

She is more emotional than the middle-class woman and has deep-seated fears of loneliness. She is also more altruistic: "pity and sympathy for the unfortunate are among the most readily experienced emotions." She is more willing to forgive others for the mistakes they make. "Doing for others—whether it be their own families or their friends—is a major motivation for the working-class woman."

She is much more discontented with her financial status than is the middle-class woman, and has little confidence in the economic future, believing that her family's fortunes are at the mercy of conditions which she cannot in any way control. "Working-class women manifest a clear case of depression phobia." She is very savings-conscious, and would, in an ideal budget, allot 40 per cent more to savings than would the middle-class woman.

She is firmly opposed to installment buying, but has no alternative. Two-thirds of those interviewed were in installment debt and feeling guilty about it.

Her taste runs to "modern" in everything; she values appliances and modern furniture more than a big house in a good neighborhood—"an expensive-looking house is vaguely frightening to these women"; many reject the idea of living near "substantial people" on the basis that they would feel uncomfortable around people who are "high toned" and "uppity."

In clothing, the middle-class woman prefers the "natural look" while the working-class woman's choice of accessories often gives her a kind of "dime-store appearance." Expenditures on her children, the study concludes, give the worker's wife greatest satisfaction; expenditures on clothing for themselves is the most satisfying to middle-class women.

Organized labor, the group that touches her life most closely, has been grossly neglectful of the worker's wife.

Frequently, all the worker's wife knows about her husband's union is that it takes up a lot of his time, if he's active, and that it occasionally threatens to deprive her of the family pay-check. For her husband, the union can provide purpose and excitement; but while he is off attending a political-action caucus of a local, department or steering-committee meeting, she sits home, working and waiting, night after night, with only the TV, her kids and perhaps *True* magazine for company.

Only during strikes, when her support is a life-and-death issue, is any real effort made to set up communications with her. In strikes at J. I. Case, Ford of Canada and elsewhere, the disgruntled housewife—unmoved by union *élan*, uninformed about strike issues and without money to run her house—has sparked back-to-work movements. These efforts, lacking leadership and spirit, have usually failed, but the undercover effect of the non-union housewife on the holding power of her striking husband cannot be measured. Perhaps it is responsible for the settlement of many strikes short of victory.

Some union people feel that the worker's wife should be consulted before a strike is called; after all, the strike affects her just as deeply and depends as much on her for its success as it does on her husband. If her consent is needed to see the strike through, it should be solicited before the strike is called. Some women, of course, do not need selling; during almost every strike there are some eager union wives who serve in the soup kitchens and around the local hall without solicitation. For some of these women, the strike serves as an exciting relief from the monotony and the loneliness of their home routines.

Union men, it is said, do not recruit union wives because they are too busy with other things. This oversight, however, is more than a matter of preoccupation, for the union man all too frequently feels that a wife's place is at home, preferably in the kitchen, doing exactly what she *is* doing.

Except among younger union members, who are perhaps more enlightened and who have not yet fallen into a pattern of conflict with their wives, there is evidence of out-and-out resistance to efforts to recruit her support. To bring women into active union life represents an invasion of the workingman's last guarded treasure: the masculine world, the world of work, protest, rebellion— his only "social club" where some would, if they could, hang up a sign as in exclusive bars, For Men Only.

The workingman, the union man, is threatened by inexorable social forces over which even his powerful union has no direct control: automation, unemployment, layoffs. His own pleasures are few enough, and his fears are great and growing. Threatened to the saturation point, he will often, in anger and impotence, strike back at his wife.

In one of the most sensitive areas of his life—politics—the worker is as distrustful of the woman voter as he is of the woman driver. He still thinks "the women" put in Ike. The truth is that his wife votes the same ticket he does, with only fractional deviations. *When Labor Votes* (Kornhauser, Sheppard and Mayer) suggests that, among union members, more men than women voted for Ike (26 per cent of men and 19 per cent of women in the sample).

The truth is also, however, that these women often fail to cast any ballots at all on election day, simply because their voting strength has not been mobilized.

When women's auxiliaries are organized in the local union (there are several hundred in the country), the union man will often complain about an invasion of jurisdiction. If the women work on political action, they are transgressing on the work of the union's political committee; if they delve into community problems, they are duplicating the function of the community-services committee. And so it goes.

In cases known to the writer, local officers have even insisted that successful political-action committees of union wives be broken up. Duplication of effort is the stated objection; the real explanations, perhaps, go deeper. Often when these women, with their bottled-up needs for expression, are let loose on an organization, they show an almost breath-taking eagerness for activity. Again, this kind of super-charged enthusiasm is threatening to men who have enough problems as it is.

These women, normally shy, even tongue-tied, in mixed meetings, very often lose all speech inhibitions in women's groups. On such occasions, they may even be more outspoken than their mates.

Also, because their approach to the labor union is less immediate, practical, job-centered than their husbands', they appear to be interested in a broader range of subjects. The underdeveloped nations, for example, are objects of real concern to the union wife— a product perhaps of her generous supply of "pity and sympathy for the unfortunate."

The final and most dangerous pitfall for the union wives' organizations is that, under pressure, these groups may become involved in local union elections. The result: headaches for the local and a misdirection of purpose for the wives.

None of these excuses are sufficient to justify the union's failure to mobilize the support and the enormous political potential of the union wife. The middle-class wife, through her frantic club activity, is an indispensable political support for her husband. Politically and otherwise, the workingman's wife is a cipher—a lonely, frightened, unhappy, frustrated cipher—and will remain so until the union, or some other group, decides that her potentialities are worth exploiting.

On the political front, the Woman's Activities Department of the AFL-CIO seems to be making some forward movement. On the research front, perhaps now that the market sociologists have begun to dig into the workingman's wife, other more disinterested scholars will continue the search.

THE EMPLOYED MOTHER IN THE U.S.S.R.

If most of the women in a society are to engage in full-time productive employment outside the home, numerous social adjustments are necessary. The society must afford women adequate education and training for such employment, numerous practical arrangements must be made (such as child-care facilities, confinement leaves for pregnant workers, etc.), and the attitudes of both men and women must be favorable to women's employment.

As the following article indicates, the Soviet Union has been fairly successful in making a number of these adjustments. Current Soviet policy seeks to maximize productive employment of women, while at the same time encouraging family life and motherhood. Success as regards the first goal can be seen in the large proportion of women working, the considerable range of occupations open to them, and the approving attitudes of Soviet citizens toward women working. As marriage counselor David Mace notes below, practical arrangements such as child care have also been handled fairly well—thus enabling the Soviet mother to work without undue worry about adequate supervision for her children. Mace's further conclusion—that male attitudes have not fully kept pace with these arrangements (since men still expect their women to take complete charge of all household tasks) —is an interesting one. It points up the significance of the attitudinal dimension, and, more important, underlines the fact that the "sexual revolution" implies changes for both sexes, not just for women.

The Employed Mother in the U.S.S.R.

DAVID R. MACE

"The Soviet Republic of Russia," said Lenin, "immediately swept away *all* legislative traces of the inequality of woman *without exception*, and immediately ensured their full equality by law."

This statement cannot be challenged. Immediately following the Revolution of October, 1917, a series of decrees was issued— on equal work opportunities, equal pay, the protection of motherhood, and the like—which gave to women a social status no other state, however progressive, had up to that time granted to them.

This action was logical. The avowed aim of Socialism was to wipe out all inequalities, and all hierarchical distinctions, between citizens. The removal of all discrimination on the grounds of sex was a fundamental article of the Revolutionary creed. Engels, the close collaborator of Marx, in a letter written in 1885, had said, "It is my conviction that the real equality of men and women can come true only when the exploitation of either by capital has been abolished." Lenin had emphasized this goal in two frequently quoted statements, that "every cook must learn to rule the state"; and that the Russian woman must be delivered from "the necessity of spending three-fourths of her life in the stinking kitchen."

While in other lands the emancipation of the woman was linked primarily with her right to vote, in Russia what was considered important was her right to earn an individual wage. Freedom from economic dependence upon any man was considered to represent the true breaking of her age-old shackles.

In the Soviet Union, therefore, the woman's "right to work" for the same pay as her male colleague has always been regarded as

Reprinted from *Marriage and Family Living*, 23 (1961): 330-333; footnotes omitted.

symbolic of her emancipation. She is not, as people in the West often imagine, *obliged* to work. There have always been Soviet women who chose to remain at home. But such women are regarded as declining to exercise their supreme privilege. They are occasionally referred to as "drones," or even "parasites." Their choice is accepted, but public opinion disapproves of it.

There is good reason for this. In the immense task of industrial development to which the Soviet Union has set itself, the labor of men and women alike is needed. While the principle of emancipation was primary, the labor shortage was a secondary motive of considerable urgency. This was dramatically argued in 1930 by O. Berukov:

> One of our basic problems is the emancipation of women and the productive utilization of their labor. Every day 36 million hours are expended in the R.S.F.S.R. for cooking alone. That means that on the basis of the eight-hour working day, four and a half million workers, or double the number that are employed in heavy industry, are occupied in cooking. Collective cooking of the same amount of food would require one-sixth of this time, and would release over four million housewives for productive labor.

The effort to emancipate Soviet women and lead them into the ranks of labor has been pursued with vigor. And it has been attended with overwhelming success. The latest available figures show that 26 million, or 47 per cent of the industrial, office and other workers in the country are women. Even allowing for the fact that the sex ratio in the Soviet Union, thrown out of balance by war casualties, shows a preponderance of about 20 million women, this percentage is very high compared with those of Western countries. During the war years it reached a peak of 55 per cent.

Needless to say, a high proportion of these employed women are wives and mothers. Though precise data are not available, there is every reason to believe that, as in the West, the trend to gainful employment affected first the single woman, next the married woman without dependent children, and finally the mother with dependent children. In the West, however, public policy has always regarded the mother's proper place as being in the home; whereas Soviet policy has from the beginning accepted and encouraged the employment of mothers. In terms of the guilt and anxiety likely to be suffered by the woman concerned, and the provision made for the care of her children, this represents a radical difference.

The Western approach to the provision of child care for working mothers has, with a few notable exceptions, been reluctant, makeshift, and sporadic. The Soviet approach has by contrast been wholehearted, and, for the most part, highly efficient.

Another principle of Soviet policy enters the picture here. The Western mind regards the creche, if not the kindergarten, as a regrettable necessity. The Soviet mind regards these institutions as a desirable concomitant of the collective way of life which is essential for the smooth running of a socialist society. In the West, the fact that mothers are employed runs counter to the accepted goals of child rearing; in the Soviet Union, it is entirely congruent with the accepted goals.

To the Soviets, therefore, the fact that mothers are employed need involve no conflict for anyone. It is considered good for the country, good for the woman, and good for the children. For this reason, it can be systematically organized into a smoothly working arrangement achieving positive values all round.

The fact that it is good for the country is self-evident. Does the woman herself, however, share in the view that by being employed she is achieving gains that do not conflict with her family obligations?

Here is a letter from one Galina Brulinskaya, printed in the magazine "Soviet Woman," "If I were asked whether I would give up my work and take up only household duties, I would say that I could not do it. In the factory, we are members of one big family,

in which I have found my true friends, my finest and kindest comrades.

"People ask if my work has any adverse effect on my life, on my
ability to bring up my children. On the contrary, it brings our family closer together, gives me equality with my husband. If I were
taken off my work in the factory, my life would at once become
spiritually poorer, and the common interests which I have with
my husband would be severed."

On the basis of many conversations with Soviet mothers, it would
be my view that this is fairly typical and widely representative.
Some, without doubt, would like to have more time with their children; but most seem to have accepted the situation. "I *want* my
children to learn the collective life, because if they don't they won't
be happy in our Soviet society," was one comment which represented a widely encountered attitude.

The arrangements made for the care of Soviet children while
their parents are at work are impressive. Undoubtedly there have
been periods when children were left with ignorant servants and
incompetent relatives, or even left to their own devices. This may
still happen occasionally in remote areas. But today in the industrial communities, and on the collective farms, very high priority
is given to the care of the children.

In a typical Soviet family all the members, with the exception
of the elderly retired, would leave home after breakfast each
weekday morning. The mother would take her baby or toddler
with her, and deliver him at the nursery attached to her place
of employment. Here he would be completely cared for by well-
trained doctors, nurses and other attendants. The mother would
know that she was within call. While nursing her child, she would
be entitled to one half-hour away from her bench or desk for
every three and a half hours, this counting as working time. In
addition, she would know that if her child was disturbed and in
need of her she would be sent for at once. If the child became ill

and required the mother's care, she would be allowed to take care of him, at home or in the creche, without loss of pay.

At the end of the working day (now seven hours in the Soviet Union) she would pick up the child again and take him home, where the family would be reunited. Older children receive their midday meal at school; and they are not normally allowed to return home until one parent at least is there to take responsibility for them. If the older children are not able to travel to and from school alone, it is customary for the fathers to take them there and bring them home again.

The time spent by the children in the creche and nursery school is by no means merely a matter of waiting until the mother finishes work. The Soviet concept is that children begin to be trained from infancy for the cooperative life with others. "Children not only play but work in the creche. They learn to act cooperatively in the interests of their own little group. Hygienic conditions of living, and education in the collective group of the creche, while keeping close connection with the child's family life, have the double advantage of allowing the child to partake of individual home life, and to share with the social communal institution in which he is educated." A Moscow child specialist elaborates this point in this way, "Persons reared individually are social burdens until they become accustomed to living on an equal basis with others and lose an egotism or selfishness which they might have acquired because of their secluded upbringing. We aim to rear children who will be socially useful even before they can talk, and for that reason we have attempted to apply collectivism not only to our children's daily chores, but also to their recreation."

Western observers have been critical of this separation of mother and young child, which runs counter to some of our cherished doctrines. However, it is hard to substantiate this criticism. It would appear, from the high degree of emotional security that is readily observed among Soviet children as a whole, that the maternal substitutes provided are adequate, and the early training effective.

The Soviet day nursery not only assists in the early training of the child, it also assumes responsibility for the training of the mother in her task as a parent. Individually and in groups, the factory mothers are taught how to handle their children at each stage of development. This is done in the permitted "rest periods" during the working day, and also after working hours.

The help given to the mother begins when she is first aware that she is pregnant. From that time she will normally be in regular touch with the medical staff at her place of work, who will arrange for her maternity leave. A Soviet woman worker is entitled to a total of 112 days away from her employment (56 days before, and 56 days after, delivery) with full pay, in addition to her annual vacation. The period can be extended on medical authority.

The working mother is also safeguarded by labor laws which are strictly enforced. Pregnant women and nursing mothers cannot be engaged in overtime work or put on night shifts. They may do no heavy lifting. When necessary they must be transferred to a lighter job. It is a criminal offense to terminate the employment of a woman who is pregnant or to lower her wages at this time.

It is clear that the State does everything possible to assist the Soviet mother so that she may exercise her right to be gainfully employed. But is her husband equally cooperative?

This is not an easy question to answer. During a month spent living with Soviet families in vacation camps, the writer gained the impression that, despite the equality of the sexes, there is still a fairly rigid differentiation of masculine and feminine roles within the life of the home. The writer noticed that the marketing, cooking, and the tidying up were nearly always undertaken by the wives. In conversation this arrangement was also tacitly accepted.

Although sociological research, as we know it, is today virtually non-existent in the Soviet Union, the author was fortunate in locating some data on this point which was produced before the purges. This material was assembled in 1931 by the Central Bureau of National Economic Accounting, and came into the hands of a competent American social scientist.

What were called "time budgets" were carefully kept by a group of 841 working men and women. From the data gathered, it is possible to make some interesting deductions. For our present purpose the writer has confined the figures in Table I to the 25-35 age group, because those would include the parents of young and dependent children.

TABLE I. *Use of Time by a Group of Soviet Men and Women*

	Men	Women	Extra Time Spent by Men	Extra Time Spent by Women
Paid Work	6	6	—	—
Domestic Work	1	4	—	3
Travel & Shopping	1	2	—	1
Personal Hygiene	1	½	½	—
Self-Education	2	¾	1¼	—
Political Activities	1	½	½	—
Rest, Leisure, Sleep	12	10	2	—
Total	24	23¾	—	—

It will be noted that although men and women were giving an equal number of hours to their paid work, the division of their time in the performance of household tasks was quite out of keeping with the concept of equality. The women were giving twice as many hours to travel and shopping, and four times as many to domestic work, as the men. This puts them four hours behind in the course of each day. They had to take two of these hours out of rest, leisure, and sleep; an hour and a quarter out of self-education; half an hour out of personal hygiene; and half an hour out of political activities. Where the final quarter of an hour came from is not specified.

Judging by these data alone, the guess might be hazarded that a large part of the additional burden of domestic work which the woman carried consisted in the care of young children. However, evidence is available to prove that this was not the case.

When we compare this 25-35 year age group with the group of 35 years and older (not tabulated here) the total number of hours spent daily in domestic duties was, curiously enough, exactly the same—one for the men and four for the women. This suggests that having older and more independent children, or even grownup children, did not lighten the domestic tasks of the parents.

There is also available an interesting record of a further group of working men and women who were designated "heads of families," and who kept similar "time budgets." As it happens, the records of this group went into greater detail. The relevant data are given in Table II.

TABLE II. *Division of Household Tasks between Soviet Men and Women*

Household Work	Men	Women	Ratio
Cooking	0.15	2.24	1:15
House Cleaning	0.07	0.62	1:9
Care of Clothing	0.09	0.61	1:7
Care of Children	0.27	0.61	1:2
Total	0.58	4.08	1:6

How a group of Soviet men and women, all heads of families, shared the household work of an average working day (rest days *not* included). All figures refer to hours or decimal fractions thereof.

The picture here is in broad agreement with that in Table I—except that the men in this group performed only one-sixth as much domestic work as the woman, despite the fact that they all without exception had family responsibilities! What is particularly interesting, however, is that in this group the time given by the woman to child care in the home—half an hour daily—is so small, and only twice that given by the man. It seems clear that in these families the real burden of child care was being borne outside the home, and that what remained was being fairly evenly shared by fathers and mothers.

As far as help in the house is concerned, these men make a poor showing. Clearly they were not domesticated. While their wives devoted more than an hour and a quarter daily to the care of clothes and the home, they got by with 16 minutes! And when it came to cooking, the wives gave nearly two and a half hours to the husbands' 15 minutes!

This fragmentary picture, thirty years old, may be far from reliable. The Soviet home has improved, prepared and packaged foods are much more readily available, and the husbands may have progressed in the direction of domestication. Yet the subjective impression which I personally gathered in the Soviet Union was that the women are still carrying the heavy end of the stick. They are proud of their emancipation and of their economic independence. They are ready to surrender many of their traditional functions in order to enjoy a fuller life. But they are paying a price in terms of longer hours of work, shorter hours of rest and recreation, and more restricted opportunities of self-satisfaction and self-development, which seriously challenges the concept of equality.

It is important to notice, however, that the extra burden which the Soviet working mother carries appears to be not that of parenthood, but of domesticity. How true would it be to say that the Soviet woman has solved the problem of being a working mother, but not yet that of being a working wife; while the American woman has solved the problem of being a working wife, but not yet that of being a working mother?

DOES COMMUNAL EDUCATION WORK?
THE CASE OF THE KIBBUTZ

*One of the most interesting experiments in family organiza-
tion has occurred in the Israeli kibbutz. The kibbutz is a collective agricultural community run along socialistic lines;
property is held in common, and all members work for the
common good. In the kibbutz an adult man and woman wish-
ing to live together merely ask for a double bedroom (formal
marriage papers at the time a child is born represent a concession to state law). Both "husband" and "wife" (in practice
these terms are avoided) are economically independent—
they contribute to the general work of the community and
are in turn supported by the community.*

*A cornerstone of the kibbutz program has been the system
of collective child-rearing, discussed here by psychologist
Bruno Bettelheim. It is this arrangement that frees the kibbutz woman to play a full role in the productive work of the
community. The unique nature of male-female and parent-
child relationships in the kibbutz have been cited as support
for an argument that perhaps the family is not really universal. Alternatively, one could say that the kibbutz shows that
there may be reasonably stable alternatives to the form of the
family with which we are most familiar.*

Does Communal Education Work?
The Case of the Kibbutz

BRUNO BETTELHEIM

Today, when there exists such widespread dissatisfaction with our educational system, a radically different one might be expected to hold great interest for us—especially one thriving among people like ourselves, of Western background. It is therefore astonishing how little attention has been paid to the fascinating educational venture embarked on some four decades ago by the more radical socialist kibbutzim of Israel: that of the communal rearing of their children—the only such experiment, outside the Iron Curtain, in a modern technological society.

Our own American Hutterites offer a less instructive case—they are tradition-bound agricultural communities, deliberately shunning modern developments. Yet the ultra-conservative, extremely devout Hutterites share with the socialist and atheistic kibbutzim one very striking feature: the children of both groups, reared communally in children's homes by professional educators rather than by their families, grow up into adolescents and adults free of the asocial behaviors that worry us most—delinquency, criminality, sexual promiscuity, homosexuality, etc. In general the incidence of severe emotional disturbance among them is extremely low as compared with our society at large. Perhaps more important, the Hutterite communities, like the radical Israeli kibbutzim, are "exceedingly effective in rearing their children to live up to the basic moral principles which they share with the larger society."

To be sure, the experiments conducted during the early days of

Reprinted from *Commentary*, February 1962; footnotes omitted. Copyright 1962 by American Jewish Committee.

the Russian revolution in the communal rearing of children failed and were discontinued. On the other hand, from Anton Makarenko's *Road to Life,* we know of his great success after the civil war in rehabilitating the wild children of Russia (*besprizornys*) through communal rearing. Reports from those who have recently visited the children's villages in the Soviet Union suggest that their young inmates are sad and passive—institutionalized—as in the earlier days of Soviet Communism. However, these observers note that the villages are badly understaffed, with untrained, indifferent adults.

We may conclude from what we know of these particular experiments that the success or failure of communal child rearing seems to depend on the size of the group, the adult-child ratio, and, above all, the attitude of those in charge of the children. Whatever has been true in Russia (or in China), we know that the children of the kibbutzim are raised in small groups and cared for by a skilled and devoted staff. What happens under such conditions is surely full of implications for our own educational methods.

In this respect the kibbutz is unique. Nowhere else during modern times has a community of highly intelligent and educated Europeans so seriously tried to free the child from a dependence on his natural parents. Within days after birth, the child enters the communal nursery. There his own age group takes the place of what we would call his family of origin—for it alone remains stable over the years; the adults who rear the children—nurses, child-care workers, and teachers—are replaced periodically. The nursery group consists of a maximum of sixteen babies—but usually fewer —all housed and cared for together. Older children are organized into smaller age groups and live in cottages within the kibbutz. Having at birth acquired full rights in the children's autonomous society, the child remains a member until his graduation from high school, at which time he is elected to adult membership in the kibbutz if he so desires—and almost all do. It must be added that the child's parents during the years of his education have no individual rights of control or decision over any aspect of his life.

Most published American critiques of kibbutz child rearing, following the general line of American psychologists and psychiatrists, declare that the children suffer severely from communal education. Judging on the basis of our own values, these critics find particularly damaging the fact that the children are separated from their parents, do not have their own mothers to minister to them, have to share the attention of their caretakers with several other children, and undergo not infrequent changes in these caretaking persons. These observers are also influenced by reports on the personality development of institutionalized children. We may take John Bowlby as their spokesman when he says that "essential for mental health is that the infant and young child should experience a warm, intimate, and continuous relationship with his mother."

But what exactly constitutes warm, intimate relations and continuity? It is true that the educators in charge of the children in the kibbutz are not always available to *all* the children in their care, and that the care by any one person is intermittent (days off, relief periods, etc.) But during the time the nursery workers are with the children, no other demands whatsoever are made on them—the child has the full attention of the mothering person. The nursery workers receive appreciation for their trained child care; they are relieved of housekeeping duties, enjoy regular periods of freedom from the children, have the stimulation of adult companionship after their day's work is done. Most important, they are not beset by a parent's typical anxieties—the hopes and fears we harbor about children who are ours. What then is truly continuous, and what is intermittent? Does not a consistent, if only intermittent, mothering nevertheless equip the child with a continuous inner image of mothering? And may it not be that a mother who spends a great deal of time with her child, but is sometimes loving and giving, and at other times demanding, or irritated, or just plain worn down—is it not possible that such a mother can just fail to give the child a permanent inner image of good mothering?

The most intimate contact between mother and infant is that of breast feeding. Now, while a vast majority of kibbutz mothers breast-feed their babies, the opposite is true of American mothers. Nearly all kibbutz mothers are able to nurse, love to do it, try very hard to stretch out the nursing period for as long as possible. When an infant seems to want to be fed, a flag is hoisted of the color known to each mother as her own. If she does not see it immediately, another member of the kibbtuz calls out to her, and she is with her hungry baby within minutes. Nursing is a social event in which the entire community takes an interest, and mothers come to the nursery four or five times a day to feed their babies. Nor does the mothering instinct seem to be interfered with by communal rearing: many who take so much pleasure in nursing their babies were themselves brought up in kibbtuz nurseries.

In contrast, bottle feeding, with much earlier weaning, is the rule of America. Where, we might ask those authors who decry the lack of intimacy between mother and child in the kibbutz, does the child experience the more "functional" intimacy with his mother—there or here? Spiro also notes that since kibbutz mothers usually "nurse their babies at the same time as well as in the same place . . . even the intimacy of mother love is not private." But what, we may go on to ask, constitutes the more intimate relation: mother and infant alone in a house—with perhaps the bottle propped up in the crib, or at best the baby held in the mother's arm—or an "unprivate" setting in which the nursing infant is held regularly to the mother's body?

Moreover, Spiro's objection to lack of "privacy" is characteristic of a whole set of attitudes and unexamined assumptions that inhere in American discussion of kibbutz child rearing. Space forbids lengthy consideration of all aspects of this child rearing, and since nursing stands at the beginning of the mother-child relation, I shall examine it further, as my principal example.

Recently, when an effort was made to study infant development in one of our large Eastern cities, only mothers who bottle-fed their children were willing to participate. The nursing mothers felt it to be indecent, if not obscene, to permit anyone, except perhaps the father, to be present when they fed the baby. But the whole issue turned out to be largely theoretical, because the percentage of breast-feeding middle-class mothers was incredibly small when compared, for example, with the kibbutz mothers we are discussing. What these findings suggest is that mother love, as expressed in breast feeding, seems more likely to exist when and where it is not kept private.

Is it possible that the privatization of so much of modern middle-class life is not the consequence, but rather the cause, of that human isolation from which modern man suffers, and which the kibbutz way of life has tried to counteract? Nor can one simply say that what is felt to be shameful is therefore made private; usually, in the history of civilization, it is the other way around. Perhaps when we consider that the nursing of infants seems to be possible for nearly all mothers in the communal setting of the kibbutz, we may see a reason for the converse condition: the large number of middle-class mothers who find themselves unable to nurse their children.

Spiro critically observes of the kibbutz mothers that "nursing becomes a social occasion in which gossip and conversation can be shared with other mothers while she shares her milk with her baby." But he adds, "in general nursing proceeds at a relaxed pace." I venture to say that it *is* relaxed for mother and infant precisely because it takes place in so pleasant and social an atmosphere.

A first important change occurs when the infant is six months old. He then may be taken from the nursery cottage to his parents' home for about an hour in the early evening. At approximately one year, the child moves from the nursery to the toddlers' house and his group gets reduced in size to about eight. At this age the child may remain with his parents in their quarters for two hours or so every evening, and most of the day on Saturdays.

The child will now live continuously with these seven others—his age peers—until graduation from high school. At about the fourth or fifth birthday, that is at kindergarten age, the group again numbers up to sixteen by the merging of two toddler groups. This enlarged group remains steadily together until they reach high school age and join with others just entering high school.

From the earliest age on, the children learn to interact with little or no adult supervision. If a child is afraid at night, or becomes ill, his companions take care of him: play with him, talk to him, bring him water, and in general reassure him. Having intimately shared his experiences, they know what he is likely to be afraid of; and the anxious child, trusting his comrades, will confide in them.

In a very short while, the child ceases to wake up afraid in the middle of the night, so absolutely secure does he feel with the other children. Group living makes it possible for the kibbutz child to enjoy much more of that inner security which we put so much stress on, but which many middle-class American infants—alone with their anxieties in their own rooms—fail to find.

Yet American observers (Irvine, Spiro) deplore "the rather unstimulating and frustrating environment of the child under three, and the limited physical and emotional content which he often has with his caretaker." They also deplore that "the child from the earliest age is expected to subordinate his own needs to the needs of the group." But are the children he lives with not a powerful stimulation? Is it frustrating to a child always to have with him a companion, a friend, some other children to watch; or is it a matter of greater contentment to be so often only with adults—or with no company at all? Are elaborate toys and equipment more rewarding than the uninterrupted company of age mates? And are not each child's own needs also those of the group? Why, one may ask, is the *coordination* of needs viewed by the American observer as *subordination?*

Perhaps such American evaluations spring from what may roughly be likened to a consumer psychology of child development. The underlying conviction seems to be that regardless of the individual's ability to enjoy or to master a thing, the more he acquires of it and the sooner, the better—be it concentrated attention, toys, food, or emotional involvement. None of us knows how much or what kind of stimulation is best for the young child. But the frequency and anxiety with which I am asked about how to get children to share with others suggests that perhaps our children do not learn the lesson early in life of how to coordinate their own needs with those of others for successful relationships.

Kibbutz children are actually much closer to their parents in some ways than most American children—if not to their parents as persons, then as members of the community. It is the kibbutz (that is, their parents' way of life) which is central to all learning, formal and informal, in the children's village. From the toddlers' school on, the children take daily hikes to visit their parents at work. At the machine shops, the barns, the olive groves, the children are stopped by adults, talked to, joked with, praised, perhaps asked to lend a hand, and when met by their parents, hugged. Thus the child is made to feel a welcome and important part of his father's and mother's occupational activities, and those of the whole community—an experience which most American children would envy them greatly. So, too, all big communal events in the kibbutz, such as holiday celebrations, are related to work that parents and children both have a part in (the festival of the first fruits, arbor day, the harvest festival, etc.).

The system of parental abdication in the rearing of the child was fashioned by the founders of the kibbutz movement out of their ideological convictions. Behind it was the idea that those who established the kibbutzim had grown up in a decadent society, injurious to human freedom and dignity. Nor could any society be regenerated, the kibbutzniks believed, except through the regeneration of the individual, who in turn was viewed as being largely the product of the education he received.

The specific objectives of this system of collective education were: (1) to abolish parental authority, particularly the patriarchal authority of the father; (2) to free the female from the impediment of being assigned only a few special roles in society, such as homemaking and child rearing; (3) to perpetuate the value system of the communal society; and (4) to provide the children with the most democratic education possible. It was hoped that freeing the parents of the need to care for and educate their children would bring the parent-child relation to rest mainly on positive emotions. Since, also, the community as a whole would be responsible for his physical well-being, the child would not be beholden to any particular person, and least of all to his parents.

Any system of child rearing can only be judged, of course, by its results, by whether or not those whom it educates behave later in life in accordance with the goals set. Now from the point of view of a communist society, an educational system is highly successful which produces citizens who embrace every tenet of communism. But can we, from our side, unambiguously recognize such a system as valid? Critics of the kibbutz tend to hold two contrary notions: that an educational system is successful if it imparts its own stated goals; and that it is successful only if it produces persons who live successfully in terms of the critics' values and standards of behavior. Because space does not permit me to review the kibbutz system in the light of both criteria, I have chosen to consider the kibbutz's own value system—which up to now most investigators have attached little importance to—as an acceptable measure of success.

Let me begin by saying that as contrasted with the vague and often contradictory goals of some of our educational enterprises, it is refreshing to encounter a system of bringing up children that

starts out with specific goals, clearly stated and commonly understood and held. Asked to rank in importance the values they wish
their educational system to instill in their children, the parents of
one kibbutz, according to Spiro, replied: First and foremost, "work";
after that, in the order of importance, "love of humanity," "responsibility to the kibbutz," "good character," "intellectualism," "socialism," "Zionism," "social participation," "patriotism," and "coop-
eration." Neither emotional adjustment nor success in competition
was mentioned: adjustment was viewed as implicit in achieving
the first four of the values given, while personal advancement was
contrary to all their values in general (and to the first in particular), since by work they meant cooperative work in the kibbutz.
Thus, queried also as to which ambitions they hoped their children
would realize, kibbutz members ranked being a good comrade
first, and being a good worker second.

From all available evidence, the results of kibbutz education
are unequivocal: the stated main goals are achieved and to a degree that has no parallel in Western education. True, this is not
what most American observers report; nearly all of them have
selected and interpreted data to support the correctness of our own
notions of child rearing and personality development. But on the
basis of my examination of the whole body of data, I am convinced
that kibbutz education has had a success of a kind that might well
lead us to reconsider some of our own assumptions and values
throughout the entire field of education.

In the kibbutz classroom, there is no competition for grades;
grading does not determine the success or failure of a student—
nor is there any grading of teachers, for promotions. The atmosphere is free; to the American observer it often seems chaotic. The
children come and go as they please, and there are no specific
assignments or homework; I am tempted to say there is only good
teaching. Youngsters of all ages are highly motivated to learn, and
study without pressure.

On waking in the morning, the children generally read until

it is time to get up; they also read at rest times and on many such other occasions. Reading books of their own choosing—generally what we would call serious reading matter—appears to be the children's favorite pastime. As they grow older, they carry increasing kibbutz work assignments in addition to their academic program. By the time they reach senior high school they are doing three hours of daily work in the field or the shops. During the two-month summer vacation, carrying a full daily work load on the kibbutz, high school youngsters also read an average of ten books of history, biography, or science. At graduation, their educational achievement is far superior to that of the average American high school graduate.

How do these habits and values carry over later on? These children, born of intellectual Jews, when they take their place in the adult kibbutz, devote themselves of their own free will to manual labor in an agricultural settlement often surrounded by hostile Arabs; frequently working ten hours a day to cultivate the desert, they live with a minimum of material possessions, and like the way they live. Both competitive ambition and long-range mobility goals, in our sense, are meaningless in their society.

But what of the primary motive for creating this educational system—that of freeing the child from dependence on his parents? Has this goal been realized too? The question must be of particular interest to American parents in view of our general concern over the emotional difficulties that we encounter in relations with our children.

The system does indeed work in making the child independent of his parents—only too well for the taste of most Western observers, since they believe that little good can come of such early and radical separation of children and parents. But it also works too well for the original founders of the kibbutz who, it seems, get more than they had bargained for.

The relations of these children to their kibbutz parents are to an astonishing degree free of those all too intense ambivalences of love and hate, of the desired and resented dependencies, which characterized relations between the founders of the kibbutz and *their* parents—and, I might add, which are also typical in the relations of white middle-class American children and their parents. But though the relations of kibbutz-educated children to their parents and to each other are amazingly uncomplicated, straightforward, and unneurotic, they are at the same time—and here is the rub—comparatively lacking in intensity. This absence of intensity is viewed with alarm both by investigators and by kibbutz parents themselves. Blood simply is not thicker than shared emotional experiences; it is the latter that tie people together. The strong positive feelings of the child who is reared communally are concentrated on his "family" of upbringing, the children with whom he uninterruptedly shared all the experiences of infancy, childhood, and adolescence.

I should like to offer here a few speculations which seem sound to me though I cannot offer any strong evidence to support them. For these kibbutz-educated children the absence of deep involvement with their parents meant there was no need to revolt or prove themselves in any way against their elders—by surpassing them economically or socially or morally—in order to achieve personal worth. Now, the need for individuation is a correlate of the fear of anonymity. In a mass society, to be more than a "number," to be "known," one has to be near unique, and once "known", one must wage a continuous struggle to remain in the limelight or at the top —even if one cares little for the opinions of others. Much that passes in our society for ambition, social climbing, the desire to get ahead of the Joneses, is basically motivated by a desperate effort simply to escape personal anonymity.

In the middle-class American family, the child's deep emotional, economic, and social dependence leads to a personality structure developed in response to the unique stresses, strains, and rewards that the family imposes. But the child then feels the need to fight free of dependence on his parents by developing a unique personality that is different from theirs. This striving becomes still more urgent where the modern mass society threatens the individual with anonymity.

Kibbutz-educated children feel no such defensive need to develop a unique personality. Each of them is safe from anonymity because he is well known to all who count in his human surroundings. He need not assert his difference from his parents because he was never so utterly dependent on them that he must now fight for his separate identity. In addition, he shares the "individuality" of the kibbutz, with which he is deeply identified, to a degree unknown and impossible in modern mass society.

It may be true that the kibbutz-reared sabras in their intimate relations and their self-realization lack the subtle nuances of an individuation they might have acquired in our society. However, they are in many ways rugged individualists who care only about living up to their own standards, about how they appear to themselves and not whether others approve of them, though with one important qualification: anyone's individuality must have been partly formed by the ethos of the kibbutz.

As noted before, much of the American discussion of kibbutz education sees replacements in the staff of the communal school as the central weakness of the system, a factor which necessarily causes emotional disturbances in the children. But if child-care workers remained the same during most of the children's infancy and childhood they would simply have turned out to be parents by another name. By entrusting the child's total education to workers who are replaced—though not too often—the kibbutz system prevents him from forming either positive or negative identifications with the whims, idiosyncrasies, or emotional constellation of one or two particular adults. Instead it forces him to organize his life along the consistent patterns and values of the *community*, held in common by all the adults: the ones who take care of him and the others living around him.

Indeed, the kibbutz idea has corrobrated many of the experimental practices we have instituted at the Orthogenic School at the University of Chicago. For example, many children who came to us near death by self-starvation (anorexia) began to eat in the confusion—and diffusion—of emotions that attended eating with a larger group of noisy and disorderly children. Alone with an adult emotionally concentrated on him, the child could not eat, even if the adult made no demands about such things as orderliness.

True, these were not typical children. But it is common knowledge that among normal children the feeding problems are often most acute with the firstborn who eats alone with his mother. By the time the table is noisy with brothers and sisters the food disappears in short order. The mother must concentrate on producing the food, not on seeing that it is consumed. Still, this is true mainly for informal meals. At dinner time in the middle class family, there is of course much pressure for decent table manners, often with repeated correcting or outright nagging.

In the children's houses of the kibbutz, during meals, there is a great deal of laughter, chatter, and singing, as there is also whining. Spiro describes such a typical meal. One child begins to sing, and soon all join in or begin to jabber; one yells, another claps his hands, and the others follow suit. One child climbs under the table, the rest yell and laugh. Such meals are social and socializing occasions, not for adults but for the children. Just as we socialize around a dinner eaten adult style, so they socialize around a meal eaten toddler style. True, the adults serving the children have little relaxation, but then they know they will soon be sitting down in peace with their own peers. Nurses seldom have difficulty in persuading the children, even those who are not hungry, to come to the table, so much do the children enjoy their mealtime.

For the individual kibbutz child, this child-centered system pays off, handsomely. Absent are the frustrations of all kinds: dependencies satisfied but made guilt-ridden; injunctions imposed, together with guilt for transgressing them; needs projected by adults onto the child, and the anxiously feared and expected developments. In their place are deep, permanent, extremely mean-ingful and mutually satisfying attachments of the youngsters to each other. These children who grew up together in the new sys-tem readily give for each other—their life's comrades—everything: fortune, even life itself.

That their interest in their parents, by comparison, is hardly equal in intensity should have been anticipated. If we remove our-selves from the lives of our children, they are not necessarily the worse off for it—in some ways perhaps even much better off; but we are then not very important in their lives. Still, this logical con-sequence is a distinct disappointment to most of the first-genera-tion kibbutz parents (and much deplored by American observers).

Yet in other respects these kibbutz parents are richly rewarded. From all descriptions, the children turn into exceptionally cour-ageous, self-reliant, secure, unneurotic, and deeply committed adults who find their self-realization in work and in marriage. Though most have some previous sexual experience, they marry in their early twenties and soon have children who in turn are brought up in the communal nurseries and schools. There are almost no divorces (about one per kibbutz) and adultery is rare and severely censured. Spiro remarks that these marriages are not only stable, but by American standards exceptionally satisfactory; marriage is, in fact, the most important and intimate relationship of kibbutz adults.

The adults are genuinely fond of children, their own as well as others, and this interest in children develops early. Young girls in kindergarten often assist their mothers who are nurses in younger children's houses; and girls in the grammar school frequently super-vise the play of nursery children. Many of the high school girls also work in the various nurseries as afternoon relief nurses and, with rare exceptions, they are warm, loving, and intelligent workers. Later, as parents, they are warm and affectionate with their chil-dren, but relaxed and unanxious. Yet they have no desire to return to raising them privately at home; they are well satisfied with the way they themselves were communally reared. Not having experienced deep emotional attachment to parents as the core of their own development, and, presently having a full life of their own, they do not feel they are missing anything by being parted from their children. Without doubt or hesitation they place their few-days'-old infants in the autonomous children's society.

We may reasonably assume that these young married couples would perhaps find their lives empty without the deep attachment of children if it were not for their work for the community, which fills such a tremendous place in their daily lives and emotions. In this connection I cannot even begin to assess what satisfactions kibbutzniks derive from living a life close to nature; and from the fact that by their labor they visibly provide for themselves and their community the things which we consider necessities but to them are cherished enrichments of living.

All that I have said, and a good deal more that remains undiscussed, suggests that a study of kibbutz education raises more questions perhaps than it answers. I feel they are questions extremely pertinent for us to think about. In particular, the study of the kibbutz educational system reveals that some of our own widely held theories on child rearing are provincial—rather than universal; though we are not therefore automatically provided with more fruitful theories for our own practice.

I am not suggesting—for all that I have said—that we adopt the kibbutz educational system. I have a great admiration for the vast expenditure of capital and human resources which the members of the kibbutzim bestow on the education of their children, and for the hardships they are willing to undergo to further their children's schooling, which is given so central an importance in the community. What we might well copy, without further study, is this attitude of seriousness toward the problems of children in their development and education.

MARRIAGE: PAST AND PRESENT

The book Marriage: Past and Present *makes available to American readers the transcript of a stimulating radio debate between two extremely well-spoken anthropologists, first broadcast by the British Broadcasting Corporation in 1931. A major point of dispute was the theory of "original promiscuity," referred to in an earlier section. Briffault espoused this theory, while Malinowski argued that nothing is more basic to human social life than monogamous marriage. Briffault further emphasized what he called "the business side of marriage," whereas Malinowski stressed the religious aspects of such a union. While it is now known that Briffault drew some unwarranted anthropological conclusions, his indignation regarding woman's subservience in conventional monogamy lent considerable force to many of his statements. On the other hand, Malinowski appears to have been on firm ground in his contention that monogamous marriage would not (and could not) be eliminated.*

The material reproduced here represents a summary of some of the points raised in the debate. As the final reading in this section on women's roles, it should serve to remind us that views on the "woman problem" relate significantly to more general values regarding marriage and the family.

Marriage: Past and Present

BRONISLAW MALINOWSKI

What have we learnt from this symposium on marriage? My task is to focus the bewildering variety of facts, arguments—I might say, almost, of sentiments—which has been put before you.

POINTS OF AGREEMENT

I shall not dwell on the points of disagreement between Dr. Briffault and myself; they have given you a good insight into the famous anthropological disputes about the origin of marriage. The points of disagreement do not matter so very much as regards modern practical questions.

But out of the discussion there have emerged clearly one or two points of agreement, and these, I think, are very illuminating as the background for discussions of present-day difficulties. In the first place there was substantial agreement as to the complexity and manifoldness of marriage. You have seen that marriage is not merely a state of sexual relationship, but that it implies a common household, joint parenthood, and a great deal of economic co-operation. Marriage, as I have insisted throughout, is essentially a legal contract which usually enjoys also definite religious, that is supernatural, sanctions. As a matter of fact, the worst errors in the theory of marriage have arisen from the confusion between the legally binding, economically founded, religiously sanctioned institution of marriage on the one hand, and casual and temporary intrigues on the other. Among the New Guinea natives whom I have studied, boys and girls are allowed by custom to go through a series of

Reprinted from Robert Briffault and Bronislaw Malinowski, *Marriage: Past and Present* (Boston: Porter Sargent, 1956), pp. 74-83.

more or less serious love affairs, settling down finally to a lasting liaison which eventually becomes transformed into marriage by the legal act of wedding. And this is a type of conduct which we find repeated in many other communities all the world over. Now, such temporary liaisons, which often take place in special communal houses, have led superficial observers to speak about the existence of actual cases or 'survivals' of group-marriage. Nothing could be more misleading, for the relationship which obtains between the boys and girls is absolutely different from marriage, and is clearly distinguished from marriage by the natives.

The second point on which there was a consensus of opinion was the value of maternity in all questions of marriage and parenthood. I personally am deeply convinced that from the very beginning it was woman who, as the mother, had the greatest influence on the forms of marriage, of the household, and of the management of children. At the same time, all my studies of primitive mankind, all my personal experiences among savages and civilised people, have convinced me that maternal affection is individual. And it is because of that, I believe, that the family and marriage from the beginnings were individual. You will remember that I laid great emphasis on the fact that maternity is individual. A whole school of anthropologists, from Bachofen on, have maintained that the maternal clan was the primitive domestic institution, and that connected with this, there was group marriage or collective marriage. In my opinion, as you know, this is entirely incorrect. But an idea like that, once it is taken seriously and applied to modern conditions, becames positively dangerous. I believe that the most disruptive element in the modern revolutionary tendencies is the idea that parenthood can be made collective. If once we came to the point of doing away with the individual family as the pivotal element of our society, we should be faced with a social catastrophe compared with which the political upheaval of the French revolution and the economic changes of Bolshevism are insignificant. The question, therefore, as to whether group motherhood is an institution which ever existed, whether it is an arrangement which is compatible with human nature and social order, is of considerable practical interest.

CLAN AND SEX

Now on this point I can be quite dogmatic. The hypothesis of group maternity has been seriously advanced by a real anthropologist, the late Dr. Rivers of Cambridge, only with regard to Melanesia. This is, in fact, the only part of the world where there were some indications that it might have existed. But having spent several years there and made special observations on this point, I can now state positively that there is not even the slightest semblance of collective maternity there. You will notice that in our debate on the subject, Dr. Briffault was not even prepared to reaffirm the existence of group maternity. In his important work *The Mothers,* on the other hand, where he exposes his views so brilliantly, group marriage and group maternity form the twofold foundation of his whole argument. And, indeed, the two are essentially connected, so that if you throw overboard group maternity you must also recant the idea of group marriage, because since parenthood, as I have tried to show you, is the essence of marriage, any form of group marriage would necessarily involve the existence of group maternity. After the present recantation, then, we can perhaps assume that it is impossible to regard the clan as the primeval domestic institution.

The clans, mind you, do exist and they are extremely important to the natives. But they fulfill special functions entirely different from those of the family, and they have nothing to do with domestic life or procreation. The only relation between clan and sex consists in the fact that membership in the same clan bars a man and a woman from marrying each other, or even from courtship. This, of course, does not make the clan into a family.

What bearing has this on modern conditions?

WOMAN'S CHOICE

If maternity has always been the central element of marriage, the inference is that in the future women will also have the last word in deciding what marriage is to be. Therefore, there are three crucial questions which the history of primitive marriage presents to the women of the future. Will women cease to be interested in becoming and being mothers, or on the contrary, will the maternal instinct remain as strong as ever? This is the first question. The second is: Will the mothers of the future prefer to carry out individual maternity and continue looking after their own children, or will they try to call into being the hypothetical primeval clan, that is, will they give over their infants into the hands of the State to be brought up as foundlings or communal babies? In the third place, will the mother of the future desire to have the father of her child as her mate and husband, or will she prefer him to be a drone? You know my answer to every one of these questions. I believe that no human impulse is so deeply rooted as the maternal impulse in woman; I believe that it is individual; and I believe that it is bound up with the institution of marriage.

The only example of real group maternity I heard of was from a farmer friend of mine; he had three geese who decided to sit communally on a nest of eggs. The result was that all the eggs were smashed in the quarrels and fights of this maternal clan of group mothers. All, that is, but one; the gosling, however, did not survive the tender cares of its group mothers. If ever another group of geese were to try a similar experiment I should like them to be aware of this precedent.

PATERNAL RESPONSIBILITY

It is a distortion of the truth to attack marriage on the plea that it is an enslavement of woman by man. The analysis of primitive marriage I gave you shows that marriage is a contract safeguarding the interests of the woman as well as granting privileges to man. A detailed study of the economic aspects of marriage reveals, in fact, that the man has to prove his capacity to maintain the woman. Often, as among the Siberian natives and certain African races and American Indians, the man has to reside with his parents-in-law for some time before marriage in order to prove that he is capable of maintaining his future wife and her offspring.

The laws of marriage and family express, among other things, the demand that the male should face his responsibility and should take his share of the duties and burdens as well as of the privileges connected with the process of reproduction.

Anthropology teaches us two things; marriage and the family have changed; they have developed; they have grown and passed through various stages. But, through all the changes and vicissitudes of history and development, the family and marriage still remain the same twin institutions; they still emerge as a stable group showing throughout the same characteristics: the group consisting of father and mother and their children, forming a joint household, co-operating economically, legally united by a contract and surrounded by religious sanctions which make the family into a moral unit.

Every society, then, teaches its members the two matrimonial commandments. The one given to the male is: if you want to possess a wife of your choice and have children with her, you will have to shoulder your share of duties and burdens. The one for the woman is: if you want to become a mother you must stick to the lover of your choosing and do your duty by him as your husband as well as by your children.

Do these anthropological conclusions profoundly modify our outlook on present and future questions? Certainly. In the first place, we do feel a considerable diffidence as regards any ambitious reforms aiming at either the destruction, or a complete re-creation, of the family by means of external coercion and legislative changes on a vast scale. The reforms of Fascist Italy and of Soviet Russia alike will, I am convinced, lead to the same result: a return to the old order of marriage and family based neither on absolute freedom nor on complete and rigid compulsion.

You can see that I am not an alarmist. I do not seriously entertain any fears or doubts as to the future of marriage or the family. On the other hand, I sincerely deprecate the mere stubbornness of the moral reactionary, who refuses to see any dangerous symptoms in our present conditions and who does not want even the form of marriage and the family changed, who opposes any discussion on divorce or family limitation or on the 'revolt of modern youth.' This attitude works against the cause of true conservatism, that is, of wise reform.

ROOM FOR IMPROVEMENT

The institution of marriage shows symptoms of maladjustment, as do all other institutions, for the simple reason that we are living in an epoch of rapid and profound change in the whole structure of our civilization. Thus a wide range of knowledge and constant stimulus given to imagination and emotion have made the modern young men and women much more alive to the need of the full sexual and erotic life. Those who believe in the institution of marriage must work not at the belittling of sex, but of showing that its full attainment can only be in a life-long relationship contracted for the fulfillment of all that sex can give, and also of all its consequences. Here I think that the work of such big educational organisations as the British Social Hygiene Council, who spread enlightenment and knowledge on moderate, but progressive, lines is of the greatest importance. The eugenics movement, again, teaches us above all that love and the falling in love is not merely a phase in human life, but a matter of the greatest moment for the future of the human race. Such movements, then, will contribute towards the establishment of the marriage relationship, the basis of knowledge and of consideration for human needs.

How far we can attempt to create a science of love and lovemaking without becoming somewhat ridiculous and futile it is difficult to see. If any ultra-modern university were to establish a Chair of Domestic Happiness or of Scientific Love-Making, I should not apply for the incumbency. But there is no doubt, however, that the pioneering work of recent contributors to the scientific study of sex are of the greatest value.

Among some other actual problems connected with marriage let me mention divorce. Here I am all for progressive reconstruction. As to family limitation, let me just remind you of the statement of the Lambeth Conference: 'in those cases where there is a reason clearly for the moral obligation to limit or avoid parenthood and where there is a morally sound reason for avoiding complete abstinence . . . other methods may be used.' The Lambeth Conference has once and for all shut the mouth of those who maintain that Christianity is incompatible with the methods of birth control, in certain cases at least.

On the whole there is nothing as important and hopeful in this question as the progressive movement on the part of conservative agencies such as the Church of England or other Christian organisations. Nor is there anything as dangerous as to identify the cause of free thought and progress with a destructive attack against marriage, with Misbehaviourism and the futile and cheap attacks against the Christian influence on marriage, attacks which have been becoming lamentably frequent in the last few years.

SACRIFICE AND SAFEGUARDS

Marriage, I conclude, presents one of the most difficult personal problems in human life; the most emotional as well as the most romantic of all human dreams has to be consolidated into an ordinary working relationship which, while it begins by promising a supreme happiness, demands in the end the most unselfish and sublime sacrifices from man and woman alike. Marriage will never be a matter of living happily ever after. Marriage and the family are the foundations of our present society, as they were the foundations of all human societies. To maintain these foundations in good order is the duty of everyone. Each must contribute his individual share, while the social reformer and legislator must constantly watch over the institution as a whole. Because, as all things alive, marriage has to grow and change. Wise and moderate reforms—reforms, however, which may go deep towards modifying the institution—are necessary in order to prevent disastrous revolutionary upheavals.

PART THREE

Birth Control

RX FOR BIRTH CONTROL

The practice of family planning is extremely widespread in the United States today. Surveys as early as the 1940s revealed broad public approval of making birth control information available (to those who desired it). More recent studies have demonstrated that the vast majority of married couples practice some form of contraception, and there is considerable evidence that even a high proportion of married Catholics employ so-called "artificial" techniques (condemned by the Church). Perhaps more significant in this matter than religious differentials are differences between socio-economic classes. There are distinct social class variations in attitudes toward, the practice of, and the effectiveness of, family planning. The results have long been seen in the fertility differentials (the inverse relationship between socio-economic status and number of children). A recent intensive interview study among working-class families (And the Poor Get Children, 1960) presented much interesting case-study material showing how the entire complex of working-class social values affects contraceptive thinking and practice.

Even where such differentials exist, there appears to be a strong desire for full and accurate information and an eagerness (at least among most of the women) to somehow bring childbearing under control. For many of the reasons discussed below, rational planning of family size is increasingly recognized as being sensible and desirable, both for the individuals involved and for society at large.

RX for Birth Control

ALAN F. GUTTMACHER

In the past generation, the practice of birth control has not only become more widespread, but the way it fits into the pattern of American family life also has changed considerably. I had a pleasant experience recently that brought these changes into focus.

A woman in her late forties stopped in my office at the hospital. "You won't remember me," she said, "but I was a patient of yours in Baltimore many years ago." I confessed my poor memory. "Well, I had been married five years and had four children." She sighed and smiled. "It finally worked out all right, thanks to you; now do you remember?"

Gradually then, as we talked, her case history came back to me. She had been an acute diabetic at the time of her fifth delivery; apparently she had no knowledge of contraception when I first met her in the obstetrical ward. But she had been told that her life would be endangered by another pregnancy. Added to her precarious physical condition was a growing anxiety neurosis focused mainly on fears for her own health and concern for her youngsters if she should die.

Of course I prescribed contraception. She returned for several annual checkups and had no more pregnancies while I knew her. Since then, I gathered, she too had moved to New York. "I discovered you were here at Mt. Sinai when I came to visit a friend," she said.

Then she added, "Doctor, would you be able to see my daughter?

Reprinted from Alan F. Guttmacher, with Winfield Best and Frederick Jaffe, *The Complete Book of Birth Control* (New York: Ballantine, 1961), pp. 14-23. Published by The Macmillan Company under the title *Planning Your Family*. © 1961, 1964 by Alan F. Guttmacher, Winfield Best, and Frederick Jaffe. Reprinted by permission of The Macmillan Company.

She plans to be married soon. I want you to talk to her about birth control *before* she's married, so that she doesn't go through what I did."

She asked if I still saw contraceptive patients regularly. I assured her I was very much interested and active in the field, but that the press of other medical responsibilities left me little time for private practice any more. However, I assured her, I would surely make a special point of seeing her daughter. I have since had a consultation with her and the young man she is going to marry.

It is always a bit of a shock to be reminded so vividly that time marches on. But I must say that when women who were former patients send their daughters for premarital consultation, I react quite differently. For, in the mother's day, it was likely that I prescribed birth control because she suffered from the physical complications of having too many children too quickly. Usually the daughters now come to me because they want to use birth control to *plan* their families in advance in order to avoid such medical problems. This is tangible and heartwarming evidence of progress.

Many developments have contributed in recent years to imbed the concept of family planning deeply in the American way of life. In the Sixties, even more than in earlier decades, physicians recognize that child spacing is good medical practice, and that medical indications for contraception include factors other than serious illness. As indicated in the last chapter, religious and social attitudes towards sex and birth control have changed markedly. As a result, birth control is prescribed by doctors and practiced in the United States today mainly to achieve these four goals: better maternal health, improved child care, financial stability, and family happiness.

A couple may practice birth control for one reason during one phase of life, and for quite different reasons later on. Let us see how these reasons—medically called "indications"—function singly or in combination.

Newlyweds use birth control to postpone the arrival of a child until they are properly established. About half of the contraceptive users in the United States begin the use of birth control before their first pregnancy. Undoubtedly this is the result of the trend toward earlier marriages: The average age at marriage has decreased since the turn of the century from 22 to 20 for women and from 26 to 23 for men. Today, more girls marry at 18 than any other age, and more men at 21. These young couples use birth control during their early years together to help them make the psychological and financial adjustments which are so important in marriage. My former patient's daughter and her husband-to-be, for example, told me they want to wait two years before having a baby. They want that time for themselves—to establish the foundation of a lasting marriage.

During their period of mutual adjustment, a young man and wife should not be concerned about an immediate pregnancy before they learn each other's needs and moods and habits in a way that only living together can teach them. The thrilling anticipation of their first born should not be blunted by forced competition with this process of sexual and domestic adjustment. Before the bride and groom share themselves with a new family member, they should have ample opportunity to share themselves solely with one another. Then, when a child is planned to arrive some time later, they will be secure with each other and ready to extend their love unstintingly toward the baby.

Many newlyweds also face problems of money, employment, continuation of schooling, or temporary family disruption because of military service. Any of these or other good reasons may cause them to postpone having babies. In order to set up housekeeping in the way they want it for themselves, and frequently to provide income so that they need not live with parents or in-laws, many newlyweds agree that the wife as well as the husband should be employed outside the home during the first phase of marriage. Several decades ago, the typical American marriage started with the bride withdrawing from any paying job or "career" she might have had and demurely hanging curtains—and shortly thereafter, diapers. Today, the popular pattern is for the new husband and wife to hang the curtains together—after they get home from work—and to aim toward a more secure financial situation before the diaper phase is launched.

Newly married couples also use this "teammates" approach to give the husband a better opportunity for job advancement. I know numerous young wives who are the principal breadwinners while their husbands are engaged in some special training or schooling which temporarily prevents them from holding fulltime jobs. This pattern is especially popular because of the increasing number of skilled occupations and professions which require years of advanced training or education.

As an obstetrician, I feel I must inject at this point a strong warning: If childbearing is postponed for too long a period, the delay may hide a physical obstacle to having children which should be treated as early as possible. Some years ago, I prescribed contraception as a routine matter for a young woman at the time of her marriage. I had known her and her family personally for years and was aware of her desire to have "lots of babies—when we are settled and ready." I had told her, "Don't wait too long—no woman knows for sure she can produce babies until she's had one." But evidently she did not take this seriously, and she and her husband found one reason after another why they weren't "quite ready" to start a family. First they quite responsibly sought to achieve a certain level of financial security before having children. Then they wanted to buy a house, "so we'll have a good place for a family"— again a worthy objective. Then there were other things. At last, when she was more than 30, they were "ready." After attempting for many months to conceive without success, the young lady came to me in panic. Examination disclosed that in the years since her marriage she had developed a tumor. To remove this growth we also had to remove her womb which, of course, made her permanently sterile.

Aside from such specific infertility problems, a woman's ability to have children normally wanes with age—at first very slightly. Many studies have shown that the decrease occurs appreciably in women after the age of 30. Two studies, carried out among rural couples who did not use birth control, investigated the relationship between age of the wife at the time of marriage and later involuntary childlessness. It was found that of wives who married before they were 20, only four percent remained childless. Of those who married between the ages of 20 and 24, six percent remained childless. And so it went, with the proportion of infertility continuing to rise with the age of the wife at marriage: 25 to 29 years, 10 percent; 30 to 34 years, 16 percent; 35 to 39 years, 31 percent; and 40 to 45 years, 69 percent. Another study analyzed the effect of the husband's age on his fertility. It showed that 75 percent of the husbands less than 25 years old were able to impregnate their wives in less than six months, while only 23 percent of the husbands aged 40 and over accomplished this.

Spacing pregnancies at desired intervals is another major reason for the practice of contraception in America today. Not long ago a Pennsylvania woman wrote this letter to the Planned Parenthood Federation of America:

> "I just feel as though I wouldn't be able to take care of another baby too soon. I am so nervous from having my children so close together and caring for so many little ones at once, that I feel it isn't fair to the children, or my husband either, to go on this way. . . ."

The letter poignantly indicates the growing recognition that child-spacing can aid not only maternal health but also human relationships within the family. In this case, of course, the Federation referred the woman—as it does thousands of others annually—to a Planned Parenthood center near her home for contraceptive help.

Fortunately, the physical hazards of having numerous babies in quick succession are not as common as they once were, because of improved medications and obstetrical and postpartum care. But some dangers still exist. Nor is the mother the only one affected by rapid-fire childbearing: According to the United States Public Health Service, "the interval between births is a basic factor in the incidence of stillbirth." For these reasons, the distinguished New York Academy of Medicine recommended in 1946 that "child spacing should be recognized as a medical indication" for contraception.

Physicians therefore often advise couples to allow two or more years between pregnancies. More often, with or without medical guidance, couples link concern for the health of the mother with other factors in deciding to space the arrival of their children.

Closely related considerations include child care and financial stability of the family. Several small children in close age sequence are simply too much for many mothers to give adequate attention to—or for fathers to provide adequate income for so quickly.

And it doesn't take a national study to discover that one of the most common—and sound—reasons for planning longer intervals between babies is plain *mother fatigue.* A young mother may be in good physical health, basically, but her cheerfulness and efficiency can be severely crippled if she has too many youngsters to cope with all at once. How many is "too many?" That depends, of course, on the individual family. I have seen mothers who seem quite able to manage without difficulty four children under the age of five (often, however, with a good deal of help from father or someone else). On the other hand, some mothers can be driven to near exhaustion and despair by two toddlers. A mother who finds herself in the latter situation has no reason to be ashamed. People just do not all have the same kinds of strengths. But she certainly does have good reason to space her children far enough apart so that she can preserve her own energies and disposition and care for her family lovingly and well.

Many of the same reasons which lead couples to space their pregnancies also cause them to limit family size. Among married couples with any offspring at all, the usual number of children per completed United States family is 3.0. Consider this alongside the statistical possibility that a woman marrying at 20 who does nothing to prevent pregnancy can bear 12 or 13 children. These figures show how vigorously Americans are curbing family size—primarily by birth control.

A good medical reason for family limitation is the rise in the risk of death for both mothers and infants after numerous pregnancies. The United States Department of Health, Education and Welfare reported in 1958 that the chances of stillbirth are almost twice as great for sixth children as for firstborn. There is a parallel, though not so steep, increase in maternal deaths when the number of term pregnancies exceeds six to eight.

Decisions to limit family size for medical reasons alone, however, appear to be much less common than decisions which combine the medical with other factors. A young man married to one of my patients recently wrapped it up this way: "We have three youngsters now and they're enough—for us anyway. Nancy's health is fine and we want to keep it that way, so that she can enjoy the kids. Having another baby would prevent us from giving the ones we have enough care and attention. We're thinking about the financial side of it too—I know we couldn't expect to give four children the things they really need." While I daresay a great many couples don't express their reasons for family planning quite that handily, many couples have a similar variety of reasons for limiting the number of their children.

Childbearing is also terminated to permit the mother to hold a paying job. The proportion of wives who are employed outside the home rose from 21 percent in 1947 to more than 30 percent in 1960. Meanwhile the postwar baby boom reached its peak. How did employment of wives and the birth rate increase at the same time? Part of the answer, of course, stems from the rising employment of women before they have children. Of at least equal importance is the increase of employment among women whose families are complete and whose youngest child has reached school age. This reflects the concentration of childbearing during the early years of marriage with the use of birth control during the later years.

The growth of family limitation in America, curiously, exists side by side with a strong tradition about the virtues and values of families with many children—the "cheaper by the dozen" philosophy. The tradition is kept honestly alive by the conspicuously large and responsible families in almost any American community —families we all respect, admire and sometimes envy. There are indications, however, that the tradition is at least partially self-defeating. Sociologists have found that children raised in *large* families, when they grow up and marry, tend to have *small* families—in fact, smaller than average. This was revealed in a University of Pennsylvania study of 100 couples with a total of 879 offspring. Of the 529 children in this group who later married and produced families of their own, only 15—*less than three percent*— had six or more children!

The study also disclosed that the parents of these large families were often less than enthusiastic. While a slight majority of large family fathers reportedly approved and were proud of their abundant paternity, almost as many merely accepted their large broods or indicated that they wished they were smaller. As for the mothers, less than a third were happy about having so many children, while a solid two-thirds majority was merely submissive or outright critical of their fertility.

The attitudes of the children themselves are even more noteworthy: Only 28 percent of these children, now grown, look back with approval on the size of their parents' families. Sixty percent were bluntly or politely critical. Another 11 percent merely accepted it.

Why is this so? The study showed, for one thing, that the older children in large broods—especially the oldest—are often given a great deal of work and responsibility as "deputy parents." These eldest children, perhaps because of their abnormal burdens and resulting lack of freedom, tended to become unhappy and poorly adjusted.

Children raised in large families also recognize from experience how largeness itself may expose the family to misfortune. Back when America was mainly agricultural, many sons were needed to till the soil and numerous daughters had household labor value. The large family tradition grew partly from this. But now, in the main, the reverse is true: In urban life, children are primarily consumers, not producers, and therefore are economic liabilities rather than assets. The large family has much less financial slack than smaller families, because a much higher proportion of its income goes for the bare essentials of food, clothing, and shelter. Unemployment, disability or death of the principal wage earner in a large family thus may be a devastating blow.

No one is more aware of these facts about large families than the children raised in them, and it is evident that this personal awareness is contributing not a little to the practice of contraception in the United States.

At this point, it may be appropriate to note that birth control is also used to produce *large families which are planned*. Not all large families are unplanned any more than all large families are full of unhappy, resentful people. In their summary remarks, the authors of the Pennsylvania study, Drs. James Bossard and Eleanor Boll, observe, "The term 'planned parenthood' has been used so largely to mean planning for a small family that it seems necessary to emphasize this other meaning of the planning process. A number of the large families contacted during the six-year period of this study may be said to be planned. . . ." The parents of some large families I know personally have practiced birth control not only to space the arrival of their children but also to limit their number. They wanted—and produced—six or seven youngsters.

Aside from the variety of reasons for child spacing and family limitation, there are several conditions which make it medically imperative that a woman not become pregnant. In the first place, *almost any serious illness makes it necessary to postpone pregnancy temporarily, or to prevent it permanently.*

Perhaps the most common ailment incompatible with pregnancy is serious heart disease. Fortunately, improvements in therapy permit a woman with only minor or moderate cardiac impairment to have a normal sized family, as long as there are no other medical complications and as long as her family care responsibilities are not too burdensome. But even in these cases medical vigilance is required. And in serious heart cases, physicians almost invariably advise against any more pregnancies.

Lung disease—namely, tuberculosis—usually calls for postponement of pregnancy until the disease has been arrested and remains inactive for a period of at least two years. Physicians may determine if it has been arrested by X-ray examination of scars to see if they are completely healed, and by examination of sputum to see if any TB bacteria are present. Pregnancy among tuberculosis patients often results in active lung lesions becoming worse. New babies are extremely vulnerable to TB germs and may die if infected by tubercular mothers.

Advanced diabetes, if severe and chronic enough to be accompanied by damage to the arteries, may also require permanent prevention of conception. This was the case of my patient from Baltimore I mentioned earlier. In such situations—and with other diseases of similar severity—sterilization may sometimes be preferable to the practice of birth control.

Any cancerous condition involving the breasts or internal organs, and which has required surgery within the past three years, calls for pregnancy postponement, at least until any recurrence of the disease appears unlikely. Kidney disease which curtails the full and normal function of these organs is another reason for preventing pregnancy. Nervous disorders, Parkinson's disease, multiple sclerosis, and the like usually dictate sterilization.

Some inherited diseases require sterilization or strict use of contraception, either to protect the mother, prevent the birth of hopelessly ill children, or both. An example of this is pseudo-hypertrophic muscular dystrophy. It directly attacks only male offspring though it is transmitted by the female. A special problem with this strange malady is that it is often impossible to predict which sons—if any—will be struck in any one generation. Those affected appear to be normal at birth, and may remain so for the first dozen years of life. But then they weaken and die before their mid-twenties.

It is gratifying that such grave medical reasons for the use of birth control involve fewer people today, by far, than 30 or 40 years ago. As our medical horizons have broadened, meanwhile, two long-range developments have figured in the use of birth control as a health measure by a much larger number of Americans.

The first is the growth of *preventive medicine*—that is, the field of medical science devoted to *preventing* physical afflictions rather than *curing* them. The difference between the situations of my former patient from Baltimore and of her daughter is a precise case in point. Contraception may well have saved her mother from death, by eliminating the crucial complication that a pregnancy might have presented in this diabetic. As far as the daughter is concerned, we are safeguarding the young lady's health by providing her with effective birth control knowledge and materials as she begins married life. She does not have diabetes, thank heaven, but use of contraception for child spacing and family limitation will surely help conserve her health. This preventive concept parallels the shift in use of contraception from merely shutting off excessive childbearing to bona fide family planning—deciding beforehand how many children are wanted and having them on a schedule regulated by birth control.

The second long-range medical development which has gone hand in hand with the increasing use of birth control is the extension of knowledge and sensitivity about mental health. By giving married couples greater control over their family growth and greater security in their sexual relationship, birth control is of tremendous value in attaining a greater degree of emotional health and maturity.

HISTORY AND LEGAL STATUS OF BIRTH CONTROL

As the following reading indicates, free access to birth control information has continually been hampered by segments of public opposition and in some instances by restrictive legislation. The present-day statutes in Massachusetts and Connecticut and the federal Comstock Act, discussed below, represent vestiges of a long siege of anti-contraceptive (and, one suspects, generally anti-sexual) pressures. As the author notes, the federal statute has been interpreted liberally in the courts. The Massachusetts and Connecticut laws would be absolutely meaningless (since contraceptives are widely sold and used in those states) were it not for their effectiveness in outlawing local birth control clinics there. This has resulted in a definite discrimination in these jurisdictions against persons of limited means—who are probably most in need of contraceptive advice, yet are least able to afford private consultations. Despite the widespread approval of family planning in the United States, related public policy measures on the local, state, and federal levels continue to arouse fierce public controversy.

History and Legal Status of Birth Control

NORMAN ST. JOHN-STEVAS

HISTORY

From the earliest times man has attempted to control conception. Anthropologists have established that both magical and rational methods were employed by primitive tribes. Amongst the civilised nations of antiquity, the Egyptians, the Jews, the Greeks, and the Romans, all possessed knowledge of contraception. Plato wished to restrict all procreation by law, confining it to men between the ages of thirty and thirty-five, and women aged twenty to forty. Aristotle also recommended the legal regulation of conception, and approved both abortion and infanticide. By scientific research, Greek physicians and medical writers greatly improved existing contraceptive techniques. Their discoveries were utilised by the Romans, but contrary to popular belief, contraceptive knowledge was not widely diffused in the Roman world, being confined in the main to medical writers, physicians, and scholars. Islamic contraceptive medicine, which owed much to the Greeks, was developed during the middle ages, but little progress was made in Europe during the same period, the attitude of the Church being unfavourable to such researches. It was not until the sixteenth century that a new advance was made with the publication in 1564, two years after his death, of Gabriele Fallopio's "De Morbo Gallico", a treatise on venereal disease. His treatise contained the first published account of the condom or sheath, which Fallopio claimed to have invented. The condom was employed during the eighteenth century, both in England and on the Continent, being mainly used

Reprinted from Norman St. John-Stevas, *Life, Death and the Law* (Bloomington: Indiana University Press, 1961), pp. 50-69; footnotes omitted.

in brothels, but also sold in shops in London and elsewhere. At the end of the century, contraceptives were still associated exclusively with immorality and vice, but by the close of the nineteenth century, this position had been deeply undermined and the way prepared for the general acceptance of contraceptives which has been so marked a feature of our own time.

Thomas Malthus, an Anglican curate, was the unwitting founder of the modern birth control movement, by means of his famous *Essay on the Principle of Population,* published in 1798. His thesis was simple. Both population and food supplies tend to increase, but since population increases faster than means of subsistence, the majority of the human race is doomed to perpetual poverty and malnutrition. Disease and war act as natural checks and so prevent a universal cataclysm. In the first edition of his book, Malthus offered no way of escape from this dreadful treadmill, but in 1803 the second edition of his *Essay* included recommendations for "moral restraint." By this Malthus did not mean that sexual intercourse should be restrained in marriage, but that marriages should be postponed to a late age or complete celibacy embraced. Far from advocating any means of contraception, he expressly condemned recourse to "improper arts."

Radical reaction to Malthus' pessimistic and conservative doctrine was sharp. Generally accepted, it would put an end to all efforts at social reform, for by his hypothesis these were automatically condemned to failure. Godwin wrote two ineffective replies to refute Malthus, but it was left to Francis Place, in his *Illustrations and Proofs of the Principle of Population,* published in 1882, to suggest that in the use of artificial contraception lay the answer to population problems. If, he wrote, "it were once clearly understood, that it was not disreputable for married persons to avail themselves of such precautionary means as would, without being injurious to health, or destructive of female delicacy, prevent conception, a sufficient check might at once be given to the increase of population beyond the means of subsistence; vice and misery, to a prodigious extent, might be removed from society, and the object of Mr Malthus, Mr Godwin, and of every philanthropic person, be promoted, by the increase of comfort, of intelligence, and of moral conduct, in the mass of the population." Place supplemented his argument by distributing amongst the working classes, a series of "diabolical handbills", recommending contraception. Despite their outlining a particular method of contraception—the use of a sponge and attached ribbon—they were not legally suppressed. Similar immunity was enjoyed by the publications of Place's disciples, Richard Carlile, Richard Hassell, and William Campion. Place's influence spread to the United States, where Robert Dale Owen was emboldened in 1830 to publish the first American booklet on birth control, *Moral Physiology*. Two years later, Dr Charles Knowlton, a Massachusetts physician, published anonymously a further treatise on contraceptive methods, curiously entitled, *Fruits of Philosophy*. Knowlton eventually served a term of imprisonment for his part in publishing this book, and later it was the subject of a celebrated English trial. Malthusian contentions were revived by George Drysdale in his *Elements of Social Science*, published in England in 1854, in which he advocated "preventive sexual intercourse."

By mid-century, Malthusian prophecies and their suggested remedies were generally discussed in educated circles, but the general public was still ignorant of contraception and the arguments for its use. In 1877, however, the trial of Charles Bradlaugh and Annie Besant for publishing an English edition of *Fruits of Philosophy* made contraception a hotly debated subject throughout the country and amongst all classes. Mrs Besant utilised a golden opportunity to spread the good news, speaking at inordinate length, and spending much of her time addressing the public on the laws of Malthus and the necessity for birth control, rather than defending herself against the charge of publishing an obscene libel. Both defendants were found guilty, but the following year the conviction was set aside for a defect of the indictment. The effects of the prosecution were startling. Before 1876 the circulation of *Fruits of Philosophy* had been only 1,000 per year, but by August 1881 no less than 185,000 copies had been sold, bearing out the words of Sir Alexander Cockburn at the trial that "a more ill advised and more injudicious prosecution never was instituted". Knowledge of contraceptive methods became widespread, and the work was carried forward by the Malthusian League, founded in 1878, with Annie Besant as its first secretary.

Of itself the Bradlaugh-Besant trial would not have resulted in a popularization of contraception, but it came at a moment peculiarly favourable to the cause. Industrialisation and the fall in the death rate had resulted in a vastly increased population, the great depression of 1873-96 led to widespread dislocation in agriculture and industry, women becoming more emancipated and unwilling to bear the burden of unrestricted families, while legislation forbidding child employment had reduced the value of children as income-earning assets. Shortly after the trial, in 1880, education for the first time was made compulsory, and this further increased the financial burden of large families. Contraception had still to win general social acceptance, but after 1878 few attempts were made to suppress *bona fide* birth control propaganda by law. The way was thus opened for a flow of publications advocating birth control. In 1879 Annie Besant published her own treatise, "The Law of Population". By 1891 it had sold 175,000 copies in England alone, at the low price of sixpence each. English law had become quiescent, but private opposition to birth control was still strong. Thus in 1887, Dr Henry Allbutt's name was erased from the medical register by the General Medical Council for publishing a popular work on birth control, *The Wife's Handbook*. In 1913 the Malthusian League for the first time published a practical handbook on birth control, *Hygienic Methods of Family Limitation,* and put it in general circulation without legal incident. After the First World War, the social restrictions on dissemination of birth control information dissolved. Marie Stopes founded the *Society for Construc-*

tive Birth Control, and in 1921 opened the first birth control clinic in London. Her work was carried on by Harold Cox, Julian Huxley, Norman Haire, Dean Inge, Lord Dawson of Penn and others. In 1930 the Lambeth Conference gave a grudging approval to family planning by contraceptives, a concession which led to a more whole-hearted approval by the Lambeth Conference of 1958. The official visits paid by the Minister of Health to the headquarters of the Family Planning Association in London, in 1955 and 1958, symbolized the nearly complete triumph of the birth control movement in Great Britain.

In the United States, the movement has not met with such unqualified success. Dr Knowlton was succeeded by other medical writers advancing the cause of birth control, including A. M. Mauriceau, J. Soule, Edward Bliss Foote, and his son Edward Bond Foote. John Humphrey Noyes founded the Oneida colony in New York and advocated his own particular method of birth control. Birth control suffered a severe setback in 1873 when, thanks to the efforts of Anthony Comstock, Congress enacted a statute excluding contraceptives and contraceptive information from the mails, declaring them obscene. Many states followed suit and passed statutes banning the sale and distribution of contraceptives. These laws were enforced with varying degrees of efficiency in different parts of the country but undoubtedly hindered the acceptance of birth control by the community. In 1912, Margaret Sanger, a New York nurse, started her life's work as a zealot for birth control. She began studying the subject and gave her first public lectures. In 1914 she began publication of a new monthly magazine, *The Woman Rebel,* and was arrested and indicted under the Comstock law. She fled to Europe and the following year her husband was imprisoned for a short term for handing out a copy of her pamphlet, *Family Limitation.* Mrs Sanger returned to the United States and on October 16, 1916, opened the first Birth Control Clinic in the United States in Brooklyn. The clinic was raided and closed by the police, Mrs Sanger and her sister both being sentenced to thirty days imprisonment in 1917. Nevertheless she continued her work and propaganda, basing her appeal on the suffering caused to women by unlimited child bearing rather than on Malthusian arguments. In 1917 the National Birth Control League was founded, and Mrs Sanger began publication of the *Birth Control Review*. National and international conferences were held and in 1921 the New York Birth Control Clinical Research Bureau was opened. Repeated efforts by Mrs Sanger and Mary Ware Dennett were made to repeal or amend the federal laws restricting birth control, but were not successful. In 1929 the New York clinic was raided and its director and assistant arrested. They were later discharged and the clinic continued its work. Public opinion gradually began to favour birth control. The gynecological section of the American Medical Association had passed a motion in 1925 recommending the altering of the law to allow physicians to give contraceptive advice: in 1931 the Federal Council of the Churches of Christ published a report favouring birth control: support also came from the American Neurological Association, the Eugenics Society and the Central Conference of Rabbis. In 1936 the Court of Appeals upheld a ruling of the District Court that contraceptives imported for a lawful purpose did not come within the restrictions of federal law. In 1937 the American Medical Association unanimously agreed to accept birth control "as an integral part of medical practice and education".

Today birth control, the Roman Catholic and Orthodox Churches always excepted, is generally approved in the United States. The courts have modified the operation of federal statutes and most State statutes have been liberally interpreted. Hundreds of different types of contraceptives are in use and contraception has become big business. In April 1958, Robert Sheehan estimated that the contraceptive trade in the United States grossed two hundred million dollars a year, no less than one hundred and fifty million being spent on condoms. Despite this activity and considerable medical research, the ideal method of contraception still does not, and probably cannot exist. Such a method should display five features: it should be wholly effective and reliable: harmless to users and to subsequent children: aesthetically acceptable: moderate in price: and unobjectionable on religious and moral grounds.

ENGLISH LAW

Traditionally, the law in England has followed the Prayer Book in recognising the procreation of children as the primary purpose of marriage. Thus in an early nineteenth century case, Sir John Nicholl referred to the procreation of children as "the primary and most legitimate object of wedlock." The continued operation of the doctrine was illustrated by a Court of Appeal case in 1946, where it was held that a man who had consistently refused to have intercourse without employing a contraceptive, against the wishes of his wife, had wilfully refused to consummate the marriage, thus entitling her to a decree of nullity. "We are of opinion," said Lord Justice du Parcq, "that sexual intercourse cannot be said to be complete where a husband deliberately discontinues the act of intercourse before it has reached its natural termination or when he artificially prevents the natural termination, which is the passage of the male seed into the body of the woman. To hold otherwise would be to affirm that a marriage is consummated by an act so performed that one of the principal ends, if not the principal end, of marriage is intentionally frustrated." Two years later, the House of Lords abandoned the principle. "It is indisputable," said Lord Jowitt, with remarkable confidence, "that the institution of marriage generally is not necessary for the procreation of children; nor does it appear to be a principal end of marriage as understood in Christendom, which, as Lord Penzance said in *Hyde v. Hyde* (1866), L.R. 1 P.&D. 130, 133, 'may for this purpose be defined as the voluntary union of one man and one woman to the exclusion of all others'.'" Accordingly a spouse has no right to a nullity decree at English law if the other spouse insists that intercourse shall only take place with the employment of a contraceptive.

As has been noted, contraceptive information was in the nineteenth century classified as obscenity, and sale of contraceptives doubtless came within the common law offence of publishing obscene matter, but this is no longer the case. Books are no longer considered obscene if they advocate or describe methods of birth control. "It cannot be assumed," said the Home Secretary in answer to a question in the House of Commons in 1922, "that a court would hold a book to be obscene merely because it deals with the subject referred to." Sale of contraceptives is not subject to common law or statutory restriction save for certain by-laws which restrict the sale of contraceptives from slot machines in public places. Advertisements for contraceptives are not *per se* considered obscene. This lack of legal restraint is not surprising since it accords with prevailing English opinion on the subject, summed up by the Royal Commission on Population when it stated: "Control by men and women over the numbers of their children is one of the first conditions of their own and the community's welfare, and in our view mechanical and chemical methods of contraception have to be accepted as part of the modern means, however imperfect, by which it can be exercised."

Under the National Health Service, however, advice on birth control can only be given in certain circumstances. The Ministry of Health allows contraceptive advice to be given in maternal and child welfare clinics to those married women for whom a pregnancy would be detrimental to health. Many medical officers refer patients outside this category to the voluntary birth clinics which are found in many areas. Local authorities may themselves, with the approval of the Minister open contraceptive clinics and give advice to nursing mothers requiring it on medical grounds. They may also contribute to voluntary organizations providing such advice. Many clinics of the Family Planning Association are conducted on the premises of the local authority or regional hospital boards. General practitioners in the Service are not forbidden to provide contraceptive advice for their patients. They may not charge for advice given on medical grounds, but may do so when no medical reason exists for limitation of pregnancies. Contraceptive appliances are not obtainable on National Health Service prescriptions, but if a patient needs them on medical grounds and cannot afford to pay for them, payment may be authorized by a local authority medical officer or hospital consultant. The Royal Commission on Population recommended that all restrictions on giving contraceptive advice to married women under public health services should be removed. Public authorities, held the Commission, should not view the furnishing of advice as a concession, but as a positive duty. This accords with its expressed view that "public policy should assume and seek to encourage, the spread of voluntary parenthood".

UNITED STATES LAW

Federal Law. Federal law restricts the distribution of contraceptives in several ways. Knowingly to deposit any contraceptive in the mails or to take such articles from the mails for the purpose of distribution is a felony under federal law. The ban extends to any information as to where contraceptives may be obtained, and any written or printed matter telling "how or by what means conception may be prevented". A further federal felony is constituted by depositing contraceptives or information where they may be obtained with an express company or other common carrier. Books on contraception are not specifically mentioned, but obscene books are included in the ban. To import contraceptive articles or obscene books is also a felony and prohibited by federal statute.

Read literally, these statutes impose an absolute and universal ban, and many attempts have been made to modify their scope by legislation. All have failed. They have, however, been modified by judicial interpretation. A first step was taken in 1930, when Judge Swan stated that: "The intention to prevent a proper medical use of drugs or other articles merely because they are capable of illegal uses is not lightly to be ascribed to Congress." Without deciding the point, he suggested that the Criminal Code should be interpreted as requiring an intent on the part of the sender that "the articles mailed or sent by common carrier be used for illegal contraception or abortion or for indecent or immoral uses." This reasoning was applied in *Davis v. United States* (1933), when an intent to use the articles for illegal purposes was held necessary for a conviction under the postal and transport statutes. The decision permitted manufacturers of contraceptives and others in the trade to dispatch their wares to druggists, jobbers, and physicians. These decisions led logically to that of *United States v. One Package* in 1936, when Dr Hannah Stone was allowed to import a package of vaginal pessaries into the United States. Judge Augustus Hand conceded that the Tariff Act of 1930 exempted only those articles excepted by the Comstock Act of 1873, but he went on to say that the court was satisfied "that this statute, as well as all the Acts we have referred to, embraced only such articles as Congress would have denounced as immoral if it had understood all the conditions under which they were to be used. Its design, in our opinion, was not to prevent the importation, sale, or carriage by mail of things which might intelligently be employed by conscientious and competent physicians for the purpose of saving life or promoting the well being of their patients." Judge Learned Hand was clearly uneasy about these verbal gymnastics, but contented himself with observing that people had changed their minds about such matters in recent years, and concurred in the judgment.

Books on contraception are specifically banned from the mails by the postal statute, but the section restricting imports mentions only "obscene" books. It is now established that a book on contraception is not *per se* considered obscene by the federal courts. Dismissing a charge against "Contraception" by Marie Stopes in

1931, Judge Woolsey stated: "It is a scientific book written with obvious seriousness and with great decency, and it gives information to the medical profession regarding the operation of birth control clinics and the instruction necessary to be given at such clinics to women who resort thereto." Such a book, he held, was not obscene, "for the reading of it would not stir the sex impulses of any person with a normal mind."

The federal statutes are accordingly by no means dead letters, but contraceptives intended for *bona fide* medical use, for the treatment or prevention of disease, and contraceptive books and pamphlets which are not written in obscene language, may be freely imported, transported and mailed. In practice this means that contraceptives must be going to or coming from doctors or other professional persons, or anyone acting at their direction or under their supervision. Druggists, jobbers and dealers, provided they are legitimate traders, thus enjoy immunity. This rule applies to contraceptive books and pamphlets going through the mails, but not to the importation of such books or to their transport in interstate commerce. Under the customs law, only obscene books are excluded, and, as has been noted, *bona fide* contraceptive manuals are not any longer within this category. To secure a conviction under the statutes an intention to use the materials illegally must be established by the prosecution. However, for administrative purposes, consignments may be stopped by the authorities temporarily, pending the production of *prima facie* evidence by the addressee that he is a privileged recipient. The Family Planning Association makes it a practice to consign contraceptives and information under a doctor's signature, and thus obviate vexatious delays. Private persons, importing, mailing or transporting contraceptives, purely for the purpose of preventing conception, with no medical indication for their employment, would still, at least theoretically, be caught by the statutes.

The Law of the States. Of the fifty American States, twenty and the District of Columbia have no legislation on the subject of contraception. Seventeen States prohibit traffic in contraceptives, but exempt doctors, pharmacists, or others operating under special license, from the statutory prohibition. Five States, Connecticut, Kansas, Massachusetts, Mississippi, and Nebraska, prohibit the sale of contraceptives and advertising. The statutes make no exceptions. Eight States have no law against contraceptives but restrict or prohibit their advertisement. In all, thirty States prohibit such advertising, fifteen making an exception for medical journals and textbooks, etc. Sixteen States regulate the trade by requiring contraceptive information to be accurate and prohibiting the sale of articles which do not comply with certain defined standards. In some States, sale of contraceptives from slot machines is forbidden.

In New York, Connecticut, and Massachusetts, considerable litigation has taken place to interpret the birth control statutes.

New York.   New York law prohibits distribution of contraceptives and birth control information, but contains the following proviso: "An article or instrument, used or applied by physicians lawfully practising, or by their direction or prescription, for the cure or prevention of disease is not an article of indecent or immoral nature or use, within this article. The supplying of such articles to such physicians or by their direction or prescription, is not an offense under this article." In 1917, Margaret Sanger was sentenced to thirty days imprisonment for violating the statute. Her appeal was dismissed, but the judge gave a liberal interpretation of the section. It protected, said the court, the physician who "in good faith gives such help or advice to a married person to cure or prevent disease". "Disease" was not limited to venereal disease, but defined as "an alteration in the state of the body, or some of its organs, interrupting or disturbing the performance of the vital functions, and causing or threatening pain and sickness; illness; sickness; disorder".

Connecticut.   The Connecticut law forbidding birth control dates from 1879, when it was dealt with as part of the obscenity statute, but since 1887 it has been a separate enactment. "Any person who shall use any drug, medicinal article or instrument for the purpose of preventing conception, shall be fined not less than fifty dollars or imprisoned not less than sixty days nor more than one year or be both fined and imprisoned." The statute is unique in that it prohibits not merely the sale but the use of a contraceptive. In 1940, two physicians and a nurse, indicted for counselling a married woman to use a contraceptive, contended that the statute was unconstitutional, unless it was interpreted to except the medical profession. The Supreme Court of Errors rejected this argument, which had been accepted by the lower court, and upheld the statute. The court confined its decision to situations where the "general health" of the woman would be endangered by lack of contraception, and left open the question whether an exception existed where "pregnancy would jeopardize life". This loophole was closed in 1942. In that year, a doctor sought a ruling whether the statute would apply where pregnancy would entail specific dangers to health because of high blood pressure, tuberculosis, or three pregnancies within twenty-seven months. The court held (3-2) that it did apply, and that abstention in such predicaments must have been considered by the legislature as an alternative to the use of contraceptives, when passing the statute. Various attempts have been made to modify the law, but all have failed.

Massachusetts. Publication of any printed matter containing birth control information and distribution of instruments and articles for preventing conception are prohibited by a statute dating from 1879. The statute was upheld as constitutional and applied in 1917, when certain pamphlets containing birth control information were held to be obscene. In 1938 the courts rejected a plea that physicians were exempt from the operation of the statute when prescribing for health reasons. In 1940, however, it was held that the distribution of prophylactics, which could also be used for contraception, did not come within the statute, unless it could be proved that the distributor intended to prevent conception rather than venereal disease, or knew that such unlawful use was intended by the buyer. As in Connecticut, unsuccessful attempts have been made to modify the law. In 1930 a Bill was introduced to give licensed physicians the right to provide information to married couples, but was later withdrawn. The following year a petition for change was signed by 7,000 laymen, 1,300 doctors, and 400 ministers of religion, but it failed to be implemented. An amendment to the same effect was defeated in the House of Representatives in 1941 by 133 votes to seventy-seven, and in the Senate by eighteen votes to sixteen. Referendums in 1942 and 1948 also failed to alter the law.

The Constitutional Question. It has been suggested that the federal and state statutes regulating birth control are unconstitutional, in that they deny the individual his personal right to pursuit of happiness and also take away the rights protected by the due process clause of the fourteenth amendment. Physicians, when the laws are strictly interpreted, are also denied a fundamental right to advise patients on professional matters involving life and health. The courts have taken an opposite view. The federal courts have upheld the federal statutes as constitutional, with an exemption for physicians and others professionally qualified. Prohibition of the sale or advertising of contraceptives or the dissemination of information on birth control has consistently been held to be within the police power of individual States. Until 1938, none of the cases had included a qualified physician as party to the proceedings, or else the statute under review contained a clause exempting physicians from its operation. In that year, however, in Gardner's case, a statute imposing an unconditional ban was upheld by the Massachusetts courts, and an appeal to the United States Supreme Court dismissed. In June 1958 five suits were filed in the Connecticut Superior Court challenging the constitutionality of the birth control legislation.

An attack on the birth control statutes may develop in the future on rather different grounds. While the police power may be exercised to protect public morals, it must be reasonable. With the general acceptance of birth control as a normal part of married life, the statutes might be held unreasonable at some point in the future. The statutes could also be challenged for violating the separation of Church and State guaranteed by the first amendment. Recent theological developments have left the Roman Catholic Church and Orthodox Churches practically isolated among Christian denominations in condemning artificial birth control. It could, then, be contended, that the birth control statutes enforce the doctrine of particular denominations at the expense of that of other religious communions. Alternatively, it might be argued that the statutes limit religious freedom.

Effectiveness of Laws. The effect in practice of the federal laws has already been described. The effect of the State laws varies in different areas. In the seventeen States which exempt doctors and other qualified persons from the operation of the laws, their effect is negligible. Birth control clinics are free to operate, provided they are in charge of someone medically qualified, and contraceptives are freely purchasable at drugstores and elsewhere. In the five States that theoretically ban all sale of contraceptives, the law has practical effects only in Connecticut and Massachusetts. There are no birth control clinics in Connecticut, although the Planned Parenthood League of Connecticut has an office in New Haven. A number of medically supervised clinics were opened in 1935, but in 1939 they were raided and after the decision of the Supreme Court in 1940 (*State v. Nelson*), all were closed and have not been reopened since. Doctors are officially barred from prescribing birth control appliances for patients, but, as has been noted: "It is common knowledge that this statute is being violated daily, except perhaps by a few high-minded doctors." Certain contraceptives may even be legitimately prescribed if they have other than contraceptive uses. Contraceptives, creams and jellies are sold everywhere, and condoms may be obtained at drugstores and even from slot machines. Supplies are sent to doctors by mail and literature on contraception is sold openly on bookstalls.

Like Connecticut, Massachusetts has no birth control clinics. From 1932-7 clinics were opened in various cities, but as a result of the Gardner case in 1938, they were closed and have not been re-opened. Thousands of doctors, in the privacy of their offices, fit and prescribe diaphragms. Condoms may legally be sold when marked "for prevention of disease" and diaphragms are sold by drugstores using devious methods of prescription. Vaginal creams and jellies are also sold, marked "for feminine hygiene." The Planned Parenthood League refers women to out-of-State clinics, and is able to tell them orally of certain new and simple contraceptives. "I am not too concerned," concludes Judge Ploscowe, "about this failure of Massachusetts and Connecticut to permit the dissemination of contraceptive information. The corner drugstore is always available for the purchase of prophylactic devices which are used mainly for contraceptive purposes. If more is desired, then the doctors in neighbouring States are available for consultation." This judgment is not shared by the Planned Parenthood Leagues, which point out that, whereas women who can afford a private consultation with a doctor, may obtain contraceptive care, poorer women cannot; that the law makes the less efficient types of contraceptive available but outlaws the more effective; and that the poor who depend on public clinics for medical advice are kept ignorant of the subject, many of them being unaware that contraceptives can be obtained at drugstores, provided they are purchased as prophylactics.

ENCYCLICAL ON CHRISTIAN MARRIAGE

The Papal Encyclical which follows is perhaps the major pronouncement of the Roman Catholic Church relating to the matters under consideration in this book. As can be seen, it touches on topics included in all three sections of this volume, and indeed the Church's position on birth control must be viewed in relation to the broader Catholic emphasis on a stable family unit, on the home roles of women, and on the restriction of sex to the marital relation.

Whereas the Church's spokesmen originally condemned contraception as such, with the discovery of the "safe period" (and the rhythm method) the opposition came to be directed more specifically against "artificial" methods of control—i.e., against contraceptives rather than contraception. In a careful study of Catholic birth control doctrine (1959), Alvah Sulloway foresaw the possibility that the new oral contraceptives might be accepted by the Church; the same hope was more recently expressed by Dr. John Rock, in his influential book The Time Has Come *(1963). Thus far, however, this suggestion has received little support from authoritative spokesmen—some of whom strongly criticized Dr. Rock (a Catholic) for the position he had taken.*

Encyclical on Christian Marriage

PIUS XI

How great is the dignity of chaste wedlock, Venerable Brethen, may be judged best from this that Christ Our Lord, Son of the Eternal Father, having assumed the nature of fallen man, not only, with His loving desire of compassing the redemption of our race, ordained it in an especial manner as the principle and foundation of domestic society and therefore of all human intercourse, but also raised it to the rank of a truly and great sacrament of the New Law, restored it to the original purity of its divine institution, and accordingly entrusted all its discipline and care to His spouse of the Church. . . .

. . . And to begin with let it be repeated as an immutable and inviolable fundamental doctrine that matrimony was not instituted or restored by man but by God; not by man were the laws made to strengthen and confirm and elevate it but by God, the Author of nature, and by Christ Our Lord by Whom nature was redeemed, and hence these laws cannot be subject to any human decrees or to any contrary pact even of the spouses themselves. This is the doctrine of Holy Scripture; this is the constant tradition of the Universal Church; this is the solemn definition of the sacred Council of Trent, which declares and establishes from the words of Holy Writ itself that God is the Author of the perpetual stability of the marriage bond, its unity and its firmness.

Yet although matrimony is of its very nature of divine institution, the human will, too, enters into it and performs a most noble part. For each individual marriage, inasmuch as it is a conjugal union

Reprinted from Anne Freemantle, ed., *The Papal Encyclicals* (New York: Mentor Books, 1956), pp. 235-243. Official English version, Vatican Polyglot Press.

of a particular man and woman, arises only from the free consent of each of the spouses; and this free act of the will, by which each party hands over and accepts those rights proper to the state of marriage, is so necessary to constitute true marriage that it cannot be supplied by any human power. This freedom, however, regards only the question whether the contracting parties really wish to enter upon matrimony or to marry this particular person; but the nature of matrimony is entirely independent of the free will of man, so that if one has once contracted matrimony he is thereby subject to its divinely made laws and its essential properties. For the Angelic Doctor, waiting on conjugal honour and on the off-spring which is the fruit of marriage, says: "These things are so contained in matrimony by the marriage pact itself that, if any-thing to the contrary were expressed in the consent which makes the marriage, it would not be a true marriage. . . ."

. . . [According to the teaching of Leo XIII,] "To take away from man the natural and primeval right of marriage, to circumscribe in any way the principal ends of marriage laid down in the beginning by God Himself in the words 'Increase and multiply,' is beyond the power of any human law."

Therefore the sacred partnership of true marriage is constituted both by the will of God and the will of man. From God comes the very institution of marriage, the ends for which it was instituted, the laws that govern it, the blessings that flow from it; while man, through generous surrender of his own person made to another for the whole span of life, becomes, with the help and co-operation of God, the author of each particular marriage, with the duties and blessings annexed thereto from divine institution.... . .

. . . That mutual familiar intercourse between the spouses them-selves, if the blessing of conjugal faith is to shine with becoming splendour, must be distinguished by chastity so that husband and wife bear themselves in all things with the law of God and of nature, and endeavour always to follow the will of their most wise and holy Creator with the greatest reverence towards the work of God.

This conjugal faith, however, which is most aptly called by St. Augustine the "faith of chastity," blooms more freely, more beautifully and more nobly, when it is rooted in that more excellent soil, the love of husband and wife which pervades all the duties of married life and holds pride of place in Christian marriage. For matrimonial faith demands that husband and wife be joined in an especially holy and pure love, not as adulterers love each other, but as Christ loved the Church. This precept the Apostle laid down when he said: "Husbands, love your wives as Christ also loved the Church," that Church which of a truth He embraced with a boundless love not for the sake of His own advantage, but seeking only the good of His Spouse. The love, then, of which We are speaking is not that based on the passing lust of the moment nor does it consist in pleasing words only, but in the deep attachment of the heart which is expressed in action, since love is proved by deeds. This outward expression of love in the home demands not only mutual help but must go further; must have as its primary purpose that man and wife help each other day by day in forming and perfecting themselves in the interior life, so that through their partnership in life they may advance ever more and more in virtue, and above all that they may grow in true love towards God and their neighbour, on which indeed "dependeth the whole Law and the Prophets." For all men of every condition, in whatever honourable walk of life they may be, can and ought to imitate that most perfect example of holiness placed before man by God, namely Christ Our Lord, and by God's grace to arrive at the summit of perfection, as is proved by the example set us of many saints.

By this same love it is necessary that all the other rights and duties of the marriage state be regulated as the words of the Apostle: "Let the husband render the debt to the wife, and the wife also in like manner to the husband," express not only a law of justice but of charity.

Domestic society being confirmed, therefore, by this bond of love, there should flourish in it that "order of love," as St. Augustine calls it. This order includes both the primacy of the husband with regard to the wife and children, the ready subjection of the wife and her willing obedience, which the Apostle commends in these words: "Let women be subject to their husbands as to the Lord, because the husband is the head of the wife, as Christ is the head of the Church."

This subjection, however, does not deny or take away the liberty which fully belongs to the woman both in view of her dignity as a human person, and in view of her most noble office as wife and mother and companion; nor does it bid her obey her husband's every request if not in harmony with right reason or with the dignity due to wife; nor, in fine, does it imply that the wife should be put on a level with those persons who in law are called minors, to whom it is not customary to allow free exercise of their rights on account of their lack of mature judgment, or of their ignorance of human affairs. But it forbids that exaggerated liberty which cares not for the good of the family; it forbids that in this body which is the family, the heart be separated from the head to the great detriment of the whole body and the proximate danger of ruin. For if the man is the head, the woman is the heart, and as he occupies the chief place in ruling, so she may and ought to claim for herself the chief place in love.

Again, this subjection of wife to husband in its degree and manner may vary according to the different conditions of persons, place and time. In fact, if the husband neglect his duty, it falls to the wife to take his place in directing the family. But the structure of the family and its fundamental law, established and confirmed by God, must always and everywhere be maintained intact. . . .

These, then, are the elements which compose the blessing of conjugal faith: unity, chastity, charity, honourable noble obedience, which are at the same time an enumeration of the benefits which are bestowed on husband and wife in their married state, benefits by which the peace, the dignity and the happiness of matrimony are securely preserved and fostered. Wherefore it is not surprising that this conjugal faith has always been counted amongst the most priceless and special blessings of matrimony.

But this accumulation of benefits is completed and, as it were, crowned by that blessing of Christian marriage which in the words of St. Augustine we have called the sacrament, by which is denoted both the indissolubility of the bond and the raising and hallowing of the contract by Christ Himself, whereby He made it an efficacious sign of grace. . . .

. . . Considering the benefits of the Sacrament, besides the firmness and indissolubility, there are also much higher emoluments, as the word "sacrament" itself very aptly indicates; for to Christians this is not a meaningless and empty name. Christ the Lord, the Institutor and "Perfecter" of the holy sacraments, by raising the matrimony of His faithful to the dignity of a true sacrament of the New Law, made it a sign and source of that peculiar internal grace by which "it perfects natural love, it confirms an indissoluble union, and sanctifies both man and wife."

And since the valid matrimonial consent among the faithful was constituted by Christ as a sign of grace, the sacramental nature is so intimately bound up with Christian wedlock that there can be no true marriage between baptized persons "without it being by that very fact a sacrament. . . ."

And now, Venerable Brethren, we shall explain in detail the evils opposed to each of the benefits of matrimony. First consideration is due to the offspring, which many have the boldness to call the disagreeable burden of matrimony and which they say is to be carefully avoided by married people not through virtuous continence (which Christian law permits in matrimony when both parties consent) but by frustrating the marriage act. Some justify this criminal abuse on the ground that they are weary of children and wish to gratify their desires without their consequent burden. Others say that they cannot on the one hand remain continent nor on the other can they have children because of the difficulties whether on the part of the mother or on the part of family circumstances.

But no reason, however grave, may be put forward by which anything intrinsically against nature may become conformable to nature and morally good. Since, therefore, the conjugal act is destined primarily by nature for the begetting of children, those who in exercising it deliberately frustrate its natural power and purpose sin against nature and commit a deed which is shameful and intrinsically vicious. . . .

Since, therefore, openly departing from the uninterrupted Christian tradition, some recently have judged it possible solemnly to declare another doctrine regarding this question, the Catholic Church, to whom God has entrusted the defence of the integrity and purity of morals, standing erect in the midst of the moral ruin which surrounds her, in order that she may preserve the chastity of the nuptial union from being defiled by this foul stain, raises her voice in token of her divine ambassadorship and through Our mouth proclaims anew: any use whatsoever of matrimony exercised in such a way that the act is deliberately frustrated in its natural power to generate life is an offence against the law of God and of nature, and those who indulge in such are branded with the guilt of a grave sin. . . .

As regards the evil use of matrimony, to pass over the arguments which are shameful, not infrequently others that are false and exaggerated are put forward. Holy Mother Church very well understands and clearly appreciates all that is said regarding the health of the mother and the danger to her life. And who would not grieve to think of these things? Who is not filled with the greatest admiration when he sees a mother risking her life with heroic fortitude, that she may preserve the life of the offspring which she has conceived? God alone, all bountiful and all merciful as He is, can reward her for the fulfilment of the office allotted to her by nature, and will assuredly repay her in a measure full to overflowing.

Holy Church knows well that not infrequently one of the parties is sinned against rather than sinning, when for a grave cause he or she reluctantly allows the perversion of the right order. In such a case, there is no sin, provided that, mindful of the law of charity, he or she does not neglect to seek to dissuade and to deter the partner from sin. Nor are those considered as acting against nature who in the married state use their right in the proper manner although on account of natural reasons either of time or of certain defects, new life cannot be brought forth. For in matrimony as well as in the use of the matrimonial rights there are also secondary ends, such as mutual aid, the cultivating of mutual love, and the quieting of concupiscence which husband and wife are not forbidden to consider so long as they are subordinated to the primary end and so long as the intrinsic nature of the act is preserved. . . .

But another very grave crime is to be noted, Venerable Brethen, which regards the taking of the life of the offspring hidden in the mother's womb. Some wish it to be allowed and left to the will of the father or the mother; others say it is unlawful unless there are weighty reasons which they call by the name of medical, social, or eugenic "indication." Because this matter falls under the penal laws of the state by which the destruction of the offspring begotten but unborn is forbidden, these people demand that the "indication," which in one form or another they defend, be recognized as such by the public law and in no way penalized. There are those, moreover, who ask that the public authorities provide aid for these death-dealing operations, a thing, which, sad to say, everyone knows is of very frequent occurrence in some places.

As to the "medical and therapeutic indication" to which, using their own words, we have made reference, Venerable Brethren, however much we may pity the mother whose health and even life is gravely imperiled in the performance of the duty allotted to her by nature, nevertheless what could ever be a sufficient reason for excusing in any way the direct murder of the innocent? This is precisely what we are dealing with here. Whether inflicted upon the mother or upon the child, it is against the precept of God and the law of nature: "Thou shalt not kill." The life of each is equally sacred, and no one has the power, not even the public authority, to destroy it. It is of no use to appeal to the right of taking away life for here it is a question of the innocent, whereas that right has regard only to the guilty; nor is there here question of defense by bloodshed against an unjust aggressor (for who would call an innocent child an unjust aggressor?); again there is no question here of what is called the "law of extreme necessity" which could even extend to the direct killing of the innocent. Upright and skilful doctors strive most praiseworthily to guard and preserve the lives of both mother and child; on the contrary, those show themselves most unworthy of the noble medical profession who encompass the death of one or the other, through a pretence at practicing medicine or through motives of misguided pity. . . .

Those who hold the reins of government should not forget that it is the duty of public authority by appropriate laws and sanctions to defend the lives of the innocent, and this all the more so since those whose lives are endangered and assailed cannot defend themselves. Among whom we must mention in the first place infants hidden in the mother's womb. And if the public magistrates not only do not defend them, but by their laws and ordinances betray them to death at the hands of doctors and others, let them remember that God is the Judge and Avenger of innocent blood which cries from earth to Heaven.

Finally, that pernicious practice must be condemned which closely touches upon the natural right of man to enter matrimony but affects also in a real way the welfare of the offspring. For there are some who, oversolicitous for the cause of eugenics, not only give salutary counsel for more certainly procuring the strength and health of the future child—which, indeed, is not contrary to right reason—but put eugenics before aims of a higher order, and by public authority wish to prevent from marrying all those who, even though naturally fit for marriage, they consider, according to the norms and conjectures of their investigations, would, through hereditary transmission, bring forth defective offspring. And more, they wish to legislate to deprive these of that natural faculty by medical action despite their unwillingness; and this they do not propose as an infliction of grave punishment under the authority of the state for a crime committed, nor to prevent future crimes by guilty persons, but against every right and good they wish the civil authority to arrogate to itself a power over a faculty which it never had and can never legitimately possess. . . .

Public magistrates have no direct power over the bodies of their subjects; therefore, where no crime has taken place and there is no cause present for grave punishment, they can never directly harm, or tamper with the integrity of the body, either for the reasons of eugenics or for any other reason. . . .

Furthermore, Christian doctrine establishes, and the light of human reason makes it most clear, that private individuals have no other power over the members of their bodies than that which pertains to their natural ends; and they are not free to destroy or mutilate their members, or in any other way render themselves unfit for their natural functions, except when no other provision can be made for the good of the whole body. . . .

The advocates of the neo-paganism of to-day have learned nothing from the sad state of affairs, but instead, day by day, more and more vehemently, they continue by legislation to attack the indissolubility of the marriage bond, proclaiming that the lawfulness of divorce must be recognised, and that the antiquated laws should give place to a new and more humane legislation. Many and varied are the grounds put forward for divorce, some arising from the wickedness and the guilt of the persons concerned, others arising from the circumstances of the case; the former they describe as subjective, the latter as objective; in a word, whatever might make married life hard or unpleasant. . . .

Opposed to all these reckless opinions, Venerable Brethren, stands the unalterable law of God, fully confirmed by Christ, a law that can never be deprived of its force by the decrees of men, the ideas of a people or the will of any legislator: "What God hath joined together, let no man put asunder." And if any man, acting contrary to this law, shall have put asunder, his action is null and void, and the consequence remains, as Christ Himself has explicitly confirmed: "Everyone that putteth away his wife and marrieth another, committeth adultery: and he that marrieth her that is put away from her husband committeth adultery." Moreover, these words refer to every kind of marriage, even that which is natural and legitimate only; for, as has already been observed, that indissolubility by which the loosening of the bond is once and for all removed from the whim of the parties and from every secular power, is a property of every true marriage. . . .

. . . Those who have the care of the State and of the public good cannot neglect the needs of married people and their families, without bringing great harm upon the State and on the common welfare. Hence, in making the laws and in disposing of public funds they must do their utmost to relieve the needs of the poor, considering such a task as one of the most important of their administrative duties.

We are sorry to note that not infrequently nowadays it happens that through a certain inversion of the true order of things, ready and bountiful assistance is provided for the unmarried mother and her illegitimate offspring (who, of course, must be helped in order to avoid a greater evil) which is denied to legitimate mothers or given sparingly or almost grudgingly.

But not only in regard to temporal goods, Venerable Brethren, is it the concern of the public authority to make proper provision for matrimony and the family, but also in other things which concern the good of souls. Just laws must be made for the protection of chastity, for reciprocal conjugal aid, and for similar purposes, and these must be faithfully enforced, because, as history testifies, the prosperity of the State and the temporal happiness of its citizens cannot remain safe and sound where the foundation on which they are established, which is the moral order, is weakened and where the very fountainhead from which the State draws its life, namely, wedlock and the family, is obstructed by the vices of its citizens. . . .

RESPONSIBLE PARENTHOOD

As early as 1930 the Anglican Bishops, meeting at Lambeth, England, held that (within a narrow range of cases) the use of contraceptives could be considered theologically acceptable. At the 1958 Lambeth Conference, Anglican Bishops from 46 countries adopted an important new statement on family planning (embodied in the report, The Family in Contemporary Society). *Such planning, the statement asserted, "in such ways as are mutually acceptable to husband and wife in Christian conscience, is a right and important factor in Christian family life and should be the result of positive choice before God." Furthermore, "it is utterly wrong to urge that, unless children are specifically desired, sexual intercourse is of the nature of sin. It is also wrong to say that such intercourse ought not to be engaged in except with the willing intention to procreate children."*

This report and the American statement reprinted here probably represent the thinking of most modern non-Catholic theologians in the United States and Britain. As the Clergymen's Advisory Committee of the Planned Parenthood Federation has stated (1960): "The ethical conviction of Protestants and Jews that family planning fulfills the will of God is rooted in the religious conviction that there are two primary functions of sexual intercourse in marriage, the unitive and the procreational. Neither is secondary, but they are different and distinguishable. The first may be rightfully sought apart from the second."

Responsible Parenthood

NATIONAL COUNCIL OF THE CHURCHES OF CHRIST

PREAMBLE

The National Council of the Churches of Christ in the U.S.A. exists in part "to do for the churches such cooperative work as they authorize the Council to carry on in their behalf," while at the same time recognizing that any member church may disassociate itself from an action of the Council.

In the present instance many member churches have already given formal expression to the same basic conviction as is contained in this statement. But differences of conviction exist which make it necessary for representatives of the Orthodox churches to abstain from voting on this pronouncement. The Council provides a meeting place for continuing study, in Christian freedom, of the implications of the Christian faith for responsible marriage and parenthood.

With these facts in mind, the General Board of the National Council of the Churches of Christ in the U.S.A. adopts and issues the following pronouncement on Responsible Parenthood.

THE CONTEMPORARY NEED

In recent decades, advances in medical science have affected marriage and family life in at least two important ways. Because of dramatic reductions in death rates, children generally have a far brighter chance to live to maturity; indeed, the persistence of large family patterns in many societies causes new and dangerous pressures upon presently inadequate means of subsistence. On the other hand, new medical knowledge of human reproduction increases the means available or potentially available to parents for regulating their fertility. In the altered circumstances of today, how is the Christian doctrine of parenthood to be made relevant to the needs of husbands and wives? Without attempting to restate the full range of parental duties, we advance certain considerations bearing on the control of procreation within the marriage bond. The concept of responsible parenthood is considered in relation to the ends of marriage, the reasons for family planning, the methods of family planning, and the task of society.

THE ENDS OF MARRIAGE

Genuine marriage, in the Biblical view, is a union whereby husband and wife become "one flesh" (Gen. 2:24, Mark 10:8, Eph. 5:31). Such a union embodies a convenant, a commitment to a dedicated common life. True marriage, however, is more than a human achievement. It has a "given" quality, expressed in the words of Jesus: "what. . .God has joined together. . ." (Mark 10:9). Hence it is a mystery according to St. Paul which symbolizes the union of Christ and His Church (Eph. 5:32) and is, in turn, illumined by this perfect union.

Since holy matrimony involves an occasion of God's grace, it is clear that the first duty of husband and wife is to nourish and care for the gift which God has given. This task is described in Christian traditions in terms of sanctification and mutual perfection. These emphasize the fundamentally spiritual character of the basic purpose of marriage, which can be served through parenthood, companionship, and vocation:

(1) Parenthood is a divinely ordained purpose of marriage for the embodiment and completion of the "one flesh" union, for the

care and nurture of children, for building the home as a true community of persons, and for the peopling of the earth (Gen. 1:28). It is participation in God's continuing creation, which calls for awe, gratitude, and a sense of high responsibility.

(2) Mutual love and companionship, rooted in the need of husband and wife for each other (Gen. 2:18), have also been ordained of God for the welfare and perfection of the "one flesh" union and for broader aspects of the sharing of life. Christians differ in regard to sanctions for the sexual expression of marital companionship, though most of our churches hold such expression right and necessary within the marriage bond, independently of procreation. All agree that Christian marriage should be free from sensuality and selfish indulgence, and that mutually accepted periods of continence can be of value in a common life of Christian discipline.

(3) Vocation, or the service of the couple in society, is another high purpose through which "the two become one." It normally includes parenthood and family life as major elements, but can assert a separate or even conflicting claim on conscience. Just as vocation may enjoin celibacy upon those to whom the gift is given (Matt. 19:11), so the calling of the couple may in certain circumstances enjoin family limitation.

Responsible parenthood, in the first instance, means to weigh the claims of procreation in relation to the total purposes of the marriage and the situation of the family in society. For most couples, the new knowledge of human reproduction and of means to avert conception affects ethical decisions regarding parenthood. But the responsibility, to be exercised in prayer and trust, has deeper roots.

REASONS FOR FAMILY PLANNING

Within the purposes of marriage ordained by God, there are a number of considerations concerning parenthood which need to be taken into account in trying to determine the number and frequency of pregnancies. These include:

(1) The right of the child to be wanted, loved, cared for, educated, and trained in the "discipline and instruction of the Lord" (Eph. 6:4). The rights of existing children to parental care have a proper claim.

(2) The prospects for health of a future child, if medical and eugenic evidence seem negatively conclusive.

(3) The health and welfare of the mother-wife, and the need for the spacing of children to safeguard them.

(4) The social situation, when rapid population growth places dangerous pressures on the means of livelihood and endangers the social order.

Reasons such as these enter into the calculations of responsible parenthood. At the same time, parents need to remember that having children is a venture in faith, requiring a measure of courage and confidence in God's goodness. Too cautious a reckoning of the costs may be as great an error as failure to lift the God-given power of procreation to the level of ethical decision.

METHODS OF FAMILY PLANNING

Christians are agreed that the limitation of procreation may be right and proper for parents under certain conditions, but differences arise in regard to circumstances and methods. The Orthodox Church follows the traditional teaching which sanctions marital abstinence as the means of family planning. Most of the Protestant churches hold contraception and periodic continence to be morally right when the motives are right. They believe that couples are free to use the gifts of science for conscientious family limitation, provided the means are mutually acceptable, non-injurious to health, and appropriate to the degree of effectiveness required in the specific situation. Periodic continence (the rhythm method) is suitable for some couples, but is not inherently superior from a moral point of view. The general Protestant conviction is that motives, rather than methods, form the primary moral issue, provided the methods are limited to the prevention of conception.

Protestant Christians are agreed in condemning abortion or any method which destroys human life except when the health or life of the mother is at stake. The destruction of life already begun cannot be condoned as a method of family limitation. The ethical complexities involved in the practice of abortion related to abnormal circumstances need additional study by Christian scholars.

Another approach to family limitation is voluntary sterilization. Because medical science cannot guarantee that the procedure is reversible it presents the Christian conscience with special problems. Responsible parenthood is seen by many as a day to day process of decision-making which sterilization may negate. On the other hand, where reasons of health or the obligations of parenthood argue for the use of the most effective means of family limitation, sterilization represents one sure method now available. Recognizing the dilemmas confronting Christian doctors and parents, particularly in some of the poorer societies where realistic alternatives seem to be lacking, we are constrained to point out the hazards in sterilization, and to stress the possibility of its use only after the most thoughtful consideration of all the factors involved. Additional study of these factors and of the moral issues entailed needs to be undertaken by Christian scholars.

THE TASK OF SOCIETY

While responsible parenthood is the moral obligation of husband and wife, the concept has implications for society also, to assist parents in the exercise of their duty. In addition to the educational and social services called for to help equip children for their fullest development and contribution to society, there are services due married couples. For most couples, family planning requires access to appropriate medical information and counsel. Legal prohibitions against impartation of such information and counsel violate the civil and religious liberties of all citizens including Protestants. Their right to means they approve in conscience does not infringe the right of others to refrain from using such means. Legislation or institutional practices that impair the exercise of moral and professional responsibilities of family-serving professions should be opposed.

As Christians and citizens in a world society, we also have the responsibility to help our fellow men overseas. Public health programs in economically less developed countries, often with substantial assistance from our government, have helped to create new population pressures. Therefore, at the request of people in other countries, we believe our government and voluntary agencies have a duty to assist with various measures to alleviate population pressures and to extend family planning. Private agencies have an important role to play, but the scope of the population problem internationally vastly exceeds their resources. Christian responsibility indicates that, when requested by other governments, governmental and intergovernmental aid for family planning should be given favorable consideration as part of a wise and dedicated effort to advance in the underprivileged regions of the earth the essential material conditions conducive to human dignity, freedom, justice, and peace.

ABORTION AND THE SOCIAL SYSTEM

Except for anthropological field reports, which collectively serve to demonstrate the apparent universality of abortion, the topic has received relatively little sociological attention. The abortion situation in the United States represents one good example of what some sociologists have termed "patterned evasion"—public insistence on proclaming a standard of behavior which is persistently violated in actual practice. A crucial aspect of the situation is the operation of supply and demand mechanisms. Repressive legislation breeds a profitable illicit traffic which provides the widely demanded services in question. Thus the legal steps taken to combat and restrict abortion, far from solving the problem, may actually create social dangers which would not exist under more permissive statutes.

In the article that follows, an attempt is made to suggest some of the "latent functions" of (and hence, reasons for the persistence of) these patently unworkable laws. Despite religious opposition to reform, there appears to be some growing sentiment in favor of extending the legal grounds for terminating pregnancies.

Abortion and the Social System

EDWIN M. SCHUR

Perhaps since the very beginnings of civilization women have used abortion—the destruction or expulsion from the womb of the unborn child, the fetus, before it attains viability—to free themselves from unwanted childbearing. After an extensive study of anthropological data, George Devereux recently found that "there is every indication that abortion is an absolutely universal phenomenon, and that it is impossible even to construct an imaginary social system in which no woman would ever feel at least impelled to abort." Though we have tried hard to ignore the unpleasant truth, even in the United States where economic and social improvements have reduced much of the burden of having children there are now probably close to a million abortions a year. Under current laws most of these abortions are illegal.

Since the law refuses to recognize most demands for abortion, highly complex illegal means of accommodating abortion-seekers have been developed, often by ruthless, inept persons. Abortion has always been dangerous when not carried out under proper conditions. While the advent of antibiotics has reduced the primary abortion death rate appreciably (even for illegal abortions), the criminal abortionist cannot possibly take all the precautions necessary for a safe operation. Hence, abortion still leads to considerable mortality and morbidity (possible complications short of death include sterility, endocrine disorders, menstrual disturbances and psychic maladjustments). Clearly abortion is a social problem of major importance.

On a more theoretical level, abortion relates significantly to many questions of policy, pattern and process which should be of

Reprinted from *Social Problems*, 3 (1955), 94-99; footnotes omitted.

interest to the sociologist. These include woman's role in our social system, family organization and disorganization, national demographic policy, and the role of informal and formal sanctions. It seems surprising that a topic which so clearly invites sociological analysis has received relatively little attention in sociological journals. A brief survey of abortion as a medico-legal, socio-psychological phenomenon may well be in order.

MEDICO-LEGAL ASPECTS

Non-surgical methods of inducing abortions are invariably dangerous. Physical techniques (e.g., falling down stairs, severe exercise, hot baths, and manipulations of the stomach) and the swallowing of chemicals (purgatives, intestinal and pelvic irritants, drugs stimulating contraction of the uterus, and poisons) are rarely effective unless undertaken so vigorously or in such dosage as would imperil the mother's life. Insertion of an irritating object into the uterus and laceration with a sharp object are similarly perilous. The latter method is often resorted to by women who attempt self-induced abortion; a partial list of the objects they use is grim testimony to the desperation of such abortion-seekers. Fisher notes the use of hatpins, umbrella ribs and pieces of wire. And Watkins, reporting on post abortion hospital patients, cites ". . . crochet hooks, nail files and syringe tips, and one patient used a nut cracker. Another introduced a case knife into the uterus."

The usual abortion operation in a hospital is dilatation and curettage. This involves widening the cervix, the neck of the womb, and introducing a "curette" (a long semi-sharp spoon-like instrument) to scrape the uterine cavity. One of the most interesting facts about our abortion situation, from a sociological standpoint, is that the relative safety of this operation has received virtually no publicity. It is true that, because of excessive bleeding when the uterine content is large, curettage should be limited to the first few months of pregnancy. But during that period, under adequate present-day hospital conditions and if performed by a skilled physician, the operation is extremely safe. As one eminent practitioner recently put it, "We feel that, if the operation is properly performed . . . , it will have no effect on either the health of the woman or her reproductive future."

Though laws on abortion vary from state to state, in this country abortion is generally illegal unless necessary to preserve the life of the mother. Abortions which satisfy this requirement are called "therapeutic." This is interesting since most physicians would probably not agree that the only therapeutic (i.e., healing or curative) abortions are where the mother's life is in direct danger; in a sense then, "therapeutic abortion" has become a legal term of art rather than a strictly medical one.

Recently hospitals have granted fewer and fewer therapeutic abortions. Scientific advances have rendered so many conditions less detrimental to the continuance of pregnancy that today there are almost no purely medical "indications" for abortion. An increase in psychiatrically-indicated abortions has not offset the overall decline. In general the attitude of hospital authorities is one of extreme caution. Some hospitals have established abortion boards which carefully screen all applicants for such operations; this usually cuts down the number of abortions granted. And although most doctors would deny that they in any way defer to political or law-enforcement pressures, fear of legal difficulties very likely holds hospitals in check; behind the reluctance of hospitals to grant abortions lies current restrictive legislation. While some physicians might admit, off the record, that their abortion recommendations are partly influenced by the patients' socioeconomic problems, no hospital will openly grant abortions on such grounds. Nor will a woman who conceives as a result of forcible rape or incest be granted an abortion, no mattter how inhumane such refusal seems. A specially perplexing situation has recently arisen regarding a possible eugenic indication for abortion. Research has shown that where the mother contracts German measles (rubella) before the twelfth week of pregnancy, there is about a thirty per cent chance the child will be born with some congenital abnormality; many obstetricians feel such a condition constitutes a valid indication for interrupting pregnancy. Yet since the mother's life is not in danger, technically the operation is illegal. Some hospitals now grant abortion in a rubella situation, admittedly in contravention of the written law; prosecutors do not interfere in such cases, accepting a broad medical "interpretation" of the statutes.

While the law has pretty effectively restricted hospital abortions (to an even smaller number of situations than many obstetricians and psychiatrists would choose), it has been unable to curb the tide of illegal abortion outside the hospital. Most state laws ban all abortions (not necessary to preserve the mother's life), whether performed by lay abortionists or physicians; in many jurisdictions the woman who submits to an abortion also commits a crime. But enforcement of these provisions is negligible. Women who submit to abortions are virtually never prosecuted. And the physician who departs from his legitimate practice to perform an occasional abortion rarely gets in trouble with the law. Prosecutors generally confine their efforts to the professional abortionist, and even here there are many serious obstacles to law-enforcement. Widespread public demand for abortion facilities makes it relatively easy for police to accept protection money from abortionists with a clear conscience.

Where graft does not block prosecution, satisfying evidentiary requirements is a major difficulty; courts usually place on the State the full burden of proving both that an abortion in fact took place and that it was not necessary to save the mother's life. Women are extremely hesitant about admitting abortions, fearing adverse publicity and possible self-incrimination. The prosecutor obtains his best leads when an abortion results in death or hospitalization. But evidence of isolated cases is not enough; a good prosecution entails use of numerous leads, long-term surveillance, and finally catching the abortionist in the act. Juries are extremely reluctant to convict abortionists, and of those who are convicted many receive suspended sentences. A supplementary sanction—revocation of a physician-abortionist's medical license—is equally weak; the abortionist needs no credentials to attract clients, nor is he likely to be cowed by the danger of prosecution for practicing without a license.

As there are no data indicating a decline in the overall number of abortions, we may assume that current negative sanctions are merely diverting abortion-seekers away from legal channels and nurturing the institutionalization of illegal means for meeting the abortion demand. Since current definitions of "therapeutic" abortion are out of line with relevant medical values, other values must be determining them. Experience in this country amply substantiates Devereux's conclusion that "social attitudes, reflecting culturally anchored value hierarchies, determine what conditions . . . constitute a *socially acceptable* 'indication,' . . . for the interruption of pregnancy." We may now wish to inquire what these attitudes are.

SOCIO-PSYCHOLOGICAL FACTORS

The argument may be advanced that killing the fetus contradicts the basic sexual function of woman—motherhood. At first glance the wide prevalence of post-abortion guilt reactions might seem to uphold this line of reasoning. Naturally an abortion will always involve some emotional consequences; indeed Helene Deutsch contends that ". . . at bottom there is hardly a woman who reacts to it with complete realism even where the rationalization is the best possible one." Similarly, a number of writers have noted the danger of adverse effects on the relationship between the parents.

While case histories reflecting such after-effects of abortion are often startling (Deutsch, for example, cites the case of a woman who erected tombstones for her fetuses, even after she had given birth to several children), we must not allow them to distort our perspective.

Additional study is needed of the etiology of post-abortal guilt; such reactions may well be socioculturally rather than biologically defined. As Simone de Beauvoir points out, this is a situation where many women "inwardly respect the law they transgress"; the fact that society labels the aborted woman a criminal may play an important part in causing this torment "by useless scruples." Similarly, the sordid clandestine dealings she must enter into (she may even have to yield to the sexual demands of the abortionist before he will operate) as well as the pain and possibility of serious complications may bring about adverse reactions.

Equally significant may be her denial of the socially defined mother role. As Talcott Parsons has noted, when the patterns institutionalized in role structure are introjected, they "become an important part of the personality structure of the individual himself, whether he conforms to them or not."

The high value we place on motherhood is inextricably tied to our insistence on monogamous marriage and emphasis on the family as a key unit in society. It is noteworthy that even in present-day American society, where opportunities for formal education are just about equal between the sexes, "The major status-giving role of the typical married woman is that of housewife." While feminist philosophy has made great strides, we should bear in mind de Beauvoir's persuasive argument that woman will achieve neither true freedom nor full creativity until she gains liberty over the childbearing function. The widespread use of abortion is striking evidence that millions of American women do want more control over deciding when they shall bear children; our laws against abortion may well serve to further woman's subservient social status. This is not to detract from the obvious values of motherhood—we would probably all agree with Burgess and Cottrell that the child is a "potent and vital factor" in family life.

Yet the potential evils attending the unwanted child, both for the child himself and the other family members, are equally well recognized. And the illegitimate child presents added problems.

Recent studies in the psychodynamics of "spontaneous abortion" (usually referred to by laymen as "miscarriage" but included in the medical definition of abortion) have thrown new light on the emotional impact of childbearing. It is now fairly well established that psychological rather than physical conditions frequently cause miscarriage, and that there may be women who are psychologically abortion-prone. Whether or not we are willing to label such a condition psychopathological, the fact remains that many women experience intense psychic conflict about accepting the role of motherhood; this is another aspect of woman's psychic makeup which must be considered in an adequate discussion of abortion.

Abortion law reflects not only the social stress on motherhood for the married woman, but also concern lest the social value of pre-marital virginity in women be undermined; in some circles, Kinsey's data have undoubtedly heightened such concern. Actually, though, most abortion studies show that the majority of aborted women are married and that many are already mothers. Similarly, the Catholic Church's rigid doctrinal opposition to all abortion is considerably undercut by the fact that many Catholic women do obtain abortions and some Catholic doctors and hospitals undoubtedly recommend non-Catholic abortion facilities. While the destruction of life violates major Western values, most thinkers would rather distinguish between different forms of life than place the life of the fetus on the same plane as the life or health of the mother.

A final factor which may in the future lend increasing support to existing abortion laws is chauvinistic pressure for a continued high birth rate. As Frederick L. Schuman has suggested, "Military and political power, rather than social and economic well-being, is the immediate objective of the economic nationalists who so largely dictate governmental policies. The patriot favors all governmental methods that seem likely to increase the rate of population growth." (And it is interesting to speculate that a particular psychological "type" may be susceptible to extreme patriotism, ethnocentrism generally, conventional sex ethics and politico-economic conservatism.) Obviously abortion can be a potent population limiter; this is borne out by recent experience in Japan where "Feticide to a degree unprecedented in modern civilization is quite legal . . ." Yet there is no reason to assume that liberalizing the legal indications for abortion need be completely incompatible with efforts to maintain a high birth rate. Sweden, for example, has fairly successfully made the concept of *voluntary* parenthood (including liberalized abortion law) part of a population policy designed to check a downturn in the birth rate. In the United States today perhaps the most pressing population problem is differential class fertility, the traditional inverse relationship between fertility and socio-economic status. Allowing abortion on socio-economic grounds could be a major step in lessening such differentials, which are often due to differences in the degree of family-planning success. Naturally, widespread use of the "perfect" contraceptive would considerably diminish the need for abortion; yet is is questionable whether we can afford to wait for the universal dissemination of such preparations. In any case, students of the abortion problem should bear in mind Frederick Osborn's statement: "Every technically advanced country in the modern world, with the exception to date of the United States, has an officially formulated and explicit population policy."

CONCLUSIONS

American abortion law today is characteristic of that legal disequilibrium which, according to Timasheff, results from "disharmony between real forces and verbal formulas . . ." This is essentially what Ehrlich had in mind when he highlighted the difference between the "living law" and the "positive law." Typical of legal disequilibrium is the widespread evasion of current abortion statutes; yet we should note that in such situations "the law is often evaded, but the behavior, while evading law, is still partly determined by law; if the law were changed, the behavior would become different." The strong influence of abortion law is seen in the refusal of hospitals to grant socio-economically indicated abortions and in the large-scale recourse to the professional abortionist in lieu of the legitimate practitioner.

Since current restrictions have not successfully reduced the number of abortions, whatever meaningful social functions they do serve may be non-purposed or latent. These perhaps include reassuring the patriot, reinforcing a subordinate status role for women, and preserving a system of sex ethics which the Kinsey reports and other sources indicate lags behind changing behavior patterns. Perhaps some illusory satisfaction is felt by maintaining formal standards to which few attempt to conform. As Radcliffe-Brown has put it: "the application of any sanction is a direct affirmation of social sentiments by the community and thereby constitutes an important, possibly essential, mechanism for maintaining these sentiments." The same might well be said of the mere existence of the sanction.

A demand for abortion is frequently viewed as a type of social deviance, and indeed most responsible physicians insist it should be satisfied only as a last resort. Yet social engineers should realize that at times abortion can be a vital instrument of social control—preventing serious family disorganization, economic hardship and diminution of physical health. Recognition of this possibility by legislators may play an important role in fostering social and economic reform.

ABORTION IN THE UNITED STATES

The 1955 national conference on abortion, sponsored by the Planned Parenthood Federation of America, served several useful purposes. It brought together specialists from various disciplines interested in the problem, and therefore produced a desirable exchange of viewpoints. Useful comparative perspective was provided by participants from Scandinavia (where relatively permissive abortion legislation is in force), and by reports of experience with the problem in still other countries. An especially interesting contribution to the proceedings was made by a former professional abortionist (a competent physician who had drifted into such practice and had since retired)—who related his personal experiences and condemned the hypocrisy underlying our current approach to the problem.

Published together with the proceedings of the conference were the report of a special statistical committee appointed to gauge the incidence of abortion, and a final statement of recommendations by the conferees (printed below). The statistical statement reported that the frequency of induced abortion in the United States, "could be as low as 200,000 and as high as 1,200,000 per year. . . ." As can be seen, the final conference statement advanced a number of general proposals—including the consideration of modifying abortion statutes so that the definition of "therapeutic" abortion would accord with good medical practice in this area.

Abortion in the United States

PLANNED PARENTHOOD CONFERENCE

STATEMENT

Cognizant of the adverse influence that the induced abortion problem must exert on the physical and mental health of the nation, the Planned Parenthood Federation of America called a conference of specialists in the fields of obstetrics, psychiatry, public health, biology, sociology, forensic medicine, the law, and demography. The group discussed the problem for two full days and evenings in April and again for a day in June, 1955.

The results of their deliberations may be summarized as follows:

The Conference participants recognized that present laws and mores have not served to control the practice of illegal abortion. Rather, this has continud to an extent ignored or, perhaps, condoned by a large proportion of the general public and even of the medical and legal professions. To keep on the books, unchallenged, laws that do not receive public sanction and observance is of questionable service to our society. Indeed, the demonstrated high incidence of terminations of unwanted pregnancies by illegal abortion could be looked upon as a disease of that society, presenting a problem in epidemiology as real and as urgent as did venereal disease three decades ago. There is a great similarity between the two, since both involve health, mores, and morals. Until comparatively recently the physicians and the public health agencies of America were constrained from facing the venereal disease problem openly without prejudice or prudery. As soon as they did, it became possible to apply medical and public health controls, and

Reprinted from Mary S. Calderone, ed., *Abortion in the United States* (New York: Hoeber-Harper, 1958), pp. 181-184.

the majority of those attending the Conference felt that the same type of frontal assault should now be made on the problem of intentional abortion.

It was recognized by Conference participants that although the effort to abtain an induced abortion may indicate that the woman is physically ill, more often it reflects one or more of a complexity of factors such as: poor social or economic environment, disturbed marital relations, psychiatric or neurotic disturbance within the family, or, quite simply, a need to keep her family at its present size. Abortion, whether legal or illegal, is a traumatic experience and in many instances its commission does not solve the basic problem. The undersigned members of the Conference recognize that the vast number of illegal abortions done each year is many times the number consistent with sound medical or social practice. The goal should be to reduce this number as far as possible, but it is apparent that this reduction cannot be effected within the framework of present attitudes and laws. The abortion problem must therefore become the candid concern of physicians, sociologists, educators, religious leaders, lawyers, legislators, demographers, and other responsible citizens. It is only by the most courageous and honest action of these groups working together that this urgent problem can be solved.

It was felt by the undersigned participants of the Conference that the following five measures would contribute to a material reduction of the high incidence of illegal abortion.

1. In view of the scarcity of reliable information concerning the whole abortion picture in the United States, medical, psychological, and social studies of the women seeking abortion should be undertaken to explore background, motivation, mechanisms, and results. Foundations and government bodies should be invited to sponsor such studies.

2. Consultation centers for women seeking abortion, modeled after the Scandinavian centers now in existence, should be established. One function of these centers would be to provide ma-

terial for the depth studies mentioned above. Their main function would be to help women realize that abortion, whether legal or illegal, may not be the best or only solution for the medical, social, or economic problems that seem so overwhelming to them. Sometimes women seeking abortion are not even pregnant. In other cases, discussion and help by informed, trained personnel who would be non-punitive in attitude may persuade a woman to follow a far more constructive course than interruption of the pregnancy. Such consultative centers would operate under joint medical and sociological auspices, perhaps through the sponsorship of state health and welfare departments.

3. It was recognized by the Conference participants that no scientific evidence has been developed to support the claim that increased availability of contraceptive services will clearly result in a decreased illegal abortion rate. The absence of such evidence, however, does not rule out the theoretical likelihood that it does. Therefore, it would be a constructive step if facilities for obtaining advice on contraception should be extended under medical supervision, to make such advice freely available to all who desire it. The undersigned members of the Conference deplore the present inequality of availability of legal abortion as well as that of contraceptive information, both of which are more readily available, even with comparable indications, to the educated and financially privileged than to the underprivileged group, whereas motivations toward contraception or abortion are the same in both groups. Examples of this undemocratic attitude were brought out at the Conference with reports of the differences in therapeutic abortion rates between private and ward patients in one and the same hospital as well as the lack of routine provision of contraceptive facilities in most hospitals serving the lower economic groups. The Conference is encouraged that the Dickinson Research Memorial of the Planned Parenthood Federation of America, the Population Council, and other agencies are supporting or conducting research toward methods of fertility control that will be at least as effective

as, and at the same time more acceptable than, those known at present.

4. There should be encouragement, through early, continued, and realistic sex education, of higher standards of sexual conduct and of a greater sense of responsibility toward pregnancy.

5. Authoritative bodies such as the National Conference of Commissioners on Uniform State Laws, the American Law Institute,* and the Council of State Governments should study the abortion laws in the various states and frame a model law that could, perhaps jointly, be presented to the states for their consideration to replace existing statutes. These bodies, in their deliberations, must be mindful that the border zone between legal and illegal abortion is at present narrow and shifts frequently, depending on personnel and locale. Such commissions should recognize that, when current statutes are interpreted exactly as written, almost no therapeutic abortions performed today are legal, since with the improvement of modern medicine it rarely becomes necessary to perform an abortion to save life. They should also recognize the mounting approval of psychiatric, humanitarian, and eugenic indications for the legal termination of pregnancy; the propriety of such indications merits extensive study and appraisal, and the commissions should engage in such study in order to be able to give careful consideration to the advisability of so modifying abortion statutes as to give to physicians latitude to include these indications in their recommendations for therapeutic abortion.

In conclusion, the Conference recommends that the professional organizations in the various fields of medicine, law, religion, sociology, and education should recognize the present importance and ramifications of the abortion problem in all its medical, legal, moral, and sociological aspects. Such professional organizations might then, by developing a body of informed opinion within their own ranks, be instrumental in developing a body of informed

---

* Since this was written a commission of the American Law Institute has drafted a Model Penal Code including laws concerning abortion.—EDITOR.

opinion among the citizens of this country, so that solutions to the abortion problem would be approached soberly, and in the most enlightened and democratic manner possible.

It is to be understood that participants came to the Conference as individuals and not as representatives of groups or organizations. The following participants have signed the Statement as an indication of their own personal agreement with it. The Scandinavian delegates felt that, as citizens of other countries, it would not be appropriate for them to sign.

Signatures

Helen W. Bellhouse	Warren O. Nelson
R. Gordon Douglas	Richard N. Pierson
Earl T. Engle	Wesley T. Pommerenke
Frederick H. Falls	John Rock
Iago Galdston	Harold Rosen
D. V. Galloway	Edwin M. Schur
Alan F. Guttmacher	Clarence Senior
Louis M. Hellman	Mack I. Shanholtz
Milton Helpern	Hilla Sheriff
Harold Jacobziner	Abraham Stone
Sophia Kleegman	Irene B. Taeuber
Lawrence C. Kolb	Christopher Tietze
Robert W. Laidlaw	G. Lotrell Timanus
Theodore Lidz	P. K. Whelpton
Charles M. McLane	Dorothy Wiehl
Robert B. Nelson	

VOLUNTARY STERILIZATION: QUESTIONS AND ANSWERS

Sterilization, or the surgical and permanent prevention of fertility, has aroused perhaps even fiercer (if less omnipresent) public controversy than have contraception and abortion. This is due partly to its permanent and ordinarily irreversible nature, further to the fact that it involves a distinct tampering with the body (as in abortion also, though not in contraception), and finally to the fact that many people today associate the eugenics movement (the desire to use scientific knowledge to improve the quality of human life) with experiments by the totalitarian Nazi regime to weed out "undesirable" elements in the population.

An important distinction which must be drawn is between compulsory and voluntary sterilization. The former procedure, which may be employed against some institutionalized mental defectives and other designated individuals under statutes in certain American states, has been subjected to disapproval by many social scientists and lawyers as well as by religious opponents of sterilization. Apart from strictly legal objections to arbitrary procedures and to cruel and unusual punishment, our uncertain knowledge regarding the hereditary nature of mental defects and other conditions felt to be undesirable in the population renders the rationale for such state action highly questionable. Sterilization undertaken at the wish of both the individual concerned and his or her spouse is another matter entirely, and it is this situation to which the following statement is addressed. There may of course continue to be strong differences of opinion as to the desirability or morality of voluntary sterilization—in general or in particular types of situations—but a dispelling of popular misconceptions about the procedure (as is attempted here) cannot but help to facilitate rational consideration of this question.

Voluntary Sterilization:
Questions and Answers
HUMAN BETTERMENT ASSOCIATION

VOLUNTARY STERILIZATION

Responsible parenthood presupposes the expectation that a child shall have proper care and normal development. When parenthood would seem to be permanently inadvisable, sterilization offers a dependable method of protection.

WHAT IS STERILIZATION

It is a method of "surgical birth control" for those who need a permanent rather than temporary method.

What is involved in sterilization?

For a woman the precedure is to make a small abdominal incision so that the tubes may be cut and tied, thus preventing the meeting of the sperm and the ovum (egg), without which no conception can occur. This operation, like an appendix operation, is always performed in a hospital.

For a man the procedure is to make a ½ to ¾ inch incision in each side of the scrotum so that the duct carrying the semen can be lifted out, cut and tied off. Usually, this minor operation is performed in the doctor's office under local anaesthesia.

Is sterilization the same as castration?

No. Castration involves the removal of the reproductive glands (the ovaries in the female, the testicles in the male). Sterilization does *not* involve the removal of any glands or organs. It merely

Reprinted from pamphlet, *Voluntary Sterilization: Questions and Answers* (Human Betterment Association for Voluntary Sterilization, Inc., New York, 1963).

closes the passageways which normally allow the sperm and ovum to meet.

WHEN IS STERILIZATION INDICATED?

Sterilization is indicated . . .

. . . When competent medical examination shows that there are physical, mental or emotional conditions which would make parenthood unwise or dangerous;

. . . When there is a medically established family history of a serious physical or mental condition which may be inherited;

. . . When other reasons, such as socio-economic necessity, make it advisable to limit the size of the family;

. . . When there is a mentally retarded child of reproductive age who needs to be safeguarded against reproduction.*

WHAT ARE THE EFFECTS OF STERILIZATION?

Will sterilization make a man impotent, prevent him from having his usual response to sex stimuli, or cause any change in his health?

No. Since vasectomy—the closing of a man's tubes—does not involve the removal of any male organs it should not change his ability to have an erection or ejaculation. Following the operation, the same amount of semen may be ejaculated as before, but it contains no sperm. There is no change in the production of the male sex hormone.

Will it produce symptoms of the menopause (change of life) in a woman?

No. It does not interfere with menstruation.

* See "To Protect the Adolescent Retarded," HBAVS publication.

Will it make a woman less feminine?

No. The characteristics which make a woman feminine are controlled by the hormones of the ovaries. Sterilization does *not* upset the production of these hormones. It merely prevents the egg from reaching the uterus.

Will sterilization make a woman frigid?

No. A woman's responsiveness depends mainly on the action of hormones, which are not affected by sterilization, and on psychological factors. With the alleviation of the fear of pregnancy, frequently sexual response is increased.

Will the resulting permanent inability to have children cause later emotional upsets or conflicts?

If a woman and her husband sought sterilization for valid reasons, with full understanding of the nature of the operation, the result should be relief and peace of mind.

Will sterilization help improve adjustment in marital relations?

Yes. If fear of pregnancy has interfered with adjustment, sterilization is likely to improve the relation.

Is sterilization permanent or may an operation undo its effects and restore fertility?

The operation is ordinarily performed as a permanent measure and should not be considered unless the couple is sure that they want no more children. Continuing research is improving the techniques for surgical restoration of fertility (reversal), but a successful reversal cannot be assured in any individual case.

WHAT ARE THE FACTORS TO BE CONSIDERED IN MAKING
ARRANGEMENTS FOR A STERLIZATION OPERATION?

Must both husband and wife agree to the sterilization?

Yes. Both must give written consent.

How much will a sterilization operation cost?

Charges vary throughout the country. To be taken into consideration are such factors as hospital arrangements; type of operation performed; coverage, if any, by an insurance plan. Costs for the female are always higher than those for the male. In certain cases of proven need, when no local resources are available, HBAVS may provide funds to help with the expenses of the sterilization.

Can a woman be sterilized soon after delivery?

Yes. It is common practice, when sterilization is desired, to close the tubes 12 to 48 hours after the baby is born. This does not materially lengthen her convalescence and makes another hospitalization at a later date unnecessary. The operation is technically easier at this time.

Can a woman be sterilized at the time of other abdominal operations?

This is possible if there is no inflammation or other condition present which makes the additional act of closing the tubes unwise.

Can a man be sterilized at the time of other operations?

Yes, with some types of operations. For example, if he needs a hernia repair, a vasectomy may very easily be done at the same time.

How long will a patient be inactive?

Usually not more than a week or two for a woman, and about one or two days for a man.

Who should be sterilized, husband or wife?

That depends on the individual family situation. Sterilization of the male is the simpler operation, but this should not be the only determining factor. The physical and emotional condition of husband and wife, the stability of the marriage, family histories, and other significant factors should be considered carefully and discussed with the physician or other counsellor.

What is the legal situation in regard to voluntary sterilization in the United States?

Human Betterment's legal counsel states: "There can be no question as to the legality of a sterilization performed upon the basis of therapeutic indications. Such a sterilization need not be a requisite for the patient's life; it is sufficient that such an operation will, in the opinion of the attending physician, be for the protection and in the best interest of the patient's well-being." Only Connecticut, Kansas and Utah are exceptions, since they have statutes requiring "medical necessity."

Can any doctor perform sterilization?

A competent and experienced specialist in this field should be chosen who is willing to explore the total situation with husband and wife prior to the operation.

Will the Human Betterment Association make referrals to a competent specialist?

Yes, following approval of the application by our Medical Committee, HBAVS maintains a roster of 1100 cooperating physicians throughout the United States. The social worker in charge of Information and Referrals is available for counsel.

THE HUMAN BETTERMENT ASSOCIATION believes that voluntary sterilization, of either the husband or the wife, is one of the methods of birth control which should be made available to those who choose it under wise and prudent professional guidance.

HUMAN BETTERMENT further believes that voluntary sterilization, in addition to proper use in limiting family size to the number of children whom the parents can love, nurture and provide for, has an important role to play as another means of birth control in bringing an exploding world population under control.

WORLD POPULATION GROWTH AND CHRISTIAN RESPONSIBILITY

For some time now, as this excerpt points out, demographers and other interested specialists have been warning of possibly grave consequences stemming from the extremely rapid growth of world population. Here again, Catholic doctrine has posed a serious problem for those who advocate launching a world-wide campaign to control this "population explosion." An intriguing aspect of this situation is that it sometimes finds Catholic spokesmen and some orthodox Marxists allied in opposing birth control measures—though clearly for different reasons (the Marxists frequently claiming that economic reform will solve all current difficulties). Yet even Marxists (as in China today) and Catholics are being forced to recognize the extreme urgency of the world population problem. A further confusion arises due to racial differences in national population composition. Thus the good faith of white Western advocates of birth control aid for underdeveloped countries has been questioned: are such "reformers" mainly seeking to limit the non-white segment of the world's population? These and other cross-currents of opinion have made the question of world population control a controversial one. It is widely accepted among disinterested experts, however, that some form of control is a vital necessity.

World Population Growth and Christian Responsibility

NORMAN ST. JOHN-STEVAS

Since the end of the Second World War, first experts, and then the public in general, have been increasingly aware of the enormous problems created by the rapid rise in world population. "The problem of population," states Sir Julian Huxley, "is the problem of our age." Numerous monographs have been published on the consequences of the rise, the United Nations has carried out an important series of investigations into the causes and extent of the increase, and in 1954 convened an international conference in Rome, to exchange information. The magnitude of the problem is stated dramatically in the United Nations publication, "The Future Growth of World Population", where the author points out that whereas the human race took 200,000 years to reach 2,500 million, it will take only thirty years to add another 2,000 million. If the present rate of increase continues, within 600 years only one square metre of earth will be left for each person to live on. In 1950, world population was 2,500 million; by 1958 it had reached 2,800 million; by 1980 a population of 4,280 million is forecast. World population is expected to double within the next fifty to sixty years, and if current estimates are correct, a world population of between 6,000 and 7,000 million can be expected by the end of the century.

Population growth is a world wide phenomenon, but is taking place faster in the underdeveloped countries of Asia, Africa, and tropical South America, than in the advanced countries of Europe,

Reprinted from Norman St. John-Stevas, *Life, Death and the Law* (Bloomington: Indiana University Press, 1961), pp. 105-115; footnotes omitted.

and even, in some cases, the United States. In some places such as Puerto Rico, the annual increase is in the region of 3 per cent compared with an increase for the United States in 1954 of 1.8 per cent. In Africa from 1951-5 the population was increasing by 2.2 per cent per year, in Asia as a whole, by 1.7 per cent, the figure being higher for individual countries, compared with a .7 annual increase for Europe. Highest rate of increase amongst the developed countries is shown by the United States, where a population estimated at 166 million in 1955 is expected to reach 204 million by 1970. Europe does not reflect this pattern of increase, the 51 million population of the United Kingdom, for example, being expected to be only 53.7 million by 1970, and France's population of 43.3 million will be 47.4 million in that year. By contrast, countries such as China and India will increase from 600 to 799 million, and from 386 to 504 million, in the same period.

Industrial and agricultural revolutions have contributed to this swift growth, but the primary cause is the reduction of disease and a fall in the death rate. Modern medical science has made decline in mortality an almost universal phenomenon, the only exception being Middle Africa, where physical and cultural obstacles remain to be overcome.

In Puerto Rico for example, the death rate fell from 11.8 per thousand in 1947 to 7.2 in 1955. The scope for further reduction is illustrated when one considers the infant mortality rates in different countries. In Britain it is now 26.5, but in India, despite improvement, it is 200. Countries appear to pass through a fourfold cycle in relation to births and deaths. First, both birth and death rates are high, and this is followed by a period of high birth rates and falling death rates. Then both birth and death rates fall, and finally the country passes into a period of low birth and death rates.

In the West, stage two of the cycle was not reached until improvements in agriculture and the industrial revolution were under way, but in the East the decline in death and disease has not been similarly matched. Thus, while the advanced countries can maintain and even raise the standard of life for their increased population, the technologically undeveloped countries, where the population by contrast is seriously undernourished, can barely maintain even existing standards, any advance being immediately swallowed up by the increased numbers. In India, for example, the average diet is only 1,590 calories per person—less than half that of the United States—and two thirds of the Indian population is underfed. In all 70-75 per cent of the world's population has insufficient to eat, 70 per cent being concentrated in Asia, and 18 per cent in Africa and parts of South America.

A world in which material resources are so unequally divided, and where the poorest parts are those where the population is increasing most rapidly raises an acute problem for the Christian conscience. The late Pope Pius XII analysed the problem in a number of messages and encyclicals; it was discussed at Lambeth in 1958; and an international Protestant study group met at Oxford in April 1959 at the request of the World Council of Churches to consider the world population problem and the related question of family planning. There is, however, no unanimity amongst Christians as to what action should be taken.

A number of Catholic writers dismiss the population problem as an illusion. They point out that the problem is theoretical rather than practical, since the prophesied catastrophe is dependent on the present rate of expansion of the race continuing into the future. Some resort to ridicule, pointing out that if the egg of every housefly was hatched, the whole surface of the globe would be covered by a mass of flies to a height of three miles within ten years. Again, projecting present population increases into the future, they show that in 5,000 years the weight of human beings would equal the weight of the earth, in 14,000 the weight of the universe, and even given stellar emigration, within a few thousand years the stars themselves would be fully occupied. This *reductio ad absurdum* is hardly helpful, any more than is the attitude of those religious writers who maintain that whatever the figures of expansion, God in due course will provide means of subsistence. Such a total rejection of reason is alien to the tradition of Western Catholicism. Others draw comfort from Thomas Doubleday's law first enunciated in 1837, stating that Nature always counteracts the endangering of the existence of a species by an increase in fertility, and this is especially so when the danger arises from lack of food. Consequently, "the state of depletion or the deplethoric state is favourable to fertility, and that, on the other hand, the plethoric state, or state of repletion, is unfavourable to fertility in the ratio of the intensity of each state." Thus, once the general standard of living is raised, the population problem will solve itself. It is of course arguable that the fall in the birth-rate amongst the better fed is due not to repletion but to an accompanying sophistication which leads to the use of contraceptives. It is also pointed out by Catholic writers that important factors in the present population increase are essentially short-term.

The growth in life expectancy brought about by a drop in infant mortality, and the increase in the life span must eventually come to an end. "Once the ultimate frontier of life expectancy will have been reached by most of the human race, and will have been implemented into the various population compositions," writes Fr. Zimmerman, "the explosion of human numbers will dissipate itself visibly and dramatically, assuming a continuation of present fertility rates." Given two doublings of human numbers before the population explosion ends he estimates factual world population at 11 billion, which would then multiply at a much slower pace.

Of course, the raising of the standard of living to the requisite level will need an intense and concerted international effort, but Catholic social scientists welcome this. They see the population problem as a spur driving mankind forward to the development of a universal community. This positive attitude is evident in the writings of all Catholic thinkers who recognize the urgency of the problem. They stress that individual States have no absolute ownership of territories and natural resources, but hold them on trust for the whole of the human race. Thus, in his very first encyclical, Pope Pius XII declared that the human race has a true unity of nature, a unity of purpose, and a unity of dwelling place on earth, "of whose resources all men can by natural right avail themselves to sustain and develop life." The goods created by God should be equitably shared and wealthier countries are bound by principles of justice and charity to share their resources with countries which are less well provided.

It follows, writes Mgr. Montini, "that a really adequate study of the relations between population and density and means of subsistence must tend to take place on a world-wide scale, while the problem to which they give rise cannot be solved except on that same scale, through the industrious solidarity of all peoples, so that those artificial barriers which divide them being removed, there may arise a more orderly circulation of peoples, of capital, and of material goods. With this subordination of particular national economic welfare to the common good of the society of nations, frontiers will no longer be valleys which divide, but bridges which unite, and material goods will be free to fulfill their natural function of satisfying everyone's needs." The Protestant and utilitarian approach of reducing population pressure by spreading contraception as a social policy is condemned not only as a violation of natural law, but as a facile avoidance of the true solution to the problem. "What an error it would be," stated Pius XII in his Christmas message of 1952, "to blame the natural law for the present miseries of the world, when it is clear that these derive from the lack of mutual solidarity of men and peoples."

Given then, a high degree of international co-operation to raise living standards, how many people could the earth support? Estimates vary from 5 billion to 28 billion, Colin Clark calculating in 1958 that the would could support 28 billion if cultivation and conservation of agricultural land were to reach Dutch standards. To achieve this a great technological effort would have to be made by the richer nations. More scientists and agricultural experts would have to be trained and made available, new methods of crop rotation and soil management introduced, and more arable land developed by irrigation, possibly using sea water. Genetic improvement of seed and stock would also help to raise yields. World food production has in fact been increasing by approximately 2.7 per cent annually since 1948, almost twice as fast as world population. Japan provides an encouraging example of how food production can be raised. During the last sixty years, food supplies have increased faster than the population, and Japan now supports 3.6 times as many people per hectare of cropland than the rest of the Far East, despite the lower fertility of her land. China has also made extraordinarily rapid progress, increasing food production by 50-100 per cent, according to Lord Boyd Orr, in the past three years. He attributes the increase to a substitution of deep ploughing for the old earth-scraping technique and the use of fertilizers and insecticides. "China," says Lord Orr, "has one quarter of the world's population but seems capable of feeding it well." Great areas of forest and scrub land could be cleared and brought under cultivation. New sources of food supplies could be developed from soil-less agriculture and synthetic manufacture, and the oceans themselves could be utilised for the vegetable substances and fungi which they contain. Expansion of fish breeding and fish catching offers a very promising and comparatively unexploited source of additional food supplies.

All this would involve astronomic expenditure, one estimate of the initial capital required by underdeveloped countries being 25 billion dollars. Huge as this figure is, it moves into the range of the attainable, when one considers that the military expenditure of the United States and the Soviet Union is probably at least four times the amount. Utilization of solar and atomic energy could speed this revolution considerably. Better use could be made of Western food surpluses, which, if distributed, could do much to ease world hunger.

A supplementary solution to world population problems stressed by Catholic writers is increased opportunity for emigration. In a letter to the American Bishops in 1948, Pius XII declared that man had a natural right to emigrate, since God had provided material goods for the use of all. "If, then," said the Pope, "in some locality, the land offers the possibility of supporting a large number of people, the sovereignty of the State, although it must be respected, cannot be exaggerated to the point that access to this land is, for inadequate or unjustified reasons, denied to needy and decent people from other nations, whenever this does not hinder the public welfare as measured on honest-weight scales." Immigration laws should be liberalized, but there are obvious limits to this process. If Australia for example were to be peopled by Indians, the maximum that could be absorbed over a long period would be fifteen million, which in 1955 represented the annual increase of India's population for only three years. Again the capacity of individuals to cross from one culture to another of a radically different nature is clearly limited, and a wholesale immigration would be destructive to the migrants and the social structure of the receiving countries.

Sharing of resources, increase of food supplies, more emigration, are the solutions put forward by Catholics for solving the problems created by world population increase. Protestants and others also support these measures, but emphasize them rather less, as they advocate the spread of family planning as a remedy. It should be made clear that while family planning in the long run may have a material effect on the population increase, it cannot be adopted quickly enough to stem the minimum increase of one billion which is likely to be achieved by 1980. Contraception is not easily spread amongst primitive peoples because they find the technique of using them difficult to master and they are comparatively expensive. This would be so even if the United Nations used its influence to encourage world wide family planning, but attempts to secure the adoption of such a policy have been blocked by Roman Catholic and Communist countries. Thus, in 1952, the World Health Organization dropped a Norwegian proposal to study contraception as part of its official programme after opposition from Catholic delegates. The United Nations has accordingly adopted a policy of neutrality on the subject, one of the agreed principles of co-operative action established at the 1954 World Population Conference, being to respect different ethical and religious values and to promote mutual understanding. This attitude of Roman Catholic countries has been severely criticized, but is not unreasonable. The United Nations is not a super-State whose majority decisions are binding on all members, but an agency for co-operation between equal partners. If delegate countries take radically conflicting stands on birth control the only possible line for the United Nations to follow is neutrality. At the same time advice and the services of experts are available in individual States on request.

A way out of the United Nations dilemma, as far as Catholic countries are concerned, might be offered by the rhythm method of birth control. Catholic theologians are generally agreed that a justifying cause for resorting to rhythm would be the social welfare of a particular community which would benefit by a reduction in population. This, of course, would mean a widespread public dissemination of knowledge about rhythm, and many moralists consider that communication should be cautious. On the other hand, these scruples might well be counter-balanced by the knowledge that the alternative would be use of unnatural means of birth control. As early as 1939, Catholic writers were advocating the foundation of Catholic medical bureaus to give rhythm advice, and the need has become very much more urgent since then. From 1952-4, with the help of the United Nations, experiments were in fact carried out in India in the use of the rhythm method. Two locations were selected, Lodi colony, an urban middle class centre, and Ramangaram, a small rural town in Mysore. The project ended abruptly in 1954. About 75 per cent of the 2,362 married couples in the two centres expressed a desire to learn about family planning, but only 13.6 per cent of the couples in Ramangaram and 28.3 per cent of those in Lodi colony proved capable of learning the method. By the end of March 1954, only 5 per cent and 7.5 per cent respectively were known to be following the method regularly. Difficulties reported were a wide variation in women's cycles, mistakes in calculations, and the reluctance of husbands to agree to long periods of abstinence. On the other hand, Dr. Abraham Stone, who went to India to give instruction in rhythm methods under the auspices of the World Health Organization in 1951, reported a success rate of 65 per cent.

India has not confined its activities to propagating the rhythm method, and, like Japan, the other Eastern country with a population policy, has sought to increase knowledge of contraception. The possibilities of wider application of rhythm, however, remain, and as scientific advance renders it a more reliable and simple method of control, it may well be more widely employed. Its major advantage is that it is the only possible method of international family planning, being acceptable to all major world religions, not only Judaism and Christianity, but also Buddhism, Hinduism, Confucianism, and Islam.

GOALS FOR A POPULATION POLICY

Whereas the current domestic population problems of the United States may not seem too pressing in comparison with those of less developed nations and with those relating to the general world population, it is unlikely that we can afford to be complacent about trends and differentials in our own population. Although these matters have been studied a good deal by social scientists (and therefore we have a considerable body of pertinent information), there has been relatively little effort in this country to utilize these data in formulating a coherent governmental population policy. Undoubtedly one obstacle to a definite national policy is the conflict bred in the United States owing to the diverse religious interpretations of population control. Also inhibiting governmental action in this realm may be a persisting American feeling that such matters are "personal" ones to be decided by the individuals involved, as well as a generalized resistance to governmental planning of any unfamiliar sort.

Many would argue, however, that a strong case can be made for a national population policy—wherein goals are established and means to such ends envisioned—a policy that could translate into some coherent actions knowledgeable judgments about such related matters as desirable family size, public birth control clinics, abortion, sterilization and artificial insemination laws, illegitimacy, and so on. Alva Myrdal's book Nation and Family *(1941), from which the following is taken, provides an excellent discussion of the general value of such over-all planning—as well as assessing specific policy alternatives for Sweden. As the author notes, such planning has been greatly facilitated in the Scandinavian countries by the close working relationship there between social scientists and policy-makers.*

Goals for a Population Policy

ALVA MYRDAL

Population has been studied far less as a problem for political action than as a problem for fact-finding research. Population policy, as well as social policy generally, does, however, require systematic thought. The Scandinavian countries have been fortunate in that they have achieved a closer collaboration between social science and politics than other countries. It is natural, therefore, to expect from them a contribution toward the clarification of the methodological problems of framing a population policy that will comply with scientific standards. The fact that academic experts are consulted on political questions under investigation and exert influence on public opinion and politics is one of the characteristics of our type of rationalistic democracy.

The distinction between truths in the theoretical sphere and recommendations in the practical sphere has on the whole been clearer in the Scandinavian countries than elsewhere. The leaders both in the social sciences and in politics have imbibed the teaching that facts make up the world of theory but that besides knowledge of facts explicit value premises are needed for rational practical action. This critical philosophy, here oversimplified, has pervaded much popular literature and influenced adult education. Whatever its importance in the realm of thought may be, we cannot overestimate its hardening and purifying influence in intellectualizing the discussion of political action. Politics has, to a considerable degree, been brought under the control of logic and technical knowledge and so has been forced to become in essence constructive social engineering.

Reprinted from Alva Myrdal, *Nation and Family* (New York: Harper, 1941), pp. 100-112; footnotes omitted. Reprinted by permission of Harper and Row, Publishers, New York, and Routledge & Kegan Paul, Ltd., London.

It has been recognized that social scientists who pretend to be able to ascertain values and prescribe social action out of pure fact-finding are just as much on the wrong track as social scientists who are so afraid of responsibility in the world of action that they hide behind an eternally insatiable "need for collecting far more detailed knowledge before practical action can be wisely planned." There is no doubt that social action is more purposeful and effective with the guidance of the experts than without it. To make their position unmistakable, scientists should distinguish clearly between the factual relations they can establish and the value judgments they will have to assume.

Two sets of premises are thus to be kept separate when discussing population policy: the *premises of knowledge* about facts and factual relations and the *premises of valuations*. The premises of facts in the population problem turn on both demographic and other social data. Various future trends are thus ascertained to be in the realm of possibility. It is these alternatives with their foreseen effects that become evaluated, marked with different coefficients of preference. In this way the goals are established. The value premises, however, become of importance not only for the goals but also for the means. When different measures are contemplated to influence the trend, these measures themselves will have to be evaluated, and human ideals and interests are again expressed. Thus the possibility exists that people who want a certain population development may not want to approve certain means for obtaining it. There is no must in the sphere of valuations.

Into people's values, as they are presented in public debate on political issues, there often enter misconceptions of facts and of their interrelations. Decline of population may, for instance, be positively evaluated because it is believed that its effect would lessen unemployment. The scientist is not on shaky ground when he reveals the false elements of knowledge in popular political thought. The positive task is, however, to establish what a man should rationally want on the ground of improved knowledge and on the assumption also of his own values. These values can vary and do vary in democratic society, but there is no need of presenting to the public a chart of all the alternatives to be inferred from all the possible sets of values. A reduction of the alternatives to be studied can be made by selecting only those values as relevant premises which seem to be held generally enough to be of political importance. It may perhaps be added that the choice of one's own values as premises, which is the same as making social propaganda, can be made in a scientifically impeccable manner if these value premises are manifestly listed and strictly adhered to. Again it must be emphasized that premises should not be hidden because that involves bias and logical confusion.

Choosing a set of value premises makes the ensuing recommendations valid for the reader only if the values are shared by him, or become shared by him, which of course is the aim of propaganda. The validity of any program of social policy is completely dependent on whether its value premises are approved. It is regrettable, therefore, that most authors do not attempt to state which value premises they have chosen. This is the practical reason why it has appeared necessary to emphasize these otherwise fairly simple principles.

To account for the general value premises underlying the Swedish program of population policy is the tedious but necessary task of this chapter. Here they can be phrased only in vague and abstract terms. The only way to make them precise and concretely determined is to relate them directly to details of means and objectives. This is a task for the subsequent discussion of population aims and measures.

THE GENERAL VALUE MILIEU

Just as in general the Swedish people take all the freedom for the individual that is compatible with social orderliness as a condition *sine qua non* for the democracy they are living in, so freedom for the individual in relation to parenthood must be protected. Only the sanction of voluntary parenthood would fit the democratic foundations of this society.

Similarly there is a positive valuation of a high level of living. That is part of the whole social philosophy of modern industrialism. In the field of population it has shown itself in deliberate efforts to raise the standard of living by reducing family size. A population policy will also have to take account of this attitude by trying to find the means by which it will be possible for families to have children without having to accept as a result an unduly depressed level of living.

Coupled with this undeniable striving toward the elevation of living conditions, there is in a democratic country like Sweden an equally undeniable positive valuation of economic equality. The cultural homogeneity of the people is no mere fact, but it is, or rather it is increasingly becoming, a vital sense of identification with the interests of others. Equality and justice, vague as ideals always are, may probably be said to be more highly valued in the Scandinavian democracies than in any other political organization. Trends toward equalizing incomes, leveling the effects of regional advantages and disadvantages, pooling of risks, cooperating instead of profiteering—all testify to the existence of some such deep-seated evaluation. In the realm of population policy these attitudes call for increased equality of opportunity for children of different social groups and for families with or without children. The tendency to regard a concentration about the average as more desirable than a wide dispersion toward extremes carries over to social sanctions in favor of families of moderate size.

Finally, there is in the general value sphere of Swedish democracy an undeniably positive valuation of children, family, and marriage. Children are liked although such an attitude does not indicate the number wanted or the degree of willingness to overcome obstacles to their procreation. The family is regarded as a value, even if some things in the exterior form of family life may have to be changed to meet needs for adjustment.

Between some of these basic values there will in actual life be many occasions for conflict. But one judgment is unanimous, namely, that quality of children should not be sacrificed to quantity. The desire for children, both as a private attitude and still more as a political attitude, will have to yield if it is in conflict with the desire to defend standards, particularly the welfare standards of children themselves. There can be no approval, therefore, of childbearing that infringes on the welfare of the children. It should be added that in Sweden the average citizen has a rather strong belief in the usefulness of social control exercised through collective agencies, such as the state, the municipalities, and the large civic organizations. At the same time, this average citizen abhors arbitrary action. He can be said to have a legalistic bent of mind. He wants to have all interference limited by specific laws and regulations that transfer a maximum of relations between the individual and the public bodies from the sphere of discriminatory judgment to one of fixed rights and obligations. He will insist upon this procedure even if the administration of justice sometimes becomes more rigid than a system which permits freer consideration of individual cases.

These generalizations as well as the more precise values which will be presented when confronting specific problems, goals, and means are intended to represent not an arbitrary choice by the author but the controlling values in actual Swedish policy. There is nothing sacred about these values. Some individuals or even whole nations may supersede one or all of them. The people, or at least the leaders, in totalitarian countries will obviously not subscribe to the first one of individual freedom nor the last one of legalism. Certain groups, especially intellectual sympathizers with the Russian family ideology of the 1920's, will not subscribe to the positive valuation of marriage and family, as they hold that society should be indifferent to the sex life of individuals. Many extreme individualists will refuse to attribute any political value to a rapidly declining birth rate, as they profess no concern for what happens to future generations. Ardent supporters of the doctrine of *laissez faire,* as well as of state socialism or communism, will deeply mistrust the Swedish pragmatic kind of variegated interventionism, which they will judge to be opportunistic.

The goals of population policy must be established as inferences from both the facts and the values. For practical purposes it is usually not necessary to determine these goals in an absolute sense. It is generally sufficient to fix only the direction toward which social action should be pointed. In generalized form the goals for which the Swedish population policy is striving include increased aggregate fertility, more even distribution of children in families, raised living standards for children and improved quality of the population stock, reduced illegitimacy, and more generally available birth control information.

These goals may seem contradictory. When the final policy is being determined, they will have to be weighted against one another. There is also the possibility that such an apparent contradiction may resolve itself when the social world is really conceived as manageable. The dilemma of wanting increased birth control, on the one hand, and increased fertility, on the other, will then be revealed as one which can be solved, one in which both horns can be seized. The new idea in what has here been called a democratic population program is that it does pay heed to the wants of the people even if they seem irreconcilable. Out of disharmony a harmony has to be created by social action. Seemingly conflicting desiderata have to be reconciled if we do not want to take the easy way of stopping on either side; that was the unresolvable dilemma in which the population problem was formerly caught.

INCREASED FERTILITY

If there was doubt whether a large enough majority of the Swedish people favored maintaining the population, the reaction observable during the recent population discussion removed all uncertainty. The prospect of a cumulative population decline was definitely classified as undesirable. Knowledge about relevant facts made it clear to almost everyone that conversion of this decline into an actual increase would be entirely outside the field of possibilities. The only alternative future trends which could be considered within reason and, therefore, the only ones to be evaluated were either that of continued, accumulated decline or that of reaching a fertility level which might maintain a constant population in the long run.

In determining the goal of keeping population constant, the various social and economic effects of population decline touched upon in Chapter 5 were taken into due account and evaluated. In addition to this indirect evaluation of the population trend by means of its effects there was also a more direct evaluation. Population constancy was felt by the average citizen to be an end or a value in itself. This direct valuation, a feeling of national self-pity at the prospect of death and a pride in the collectivity of the national culture, was presented in various forms. Its common minimum basis was an attitude that "our society is too good not to be preserved." This certainly is nationalism but just as certainly it is not nationalism of a militaristic and expansionist type. The reaction may rather be intellectualized in terms like these: "It is not going to be so stimulating to work for a national culture that is under liquidation. It is not going to be so satisfying to build up a social structure which our children are not going to inherit. The risk is great that a depopulated country with rich natural resources and a wide coverage of social security will attract foreign peoples. It is practically certain that these peoples are not going to be our culturally related Scandinavian neighbors. They will constitute an overflow from larger nations, and it is then virtually inevitable that in their strong clasp our cultural heritage will be completely submerged. This we dislike."

It must be stressed, however, that this recent anxiety has been focused not on the size of the nation which should be considered as optimal but on the prospect of incessant decline with its inescapable effect in the near future of an aging society and its possible long-range result of allowing a culture and an economy to decline. Stopping this process has seemed the important thing. If stabilization of the population could be achieved at all, which would involve making up the present 25 per cent deficiency in fertility, there is reason to suppose that Sweden could adjust to various magnitudes of population. In a country with plenty of natural resources the quantity of population cannot in itself, within practically relevant limits, be conceived to have any important effects on the general welfare or the standard of living of the people. The available number of producers could work for the available number of consumers. The crucial factors of population thus are direction and rate of change rather than any optimal size.

Since the imperialistic days of the seventeenth century, the Swedish citizen has not complained because his nation is small. He has fortified his mind against the confusion of "great" and "big"; and, besides, he has increasingly felt the whole world open for his cultural and economic ambitions. There is a considerable degree of indifference in regard to all total figures of future population in Sweden. The only cause for worry is the trend toward an ever smaller nation that would be threatened with self-liquidation. In view of the contemporary psychosis of militant nationalism, this fact cannot be stressed too strongly.

Constancy thus becomes the goal of a population policy for which public opinion can be mobilized. This constancy will demand a policy because population maintenance involves in the long run not a mere *status quo* of fertility but a considerable increase. Increased fertility becomes the main desideratum.

MEDIUM-SIZED FAMILIES

This goal of permanent maintenance of population can be translated into terms that show more precisely the implied demands on the fertility of the individual family. Assuming the record low mortality figures for different age groups in 1933, every woman reaching 15 years of age would during her later fertility period have to have on the average 2.21 children. If only those marrying are supposed to have children, that would require, with the low nuptiality rate of Sweden, 2.95 children per married woman. In all marriages which last to the 50th year of the wife, 3.14 children would be necessary, allowing a margin for marriages which are dissolved earlier (no allowance being made for illegitimate child-bearing). This is evidently equivalent to the popular estimate of three children to keep the next generation as numerous as the present one. This holds true even if the present rate of illegitimacy should be maintained. In those Swedish marriages in which the wife has in recent years just reached the end of her fertility period the average number of children has been around three. In the younger marriages the average number of children is so small that there is doubt that a final average of even two children will be attained.

This method of considering averages is, however, an unsatisfactory one. No account has been taken of sterility; no allowance has been made for other personal variations. The question as to what percentage of marriages must be excluded from average fertility computations on account of involuntary sterility naturally arises. Taking into consideration the scanty data available about physiological sterility and spontaneous abortion and allowing a certain margin, it is estimated that 10 per cent of all marriages in Sweden will be completely childless, 7.5 per cent will have only one child and 5.0 per cent only two children owing to involuntary causes. The remaining 77.5 per cent must then be divided between 3- and 4-child families, but mostly the latter (65 per cent of all families, while only 12 per cent could have as few as three children) to maintain the population at the present level. Even if nonmarital fertility should be calculated to remain on a high level, only a slight reduction in the number of chidren within marriages could be allowed. Now it is scarcely possible to assume that the number of small families, with none, one, or two children, can ever be kept close to the minimum. For various reasons, such as late marriages, hereditary considerations, and economic distress, some families will always remain childless or have but one or two children. The 4-child family and not the 3-child family evidently will have to be the practical minimum aimed at in all nonsterile families.

In order to settle which of these or other distributions should be chosen as a goal for population policy, we must again resort to certain value premises. One of these has to do with individual values as norms for behavior. Another is concerned with the attitude as to what size of family is preferable for society as a whole. According to the first value premise, parenthood should be voluntary. Knowledge of prevailing conditions then reveals that with planned parenthood most of the very large families are not going to come into being. The only choice, then, seems to be such a distribution of families that a large majority become middle-sized rather than that many be undersized and some oversized. How does this goal conform with the natural inclination of parents? If ignorance did not operate to increase the number of children and economic difficulties work to decrease them, would it seem normal or abnormal to parents that families should cluster around the average of three or four children which is "normal" in the demogaphic sense of being implied in the established goal of population constancy? Here an extremely difficult conjecture is necessary in order to arrive at any generalization as to the number of children families actually want.

A desire for children has to be taken for granted, but it is not quantitatively circumscribed. The wish for offspring is no imperative craving like hunger or sex. The demand is highly elastic. A survey was made of the existing literature on the subject of marital happiness under different family constellations, of the psychological and educational situation in families of different sizes, and of position psychology in regard to the influences of family size and birth order on mental and moral development. Only vague conclusions could be drawn from this survey. It would seem natural for the variegated desires and considerations of parents to converge on three or even four children in the family if economic conditions and educational stimulations were readapted for the family size that society wants. The 1-child situation contains certain risks and problems which are neutralized in families of a somewhat larger size. In the very large family, on the other hand, certain hardships mount. In the marginal reasoning about preferences for two or three or four children, nuances are many, and any one conclusion is difficult to draw. The additional burden and displacement of family arrangements that result from having three children instead of two, or from having the fourth child when there are already three, would not seem to be prohibitive, particularly if to the balance of motivation should be added the general appreciation that it is socially valuable to reach that average.

This social valuation on the part of individuals as citizens would seem to be not only that children should accumulate to the number needed for a constant population but also that a more general clustering around the average would be preferable. It would also seem to correspond to a basic Swedish ideal that equalization as to the number of children in itself would be a good thing. Such a democratic leveling of family size to produce more middle-sized families thus can be specified as a goal for population policy.

IMPROVED QUALITY

A basis for a consensus with regard to population policy further develops out of the concern for human quality. Improved quality of succeeding generations, and particularly improved growth conditions for children, can be fixed as a goal for the population program.

The available facts do not funish much of a basis for attempts to encourage selective breeding by particular social groups with supposedly superior hereditary worth. In any case common valuations do not permit such a policy. As opposed to this so-called positive eugenics, negative eugenics is commonly accepted but how far interference with individual freedom should go in the interest of the quality of the offspring is a delicate problem. Here is a real conflict of values which cannot, like many others, be eliminated through induced social change. To decrease the fertility of mentally deficient people seems to be the minimum formula that will win common approval.

Similar difficulties appear in deciding how far strivings for improved environmental conditions should be carried. In Chapter 6 the conflict between qualitative and quantitative goals was revealed. Most families have to pay for an extra child with a lowered standard of living for the rest of the children. In a society giving primacy to quality rather than quantity this dilemma would block a population policy of the type here discussed, if it were not possible to reunite the two goals by social reform. When as in Sweden the primacy is definitely given to quality, there is still room for a certain indeterminateness: how small a risk for quality shall take precedence over how large a gain in quantity. Obviously the intention cannot be to follow the rule to the extreme, for example by spending the money and time to care for the health of one child that could secure a decent living for ten children.

In order to arrive at some determination of this goal of quality, the minimum is here interpreted as the desire to safeguard for all children, born and unborn, what are now average environmental conditions for children with regard to housing, food, medical attention, schooling, and so forth. Such a policy has strong moorings in our predilection for greater social justice. If the nation's resources or the social ingenuity for redistribution cannot ensure such average conditions for all children, no additional children should be sought. If, for example, the average nutrition for children can be ascertained, a national policy would set as its goal making available the average for all children. Sometimes it will seem reasonable to set the goal even higher than such a level. Thus the minimum level for infant mortality, which is technically possible as evidenced by the low rate in a favored social group, can be set as the practical goal for all groups.

Even if these attempts to state the qualitative goal in terms of definite levels are of necessity somewhat arbitrary, the general direction is not, and neither are the principles of primacy. On this basis population policy can obviously be directed toward fairly concrete social planning.

REDUCED ILLEGITIMACY

Parallel with the goals of increasing the number of children born and safeguarding their quality is that of having more births take place within marriage and fewer outside marriage. The fate of illegitimate children is so generally deplored that a mere statement of this value premise is enough to justify the goal that illegitimacy be reduced.

Closer examination reveals that generally the most tragic aspect of illegitimacy is that children are born without a home, without being parts of a loving complete family. The goal, therefore, is to reduce the number of children born out of wedlock to such an extent that they can all be assured a good home. This can be achieved by decreasing the number of illegitimate children born, by making it possible for more parents to live with their children, and by increasing the number of really good foster homes where the children are welcome. The goal would be fixed not at a certain percentage of illegitimate children nor at a certain extramarital fertility but rather would depend upon society's ability to take care of the children. This formulation of the vague values of the general public is offered as a more solid goal than any other yet advanced, difficult as it is to find a common denominator in this field of varying moral judgments.

THE PRINCIPLE OF VOLUNTARY PARENTHOOD

From value premises directly avowed by the Swedish people, it follows that a population policy should not interefer with voluntary parenthood. An honest recognition of birth control and family planning is implicit in our democratic population policy. In this connection it is necessary to explain why birth control can so categorically be stated as a common value attitude, when verbalized public opinion has so often been to the contrary.

The relation between private attitudes and political attitudes is beclouded here and the fixing of the goal thus made difficult. Most individual families will reserve their private right of planning their childbearing. Birth control of some sort and with some degree of effectiveness is practiced in almost all nonsterile marriages, but many people have been unwilling to proclaim as a social value the attitude that voluntary parenthood should be sanctioned as normal for the whole people. This obvious inconsistency between private behavior and public principles was exposed in the recent population debate in Sweden. It appeared incompatible with enlightened and honest democracy to reserve birth control rights for oneself and at the same time to support a public policy denying the same rights to other citizens. Where such an attitude is not sheer hypocrisy, it implies a denial of equal rights and an attempt to preserve a kind of moral class privilege. It is impossible to maintain such a position for long in a democracy. Inevitably the individual's use of birth control practices becomes reflected in a social opinion that voluntary parenthood is the right thing for all.

In the foregoing conclusion many practical arguments are included. Not only is the assertion of individual freedom involved but also the necessity of spacing children, of sparing mothers' health, and of not transmitting hereditary taint. In addition there is the problem of not augmenting the family beyond the available means for maintaining a satisfactory level of living.

Recognition of the right to voluntary parenthood as a superior value premise related to the principles of democracy has, however, been carried beyond a mere policy of *laisser-aller*. It is definitely felt that equal rights are not wholly realized if equal opportunities are not afforded. A lag in the spread of effective knowledge of birth control should be overcome and easy access to contraceptives be secured for everyone. It is the duty of society to see to it that every man and women reaching maturity receives realiable information about birth control and has individual advice and good technical resources available for its practice.

The premise of voluntary parenthood, which is fundamental to a democratic population policy, is of paramount importance in evaluating the means for executing such a policy. This premise excludes a number of alternative measures which would otherwise be possible. Any obstacle to providing knowledge about birth control to certain groups thus becomes indefensible. Futhermore, no force or coercion can be allowed with regard to matters of matrimony and parenthood. While this problem is one of little practical concern in its positive sense—"forced" childbearing is never proclaimed by any state—it becomes more important in the negative sense. In a democracy it would be just as inconsistent to compel people not to marry or have children. Forced celibacy for anyone who has reached the legal age for matrimony becomes an absurdity. The desire to marry and the desire to have children are felt to be fundamental human rights, which neither state nor church nor employer nor parents should interefer with. In Protestant Western society this becomes of practical significance only for women. Employers should not have the right to dictate to their employees with regard to marrying or bearing children through the exercise of discriminatory practices. It would thus be consistent with this general value premise to formulate the goal that both men and women be guaranteed freedom of choice as to family status and family size. Interference in these rights should be outlawed.

Moreover, any propaganda for families and increased families should be honest, should start from the true interest of the individual himself, and in any case should not divert him from clear thinking about his own values and motives. Exhortations to duty, to patriotic glorification, or to religious obedience are at least believed to be undemocratic in the country under study. The state should appear for what it is and voice the reasons it has as the collectivity of individuals for wanting more or fewer children; but it should not confuse the issue by donning consecrated vestments of superindividual powers. In order not to disturb the individual's democratically free choice as to marriage and parenthood, all measures intended to encourage the founding of families should be devised fundamentally to aid the family. In this connection it may be pointed out parenthetically that certain other values than those explicitly stated above may also negate one or another measure of population policy. Thus respect for merit only as the prerequisite for positions in administrative, political, and civic offices would make it impossible in Sweden to imitate the laws of some totalitarian countries, which make a certain family status or number of children a condition or an advantage for obtaining posts within the civil service.

We may draw certain practical conclusions from the value premises of individual freedom with regard to family status. People should neither be forced nor, through ignorance or otherwise, be lured into marriage or childbearing. Measures to encourage families should take the form of honest education and of attempts to remodel the social and economic foundations of the family institution.

The moral revolution which the acceptance of these principles implies is, of course, not completed. Individuals or even groups can easily be found who hesitate before some of the logical inferences from our ideals of enlightened rationalistic democracy, but responsible representative bodies have openly endorsed them. The Population Commission particularly has been commendably explicit on these points. As a result of the open fight that was waged, public opinion has also been moving rapidly. As elsewhere it has again been proved that the average man has quite a capacity for honesty and common sense even in sexual matters and that politician, administrator, writer, preacher, and teacher are likely to make a serious mistake when they underestimate the masses and assume that public opinion is not sufficiently "mature" to support their own advanced views. The era of public hypocrisy is nearing its end in Sweden.

MERGING THE GOALS

The cleavage of public opinion about birth control into two camps, with one talking only of the individual's right and need to limit childbearing and the other condemning such family limitation as immoral and ruinous for the nation, has made it difficult for people to keep two ideas in their heads at the same time, namely, that parenthood can be made voluntary and that society can remodel its very basis so that more children can still be welcomed. The illusion that society is static and therefore condemned to remain in its present dilemma between children and poverty has paralyzed intelligent thinking. By regarding society rather as a household that the citizens can operate for their common welfare, it is at once seen to be possible to join voluntary parenthood with positive population interests, to join birth control and fertility increase. Birth control means family planning; only social ignorance construes planning to mean reduction exclusively.

The harmonizing of the two goals of quality and quantity is also more feasible than it appears. Only by selecting for population policy a certain set of social reforms, however, can such a harmony of interests be achieved. These reforms should directly improve growth opportunities for children and at the same time reduce the individual's reasons for not taking on the burden of children. This consonance of population goals will require a much more detailed discussion as it is the main principle in determining the means of population policy.

Some Further Readings

Anshen, Ruth Nanda, ed., *The Family: Its Function and Destiny*. New York: Harper, rev. ed., 1959.

Beard, Mary R., *Woman as Force in History*. New York: Macmillan, 1946.

Bebel, August, *Woman and Socialism*. New York: Socialist Literature Co., 1910.

Bell, Norman W., and Ezra F. Vogel, eds., *A Modern Introduction to the Family*. Glencoe, Ill.: The Free Press, 1960.

Bertocci, Peter A., and R. M. Millard, *Personality and the Good: Psychological and Ethical Perspectives*. New York: David McKay, 1963.

Borgese, Elizabeth Mann, *The Ascent of Woman*. New York: Braziller, 1963.

Calverton, V. F., and S. P. Schmalhausen, eds., *Sex in Civilization*. New York: The Macauley Co., 1929.

Cavan, Ruth Shonle, *The American Family*. New York: Thomas Y. Crowell, 3rd ed., 1963.

Cole, William G., *Sex in Christianity and Psychoanalysis*. New York: Oxford University Press, 1953.

———, *Sex and Love in the Bible*. New York: Association Press, 1959.

Coser, Rose Laub, ed., *The Family: Its Structure and Functions*. New York: St. Martin's Press, 1963.

Cyrus, Della, "Problems of the Modern Homemaker-Mother," in J. and M. Landis, eds., *Readings in Marriage and the Family*. Englewood Cliffs, N.J.: Prentice-Hall, 1957.

Davis, Kingsley, "Illegitimacy and the Social Structure," *American Journal of Sociology*, 45 (1939): 215-233.

———, "Prostitution," in R. Merton and R. Nisbet, eds., *Contemporary Social Problems*. New York: Harcourt, Brace and World, 1961.

———, "The World's Population Crisis," in Merton and Nisbet.

423

Devereux, George, *A Study of Abortion in Primitive Societies*. New York: Julian Press, 1955.

Ditzion, Sidney, *Marriage, Morals and Sex in America*. New York: Bookman Associates, 1953.

Drummond, Isabel, *The Sex Paradox*. New York: Putnam, 1953.

Ellis, Albert, *The American Sexual Tragedy*. New York: Lyle Stuart, 2nd rev. ed., 1962.

Ehrmann, Winston W., *Premarital Dating Behavior*. New York: Holt, 1959.

Fairchild, J. E., ed., *Women, Society and Sex*. New York: Sheridan House, 1956.

Fitch, Robert E., *The Decline and Fall of Sex*. New York: Harcourt, Brace, 1957.

Ford, Clellan S., and Frank A. Beach, *Patterns of Sexual Behavior*. New York: Harper, 1951.

Freedman, Ronald, P. K. Whelpton, and A. A. Campbell, *Family Planning, Sterility, and Population Growth*. New York: McGraw-Hill, 1959.

Freeman, Lucy, with Dr. X, *The Abortionist*. Garden City: Doubleday, 1962.

Friedan, Betty, *The Feminine Mystique*. New York: Norton, 1963.

Fromm, Erich, "Sex and Character," in Anshen, *The Family: Its Function and Destiny* (see above).

Gebhard, Paul H., et al., *Pregnancy, Birth and Abortion*. New York: Hoeber-Harper, 1958.

Geddes, Donald P., ed., *An Analysis of the Kinsey Reports*. New York: Dutton, 1954.

Genné, Elizabeth and William, eds., *Foundations of Christian Family Policy*. New York: National Council of Churches, [1961].

Grabill, W. H., C. V. Kiser, and P. K. Whelpton, *The Fertility of American Women*. New York: Wiley, 1958.

Hacker, Helen, "The New Burdens of Masculinity," *Marriage and Family Living*, 19 (1957): 227-233.

Harper, Fowler V., and Jerome Skolnick, *Problems of the Family*. Indianapolis: Bobbs-Merrill, 1963.

Hiltner, Seward, *Sex Ethics and the Kinsey Report*. New York: Association Press, 1953.

Himelhoch, Jerome, and Sylvia Fleis Fava, eds., *Sexual Behavior in American Society*. New York: Norton, 1955.

Hunt, Morton, *The Natural History of Love*. New York: Knopf, 1959.

Kirkendall, Lester A., *Premarital Intercourse and Interpersonal Relations*. New York: Julian Press, 1961.

Kolb, William, "Sociologically Established Family Norms and Democratic Values," *Social Forces*, 26 (1948): 451-456.

Komarovsky, Mirra, "Cultural Contradictions and Sex Roles," *American Journal of Sociology*, 52 (1946): 184-189.

——, "Functional Analysis of Sex Roles," *American Sociological Review*, 15 (1950): 508-516.

Krich, A. M., ed., *Men: The Variety and Meaning of Their Sexual Experience*. New York: Dell Books, 1954.

——, ed., *Women: The Variety and Meaning of Their Sexual Experience*. New York: Dell Books, 1953.

Kronhausen, Phyllis and Eberhard, *Sex Histories of American College Men*. New York: Ballantine Books, 1960.

Levy, John, and Ruth Munroe, *The Happy Family*. New York: Knopf, 1938, 1959.

Lewinsohn, Richard, *A History of Sexual Customs*. New York: Longmans, Green and Harper, 1958.

Lippmann, Walter, *A Preface to Morals*. New York: Macmillan, 1929.

Mace, David and Vera, *Marriage, East and West*. New York: Doubleday, 1960.

Maccoby, Eleanor, "Effects upon Children of Their Mothers' Outside Employment," in National Manpower Council, *Work in the Lives of Married Women*. New York: Columbia University Press, 1958.

Malinowski, Bronislaw, *Sex and Repression in Savage Society*. New York: Harcourt, Brace, 1927.

——, *The Sexual Life of Savages*. New York: H. Liveright, 1929.

Mead, Margaret, *Male and Female*. New York: Morrow, 1949.

Montagu, Ashley, *The Natural Superiority of Women*. New York: Macmillan, 1952.

Moore, Barrington, Jr., "Some Thoughts on the Future of the Family," in *Political Power and Social Theory*. Cambridge: Harvard University Press, 1958.

Murdock, George, *Social Structure*. New York: Macmillan, 1949.

Murdock, G. P., L. Woodward, and F. Bolman, "Sexual Behavior, What Is Acceptable?" in J. and M. Landis, *Readings in Marriage and the Family*. New York: Prentice-Hall, 1952.

Myrdal, Alva, and Viola Klein, *Women's Two Roles: Home and Work*. London: Routledge and Kegan Paul, 1956.

National Manpower Council, *Womanpower*. New York: Columbia University Press, 1957.

————, *Work in the Lives of Married Women*. New York: Columbia University Press, 1958.

Nye, F. Ivan, and Lois W. Hoffman, eds., *The Employed Mother in America*. Chicago: Rand McNally, 1963.

Parsons, Talcott, "Age and Sex in the Social Structure of the United States," *American Sociological Review*, 7 (1942): 604-616.

Petersen, William, and David Matza, eds., *Social Controversy*. Belmont, Calif.: Wadsworth Publishing Co., 1963.

Queen, Stuart, Robert Habenstein, and J. B. Adams, *The Family in Various Cultures*. New York: Lippincott, 1961.

Rainwater, Lee, with Karol K. Weinstein, *And the Poor Get Children*. Chicago: Quadrangle Books, 1960.

————, Richard Coleman, and Gerald Handel, *Workingman's Wife*. New York: Oceana, 1959.

Reiss, Ira L., *Premarital Sexual Standards in America*. Glencoe, Ill.: The Free Press, 1960.

————, "The Treatment of Pre-Marital Coitus in 'Marriage and the Family' Texts," *Social Problems*, 4 (1957): 334-338.

Rock, John, *The Time Has Come: A Catholic Doctor's Proposals to End the Battle Over Birth Control*. New York: Knopf, 1963.

St. John-Stevas, Norman, *Life, Death and the Law*. Bloomington: Indiana University Press, 1961.

"Sex Offenses," *Law and Contemporary Problems*, 25 (Spring 1960), entire issue.

Spiro, Melford E., *Children of the Kibbutz*. Cambridge: Harvard University Press, 1958.

————, *Kibbutz: Venture in Utopia*. Cambridge: Harvard University Press, 1956.

Stephens, William N., *The Family in Cross-Cultural Perspective*. New York: Holt, Rinehart and Winston, 1963.

Sulloway, Alvah W., *Birth Control and Catholic Doctrine*. Boston: Beacon Press, 1959.

Taeuber, Conrad and Irene, *The Changing Population of the United States*. New York: Wiley, 1958.

"The American Female," *Harpers*, October 1962 (special supplement).

The Wolfenden Report. Report of the Committee on Homosexual Offenses and Prostitution (U.K.). New York: Stein and Day, 1963.

Thomas, John L., *Catholic Views on Sex, Love, Marriage*. Garden City: Hanover House, 1958.

Towards a Quaker View of Sex. By a group of Friends. London: Friends Home Service Committee, 1963.

Vogt, William, *People! Challenge to Survival*. New York: W. Sloane Associates, 1960.

Waller, Willard, "The Rating and Dating Complex," *American Sociological Review*, 2 (1937): 727-734.

Whelpton, P. K., and C. V. Kiser, eds., *Social and Psychological Factors Affecting Fertility*. New York, Milbank Memorial Fund.

Winter, Gibson, *Love and Conflict*. Garden City: Doubleday Dolphin, 1961.

"Women and Work," *Marriage and Family Living*, 23 (November 1961), entire issue.

"Women's Opportunities and Responsibilities," *Annals of the American Academy of Political and Social Science*, 251 (1947), entire issue.

Wylie, Philip, *Generation of Vipers*. New York: Rinehart, 1942.

3